The End of Politics

CRITICAL PERSPECTIVES
A Guilford Series

DOUGLAS KELLNER, Editor
University of Texas at Austin

Recent Volumes

THE END OF POLITICS: CORPORATE POWER
AND THE DECLINE OF THE PUBLIC SPHERE
Carl Boggs

THE TWO-FOLD THOUGHT OF DELEUZE AND GUATTARI:
INTERSECTIONS AND ANIMATIONS
Charles J. Stivale

THE POSTMODERN TURN
Steven Best and Douglas Kellner

POSTMODERN WAR
Chris Hables Gray

REVOLUTION OF CONSCIENCE: MARTIN LUTHER KING, JR.,
AND THE PHILOSOPHY OF NONVIOLENCE
Greg Moses

SIGN WARS: THE CLUTTERED LANDSCAPE OF ADVERTISING
Robert Goldman and Stephen Papson

LEWIS MUMFORD AND THE ECOLOGICAL REGION:
THE POLITICS OF PLANNING
Mark Luccarelli

ROADS TO DOMINION: RIGHT-WING MOVEMENTS
AND POLITICAL POWER IN THE UNITED STATES
Sara Diamond

THE POLITICS OF HISTORICAL VISION:
MARX, FOUCAULT, HABERMAS
Steven Best

AFTER MARXISM
Ronald Aronson

MARXISM IN THE POSTMODERN AGE:
CONFRONTING THE NEW WORLD ORDER
Antonio Callari, Stephen Cullenberg, and Carole Biewener, Editors

POSTMODERNISM AND SOCIAL INQUIRY
David R. Dickens and Andrea Fontana, Editors

The End of Politics

CORPORATE POWER AND THE
DECLINE OF THE PUBLIC SPHERE

Carl Boggs

THE GUILFORD PRESS
New York   London

To the memory of my father,
one of the first atomic victims

320.973
B

©2000 The Guilford Press
A Division of Guilford Publications, Inc.
72 Spring Street, New York, NY 10012
http://www.guilford.com

Printed in the United States of America

This book is printed on acid-free paper.

Last digit is print number: 9 8 7 6 5 4 3 2 1

Library of Congress Cataloging-in-Publication Data

Boggs, Carl.
    The end of politics : corporate power and the decline of the
  public sphere / Carl Boggs
      p. cm.–(Critical perspectives)
    Includes bibliographical references and index.
    ISBN 1-57230-496-0
    1. Political participation–United States. 2. Political culture–
  United States. 3. United States–Politics and government–1989–
  4. United States–Social conditions–1980- 5. Political leadership–
  United States. I. Title. II. Critical perspectives (New York, N.Y.)
  JK1764 .B64   2000
  320.973′09′048–dc21   99-048588
                                                        CIP

CONTENTS

PREFACE

In this book I reflect on what might appropriately be called "a crisis within the crisis"—the profound deterioration of political discourse and action in the United States over the past two decades or so, in a country that has historically celebrated the virtues of open dialogue, citizenship, democratic participation, and public access to governmental decision making. My core argument is that by the 1990s American society had become more depoliticized, more lacking in the spirit of civic engagement and public obligation, than at any time in recent history, with the vast majority of the population increasingly alienated from a political system that is commonly viewed as corrupt, authoritarian, and simply irrelevant to the most important challenges of our time. This deterioration has occurred, ironically and ominously, at a time when deepening social problems—environmental degradation, the decline of urban life, eroding public services, widespread civic violence, increased threats to privacy—will surely require extensive and creative political intervention. In such a historical context the deterioration of the public sphere has potentially devastating consequences for citizen empowerment and social change, not to mention the more general health of the political domain itself—hence the "crisis within the crisis." Further, the deterioration has taken place during a period of accelerated growth not only of the national economy but of higher education, informational resources, and communications. Sadly, despite the much easier access to educational facilities and technological outlets, most people seem to have lost hope for remedies to social problems within the existing public realm. Theirs is a predictable enough reaction to a badly atrophied political system in which differences between the two major parties are narrower than ever and citizenship is in a spiraling decline—as reflected in lower voter turnout, a collapsing sense of political efficacy among ordinary citizens, and declining knowledge (or concern) about the social and political world.

This epochal triumph of antipolitics is not merely a matter of failed

leaders, parties, or movements, nor simply of flawed structural arrangements, but also mirrors a deeper historical process—one tied to increased
corporate colonization of society and economic globalization—that shapes
virtually every facet of daily life and political culture. Depoliticization is
the more or less inevitable mass response to a system that is designed to
marginalize dissent, privatize social relations, and reduce the scope of
democratic participation.

While the organizing theme, or leitmotif, of this volume is clearly
"politics," my approach is not informed solely by the discipline of political
studies or political science—or indeed any other modern field of academic
inquiry—since my argument does not follow any specialized mode of
discourse. The fragmented, professionalized, and insular character of established scholarly fields (and subfields) has the effect of blocking system
analysis of the contemporary impasse; in fact, academic preoccupations
more often obfuscate or distort rather than illuminate by chopping up social reality into manageable (and usually quantifiable) disciplinary texts,
discourses, and "methods." In most academic fields one finds a growing
aversion to "macro," or global concerns that inevitably possess some historical sweep or cut across often artificial disciplinary boundaries. The
arid texts in most areas of political science are especially deficient for the
task I have set out to accomplish here (which is ironic, given that political
science is ostensibly a "political" discipline that should be abundantly rich
in sources and insights for a study dealing with the phenomenon of depoliticization and its enormous consequences). Of course, some works
authored by political scientists have proved helpful to this enterprise, but
the bulk of the literature is too imbued with conformist ideology, too restricted in scope and methodology, and too detached from other fields
and discourses to be of significant help. These shortcomings are all the
more intellectually disturbing at a time of intensifying economic and technological (as well as political) globalization. In fact, the very *definition* of
politics that informs not only political science but most of the social sciences is far too theoretically narrow and ideologically conservative to allow for the kind of far-reaching critique that I set out to develop in the
present volume.

By invoking "the end of politics" in my choice of the title, I do not
have in mind any literal demise of the political enterprise—nor anything
resembling an "end of ideology" or "end of history"—but rather a meta-
phorical reference to the zeitgeist of antipolitics that seems to define so
much of U.S. society at the turn of the new century. Of course "politics" in the ordinary meaning of the term—encompassing elections, legislative activity, public policy, lobbying, presidential directives, and so
on—has by no means disappeared from the landscape, nor has it lost its
capacity to attract significant media and popular attention. Further,

manifestations of citizenship and a participatory culture—a hallmark of political vitality—can surely be observed in various forms of community organizing, grassroots struggles, and social movements that, while generally scattered and isolated, remain important parts of U.S. political and intellectual life. Yet, while politics has not completely vanished from the scene, the once vibrant discourse that focused our attention on such values as citizen participation, the public good, political obligation, social governance, and community—part of an ongoing tradition stretching back to the ancient Greeks—has atrophied beyond recognition. This traditional civic-mindedness has been subverted by an array of overpowering forces, first and foremost by corporate power and the growing impact of economic globalization. Yet, owing to the explosive contradictions of the system and massive social problems on a world scale, the sense of finality that might be associated with a concept like "the end of politics" must be emphatically qualified. Whether the nearly all-consuming process of depoliticization that will be explored in these pages can be eventually reversed and possibly overturned—that is, whether we can expect a turn toward political revitalization—cannot be fully addressed at this time.

This study could not have been carried out in its present form without access to a wide variety of sources, both scholarly and nonscholarly; such an eclectic choice of sources is dictated by the inevitably multifaceted nature of the problem. While this admission might be read as a concession to certain "postmodern" sensibilities, it is really more an acknowledgment of the fact that politics never stands in isolation but sooner or later intesects with every dimension of human life. Political analysis that is not informed by history or economics, or even psychology, is bound to be lifeless, perhaps even pointless. My hope is that this volume will benefit from this intellectual eclecticism that goes against many academic conventions, striving as it does to incorporate methods, analyses, and visions from a wide spectrum of discourses. Above all, I wish to thank those who gave so generously of their time to help with parts or all of the manuscript during its lengthy journey toward completion. Chief among these contributors are Steven Best, Douglas Kellner, Lauren Langman, and Karen Lucas, along with other members of the *Theory and Society* editorial board, whose insightful comments and criticisms helped me revise my manuscript "The Great Retreat"—a much condensed predecessor to this volume—which appeared in the December 1997 issue of the journal. Two of my collaborators at UCLA, Tina Dirmann and Eric Magnuson, also helped me rethink and refine portions of the argument. I am grateful to colleagues and friends throughout the country who have had a long-standing interest in my work and who have been intellectually and politically supportive, including Barbara Epstein, Dennis Judd, George Katsiaficas, Peter McLaren, and Fred Schiff. My regular late-night conversations with Darrell Hamamoto, touching on countless topics but often returning to the sorry state of U.S. politics, have been a special source of intellectual reflection and personal inspiration. My colleagues at National University have offered invaluable support; though most of them work in fields of study far removed from my own, they remained interested in the progress of my book: Mona Afridi, Hans Bertsch, Monica Carbajal, Douglas Hadsell, Teresa Larkin, Cherie Lewis, Karen Offitzer, Tom Pollard, Fran Rosamond, James Roseboro, Igor Subbotin, Doug Slawson, David Steinman, and Ross Talarico. I am further indebted to National University for granting me sabbatical leave during much of 1997 so that I could finish this project unencumbered by teaching and other university-related duties.

Many of the ideas developed in this text were first presented, and then further revised, while I was a columnist for the alternative weekly *L.A. Village View* over a two-year span beginning in late 1994. The close relationship I had with one of the *View* editors, Danny Feingold, was particularly influential during that period. Several students in the UCLA sociology department (where I taught from 1993 to 1996) were generous and helpful in providing research and assistance, in particular, Loan Dang, Tina Dirmann, Aderonke Epps, Ben Frymer, Allwyn Gustafson, Christina Hazan, Eric Magnuson, Mark Nagel, Max Stevens, and Denise Sze. In certain ways the most enduring support has come from friends who frequently provide some of the sharpest commentary on my work—along with plenty of inspiration: Cynthia Pena, Mary Jo Johnson, Lee Meihls, Danny Postel, Marina Brennan, John Sanbonmatsu, Randye Sandel, Brady Sullivan, and Milt Wolpin. My ongoing and generally spirited political discussions with Brady Sullivan over a period of nearly 15 years, generally while huddled in one or another westside Los Angeles cafe, have often forced a rethinking of seemingly taken-for-granted premises. The contributions of Peter Wissoker and William Meyer at The Guilford Press—their patience, support, and editorial suggestions—have been invaluable. Most of all, I wish to thank Dory Lewis for her constant encouragement and support for a project that must have seemed as though it would continue indefinitely.

INTRODUCTION

As the twenty-first century dawns, American politics is in an increasingly pathetic condition. Elections have become more meaningless than ever, significant differences between Republicans and Democrats are scarcely discernible despite all the political hue and cry, public discourse is drawn increasingly toward trivial concerns, and legislatures at all levels are in gridlock. Meanwhile, citizens in ever greater numbers have retreated from political involvement out of justifiable feelings of disgust and pessimism. Measured by virtually any set of criteria, the political system is in a (potentially terminal) state of entropy, out of touch with the needs and aspirations of the vast majority of people; citizenship—its rights and obligations—has decayed beyond recognition. While at one time in the not-too-distant past complaints about a declining public sphere, or "commons," was the distinct province of Burkean conservatives, nostalgic liberals, and republican communitarians bemoaning the disappearance of a more simple associational life, today it is a refrain heard loudly across the ideological spectrum. Indeed the seemingly irreversible depoliticization of American society—perhaps the dominant motif of our times—is no doubt most harmful to *progressive* social movements that have a vested interest in critical public dialogue and broadened civic participation leading (so it is hoped) to far-reaching change. In the 1990s "politics" has been met by an increasingly cynical populace with a sense of deep anger and futility, linked in the popular mind to media spectacles, ever present scandals, campaign deceits, bureaucratic machinations, PAC (political action committee) and corporate influence peddling, and just plain corruption—an almost planetary remove from the more noble vision of political enterprise championed by the ancient Greeks, by diverse political thinkers such as Rousseau, Paine, Jefferson, Dewey, and, more recently, by the empowering vision of civil rights leaders like Martin Luther King, Jr., and Stokely Carmichael. In contrast to the naive, almost romantic, view of government presented in most high school civics

1

classes and even college political science courses, we appear to have arrived at what one observer refers to as the "Darwinian organization of politics."[1] The modern crisis of politics blocks the capacity of ordinary people to intervene in the worsening social and ecological problems of our day.

Surely the most dramatic sign of the times was the White House sex scandal that led to the impeachment of President Bill Clinton by the U.S. House of Representatives in December 1998. The scandal degenerated into one of the great overblown media spectacles of the twentieth century. It was accompanied by byzantine legal maneuvers, a sexual McCarthyism that blurred public and private boundaries, fierce personal rivalries, and quite possibly (following the now famous plot of the movie *Wag the Dog*) a manufactured global military crisis that served as a pretext for missile assaults on presumed terrorist encampments and eventually on Iraq. As fateful episodes unfold well beyond their surreal origins, the public sphere becomes saturated with loud and shrill voices from all sides, the louder and shriller the more emptied of political substance—and all the less relevant to what is actually happening in the world or to any conceivable policy outcomes. As time passes, the political terrain winds up littered with informational and propagandistic debris fanned by endless charges and countercharges, spins and counterspins, which pass through all the established conduits of mass media and popular culture: talk shows, TV sitcoms, network news, the Internet, and movies. If public discourse (in or outside of the spectacle) has sunk to new levels of personalized and trivialized blather, politics has in many ways been transformed into yet another dimension of show biz that remains so central to the commodified media culture of contemporary American society. In the midst of scandal it is easy enough to see how the devaluing of politics converges with the spectacular growth of the media–entertainment complex.

SEX SCANDAL AND POLITICAL ENTROPY

At the pinnacle of the heralded information revolution, with its hundreds of cable TV alternatives, one searches in vain for a single channel (or even a single program) devoted to the role of corporations in the United States or the world, the impact of mergers, deregulation, corporate abuse, crime, and exploitation, and the culpability of multinational firms in rain-forest destruction, global warming, atmospheric radiation, and food contamination. What passed for "dialogue" in the national obsession with the scandal took over nearly every media source around the clock, producing little, however, in the way of analysis or perspective. Instead of encountering useful or empowering "information," mass publics typically confront a situation in which the crucial social problems of our time end up shrouded in denial, suppression, mystification, and hypocrisy while the media fixate unendingly on every tidbit of sexual scandal.

The White House sex scandal actually served to both reflect and perpetuate the deep sense of political malaise that has gripped American society in the 1990s—a malaise deeply rooted in historical processes that have given rise to unprecedented levels of popular distrust, hostility, and alienation toward the political system, politicians, and indeed "politics" in general. Public confidence in the federal government declined from 75 percent in 1964 to 35 percent in the late 1980s and, finally, to less than 25 percent by the late 1990s, by far the lowest figure for any of the major industrialized countries, according to a 1999 Gallup Poll. Even such a mainstream political commentator as Jeff Greenfield (a senior analyst at CNN) was moved to remark, in the context of the scandal; "The most striking thing is that the public—which was supposed to go into a state of panic, shock, horror—seems to be treating this with all the impact of the score of the latest Rams game. My guess is that it shows that for most people this country's national politics have become less important than at any time in this century. It is irrelevant to most people." During a lengthy interview with the *Los Angeles Times*, Greenfield added: "And most people in need of [taking part in] decision-making have totally opted out of the electoral process. The voter turnout, based on income and education, has widened into a chasm. People look at Washington and see one bunch of loudmouths in suits screaming at another group of loudmouths in suits. Impeachment seems like sort of a sideshow." People could hardly be blamed for their tenacious indifference, since "you had members of the House engaged in what may be one of the most important things they ever do, [and] half of them marched up to the podium and didn't know what their staff wrote for them. Some of them had not even seen the speech they were reading."[2]

Widespread disaffection with politics has no doubt been deepened by fallout from the scandal, as indicated by the extremely low voter turnout (36 percent) for the 1998 congressional elections, the lowest in a national election since 1942, in fact. Young voters turned out in even smaller proportions in 1998. What the scandal has revealed, perhaps more than anything else, is the poverty of public discourse in American life; more and more citizens have been turned off not only by the recurrent lies, false promises, and corruption, but by the shrill negativism of electoral campaigns and the intrusion of government into the private lives of politicians. There is an evolving consensus that governmental service is no longer the noble calling it once was, that politics has less and less to do with ideas, beliefs, and commitments—with a vision of the future. Organizers for both parties who tried to mobilize voters for the 1998 elections found the going rougher than ever. In the words of one political operative: "I try to get them to vote. They say: 'On what issues? On the scandal? On the President's sex life?' That doesn't give them anything to vote for."[3] Implicit here is the pervasive sense that American politics has lost all meaning, that it has abandoned any rational ordering of social priorities.[4]

Such visceral hostility to politics bespeaks nothing less than a deep suspicion of the political enterprise as such—beyond any specific politicians, parties, or administrations—which helps to account for the growing weakness and vulnerability of politicians that was originally set in motion by the Vietnam war and then Watergate. President Clinton's immense "popularity" amid his own scandals and impeachment must be understood in this larger context. That an extraordinary 72 percent of the American public (as shown in various national surveys) approved President Clinton's performance in office after the House of Representatives moved to impeach him may suggest at least a mild endorsement of his policies and his capacity to govern, but mostly it appeared to signify massive indifference (or, even better for the Democrats, antipathy) of the American people to the Kenneth Starr investigation and the House Republicans' virulent anti-Clinton agenda. Although Democrats and Republicans may spite one another, the vast majority of Americans felt that impeachment would make no difference in their lives, one way or the other; they generally believed, as well, that President Clinton's remaining in office would never be a threat to the orderly functioning of the economy, or society as a whole. The inescapable irony in all this is that President Clinton has pursued largely conservative policies at a time when the *real* ideological gulf separating Republicans and Democrats had narrowed beyond recognition.[5]

This pathetic state of American politics could be dismissed as yet another manifestation of the theatrical spectacle—irrelevant but still amusing—were its impact on economic and social life not so destructive or debilitating. The Clinton sex scandal, like the O. J. Simpson trial and countless other media spectacles before it, effectively diverted public discourse from the major social problems of our time, permitting corporations to continue their depredations with but minimal interference. Social issues of real consequence end up being ignored or trivialized while popular attention remains fixated on media-generated "controversies," crimes of the rich and powerful, and the personal foibles of leaders. While the Clinton sex scandal dominated the airwaves throughout 1998, for example, the nation's $220-billion electric power industry was being rapidly deregulated in the absence of any real public debate. As a result, corporations and utility lobbyists (mainly working behind the scenes) were able ti exercise undue control over the process, especially as compared to community, consumer, labor, and environmental groups. The long-term consequences of utility deregulation for the average citizen will surely dwarf those of the scandal, whatever Republicans might claim about Clinton's sexual behavior or his alleged flaunting of the "rule of law."

Consider further the urgent problem of U.S. nuclear strategy in the context of a fully transformed NATO alliance following the 1989–1991 collapse of the Soviet Union and other communist governments. While the need for a massive (first-strike) nuclear presence in Europe and around the world now appears to require a thorough rethinking, American military planners in fact have moved to further stockpile nuclear weapons without even a nod toward abandoning the antiquated doctrine of first use justified by the Soviets' postwar military buildup—all without even the semblance of political discussion or input from interests outside the Pentagon.

Even more troublesome is the extent to which different aspects of the mounting ecological crisis have been obscured or ignored in mainstream political discourse. By the late 1990s scientific research had conclusively demonstrated that global warming was a real and urgent problem—that is, the massive threat to the world's ecosystem posed by continued high levels of certain manufactured gases and burnt fossil fuels had reached a critical point. Moreover, tremendous increases in greenhouse gases were expected in the early twentieth-first century, with potentially disastrous implications for weather patterns (most likely, oscillations between droughts and floods) and food production. Yet, in the United States, which produces more than 25 percent of all fossil-fuel emissions, public awareness and discussion of this issue have been virtually nonexistent, the issue having been largely co-opted, or hijacked, through corporate propaganda and greenwashing.[6] In this situation American elites, committed unreservedly to an economics of growth and expansion, remain adamantly opposed to significant reductions in fossil-fuel use or to any serious reorientation of production and consumption patterns that would be consonant with mere "sustainable development" (which is what ecologists urge). The grim ecological outlook forecasted by scientists and other researchers, and commonly accepted elsewhere in the world, is steadfastly minimized by agenda setters in the very country that is most responsible for the problem—and that has the most depoliticized public sphere. Most American agenda setters in 1998 were far more interested in the details of President Clinton's sex life than in the prospects for life on earth after 2010.

No less a onetime Washington insider than Robert Reich has lamented the sad state of American politics that he experienced firsthand as secretary of labor during President Clinton's first term, between 1993 and 1996. The main problem, as Reich came to understand it, is the colonizing influence of large corporations and wealth throughout every area and level of government, often rendering the public sector incapable of serving even the most minimal general interest. The intensification of "economic apartheid" in American society, even in the midst of seemingly unprecedented material growth and prosperity, threatens to erode the democratic core of our politics as it produces growing concentrations of economic and governmental power; participatory ideals have been reduced to a hollow myth while the elites (conservatives and liberals alike) continue to trumpet the virtues of citizenship. It hardly matters which party is in power, according to Reich, since big business essentially "owns" both of them, and in any event they carry out basically the same policies. Much like the Republicans, Democrats do the bidding of Wall Street—even as they make campaign promises to bolster the living standards of the poor and the working majority.

Reich points out that the elites' stranglehold over political discourse has made it impossible even to carry on rational debate about such a pressing issue as how to rebuild a rapidly decaying social infrastructure. The media-trumpeted concerns of these same elites—whether the trivia of sex scandals, celebrity trials, or imagined foreign demons—end up crowding out far more urgent societal priorities, while "serious" debates generally revolve around such matters as how to more efficiently wage the war on drugs, maintain law and order, reduce government spending, or balance the federal budget. "But what about public investment?" asks Reich incredulously. "It's now a tiny morsel of what we originally sought [in 1993]. This budget proclaims to all America that the way out of all our economic problems is to cut the budget and reduce government borrowing, regardless of what the borrowing is for. There's no boundary to this logic, no way out. The conceptual prison is complete . . . [meaning that] a balanced budget will require massive cuts in spending."[7] Meanwhile, as the cities continue to fall apart, the tremendous gulf between rich and poor in the United States expands with each passing year. As Reich observes: "Most workers in the bottom half continue to experience shrinking paychecks. The gap between the best-paid ten percent of Americans and the lowest-paid ten percent is wider than in any industrialized nation. *Every* rung on the economic ladder is growing wider apart."[8]

THE AGE OF CORPORATE COLONIZATION

The depressing reality is that most Americans have become accustomed to viewing politics thusly; the very idea that government or politics could be something positive, could serve progressive ends, typically is now seen as quaint, archaic, far removed from the cutthroat world of business competition and bureaucratic scheming. Citizen participation, which once defined the very essence of liberal-democratic politics, now seems thoroughly undermined by a culture that glorifies the singleminded pursuit of (economic) self-interest. Yet, there is an altogether different understanding of politics—one that is actually more relevant to the massive national and global challenges ahead; it draws on roots in a long tradition going back to the ancient Greeks. A tradition that is more empowering and visionary than cynical or despairing, it celebrates the positive ideals of citizenship, the public sphere, community, and social governance that are the sine qua non of any thriving democratic society. It counters the dominant minimalist view, championed endlessly by opinion-making elites, that has largely abandoned even the pretense of striving for a political system grounded in broad-based civic participation and popular decision making. This tradition regards politics as a uniquely inclusive and activating enterprise, vital to the life of any social order. In Aristotle's words: "All associations aim at some good; and the particular association which is the most sovereign of all, and includes all the rest, will pursue this aim most, and will thus be directed to the most sovereign of all goods. This most sovereign and inclusive association is the polis . . . or the political association."[9] For Aristotle, human beings are designed by nature to live and be active in the polis, which "exists for the sake of the good life."[10] Outside of the public realm, confined strictly to their own private or parochial concerns—believing perhaps that they are completely self-sufficient—people inevitably become a "poor sort of being." In such a state they are "either a beast or a god."[11] There are no apologies for one's thorough immersion in the affairs of the polis. On the contrary, politics constitutes a unique public sphere in which people come together, interact, make decisions, forge citizen bonds, carry out the imperatives of social change, and ultimately search for the good society insofar as "justice belongs to the polis."[12] In the Aristotelian conception, then, politics represents a source of broad human governance that is indispensable to the pursuit of meaning, direction, and purpose in life.

Many centuries later the Italian Marxist Antonio Gramsci, in his famous commentary on Machiavelli in *The Modern Prince*, wrote passionately about the epic role of politics in furnishing new collective identities, creative forms of statecraft, and a revolutionary vision of the future. For Gramsci (as for Machiavelli), "only politics creates the possibility for maneuver and movement," only politics serves to enlist popular energies and passions behind action needed to achieve some ideal—in Gramsci's case, of course, socialism. Thus, "what Machiavelli does do is bring everything back to politics," to the art of governing, founding "great states," "making history."[13] It is precisely through politics that a human being can become the "protagonist of a real and effective historical drama."[14] In the Machiavellian tradition, which Gramsci refused to equate with the common definition of amoral scheming and manipulation, politics belongs to the realm of neither religion nor science but to that of concrete secular action which sets out to create a better society. Gramsci further adds that it is on the terrain of politics that a "critical understanding of self" takes place, that deep human emotions about the present and future are engaged, that people are brought into the historical process.[15] Although writing squarely in the Marxist tradition, Gramsci—like Lenin and the Bolsheviks during roughly the same period—never went so far as to devalue politics by regarding it as little more than an epiphenomenal function of deeper class or material forces. These views, spanning the classical and modern periods, were later reformulated by Hannah Arendt in her classic *On Revolution*, which incorporates some of Rousseau's sentiments on the linkage between politics, the general will, and community erected on a foundation of the social contract.

Arendt's main emphasis was on the dynamic role of the public sphere in giving leverage to the historic process of democratization, to popular struggles against concentrations of both private and governmental power. In her words: "The only remedies against the misuse of public power by private individuals lie in the public realm itself, in the light which exhibits each deed enacted within its boundaries, in the very visibility to which it exposes all those who enter it."[16] It is precisely this visionary and empowering sense of politics that seems to have vanished from the American landscape—on the left no less than on the right. To speak of such an epochal decline of politics, however, is not to suggest that "politics" in all of its colloquial urges (including the exercise of state power) has disappeared from our vocabulary or from our everyday social reality. "Decline" in the sense I employ it, refers to a deeper historical process of depoliticization, to the loss of citizen participation and social governance, to the narrowing of public discourse, to the eclipse of political community that held so much value for the Greeks, Rousseau, and even for Americans like Paine and Jefferson. The disintegration of politics in the modern world (and not just in the United States) ultimately reflects the profound failure of major ideologies to continue to furnish visions and guideposts for the future, to address people's needs and aspirations—indeed to offer the kind of political language required to confront new situations, conditions, and challenges. Universal appeals to socialism (however that belief system is defined), nationalism, or religion have little resonance today in highly industrialized countries. At the same time, liberal capitalism—the presumably reigning ideology of both American society and the "new world order"—is beset with such deep contradictions that its legitimacy now rests on the most fragile underpinnings. None of these worldviews provides the basis of sustained moral purpose, commonality, and engagement with a turbulent world needed to revitalize politics and confront pressing issues.[17] We are now moving inexorably into a Hobbesian universe that the conventional ideologies can no longer hope to grasp.

The underlying historical causes of this impasse are many, but they tend to revolve around one overriding condition, namely, increased corporate penetration into virtually every corner of modern American life (what I call "colonization"), a phenomenon that has been speeded up and intensified by such forces as economic globalization and the information revolution. In many ways the predatory system of privilege and power is devouring its own (increasingly precarious) foundations. The grandiose ambition of American elites to extend their dominion throughout the world, while ostensibly a sign of great national economic, political, and military strength, has turned into a deadly bargain for the population as a whole, auguring long-term political weakness rather than the heightened power that now seems to be the most visible outcome.

Nothing has undermined the public sector or eviscerated political discourse more than this process of corporate colonization. Without doubt corporate power and wealth shape politics in the United States today more than ever—in corporations' very growing presence in the economy, their extensive lobbies and influence over legislative activity, their ownership and control of the mass media, their preponderant influence over election campaigns, their capacity to secure relief from myriad regulatory controls, their massive public relations apparatus, their general subsidies to the two major parties and the convention process, and so forth.[18] At the dawn of the twenty-first century American politics has become full-blown capitalist politics to an extent that even Marx might not have anticipated. Surely C. Wright Mills's prediction, in *The Power Elite* (1958), of a thorough convergence of economic and political strata has by now come to pass.[19] From this standpoint, the deterioration of the public sphere can be understood as a deep manifestation of advanced capitalist development.

The economic, political, and cultural signs of corporate colonization are increasingly abundant and readily visible in the contours of daily life. Consider, for example, the unparalleled growth of such corporate media giants as Time Warner, Disney/ABC, Bertelsmann, Viacom, and Rupert Murdoch's News Corporation, which preside over a new era of communications globalization.[20] These corporate behemoths control not only mass communications to a surprisingly large extent, exercising vast influence over film production, cable TV, radio, and book publishing and other forms of print journalism; their capacity to maintain ideological hegemony in and through the public sphere has reached qualitatively new heights. The corporate stranglehold over political dialogue, whether such dialogue is labeled "liberal," "conservative," or "independent," has disastrous consequences for democratic participation that will be elaborated on later. What deserves further comment for now, however, is that this very process has unfolded outside the realm of popular involvement or political debate. As one observer writes, "What is tragic is that this entire process of global media concentration has taken place with little public debate, especially in the U.S., despite the clear implications for politics and culture."[21] Mass media that are the direct extension of corporate power and wealth can be expected to trumpet, in one fashion or another, those virtues or attributes most consonant with perpetuation of that very system of power and wealth, namely, free markets, consumerism, personal responsibility, competitive individualism, and lessened reliance on the public's input or state governance. Under these circumstances, dominant media players will foster a discourse that focuses on the "economy," on such distinctively material factors as gross domestic product, levels of growth and productivity, interest rates, corporate performance in Wall Street's eyes, budgetary concerns, and inflation, to the virtual exclusion of such social concerns as the quality of work, subordinate authority relations, the environment, the gulf between rich and poor, and human needs (such as housing, health care, and sanitation). A strictly economic language functions to distort, perhaps even obliterate, specifically public concerns that remain silent where corporate priorities hold sway. Self-interest and greed become the readily accepted standards of behavior at a time when the media chooses to serve as a watchdog over the supposed moral foibles of politicians and other celebrities. In this vein Disney's ABC network in February 1998 aired a special program on "greed," hosted by John Stossel, that surpassed even the classic laissez-faire doctrines of Adam Smith in its strong claim that old-fashioned self-interest can secure the common good far better than any set of ideas set forth in the public sphere. Citing such billionaire success stories as Ted Turner, Bill Gates, and Michael Milken, the program extolled greed for its role in generating wealth, innovation, goods, and jobs, in giving people "what they want," in giving rise to a dynamic economy. Greed thus advances the flow of capital and helps make the world go around. Lost in ABC's one-sided tribute to a mythological free market rooted in competitive greed was any sense of larger social outcomes or human ethics. A more ruthless capitalism might well create massive wealth for a few, but what are its implications for the general distribution of resources, for democracy, for the environment—indeed, for the manner in which people ought to conduct their lives? Such wholesale resurrection of antiquated capitalist dogma has become an article of faith for elites in the contemporary public sphere.

While the era of "big government" has supposedly come to an end, as both Democrats and Republicans like to repeat ad nauseum, the era of big corporations has taken center stage with a vengeance. Corporate gigantism underpins deterioration of the public sphere and, with it, a deepening mood of antipolitics that has few parallels in the twentieth century. The very absence of political debate, much less protest, over such impoverishment of American social life testifies emphatically to the pervasiveness of this mood. The issue of corporate power, manifest today in every area of social life, has never been placed on the public agenda, owing not only to the vast power of corporations but surely also to the profound cynicism among so many people convinced that the political game is rigged in favor of the dominant interests. Youth in particular have decided in greater numbers than ever simply to ignore or sidestep the political realm as reflected in their disaffection with the 1998 elections. (While the vast majority of Americans were opposed to President Clinton's impeachment on grounds that his behavior did not rise to the level of a "high crime or misdemeanor," the low turnout suggested that the Clinton sex scandal itself did not generate much *political* interest.) More and more adults, at the same time, have chosen to disengage themselves from the public realm by opting for intensely privatized lifestyles that may include trips to the shopping mall, greater fixation on TV, surfing the Internet, and, most ominously, a move into gated communities of "fortress America" replete with private security forces and electronic monitoring devices.[22]

If modern liberal capitalism has trumpeted the virtues of free and open access to the public sphere linked to classical Lockean ideals of individual competition and social autonomy, the reality of corporate colonization has produced more or less the opposite: a Hobbesian world of chaos and fragmentation where democratic participation has become a chimera. The public sphere has become thoroughly depoliticized.[23] Indeed, the very matrix of the liberal-capitalist state is now in the process of being dismantled, a victim of those forces of greed, competition, aggression, and predatory violence unleashed by global capital in its mania to dominate all sectors of human life. As a zone where people could enter into discourse with others, exchange ideas, mount debates, and influence collective decision making—where, in fact, important problems of common concern could be addressed—the public arena has degenerated well beyond even those minimal standards of liberal capitalism. This dismal state of a public sphere that has been taken over and gutted by huge private interests can be viewed as the defining crisis of American society at the end of the twentieth century.[24]

Of course the phenomenon of corporate colonization has been with us for many decades; what is new about the contemporary situation is the solidification of a neoliberal global order made possible by the tremendous growth in power of multinational corporations over the past two or three decades. Today business elites are not only stronger and more aggressive than before, they face considerably less organized political opposition—owing in no small measure to their much enhanced international mobility and to the success of their propaganda, which trumpets the inevitability of "free market" economics as the only rational alternative in a world that has seen the collapse of communist and socialist alternatives. Corporate domination is thus facilitated by a thoroughly depoliticized public that is consumed by spectacles and carnivals that take the place of serious political debates, that substitute for genuine popular involvement that might conceivably pave the way toward greater self-governance. Hence the neoliberal order, geared far more toward maximizing profits for the leading multinational firms than toward values of democracy or the free market, has come to depend on an atomized society of disengaged individuals who feel alienated and powerless.

THE LOGIC OF ANTIPOLITICS

Over the past two decades the spreading national ethos of what might best be labeled antipolitics has deepened even further. A definite majority of Americans has come to feel, justifiably enough, that it is almost completely powerless in the face of incredibly rapid (and seemingly unfathomable) economic and cultural changes; the established political system offers fewer and fewer outlets or resources, less space for genuine participation, and little hope for the future. No observer should be even the least surprised, therefore, to find that, in David Croteau's words, "the reigning political mood in America is a combination of disenchantment, cynicism, and alienation."[25] At the core of all this is a perpetually eroding language of the "public" that can be detected in every arena of life: TV news, talk shows, the Internet, schools, cafes, popular culture, elections, even social movements that have adapted to what in American political culture has become a seductive and increasingly overpowering pull of antipolitics. "Politics" has become the most denigrated and devalued of all enterprises, robbed of the visionary, enobling, and transformative qualities that not so long ago were associated with the great popular movements of the 1960s and 1970s (which found their original inspiration in the earliest civil rights demonstrations).

The depoliticization of American society appears to be deepening with each passing year, reflected in surveys indicating that younger respondents seem to grow ever more disaffected with politics. A 1997 UCLA poll of 252,082 freshmen at 464 colleges and universities around the country showed a precipitous decline in student knowledge of and interest in politics—signs of what could be described as the "disengaged generation." Only 26.7 percent of respondents said that it was important to keep up with public affairs, the lowest tabulation ever and far less than the 57.8 percent reported for 1966. Two main culprits in this downward cycle, according to poll director Alexander W. Astin, are television and computers: "It's the whole electronic thing, the wired society, people sitting in front of their screens, playing video games, watching TV. It is encouraging all of us to be independent, isolated individuals. That is going to lead naturally to disengagement."[26] Perhaps the depressingly bleak vision of the future portrayed in Terry Gilliam's brilliant film *Brazil* may have to be taken seriously after all. The film depicts a dystopian society of docile, mindless, willing victims of a pervasive, numbing, and destructive technological order that in some ways goes even beyond the nightmare of George Orwell's novel *1984*.

As the national mood of antipolitics builds in reaction to closure of the public sphere, long-standing forms of civic participation often give way to a variety of popular responses that might be summed up under the heading "retreat from politics." While such responses include the widespread embrace of privatized lifestyles (abetted by TV and computers, to be sure), they also extend to more distinctly *social* phenomena where empowerment is sought, but mainly outside of and against the public sphere: millenarian new-age groups and cults, gangs, militias, back-to-the-country environmental movements, a multitude of therapeutic fads, and postmodern intellectual culture. This volume explores both the historical context and the general constituent elements of political decline, which has become one of the dominant motifs of American life during the rise of post-Fordist globalized capitalism.

It might well be argued that American politics has *always* been the domain of elites, quite remote from the life rhythms of ordinary citizens—the province of exploitative and manipulative private interests rather than a mechanism of empowerment for workers, minorities, and other disenfranchised groups. There is, of course, much truth to this generalization. The promises of democracy have mostly run hollow throughout U.S. history; a liberal-capitalist power structure has penetrated and transformed every aspect of daily life, and politics has all too often degenerated into an authoritarian, semiadministered charade where real choices and alternatives have been obliterated. Yet this is only one portion of the truth. There is no denying that over the past two centuries new participatory spaces have opened up, chipping away at many of the structural and ideological barriers to inclusive citizenship—the result mainly of a series of popular struggles (by labor, feminists, civil rights activists, the New Left, and so on) that helped to democratize the political culture. By the 1960s and 1970s that culture wound up far less elitist and authoritarian than before, far less closed off to democratic inputs from within civil society—and far less racist and patriarchal. Owing to those important struggles, not to mention the explosive movements of the 1960s and later, the public sphere was broadened well beyond the confining parameters of a republic enshrined in the Constitution and in documents such as *The Federalist Papers.* The problem today, as I emphasize in the following pages, is that this precarious social and political space won through hard battles has progressively narrowed since the late 1970s, when the public sphere became increasingly subject to the ravages of corporate colonization. In this setting the decline of politics amounts to nothing less than a harsh turn backward, toward a more regressive and antidemocratic order, to a degree that calls into question the very foundations of American civic life. The simple democratic optimism of Alexis de Tocqueville's mid-nineteenth-century account of the nation's political life runs aground on the turbulent, dystopic realities of late-twentieth-century global capitalism, where a democratic institutional facade barely conceals deep underlying Hobbesian currents.

The proliferation of antipolitical tendencies, with the inevitable connotations of irrationalism, mysticism, conspiracy theories, and local self-absorption, may seem totally out of place in a modern society characterized by the outward Weberian features of bureaucratic rationalization and administrative control. As with the seemingly permanent control of government by elites, the retreat from politics among mass publics may be viewed as something more attuned to earlier times and other (mainly preindustrial) places. As Michael Parenti has observed, the United States has always been a land of idols and myths that function, whether or not by overt design, to discourage popular mobilization and social protest against vested interests. "In the struggle for social justice and democracy," writes Parenti, "we must traverse a land of idols."[27] The crucial difference today is that such tendencies appear to be growing dramatically throughout the population—owing in part to the immense concentration of corporate and state power, which so often pushes public anger and frustration outside the political terrain, toward more immediate, micro, psychologically gratifying, and typically privatized modes of resistance. To be sure, this type of extrainstitutional resistance can lay the groundwork for what James C. Scott calls "the infrapolitics of subordinate groups"—a stage in the possible evolution toward a more full-blown oppositional politics.[28] In the United States, however, the chronic absence of a viable oppositional politics only reinforces the inclination to look elsewhere, outside the public sphere, for individual or small-group answers to pressing social challenges. The worship of idols (mystical or irrational beliefs) is commonly associated with a profound fear of politics, with avoidance of harsh or threatening social realities even when such realities may come to dominate the social landscape. The opposite of this—broad development of a modern oppositional politics designed to bring about social transformation—suggests some measure of ideological coherence and organizational leverage of the sort long identified with socialist movements and parties, but it goes far beyond forms of electoral and legislative activity that define the conventional liberal-capitalist view of politics. The conception of politics (and the public sphere) that informs this book does indeed encompass electoral activity, but it also extends well beyond it, into the comparatively murky realm of social movements and the wide range of discourses that enter into and help constitute the whole terrain of public life. In a world of intensifying corporate colonization, where ideological hegemony permeates every aspect of life, governmental institutions alone can never be the centerpiece of analysis and vision. The diffusion of antipolitical tendencies, however, is not simply a manifestation of irrational or metaphysical impulses disconnected from real historical forces at work; antipolitical tendencies also unfold at the very center of highly institutionalized public spaces. What seems uniquely interesting about contemporary circumstances is the prevalence of popular "escapes" from politics, if not from society altogether: the sublimation or deflection of public concerns in a mystical or privatized mental enclave, privatized forms of withdrawal, a focus on vague planetary (or interplanetary) conspiracies, social empowerment through membership in gangs and cults, a quasi-religious obsession with technology, to name some alternatives.

One of the most fetishized "idols" of our time turns out to be the information revolution, which in some circles has become a panacea for solving virtually any social problem: economic crisis, military conflicts, learning disorders, health ailments, environmental decay, even political cynicism or apathy. As computerized technology transforms the global economy, the "knowledge industry" is part of an unprecedented worldwide integration of production and financial, political, and cultural processes; communications has become more rationalized, more far-reaching in its human consequences. But this is in many ways a chimera of a revolution. The irony is that the collapse of the public sphere in modern society is taking place at exactly the time when the information revolution is in full swing, when people (especially in the industrialized nations) have become inundated with huge mountains of data—and are blessed each year with more sophisticated computers. In fact the rapidly increasing availability of new machines, not to mention the proliferation of media outlets, cable TV channels, publishing houses, books, magazines, and video productions might indicate something of a *negative* relationship between the massive spread of techniques or "facts" and the prospects for deep citizenship, flourishing public dialogue, and diffusion of critical thinking. This notion is hardly a new one; the authoritarian, even repressive, consequences of modern technology were analyzed in the 1960s by Herbert Marcuse in *One-Dimensional Man,* as well as in the more recent works of Langdon Winner (*Autonomous Technology*), Theodore Roszak (*The Cult of Information*), Neil Postman (*Technopoly*), and David Noble (*The Religion of*

Technology).[29] A revitalized politics will ultimately depend on a subversion of instrumental rationality, which is one of the hallmarks of contemporary technological discourse. If the British activist Hilary Wainwright is correct in suggesting that democratic transformation requires a sustained popular attack on instrumentalism (technocratic ideology expressive of the status quo) in the name of a "new politics of knowledge" linked to grassroots struggles, then the development of much anticipated cyber machines of the twenty-first century will necessarily constitute a primary setting for fierce cultural and political battles in which the force of technology will have to be demystified so that it can be seen simply as a vehicle of social progress.[30] Technology in its present incarnation is much too well assimilated into the prevailing corporate structure to represent, in itself, anything close to an emancipatory mechanism.

Utopian hopes and dreams originally invested in the "digital revolution" (not long ago celebrated by *Wired* magazine, futurists Alvin and Heidi Toffler, and thousands of computer aficionados have already foundered on a stubborn corporate reality; Internet culture has become deeply enmeshed in mainstream economics and culture. By the late 1990s one was hearing less and less about the historic benefits of computer technology and how these would lead to unprecedented levels of freedom, democracy, and creativity. In fact, the Internet—like other arenas of global communications—exists as a vessel for anything that takes place in society (whether daily personal interactions, corporate transmissions, news accounts, pornography, dating services, or political activity). Such bottom-line-oriented firms as Microsoft, Disney, Time Warner, and America Online have a comparative stranglehold over cyberspace that can rarely, if ever, be matched by even the most resourceful individuals and small groups. If the Internet was once theorized by the intellectual "digerati" as a kind of technological playground, in practice it has evolved into yet another extension of the corporate multimedia complex, reinforcing predominantly middle-class values and benefiting traditional businesses.[31] With nearly 60 million users on-line (as of early 1999) and with its use growing rapidly, the Internet has assumed a specific modus operandi, namely, business-as-usual. To the extent that this is the case, the much celebrated informational revolution too becomes a vehicle of depoliticization.

CAPITALISM VERSUS DEMOCRACY

A critic of this line of thinking—that is, regarding the whole process of depoliticization that is the main focus of this volume—might object that my analysis is much too relentlessly pessimistic, that it involves a harsher and more sweeping account of the forces in motion than the actual reality implies. Leftists in particular may prefer a more "balanced" interpretation that effectively takes into account the wide array of systemic contradictions and emancipatory possibilities. The problem is that, while such contradictions do persist and have even intensified, the likelihood of fundamental social change in the near future seems increasingly dismal, all the more so in industrialized countries. My belief is that such objections ignore deep transformations in American political culture that are no longer hidden from public view—whether one is watching TV news, following election campaigns, partaking of popular culture, participating in community groups, or simply keeping up with current events. Closure of the public sphere, especially as it affects social policy, has become an unassailable fact of contemporary life—denied only by those who continue to believe that interminable debates over the federal deficit, sex scandals, personal responsibility, and the drug war will make much difference to people's quality of life, or by those with millenarian ideologies who in the end have little interest in engaging the existing public sphere. As social and ecological crises worsen, there is no sign that the political system is capable of addressing, much less solving, these megaproblems. The spread of antipolitical currents across regional, class, racial, and gender divisions seems also impossible to ignore, as it throws up new barriers to radical democratic change. To deny all this—to forget that we live in a thoroughly depoliticized society—serves only to obscure the real (and global) challenges at hand. Any historical analysis that blurs or dismisses basic developmental truths for the sake of a more uplifting vision can never produce a viable political strategy. As Marx insisted, nothing short of a relentless and total critique of prevailing social reality will be adequate for a theory and practice of historical transformation. And to paraphrase Gramsci's well-known motto, which appeared on the masthead of his journal *Ordine Nuovo*, political optimism is never subverted by "pessimism of the intellect" but more likely will be informed or served by it. The cause for "pessimism" in Gramsci's time was, among other things, a series of crushing blows to the socialist Left followed by the rise of fascism. In our own time it could refer to mounting global problems and, more immediately, to the eclipse of politics itself with its vast implications for the future of citizenship, democratic participation, state governance, and social change. Less than two decades after the fascist conquest of power in Italy the system disintegrated, triggered by a losing war effort, the collapse of Mussolini's legitimacy, and the rise of explosive popular movements linked to the Resistance. In the United States today, any revitalized politics will have to take serious stock of the immense (and in some ways novel) obstacles and challenges that lie ahead— obstacles and challenges that demand above all a *political* revitalization.

The historical forces that feed into the recurrent cycle of antipolitics cannot be isolated from *systemic* features of global capitalism any more than we can explain the influence of mass media and popular culture without referring to the growing colonization of American life by mammoth business interests. While the global reach of market capitalism gives the appearance of solidified U.S. *national* power, the overall developmental consequences are far more complex. Multinational corporations operating in diverse regions of the world yield extraordinary profits and material affluence for some, but they may also give rise to massive social decay in society as a whole. Alongside the postwar trend toward increasingly large international industrial and banking firms, the United States has emerged, since the 1960s, as a *declining* global world power even though it emerged as the world's only genuine military superpower at the end of the cold war. In pouring such vast resources into the global economy—not to mention a far-flung military support system—the United States appears to have exhausted the limits of its hegemonic position, much along the lines argued by Paul Kennedy in *The Rise and Fall of the Great Powers*.[32] Not only has the United States lost some of its competitive advantage relative to other industrialized powers, but it has, more significantly, allowed vast resources to be drained away from the domestic infrastructure. Global power in this scenario turns out to be illusory: high levels of material growth are translated into a pattern of highly uneven development, marked by the loss of quality jobs, eroding social services and welfare functions, the disintegration of urban life, increasing crime rates and substance abuse, and generalized environmental blight. The idea of an "American Century" in which all (or even the majority of) citizens could share in the fruits of economic growth guaranteed by a dynamic capitalist regimen has finally revealed its limits, despite stepped-up elite propaganda about the virtues of a "free market," globalization, free trade, and so forth. In the words of James Petras and Morris Morley: "As the U.S. overseas capacity grows amid rising competition, a zero-sum game emerges: what is spent or invested abroad is largely at the expense of the domestic economy."[33] From this perspective, the U.S. invasion of Panama along with Persian Gulf and Yugoslavian involvements may be seen as evidence of national weakness rather than strength—a forced resort to imperialist bavura largely for the sake of domestic political one upsmanship.

The origins of an eroding public sphere in the United States are thus entirely systemic, and the consequences are global in character. Most of the great challenges we face—the ecological crisis, for example—have become increasingly global in scope, meaning that the political discourse required to dissect and confront them must be global as well. While traditional ideologies such as liberalism, nationalism, socialism, and communism lose their contemporary resonance, the institutional routines of normal politics have become a site of mounting futility and despair. In the United States, at least, a distinctly political enterprise that might help citizens cope with a rapidly changing world scarcely exists in any recogniz-able public sphere. (One might compare the depressing American circum-stances with developments in such countries as Germany and Italy, where oppositional politics—pitting Greens, radicals, and former Communists against one another—has been able to carve out a comparatively strong na-tional presence.) In many respects, therefore, the pervasive mood of antipolitics in American society embraces a certain imposing logic of the times. In cases where that mood does not lead to withdrawal from politics altogether, it frequently leads one to a furtive pursuit of "alternatives"—that is, an oppositional outlook and vocabulary—in a context where the "public" domain, however, is viewed as hopelessly corrupt or insufficient.

Any widespread retrieval of politics at this juncture will surely re-quire something of a paradigmatic shift toward what William Ophuls suggestively calls "ecological politics"—recognition that even the most significant local or "micro" problems we face have a global dimension, that politics too must adapt to this holistic reality or wind up further degraded and impotent.[34] One of the great ironies of the past two de-cades is that large-scale, macro, and global issues are increasingly met with local, often individual or privatized, outlooks and "solutions" which is yet another testament to political futility. Problems are typi-cally addressed in isolation, as single manageable concerns, in a way that detaches both discourse and action from the all-important interrela-tionships among them. But, as Ophuls writes, "Even if modern civiliza-tion could find the means to solve any one of these problems in isola-tion, it cannot expect to overcome all of them simultaneously: like Gulliver trussed up by the Lilliputians, industrial civilization will find it-self more tightly bound up with the web of interacting forces that make up ecological scarcity."[35] Of course, any significant detour from this lo-calized mode of thinking—and in the direction of well-developed critical consciousness—is precisely what a depoliticized order nullifies, in great measure by design, at every turn.

Despite its official ideology, liberal capitalism has always stood op-posed to genuine forms of democratic governance insofar as such forms present a serious threat to privileged interests; democratization has oc-curred largely through the energies of popular movements and insurgen-cies.[36] The quasi-Hobbesian character of contemporary society further im-pedes democratic possibilities (not to mention grassroots radicalism), since social fragmentation, moments of chaos, and civic violence all serve to undermine prospects for collective solidarity. The crisis of modernity tied to post-Fordism has given rise to what Ron Inglehart calls a "postmaterialist" (or postmodern) shift among a growing sector of the population in every major industrialized society, including the United States. While this situation opens up new social challenges and responses, from a strictly political standpoint it has generated much local dispersion and ambiguity, imposing limits on development of oppositional struggles.[37] In any event, a central thesis of this text is that the future of American society will depend greatly on how the deepening crisis of the public sphere is resolved. This epochal challenge will demand nothing less than a fundamental reinvention of politics, going beyond old-fashioned pragmatic "realism," absorption in electoral tactics, the *haute politique* of statecraft stratagems, the effort to win momentary reforms, and the like—that is, beyond a strictly modernist phase where industrialism delimits the forces at work. In Ulrich Beck's words: "Reinventing politics means a creative and self-creative politics which does not cultivate and renew old hostilities, nor draw and intensify the means of its power from them; instead it designs and forges new content, forms, and coalitions."[38]

AMERICAN EXCEPTIONALISM REVISITED

The seemingly pessimistic character of the analysis that follows requires something of a disclaimer: I do not intend to suggest that we have literally reached an "end of politics," much less an "end of history" or an "end of ideology," or that depoliticization is so all-embracing or monolithic as to obliterate forever the prospects of a coherent political opposition. If the prevailing forms of hegemony (market liberalism, technological rationality, nationalism) seem to be more deeply entrenched than ever, they are far from being so one-dimensional as to completely negate the presence of grassroots insurgencies rooted in local communities, labor groups' efforts, and the multiple social movements that have retained some dynamism even in the conservative 1990s. I address this important concern at length in the Conclusion, where I argue that globalized corporate capitalism can never attain genuine stability, nor rid itself of conflict and insurgency, while major social contradictions persist in a decaying, harshly inegalitarian order. Indeed, these very contradictions can be expected to become all the more explosive as the fractured, depoliticized system suppresses or in other ways fails to confront them. If today's hegemonic institutions and discourses function to subvert critical thinking and political opposition, their long-term staying power can never be guaranteed. Supposedly stable or monolithic ideological fortresses have been known to crumble almost overnight, as we have seen in Eastern Europe, the Soviet Union, and South Africa just in the past decade or so (and such countries as Mexico, Brazil, and Indonesia may currently be on the verge of similar radical change). The epic upheavals of the 1960s burst on the political scene will little advance warning. Resistance is built into the very logic of multiple structures of domination tied to hyperactive economic growth, uneven development, and widening class and social divisions—phenomena that remain very much a part of the American experience. Despite the awesome, intimidating power of vested interests pitted against them, large groups of people do often begin to respond critically to the world in which they live; they will commonly agitate, resist, fight back, and organize under even the most difficult circumstances, and they will forge a variety of social movements. Indeed, American history is replete with examples of such populist mobilizations directed against the power structure. Clearly not all human reaction to conditions of hardship and alienation is channeled into legitimate modes of discourse and institutional practices, nor does it inevitably succumb to the pressures of depoliticization.[39] What does make the American predicament historically unique is the development of a more deeply ingrained culture of antipolitics than exists in any other industrialized society.

This peculiar state of affairs has deep roots in the American political tradition, with its overriding attachment to such values as competitive individualism, minimal government, economic self-sufficiency, and local autonomy. It also has a basis in the daily experience of ordinary Americans long frustrated by an increasingly remote and impotent political system. After all, it should now be abundantly obvious to all but the most privileged sectors of the population that the corporations, consumed with protecting their wealth and power, have an unprecedented stranglehold over government and most of what passes for political activity. Political institutions and practices have been shrouded in corruption, deceit, hypocrisy, and manipulation to such a degree that a mockery has been made of such time-honored ideals as citizen participation. Governmental power is almost universally viewed as more alien, inaccessible, and repressive than at any time in recent memory, while the familiar American fascination with conspiracy theories—commonly linked to presumed machinations of the state—seems to have more currency today in the wake of political assassinations, the Vietnam debacle, Watergate, the Iran–Contra controversy, the savings-and-loan bailout, and of course the more recent Clinton sex scandal. The ordinary person is not necessarily paranoid to believe that the IRS, FBI, and other government agencies employ increasingly heavy-handed methods, nor to focus on how the *repressive* side of the state (law enforcement, the prison system) has grown so dramatically over the past two decades. And many people are understandably alarmed about the widespread invasion of their privacy, which has often justified by the long-standing federal war on both drugs and terrorism. Where government is so authoritarian and corrupt, people have legitimate reasons for being distrustful of it and for turning away from it as a potential agency of political activism, redress of grievances, or social change.

Insofar as such an ethos of antipolitics makes sense in American

society at this time, any future retrieval of politics will have to be built
on foundations that extend far beyond the parameters of existing state
institutions since these have already been profoundly weakened as
agencies within the public sphere. The traditional reformist idea of simply taking over and perhaps turning around or refurbishing the national governmental apparatus unfortunately cannot work, for both institutional and ideological reasons. The entire structure of power will
have to be *transformed*, not merely conquered, from the grassroots to
the summit, meaning that the struggle for a democratized system of
governance must coincide with a more egalitarian economy and social
structure; neither the state nor politics can be understood as "autonomous." This process naturally involves much more than just adding to
the functions and powers of "big government." Repoliticization will
therefore depend on a historic outpouring of popular-movement energies and discourses made possible by an expanded, more invigorated
public sphere. For such outpourings to be politically empowering and
transformative, the very concept of the "public" will have to be revived
and brought to the forefront of distinctly common agendas that will
shape the twenty-first century. Community, social infrastructure, economic planning, the environment, public welfare, and a revitalized
sense of citizenship will all be prime concerns.[40] To what extent we
can transform this increasingly fragmented, repressive, depoliticized
Hobbesian culture into something much better will no doubt be the
most urgent question of the coming decades.

DIMENSIONS OF THE PROBLEM

A central aim of this book is to identify the origins, components, and implications of political atrophy in the United States—an epochal trend that
shows few signs of abating. The pervasive and deep mood of antipolitics
is associated with feelings of cynicism, despair, uncertainty, and even fear
about the future, and such feelings cannot be disregarded by observers as
simply "irrational" or "escapist." A depoliticized public may generally be
said to have elements of five broad features in common: an unmistake-
able retreat from the political realm; a decline in the trappings of citizenship and with it the values of democratic participation; a narrowing of
public discourse and the erosion of independent centers of thinking; a
lessened capacity to achieve social change by means of statecraft or social
governance; and the eventual absence of a societal understanding of
what is uniquely common and public, what constitutes a possible general
interest amidst the fierce interplay of competing private and local claims.
Of course, our contemporary predicament did not appear suddenly, out

of thin air, but rather is the product of complex, interlocking historical factors that can be traced back to the earliest days of the nation.

As we explore the intricate dynamics of antipolitics in recent American history, several patterns become immediately visible. There is of course a wide range of political escape mechanisms available in the routines of everyday life—mechanisms that involve largely *personal* or privatized options for dealing with alienation (i.e., such options as overindulgence in drugs, alcohol, watching TV obsessively, and so on). My concern here, however, is with more explicitly *social* phenomena that, in many instances, are embodied in a popular movement or interest group. In this category the main forms of antipolitics include: (1) an inward preoccupation with self-actualization consistent with the features of a therapeutic culture; (2) the metaphysical pursuit of individual or spiritual values defined in largely transcendent terms; (3) insular localized struggles for community; (4) spontaneous outbursts of collective action that may be unfocused and short-lived; (5) isolated acts of terrorism or random violence; (6) faith in technological solutions or "fixes" to social problems; and (7) intellectual schemes (postmodernism as one example) that are preoccupied with such themes as nihilism, social retreat, and pessimism. These expressions of a depoliticized outlook remain fluid and changeable, subject to reconceptualization as historical conditions open up new *political* opportunities.

The contemporary flight from politics occurs at a time of mounting social (and ecological) crisis on a world scale—indeed at a time of intensifying global disorder—as well as deterioration of classic ideologies (nationalism, communism, socialism, liberalism) that once provided tens of millions of people guideposts for thought and action. For better or worse, the grand historical discourses that shaped the public sphere for well more than a century have left an enormous void that no alternative ideology or social force has been able to fill. It is in this context that the forms of antipolitics outlined above have made their appearance and taken on new meaning; they clearly benefit from the obsolescence of traditional belief systems. In the absence of a vibrant and democratic public sphere where alternatives can be voiced and heard, oppositional politics is doomed to remain a distinctly marginal activity, at best, while the ruling elites are comparatively free to perpetuate their hegemony—at a time when various global crises are looming.

CHAPTER 1

THE DEPOLITICIZED
SOCIETY

The steady erosion of political debate and the weakened capacity of governing institutions to address urgent social challenges even minimally is rooted in recent historical developments that appear to devalue the very meaning and significance of citizenship. To be sure, these developments converge with some long-standing elements of the American political tradition, but by the 1990s they had begun to systematically transform the most of the public landscape. The crisis of citizenship has assumed several forms, including the loss of civic values and trust, a decline of the sense of political efficacy, lower voter turnout, decreased levels of social knowledge, mounting hostility to government, and the embracing of privatized lifestyles and identities. What this augurs for the future of the American two-party system, however, might be less devastating than is commonly believed insofar as the "stability" of the system (as political scientists frequently remind us) can actually be reinforced by the phenomenon of a disengaged citizenry; a generalized disinterest in politics effectively gives elites more space to maneuver and hence more power.

THE PARTY SYSTEM AS FACADE

Before exploring this situation I wish to address a theme that goes to the core of recent antipolitical trends, namely, the shrinking of public discourse in the fullest possible sense. Corporate liberalism now maintains a strengthening hegemony over the political life of the country, made possible above all by a growing concentration of economic and political power. This reality alone imposes strict limits on public debate, or at

least on those exchanges and deliberations that have direct policy implications. Even classical liberalism, with its emphasis on civic virtues and
democratic participation, seems nearly obsolete in the new circumstances. Progressive alternatives too have been increasingly marginalized:
populism, socialism, communism, even the great social movements of
the past few decades. Such an epochal shift in American political culture
would seem to be captured by Francis Fukuyama's "end of history" thesis,
perhaps even by the familiar "end of ideology" argument fashioned before the era of 1960s radicalism, but that would be a false reading in that
many forms of social conflict do persist—and may even be intensifying—
amid current depoliticizing trends.[1]

Familiar ideological traditions—liberalism, socialism, nationalism, fascism, communism, perhaps even conservatism—have lost their points of
contact with rapidly changing global conditions; with few exceptions, they
no longer offer a source of analysis or vision of the future.[2] What indeed
has "socialism" meant to the ruling parties of France, Spain, and Greece,
or "liberalism" in the case of Great Britain and the United States? What is
the contemporary significance of "communism" in China, North Korea,
and Cuba? Moreover, how are we to understand the substance of presumably "conservative" alternatives to corporate liberalism, with their archaic
appeals to a free market, individualism, and traditional virtues that can offer no policy or developmental guidance in the modern world? Elites have
been freed to articulate their own (generally esoteric and instrumentalized) discourses, insulated from the pressures of mass consciousness
and the actualities of daily life.[3] In this setting a multiplicity of far-fetched
promises and appeals may come to the fore, including the return to a laissez-faire economy, the celebration of idealized family values, the extermi-
nation of "drugs," and the wholesale export of democratic institutions on
a global scale. None of these possibilities is sufficiently grounded in historical reality to warrant being taken seriously as an element of rational government policy. The ofttimes ready resort to facile "solutions" is simply
one reflection of how politics has declined as a source of meaning and
identity—and how it has ceased to perform the critical function of mass
mobilization in the advanced industrial world.

Looking at the evolution of American politics, it is possible to show
the degree to which differences between Democrats and Republicans
have mostly collapsed—or, to put it more succinctly, how Democrats have
increasingly assimilated the Republican belief system. From the 1930s
through most of the postwar years Democrats argued for a Keynesian liberal agenda with its broad commitment to social justice, redistribution of
wealth, public welfare, regulation of the economy, and expanded social investment. The New Deal coalition was rooted in a mixture of progressive
constituencies (labor, minorities, the poor) that was galvanized by an

ethos of political struggle (in capitalist boundaries, to be sure). By the
1990s this coalition had broken down, giving way to a collection of narrow, sectoral interests working to push the party toward the "dynamic
middle" and away from a politics of struggle. Today the Democratic Party
has taken on a distinctly procorporate, interest-group outlook that fully
meshes with the antipolitical mood of the times, invoking such traditionally conservative ideas as the free market, free trade, family values, deregulation, welfare overhaul, lowered public investment, the war on drugs,
and so forth. This turnabout perfectly reflects President Clinton's dictum
that "the era of big government has come to an end." Beneath the rhetoric of a common vision made possible through local initiative and personal responsibility one can detect a more imposing agenda: Democrats,
like Republicans, are thoroughly enmeshed in the all-consuming interests
of Wall Street and the multinational corporations, part of what Robert
Borosage calls the "suffocating consensus."[4] After his 1996 reelection,
President Clinton outlined a new Democratic program designed to occupy the "vital center" (neither conservative nor liberal), freeing his energies to complete his task of "preparing America for the twenty-first century." This regimen amounts to a thinly disguised conservatism—a
balanced budget, free trade, reduced social spending, an emphasis on personal responsibility, getting tougher on crime—under the old Democratic
label. It does nothing to reverse huge Pentagon outlays, the ongoing loss
of jobs from capital flight, worsening urban decay, or the same harmful
growth and allocation patterns. President Clinton's "alternative" is neither
liberalism nor centrism but simply a formula for capitulation to time-honored Republican agendas.

In view of all this, is it any wonder that most political discourse is reduced to either media formulas or empty posturing that, among other
things, conveniently allows elites to sidestep the social and political consequences of corporate domination. If the power of corporations has
reached new peaks, such power has nonetheless managed to disappear in
the fog of public debate. It is true that the issue of corporate power has
been taken up by a number of third-party campaigns and progressive coalitions such as the Citizens Party, the Rainbow Coalition, Libertarians,
and Greens, but their ambitious efforts were quickly neutralized by the
workings of the winner-take-all electoral system, an indifferent or hostile
mass media, and of course the culture of antipolitics itself. One of the
ideological effects of a depoliticized society is a widespread loss of interest
in alternatives, where even the most "pragmatic" forms of opposition may
seem futile, a waste of time and energy. Here, as elsewhere, we appear to
have reached a historical devaluing of that very sense of public obligation
and civic participation that the high school textbooks inform us is the sine
qua non of democratic politics.

This development can most visibly be detected in the steady erosion of the two-party system itself—a system that, unique to the industrialized world, has been a defining feature of American politics since the mid-nineteenth century. While Democrats and Republicans surely retain a hold over official public discourse, elections, and legislative activity, their organizations now perform less and less of the functions traditionally associated with parties: offering a real choice, framing identifiable programs and policies, articulating (noncorporate) social interests, providing forums for public debate, mobilizing popular constituencies. Over the past few decades, according to Martin Wattenberg, the American public has been gradually drifting away from the major parties, which, as we have seen, converge more than ever around shared interests and ideas.[5] Opinion polls (taken in 1995) show that as many as 52 percent of all citizens identify themselves as "independent," a sentiment found mostly among the working class, the poor, and minorities. Surveys indicate that most people's attitude toward party rivalry is largely one of boredom and detachment, apparently a key factor in the sharp downturn in voter turnout since the 1950s. One illustration of this trend was the audience's response to Vice President Al Gore's visit to Locke High School in south-central Los Angeles during the 1996 presidential campaign. As Gore spoke, a large number of students roughhoused in front him, talked loudly, and joked around as he was desperately sought their attention. The students then complained that the real main attractions (for them)—Magic Johnson and Kareem Abdul Jabbar—had failed to appear. Most students expressed little or no interest in the vice president's appearance despite his exalted status and the fact that elections were only a few weeks away. Even a hard-hitting defense of besieged affirmative-action policies (before the largely black audience) inspired little support. Said one student, a senior: "He's saying a lot of things, but, honestly, I don't think it relates to me. Personally, I don't think it matters who is president. How does it affect me?"[6] As Wattenberg comments: "Once a central guiding force in American electoral behavior, the parties are currently perceived with almost complete indifference by a large proportion of the population."[7]

Neither major party has any clearly defined ideology, constituency, or goals. Although such diffuseness may once have been considered to be the essence of American political genius—even today it fits nicely in a corporate agenda that *does* have all the coherence the party system lacks—diffuseness (along with the single-member electoral format) impels the parties to move toward the "center" in order to maximize voter support, which of course guarantees ideological moderation. Because structural diffuseness and ideological moderation are so integral to American electoral politics, the problem is not one of corruption or dishonest politicians or even poor candidates, although these factors are present. The parties have been taken over by their professional campaign staffs, media and technical specialists, pollsters, and fundraisers—groups scornful of anything resembling "ideology" and dedicated to the idea of politics as a marketing enterprise. There is now in place a massive campaign industry that proceeds on the basis of recycling time-honored electoral formulas. The role of parties is to aggregate millions of atomized voters who are not expected to participate beyond the ballot box, with any connection between parties and social forces, elections and daily life, having been effectively dissolved. This state of affairs is not democracy but pluralism of elites, or what Macpherson calls "equilibrium democracy," and would be characterized far more effectively by "elite" theorists (Michels, Mosca, and Pareto) than in classical or even modern liberal terms.[8]

One cannot rule out a future popular turn away from the sphere of normal politics that might result in a dramatic boost to third-party efforts; atrophy of the two-party system could be a catalyst for revitalized citizen activism. Signs of this are already visible, as in the appeals of independent party campaigns (including those of billionaire Ross Perot in 1992 and 1996). In 1992 there were no less than 74 minor parties registered in the United States, a figure all the more astonishing given the historical record of third-party futility. More often, however, the declining strength of Democrats and Republicans is accompanied by a deepening alienation from politics *tout court*, as if the two-party failure grows out of a more basic flaw in the whole political enterprise. Disaffection with the major parties can be, and to some extent has been, transferred to the larger political realm. Here the decline of the major parties and the accelerated drift toward antipolitics is temporally linked, reinforced by the pervasive corruption of the Reagan, Bush, and Clinton administrations, revelations of the Iran–Contra scandal, broken promises of politicians, boring and irrelevant party conventions, and the glaring failure of the political system to address urgent social problems. There is also the ongoing rhetorical assault on "big government" waged by the major parties as well as by leading sectors of the media, popular culture, and the intelligentsia, an assault that has effectively discredited the idea of "public" engagement, particularly at the national level. In Dionne's words, "If things are going wrong in society, it's far easier to blame government, a big obvious institution, and politicians, whom no one much likes anyway, than to talk about important but rather vague forces such as 'the global economy.' "[9]

American parties are structured in such a way as to tone down or trivialize debate over substantive issues—a phenomenon that goes back well before the days of TV or the mass media. Yet, both Democrats and Republicans, while ideologically moderate on the surface, are anything but inert, purposeless entities drifting aimlessly about the political scene; each, in different ways, serves as a conduit of corporate domination and privileged interests, and each represents a case study in the decisive role of wealth and money in politics. Consider the 1996 elections. The AFL-CIO contributed $35 million to Democratic campaigns, while large business interests outspent organized labor by more than seven-to-one, with business raising about $250 million for mainly Republican candidates. Given the hegemonic role of corporations, along with mounting disparities between rich and poor, it is hardly surprising to find that money works so effectively through the party system to shape conservative outcomes. Business interests spend money with the idea of securing low taxes, less government regulation, economic privatization, and cuts in public spending (at least *social* cuts)—all perfectly compatible with the Republican agenda. Democrats who receive corporate largesse will be more inclined to curtail traditional liberal programs. In many cases, of course, business donors, PACs, and lobbies may simply want to purchase access to decision makers. In fact, the Clinton campaign was able to raise $135 million in 1996, most of it from sources that have little interest in progressive movements or goals, as the 1997 investigation into Clinton fundraising activities clearly revealed. To the extent politics is driven by money, progressive challenges to business-as-usual in the public sphere will easily be blocked: the need to raise big money inevitably puts severe limits on what can be taken seriously in the political arena, since few politicians are financially independent enough to carry out independent strategies, especially anticorporate strategies.

CITIZENSHIP IN DECLINE

One of the more visible and easily measurable signs of depoliticization is sharply fading voter participation. Always a highly problematic area of American politics, electoral turnout in recent years has fallen to all-time lows in both national and local campaigns. The percentage of registered voters who cast ballots in the Bush–Clinton contest in 1992 dropped to 48.6 percent, compared to turnouts of 52.6 percent in 1980 and 62.8 percent in 1960. The turnout rate for the hard-fought 1994 congressional elections—which heralded in the so-called Gingrich Revolution—was an even more dismal 38.6 percent, meaning that more than 80 million potential voters decided to sit out the election. It is not unusual to see fewer than 30 percent of eligible voters going to the polls for local and municipal elections. Although citizen alienation from politics may be a worldwide phenomenon, especially in the industrialized countries, U.S. voter participation rates remain abysmally low when compared to rates in other countries. In settings where the party system presents clearer choices—that is, where a viable left alternative exists—electoral involvement is predictably much greater. Using 1984 as a benchmark, the turn-out rate for national elections in Australia was 94.2 percent, in Belgium 93.6 percent, in Sweden 89.8 percent, in West Germany 89.1 percent, in Italy 89.0 percent, and in Israel 78.8 percent. For the 1995 general elections in Quebec the turnout rate was 93.5 percent.[10]

Although voter participation in the United States has always been low in comparison with other liberal-democratic countries, it had nonetheless reached all-time lows by the 1990s, surely a testament to the empty spectacle that American politics has become. There seem to be few, if any, compelling reasons for citizens to express themselves politically through the ballot box. Disinterest in the traditional electoral process is particularly evident among the poorer, less educated strata: among the poorest one-fifth of the population in 1996 the turnout rate was less than 35 percent overall, compared with 75 percent among the most affluent one-fifth. The blue-collar turnout for presidential elections declined from 59 percent in 1968 to 45 percent in 1980 to 34 percent in 1994, while the rate for both Latinos and blacks—always very low—dipped well below 40 percent. Such data suggest that the mood of antipolitics, when measured by voting statistics, has deepened among lower-status groups fed up with ritualized election campaigns and empty promises.[11] In fact, this mood coincides with the definite *preference* of elites, who clearly realize—despite their nominal appeals to civic duty—that low voter participation among the poor, minorities, and labor gives those who rule greater flexibility and power.

The magnitude of this downward spiral in American voter turnout is illuminated by the following facts: (1) registered voters in 1996 totaled 96 million (48.8 percent) of the 196 million potentially eligible to vote, with only 23.9 percent of the voting-age population supporting President Clinton's reelection; (2) the 1996 voter participation rate was the lowest since the elections in 1924, despite the vast amounts spent on political advertising, which (in theory at least) reached more people than ever; (3) only 39 percent of viewers watched election returns on TV, less than half the 1968 number; and (4) no matter what person or party or political issue was cited, no more than 25 percent of the population expressed any support of it.

An equally revealing indicator of increasing political indifference is the sharply declining knowledge of (and interest in) social and governmental matters—part of a more general waning of sense of civic obligation. There is actually nothing inevitable about this trend; given some of the powerful cultural developments at work in American society throughout the postwar years, one might even hypothesize that there would be a marked *upward* shift in the measures of political interest and knowledge. The number of college graduates has quadrupled since 1945, while libraries, bookstores, and publishing houses have flourished as never before, saturating the culture with books and periodicals on every conceivable topic. By the 1990s Americans were reading more than ever and were far more educated than at any time in history. Far more people go to college in the United States than in any other country: in 1995, about 45 percent of all high school graduates were able to enroll at institutions of higher education, compared with average rates of less than 10 percent in European countries. Modes of communication are far more sophisticated and accessible today than ever, reflecting the high-tech revolution with its proliferating information networks, as well as increased computerized data processing, enhanced mass media, and general technological expertise. There is an unprecedented amount of data and information for public consumption available in all important areas of life: education, science, health and medicine, the arts, family and sexuality, the environment, race relations, foreign affairs. Never in human history has so much information been so readily available to the public. Advancing together with the new technology is a sprawling media culture featuring hundreds of TV and cable outlets, countless film and video productions, thousands of radio stations, an explosion in print materials, and now, with the Internet, a mind-boggling array of multimedia products—often relatively cheap and accessible even to people on the lower end of the income scale.

The extent to which this rapidly snowballing wealth of technological and cultural resources winds up being translated into knowledge for empowerment, however, is yet another matter. In fact, the *political* results are strikingly at odds with what might be expected; as college attendance, book purchases, exposure to media, and access to informational technology reach peak levels, we find the process of depoliticization in full swing. American society has experienced a dramatic erosion of knowledge about and interest in public affairs, especially among young people. Thus, in 1989 only 29 percent of U.S. respondents could name their congressional representative (compared to 38 percent in 1954), while just 25 percent could identify the two senators from their state (compared to 35 percent in 1945). According to the same poll, in 1989 only 36 percent of respondents knew which party controlled the Senate, and only 18 percent knew that the first 10 constitutional amendments make up the Bill of Rights. As the two authors remark about this survey, "It is certainly hard to imagine that a citizen can have a meaningful grasp of or play a vital role in politics of the day without knowing which party controls Congress, what a recession is, what the Bill of Rights is, or says, and so forth."[12] This dismal knowledge deficit only worsens when it comes to awareness of international affairs. In a Gallup poll conducted in 1989, asking people from several countries to locate 16 places on a world map, the average measure for U.S. citizens was 6.9—easily the lowest among all nationalities surveyed. The results demonstrated a sharp decline in geographical knowledge over a span of 40 years, especially among 18- to 24-year-olds. For example, only 25 percent of Americans could identify the Persian Gulf on a map (an area that since the late 1970s has been a focal point of explosive global conflict). Another Gallup poll, conducted in 1988, revealed that an astonishingly small number (roughly 30 percent) of Americans understood the rudiments of reading a map. More than half did not know that Nicaragua (another target area of U.S. foreign policy) was a country where Sandinistas and Contras were in conflict, while 45 percent had no idea that a system of apartheid existed in South Africa. One-third could not name a single NATO member, and fully 25 percent could not find the Soviet Union on a map.

This pathetically low level of political awareness, most pronounced among the poorer income groups, extends even to college youths from more affluent backgrounds. In a 1995 UCLA Higher Education Research Institute poll, conducted among 240,000 university freshmen around the country, less than one-third said that keeping up with public affairs was important to them in their future as students. Only 16 percent reported that they ever discussed politics. The smallest proportion of university students since data were first available, about 20 percent, chose to define themselves as "liberal," or concerned about social change or legislative reforms—this among students with the greatest access to library resources, bookstores, informational technology, and popular culture than among any previous cohorts. The contrast with students of the 1960s and 1970s (even 1980s) could not have been more stark. Commented the survey director, Alexander W. Austin: "The year's college freshmen are more disengaged from politics than any previous entering class. When people become disengaged they don't bother to inform themselves and they make themselves more vulnerable to manipulation." He concludes by describing the freshmen of 1995 as "people who don't see themselves as being part of the democratic process, who don't even understand how democracy works."[13] What I would add to Austin's statement is that, given the nature of contemporary American political life, truly candid freshmen (or members of any other class) could hardly view themselves otherwise.

What we seem to be experiencing in the United States, ironically, is an inverse relationship between the amount of knowledge and "data" available to most people and the extent to which they actually internalize and process it, making it meaningful in their everyday lives. Social and political knowledge of the world may not be perceived as significant or even relevant by people already inclined to withdraw from the public arena. Data networks, information, technological acuity—these specific components do not necessarily contribute to higher degrees of civic consciousness, nor do they automaticaly translate into basic citizenship skills.

Rather, when normal public discourse is so commodified, instrumentalized, or otherwise translated into official rhetoric as to be politically barren, they might work in just the opposite direction. The fact is that high levels of civic awareness and social involvement are, in the United States at least, reserved mainly for economic, political, and cultural elites in the "knowledge industry" (probably no more than 15 percent of the population), who are highly educated, aware, and experienced enough to manage or influence the system that helps to preserve their privileged status. As for the great mass of people, their civic involvement will depend far more on what Putnam calls "social capital"—everyday social and cultural resources needed to sustain popular associations—than all the technological and informational paraphernalia in the world.[14]

Where there is such a dearth of *political* knowledge and interest throughout the population as a whole, we can also expect to find a declining sense of efficacy—the feeling that one can make a difference through individual or collective action, that the expenditure of time and resources toward public commitments is somehow logical. Obviously, rather high levels of efficacy are needed for collective initiatives to have a chance of success, whether in the form of legislative work, social movements, or some broader insurgency directed against the power structure. In the United States, for many years data regarding public attitudes have shown a waning of popular efficacy, reflected in increasingly pervasive anger directed against "politics" and politicians, widespread feelings of cynicism and despair, the spread of conspiracy theories, and greater movement toward privatized lifestyles. These phenomena involve a number of interrelated common perceptions:

- That political debates are meaningless and the parties fail to offer real choices;
- That government is filled with corrupt, self-seeking politicians who cannot be trusted;
- That, in an age of ideological malaise, people are extremely pessimistic about the future;
- That, owing to the vast power of corporate interests, the system is far too rigid for those without abundant resources to have any influence;
- That, with the breakdown of community, people are concerned with their own self-interest first and foremost, vastly diminishing prospects for collective action and the achievement of common goals;
- That changes made possible by political action turn out to be inconsequential in terms of what actually matters to most people; and
- That the overwhelming force of bureaucracy, especially in national politics, means that "you can't fight city hall."

This syndrome of pessimism and hopelessness, which afflicts mostly those who are already impoverished or marginalized, may be seen in such conduits of popular culture as talk radio, TV sitcoms, and films like *JFK*, *Falling Down*, *Forrest Gump*, *Wag the Dog*, *Primary Colors*, and *Bullworth*. (Even progressive, sophisticated documentaries like *Roger and Me* and *American Dream* exude an overpowering sense of working-class futility in the face of massive layoffs at General Motors and a militant strike at Hormel, respectively.) In such a milieu a disinterest in and even disavowal of the public sphere—voting, joining organizations, getting involved in election campaigns or legislative work, going to marches and demonstrations, even discussing issues with friends—can seem perfectly natural and rational. The social space in which to address and debate vital issues diminishes.[15] Such a void can also serve to discourage participation in social movements, where the average person is easily put off by the intimidating presence of "leaders" and "experts" or by the perceived "extremism" of activists who may express contempt for mainstream social and cultural conventions. It could be, too, that the vast majority of people will be alienated from the outlooks and lifestyles of political activists in virtually *any* party, interest group, or movement owing to tremendous gaps in education, income, and status. This gulf can be broadened even further in the case of new social movements, given the tendency toward a more elevated "postmaterialist" outlook among participants in those groups. Similarly, the extremely rapid development of informational culture, with its deep attachment to machines, skills, and knowledge largely at the disposal of the most educated and affluent citizens, has already exerted something of a divisive impact, with disempowering consequences for those left outside the high-tech orbit. Again, those with the most resources and greatest self-confidence, including people most familiar with the corridors of power, will surely be more prepared, materially and psychologically, to exercise a broad range of citizen rights. This upper echelon of citizens includes elements of the professional–managerial stratum, among them lawyers, high-level bureaucrats, technical people, marketing experts, financiers, and media or cultural workers.

The sense of political efficacy is far more honed among the privileged strata, a phenomenon that takes on added meaning in the United States with its ever enlarging material inequalities. To be effective, citizen participation requires at least a minimal amount of time, money, and access, most of which is acquired in the world of business, professional life, and elite higher education. Those removed from this domain—that is, people who have the greatest objective interest in far-reaching social change—will often view political activity as an irrational expenditure of their (more limited) resources. The popular mood of alienation corresponds to the attitude that it makes better sense to look for meaning and identity *outside* of

politics, in the private sphere. As suggested earlier, the elite stratum cannot be too unhappy with this state of affairs. For progressives whose goal
is to mobilize grassroots constituencies for social change, however, the
consequences are devastating. As David Croteau observes, the historic
goal of the Left has been to "socialize the state and politicize society," but
achieving the goal is made difficult when the public sphere is so hopelessly narrowed, fractured, and colonized by powerful interests with their
own aggressive designs. A loss of efficacy is all too often tied to the perception that, given a deeply entrenched power structure, nothing the average person does or could possibly do is likely to make any difference;
"democracy" is reduced to an abstract principle, devoid of action consequences. In the end, as Croteau suggests, "This belief often leads to a
sense that social and political problems are inevitable and that resignation
is the only sane response."[16]

The broadest measure of a depoliticized society—one that incorporates many of the earlier cited factors—is the overall decline of civic consciousness. A civic culture (understood in the broadest sense) requires extensive processes of interaction in the public sphere, sense of community,
general citizen access to decision making, and social obligation, but historical trends in the United States have worked inexorably against such a culture. In its place has emerged a phenomenon quite different, an ethos of
extreme individualism, consumerism, and parochialism that devalues not
only politics but any form of civic involvement. Contemporary urban society reproduces a world of atomized egos and localized defense of turf,
which can easily produce certain Hobbesian extremes where communal
values lose out to the incursions of corporate power, top-heavy bureaucracies, and the culture industry—all exaggerated by the complex vastness of
the city itself.

Social commentators and pollsters have for many years documented
a loss of civility in American society—a far remove from the more celebra-
tory discourse of Tocqueville's classical analysis of the political landscape:
the culture of violence; breakdown of the family and neighborhoods;
weakened popular support for public services and programs; private retreat into consumerism, TV, and home technology; and proliferation of
gangs, militias, and kindred antisocial groups. One finds a marked atrophy of civic activism and solidarity, reflected in the impoverishment of
community forms, neighborhood associations, and even many local movements, along with the rise of more artificial forms of public engagement
(talk radio, consumer malls, cyberspace, and so forth).

Antipolitical sentiment is not only deeply rooted in American culture
but appears to be more or less evenly distributed on the ideological spectrum. Government, politics, politicians—the whole domain of public discourse and activity—is often regarded as the work of the devil, to be dis-

missed in the harshest of terms as hopelessly corrupt and meaningless, beyond any hope of redemption. Historically, the retreat from politics has taken many forms: the New Left and counterculture of the 1960s, the new social movements, identity groups, neo-conservatives and neoliberals, populists, libertarians, new-age worshipers, Republicans who seek a return to laissez-faire ideals, right-wing militia members, and (perhaps most numerous of all) just average citizens fed up with the routine of normal politics. The only remaining bastion of governmental activism, it seems, is the shrinking nucleus of old-fashioned Keynesian liberals committed to expanded federal and state-funded social programs. (To be sure, many forms of *ideological* antistatism are more than ready to coexist with huge outlays for the military, law enforcement, the prison industry, and the always voracious drug-war machinery.) The erosion of civic values is no momentary phase but is rather the product of deep material and cultural forces at work since at least the 1950s. Vital elements of the political enterprise—participation, community, governance—have been distorted or obliterated by postwar depoliticizing trends, creating a mockery of the Aristotelian ideal of *homo politicus* and the Rousseauian hope for community grounded in human solidarity. Here politics, atrophied beyond recognition, can no longer transcend the limits of strictly local, provincial, and centrifugal interests, cannot move beyond identities and loyalties that remain implacably hostile to *any* conception of the public good or general interest.

As civic culture deteriorates further, the psychological traits and habits necessary to support viable citizenship begin to vanish; political structures and practices become increasingly hollow and inert, lost in a thicket of privatized retreat or (in the worst case) Hobbesian chaos and strife. Gestures and images, always part of an expanded media culture, easily overwhelm stirrings toward collective action, while organizations dedicated to social change run up against the limits of mainstream politics. The public sphere is corroded by a profoundly diminished feeling of social belonging—to neighborhood, community, movement, group, party— that might lend transformative meaning to the quest for identity, recognition, and change in everyday life. What emerges instead are more abstract forms of identity bound up in momentary expressions of patriotism, ethnic or racial loyalties, conceits over the control of local turf, and the familiar media spectacle.

This deep transformation of long-established patterns of daily life often gives rise not only to privatized retreat but to romanticized journeys into nostalgia. The resurgence of interest in "family values," personal "roots," ethnic identities, and mythologized earlier historical periods (as with certain feminist practices of goddess worship) makes sense in this context. Whatever its origins, the yearning for a more insular, pastoral, comfortable private sphere is often accompanied by a strong revulsion against civic life, even as the modern setting remains implacably hostile to such traditionalism. Of course, the thoroughly altered character of gender and sexual relations alone would preclude such a return. It was, after all, the feminist movement that affirmed the equation personal = political, thus opening up such subjects as family matters, parenting, relationships, and sexuality issues to public discourse and making them an integral part of the civic culture.[17] The turn toward traditionalism since the early 1980s marks an effort to depoliticize these types of subjects once again, to re-move them from the public sphere. This backlash, therefore, has been just as much a revolt against the integrity of the "public" or "political" as against feminism. Hence the important dialectic that had developed relat-ing everyday life struggles to the broader social governance issues raised by the women's movement is being largely suppressed these days, as part of the general trend toward antipolitics.[18]

The downward spiral of public life cannot be measured simply in terms of passivity and cynicism, or even in terms of the more general re-treat from politics. There is also the phenomenon of citizen anger—an an-ger that is deep-seated, increasingly overt, sometimes directed against hated or feared "others," most commonly focused on "government" but rarely channeled in the direction of the military–industrial complex or "private" corporations. Expressions of anger, whether in the form of tax-payer rebellions, the militias, domestic terrorism, gangs, urban strife, or simple anti-IRS sentiment, have been fueled by hyperreal images of con-flict and violence disseminated constantly through the media and popular culture. Issues range from jobs and taxes to abortion, gun control, crime, and the death penalty. Social hardships frequently give rise to a hardened identity politics, as in the case of the familiar "white male anger" that, more often than not, emanates from a deeply emotional backlash against the social gains won by women and minorities.[19] Popular surveys reveal that hostility to government has reached all-time peaks, reflected in such events as the L.A. riots, the Branch Davidian standoff at Waco in 1993, the Oklahoma City bombing in 1995, and a wave of local terrorist acts— not to mention the general increase of membership in gangs, cults, mili-tias, and outlaw groups. During the 1990s threats to government workers became a much more common phenomenon, with threats involving bombs and other weapons no longer so rare an occurrence. (In the first ten days after the Oklahoma City events the federal government received more than 140 bomb threats.) Public officials, especially in the west and Midwest, were increasingly confronted and verbally assaulted at their workplace and in open meetings. Intense anger has provoked many white men to fantasize about Rambo-like scenarios, where individuals or small groups of ordinary citizens embrace methods of direct action to take on a hard, oppressive, parasitical government by themselves, mobilizing their own grassroots resources. While dramatic confrontations like the Ruby Ridge, Waco, and Montana Freemen standoffs with federal agents are still the exception, the *sentiment* underlying these actions is surprisingly widespread: a 1997 Gallup poll found that nearly 40 percent of Americans believe the federal government poses a threat to people's basic rights.

Strong antigovernment feelings, of course, can be a prelude to mobilization for radical change—but only where such feelings take shape in a milieu of widely shared values of public engagement and collective action. In an environment where politics is routinely denigrated, however, mechanisms of social transformation are undermined, that is, anger is depoliticized, often being channeled in starkly antisocial directions. If the future of any society importantly depends on how institutional power is exercised, then the steady erosion of civic culture with an attendant deep aversion to politics will have long-term implications, since elites will feel freer to pursue their own or corporate agendas with a minimum of interference from below.

MAX WEBER MEETS THOMAS HOBBES

The modern American dilemma has two sides: a political system increasingly remote from a looming social crisis and a depoliticized mass public seemingly incapable of forging any coherent political opposition. If widespread alienation from the public sphere were simply a matter of class division or a sign of mounting popular insurgency, then hostility to government or "politics" might be regarded as an expression of a healthy civic life. But this is far from the case today. In the contemporary American political scene, class consciousness remains weak, organized labor (despite some signs of reawakening in the 1990s) remains shackled by its own conservatism, and popular movements (though still numerous) have fallen victim to the corrosive logic of antipolitics. The sad reality is that in a depoliticized society mobilizing people around common goals is extremely difficult to achieve; the ideological and organizational capacity for planning, for initiating processes of social transformation, is badly weakened by the myriad forces at work. Indeed, the very language of politics has become so corrupted that it conveys little beyond norms of commodified exchange and instrumental rationality, sometimes laced with elements of social Darwinism

This deterioration of political life parallels a general decline in the social and psychological capacity of ordinary people to forge collective identities, establish notions of the public good, democratize the power structure, and carry out badly needed reforms. It means the loss of what

Antonio Gramsci frequently focused on, namely, politics as the passionate connecting link between philosophy and everyday life, between history and democratic participation. The depoliticized society, like the one-dimensional system long ago anticipated by Marcuse, is one where opposition to the status quo has been dispersed if not extirpated altogether.[20] Citizenship, empowerment, democracy—all these long-cherished values take on an illusory character when public discourse and action have such truncated political consequences. The erosion of political terrain thus takes place on two levels, reflecting the dualistic nature of modernity in general: a rationalized corporate-state order coexists with an atomized civil society, the world presented by Max Weber tensely juxtaposed against the world described by Thomas Hobbes.

CHAPTER 2

SOCIAL CRISIS
AND POLITICAL DECAY

The American political tradition has undergone dramatic and far-reaching changes since the founding of the Republic, despite the presence of strong elements of continuity and stability. As theorized in *The Federalist Papers* and elsewhere, an emergent constitutional regime—influenced as much by Burkean conservatism as by Lockean liberalism—was designed as a bulwark against not only elite tyranny but also the "mob rule" that elites feared would lead to extreme partisan activity, political fragility, and the possible breakdown of new republican institutions. The founders viewed the world, quite understandably, in Hobbesian terms, with images of chaos and anarchy always close at hand, and this collective state of mind reinforced the public mood of anxiety and vulnerability. During this early period the state therefore became an object of considerable ambivalence, with the ideal of citizen participation honored mainly in the abstract. As is well known, suffrage was limited to white male property holders, a comparatively small minority at the time. The political system amounted to essentially what C. B. Macpherson labeled "protective democracy"—an elitist pluralism designed much less for popular decision making than for a defense of embryonic (but still formidable) privileged interests. As Macpherson observes: "In this founding model of democracy for a modern industrial society there is no enthusiasm for democracy, no idea that it could be a morally transformative force; it is nothing but a logical requirement for the governance of inherently self-interested individuals who are assumed to be infinite desirers of their own private benefits."[1] For all but a few radical democrats like Thomas Paine, democracy came to mean little more than a "market mechanism" in which the "voters are consumers and the politicians are the entrepreneurs."[2]

LIBERALISM IN DISARRAY

Beginning in the mid-nineteenth century, this oligarchical system broke down with the gradual introduction of universal suffrage, extended mass participation and individual rights, and a public sphere that by the early twentieth century developed into an enlarged arena of social conflict and popular intervention. In the United States, as in other capitalist democracies, a special discourse of politics emerged that was based on distinctly public and common aspirations, needs, demands, and visions that were revisited and renewed over time. The realm of political language and action eventually became more open and democratized in a way that more clearly approximated classical liberal ideals. Even during the 1840s and 1850s, as Tocqueville amply documented, civic associations flourished and the sense of citizen obligation, while clearly limited, was taken far more seriously than in most European countries. The historic American suspicion of governmental power was directed into a broad culture of civic participation and local self-directed activity. Movements, interest groups, grassroots organizations, parties, even urban machines all sought to extend the terrain of politics, making the state more accessible to such disenfranchised groups as labor, the rural poor, minorities, and eventually women. Even taking into account the obscurantist myths about American democracy that Richard Hofstadter, Mark Roelofs, Howard Zinn, James Morone, and others have rightly stressed, there can be no question that the ideal of *homo civicus* reached a level of ascendancy scarcely imagined in preindustrial society.

The positive side of liberalism consisted in its encouragement of a framework that allowed for broadened mass participation—an institutional and ideological domain in which popular struggles against authoritarian rule could be waged and legitimated. From this standpoint, politics signified the capacity of ordinary people—the same laboring and marginalized strata championed by Paine and Jefferson—to make their own decisions, to become actively engaged in the course of events, to shape history. Liberalism offered a counterforce against rigid, centralized structures while upholding Enlightenment universalism in its dedication to the norms of freedom and economic rationality. Yet, liberalism simultaneously embraced a darker, more undemocratic side that became more clearly visible in the United States than in Europe, coexisting in American with a protracted legacy of political and military horrors that included slavery, the annihilation of Native American lands, culture, and people, the forcible conquest of Mexican territories, and the rise of global militarism set in motion by the Spanish-American War. Liberalism also proved to be compatible with a highly restrictive suffrage that excluded minorities, women, and the poor from citizenship, transforming the idea that "all men are created equal" into a sad hoax.

In a solidifying American liberal tradition the same antistatism that nurtured healthy democratic instincts eventually came to foster a fierce individualism and social Darwinism that opposed any extensive regulation and planning of the economy. And the same defense of localist pluralism served to encourage a highly fragmented and privatized political culture in which the interests of a privileged few would hold sway over the common good. Despite its strong rhetoric of democratic process and civic obligation, liberalism in many ways turned into a caricature of those participatory values that Tocqueville saw as being central to the early American experience. If classical liberalism helped enlarge the public sphere as it subverted traditional institutions and social relations, it also imposed definite limits: the state was designed to protect the free reign of capitalist economic interests against the inevitable encroachment of mass politics. All the celebration of popular sovereignty and local communitarianism served as a facade behind which elites were effectively able to remove politics from the domain of popular determinance. The language of laissez-faire capitalism, possessive individualism, and rational self-interest led, ultimately, to an impoverished political discourse that was bound to negate the requirements of an active citizenship. As Bellah and his collaborators have persuasively argued, the Lockean tradition of individual self-interest that so profoundly shaped American political culture always served to privilege the "private" over the "public" realm, favoring the narrow logic of economics.[3] In the historic struggle between the espoused ideals of democratic participation and the harsh logical requirements of capitalist accumulation—namely, a more rigid social hierarchy, greater division of labor, enlarged bureaucratic control, and widening gap between the rich and the poor—the latter came to prevail, even if in an attenuated and compromised form.[4] The result was corporate liberalism.[5] Efforts to retrieve politics from the corruptions of power from the late nineteenth century onward have in fact been largely directed *in opposition to* the liberal tradition, whether in the guise of populism or progressivism, the militant contemporary labor movement, or the emergence of popular struggles (civil rights, feminism, antiwar mobilizations, the New Left) later in the twentieth century. Such alternatives sought to broaden the public sphere by embracing government as a dynamic mechanism of social change, by pressing for more inclusionary policies, or by expanding the very boundaries of politics itself. The kind of normal politics associated with modern liberalism (electoral and legislative activity, interest-group lobbies, bureaucratic machinations, and so on) has, with the passage of time, militated against expanded citizen participation. Thus, populism and related grassroots movements that drew on the energies of disenfranchised groups were ultimately forced to combat the very logic of corporate liberalism. This is precisely what happened in the 1960s and 1970s, when the radicalism of the New Left and new social movements exploded the boundaries of the public sphere and challenged the emaciated form of politics known as coldwar liberalism, which stigmatized even the most tepid dissent as communist subversion.

The proliferation of social movements reshaped the political landscape insofar as it brought a wide range of new ideas into the public arena and opened up for debate what previously had been dismissed or met with silence. It helped to legitimate new ways of defining the world. Thus, in the 1960s, the civil rights movement forced an ongoing national encounter over race relations; antiwar struggles pressed for a more critical assessment of U.S. foreign policy; the New Left refocused discussion around the very nature of democratic participation; an embryonic women's movement posed subversive questions about gender equality, the family, and sexuality; and the first stirrings of modern environmentalism raised consciousness about the destructive impact of industrial growth on the global ecology. In each case it was possible to identify a renewal of language, involving new concepts, analyses, and visions of the future—new ways of grasping social reality. The cumulative effect of all this, by the early 1970s, was the perceptible erosion of general support for an economic and political system that could now be said to have incurred something of a legitimation crisis. One sign of this was George McGovern's candidacy for president in 1972—a candidacy that predictably failed but which did manage to bring progressive values and ideas into the national public arena to a degree probably unmatched in modern times. It was a phenomenon that extended well beyond the university ghettos of the "great refusal" (to serve in Vietnam) and the esoteric subculture of the New Left. In fact, the new social movements of the 1970s reached out to tens of millions of people, urban and rural, young and old, white and minority, liberal, independent, and radical.

Such a historic turn has had a sharply divided legacy: the very assault on liberalism that disturbed the political tranquility of American society simultaneously encouraged a widespread retreat from the public sphere. Such a retreat, as we shall see, combined a healthy revolt against hierarchical structures and social injustice with a more problematic sense of futility regarding the very efficacy of *political* action. The crisis of corporate, coldwar liberalism emanated from several sources—the growth of concentrated corporate power and wealth, increased bureaucratization of social life, popular disillusionment born of contemporary events (Vietnam, political assassinations, Watergate, and so on), and the diffuse ideological challenge presented by the New Left itself.[6] Some radical elements in the New Left and counterculture imagined a cultural revolution that would somehow bypass politics as it glorified a return to spontaneity, local community, authentic personal experience, and nature—the realization of "free" personalities liberated from the burdensome oppressions of "the system." In adopting a stance of cultural defiance tied to a thoroughgoing consciousness transformation, the new radicalism was often militantly antistatist and even anarchistic in its outlook. Liberalism, in this heady milieu, was increasingly regarded as an outmoded belief system that was surely no longer capable of furnishing an analysis of the present or a vision of the future.[7] The erosion of liberalism, which in fact had been building for at least a century, marked a critical turning point in contemporary American public life. What had emerged by the late 1970s was a transformed political culture in which a powerful ethos of antipolitics began to gain widespread currency, where the (liberal) connection between ideas and reality, between beliefs and action, was finally and unquestionably broken.

THE SHRINKING PUBLIC SPHERE

If the decline of American liberalism was inevitable enough, it nonetheless produced an ideological void that neither socialism nor any other alternative has been able to fill. (The socialist Left, in any of its incarnations, was never able to establish a truly mass presence in the United States, even during the peak years of the Socialist Party.) The New Left and successive popular movements did make inroads into the political culture, forcing new issues and provoking new debates, but their fragmented character along with a deep antipolitical outlook helped restrict their development far short of a coherent, organized attack on the status quo. Even with the growth of local radicalism in the 1960s and 1970s, therefore, political space was available at the level of national institutional life for a powerful conservative backlash—indeed for a right-wing appropriation of antistatism that, shaped by a return to laissez-faire free-market ideals, had always been central to capitalist hegemony before the Keynesian revolution of the 1930s. In this sense, at least, elements of the liberal tradition remained very much alive. Ronald Reagan's victory in 1980 can be seen as a historic breakthrough of conservative ideology that fit the general mood of antipolitics that the ideology, in turn, helped to further encourage. Since the early 1980s, thanks largely to the "Reagan revolution," the public sphere in the United States has been shrinking steadily and dramatically.

By the 1990s one could argue that American society had become more depoliticized than ever—an ironic development given a deepening social crisis that has persisted along with the rapid growth of higher edu-

cation and the accelerated information revolution. The vast majority of
the population—middle strata, working class, the poor—has become politically demoralized, increasingly bereft of hope for remedies to social problems in the existing public sphere. In the words of William Greider: "Behind the reassuring facade, the regular election contests and so forth, the
substantive meaning of self-government has been hollowed out. What exists behind the formal shell is a systemic breakdown of the shared civic values we call democracy."[8] There can be little doubt that the political system
has atrophied markedly, resulting in much reduced levels of citizen involvement, whether at the ballot box, in formal party activities, in the corridors of power, or even in local community life. Of course, it would be
foolish to argue that popular movements have completely disappeared,
but they suffer from dispersion and impotence, just as most interest
groups have become absorbed in the labyrinthine web of institutional
power. The triumph of antipolitics is not a matter of failed leaders, parties, or movements, nor of flawed structural arrangements, but rather reflects a deeper historical process that shapes every facet of daily life and
political culture. Depoliticization is the likely popular response to a system
that is designed to marginalize dissent, privatize social relations, and reduce the scope of popular participation. As Greider observes: "If citizens
sometimes behave irresponsibly in politics, it is the role assigned them.
They have lost any other way to act, any means for influencing the governing process in positive or broad-minded terms."[9]

For politics to be truly participatory, it must be organically connected
to social relationships, community life, forms of collective action, and
popular aspirations toward social governance.[10] American society in the
1980s and 1990s, however, has departed radically from this model, as
Sandel, Greider, Dionne, Roelefs, and Ophuls among others have con-
vincingly shown. This condition might even be worse than the literature
suggests: private agendas have triumphed over any semblance of a general
interest, passivity and cynicism have engulfed the political culture, and citizenship winds up more devalued than ever. Indeed, the very material and
cultural factors essential to the reproduction of citizenship seem to be
vanishing. Politics has degenerated into a concatenation of interest-group
machinations, bureaucratic intrigues, and electoral rituals even as urban
life continues to disintegrate, health care and education worsen, and the
ecological crisis veers out of control. While none of these developments is
especially novel, taken together they have given rise to a truncated party
system, depoliticized citizenry, and a trivialized discourse of politics that
hardly does justice to even minimal norms of liberalism and "protective
democracy." The result is that "politics" has increasingly become the domain of corporate and governmental elites whose overriding ambition is
to perpetuate their quasi-oligarchical status.[11] The decay of politics and

citizenship means that the average citizen has lost faith that any level of government can appreciably serve common interests—a loss of faith that, while distressing, contains its own decipherable logic. In Dionne's words: "Politics has stopped being a deliberative process through which people resolved disputes, found remedies, and moved forward. When Americans watch politics now . . . they understand instinctively that politics these days is not about finding solutions. It is about discovering postures that offer short-term political benefits."[12] As Eliasoph argues, the famous "cool minimalism" of liberal politics masks—but just *barely*—a strong popular reluctance, even fear, of engaging the public sphere.[13]

Political dialogue in the United States has degenerated into a welter of rhetorical flourishes and abstract platitudes invoking such hallowed notions as the free market, family values, personal responsibility, and economic growth that, in the end, have little to do with either social welfare or public policy. The gulf between words and reality seems to widen with each passing year. In place of an active, engaged citizenry once associated with populism, the civil rights movement, and feminism, for example, we encounter a dispersed, alienated population increasingly devoid of civic trust or obligation and enmeshed in private preoccupations (whether excessive television viewing, Web surfing, or "shopping 'til you drop") whose claims on our time make the public sphere seem altogether irrelevant. Meanwhile, the corporations, state, and military intensify their hold on public life as their priorities—with a few notable exceptions, such as the tobacco industry—go more or less unchallenged. The system retains all the external trappings of democracy, legality, and citizenship, but it is strongly repressive and antidemocratic in practice.[14] It functions precisely to corrupt all significant manifestations of political agency at the mass level, and it has performed this task rather well over the past two decades or so. In this context, it might be argued that the most pressing crisis of our time is the crisis of citizenship, or empowerment, since without resolving this challenge it will be difficult if not impossible to confront the mounting social problems of the day.

ASSESSING THE DAMAGE

Assuming that the thesis of a depoliticized society is more or less valid, we still need to determine and measure more exactly what this means. What are the various indices of political decline? There are indeed several indicators pointing toward a drastic narrowing of the public sphere— lower voter turnouts, a decreasing sense of political efficacy, waning popular trust and obligation, eroding knowledge of and interest in political issues, the decline of party and/or legislative functions, and the convergence of the two major parties, ideologically to name some of the most important. Before exploring these areas, however, it might be useful to show how critical social problems are either suppressed or distorted in what passes for American political debate. If it can be demonstrated that public discourse excludes, trivializes, or massively distorts so many issues that are central to the well-being, even survival, of ordinary people, then what does this say about the healthful vitality of the body politic? In the absence of truly vigorous, open, critical dialogue how can we address, much less remedy, the great challenges ahead?

The restricted nature of debate goes to the heart of the problem—to the colossal banality of politics itself: the corruption, deceit, propaganda, and false promises that shape the whole terrain and that inspire increasing popular revulsion against the public sphere. Enshrouded in the great myths of American democracy is a political system that responds far more to wealth and influence peddling than to any form of citizen initiative. Despite the indispensable procedural elements of liberal democracy, the most important areas of decision making (finances, corporate agendas, investment policies, foreign and military policy) remain the preserve of a small stratum of economic, political, and military decision makers who seek to legitimate their rule by invoking the time-honored concept of the "inevitability of elites." As Roelofs points out, elites work assiduously "to promulgate the relevant myths, including most importantly the myth of their own and their office's importance."[15] The more that systemic rituals like voting, candidate debates, and legislative maneuvering become detached from the realities of social life and the more they seem to be trumpeted as the necessary features of a democratic order, the more they function to obscure genuine debates and block alternatives to the status quo.

The eclipse of modern citizenship is reflected in the degree to which the vast majority of people are effectively inhibited from giving meaningful political articulation to their interests and concerns. Forced alienation from the realm of government and politicians does not, under these circumstances suggest true indifference to what matters in people's daily lives—jobs, health care, education, civic violence, the environment, indeed the capacity to be heard and to have influence. The point is that an institutionalized corporatist system presided over by a narrow stratum (of white males, predominantly) will naturally set limits to the scope of debate, to what is regarded as "legitimate" or "respectable" opinion on important public issues. The word "citizen" seems to have lost resonance in the culture today (apart from being a fixture of Fourth of July rhetoric), and glowing references to pluralism and diversity are but prettified platitudes to the extent that elite-driven politics is allowed to close off real *ideological* differences that might incite departures from established practice. Today's public is confronted by simplistic buzzwords and vague promises that, in any case, politicians rarely keep. For example, the public is treated to perpetual fanfare about the inevitability of economic globalism and its presumed benefits (linked, of course, to the communications revolution)—but one might ask what is meant precisely by such "globalism" and, further, what it augurs for the lives of the vast majority of people around the world. Is global integration simply another catchphrase that obscures more than it reveals? Who makes vital decisions—and on the basis of *whose* interests? Who benefits from globalization and who loses? What is it likely to mean, over the long term, for the future of jobs, health, the environment, and the relationship between rich and poor countries—for the very conduct of politics? Instead of relatively open debates that might be expected to touch on such life-and-death topics, we are beguiled with flashy advertisements for the informational revolution, invocations of a "new world order," and oft-repeated proclamations of a new era of interdependence, growth, and prosperity that ostensibly will benefit all. What we get, in other words, is essentially one form or another of corporate propaganda—propaganda, however, that is eagerly embraced by mainstream politicians, the mass media, and leading academics alike. The almost certain harsh consequences of "globalism" are essentially swept from view—and thereby excluded from the realm of public debate and decision making.

Where politics is so devalued, public forums that allow for critical discussion of established priorities are largely absent. Thus, we have seen few civic arenas where the destructive effects of globalization, or of the corporate economy itself, might be addressed or in some way connected to policy concerns. A stringently econometric discourse often prevails at the government's policy-making levels, with the greatest attention focused on growth rates, productivity, trade balances, interest rates, and other aggregate data—in short, the working vocabulary of Wall Street, multinational corporations, perhaps the military planners. Meanwhile, the economy produces such massive dysfunctions as rampant plant closings, worker layoffs, the gutting of social services, decaying inner cities, environmental devastation, and growing divisions between rich and poor. Typical elite responses to all this have been to stimulate heightened global competition, give tax breaks to multinational corporations, downsize the public sector, dismantle the "welfare state," and intensify the war on crime and drugs. Globally focused initiatives are more apt to aggravate domestic dysfunctions than to cure them, and thus they push the system further along its downward spiral.

This predicament is worsening year by year. Capitalist flight, downsizing, growing poverty and social dislocation, and ecological crisis are all built into the current phase of capitalist development—an ad hoc post-Fordism managed by banking systems, global corporations, the federal government, and international bodies set up to maximize the free flow of capital around the world. In the 1990s, as major companies downsize by laying off thousands of workers, many of their CEOs receive huge pay raises, bonuses, and stock options as their reward for cost-cutting, while Wall Street rejoices and the media join in the refrain (singing the praises of "globalization"). Consider, for example, AT&T chairman Robert Allen, who fired 40,000 workers in 1995, a year in which he received $3.4 million in total compensation. During the same year IBM chairman Louis Gerstner was awarded $2.6 million despite management's embarrassment in opting to lay off 60,000 workers (in a once layoff-free company). Meanwhile, Sears gave walking papers to 50,000, General Motors 74,000, Boeing 28,000, and McDonnell-Douglas another 17,000. Jobs vanished as a function of the speeded-up imperatives of global competition, merger mania, technological restructuring, and just plain old-fashioned cost cutting. At the same time, the accelerated trend toward concentration of power in many global industries, including above all energy and communications, has made political intervention by nation-states and other bodies all the more difficult. Attempts to force corporations to shoulder "public interest" obligations on jobs, pricing, the environment, and human rights issues (for example, the role of Shell Oil in destroying tribal lands in Nigeria or of Nike in setting up global sweatshops) are routinely deflected through the enormous power exerted by market ideology.

It might be argued that the ethos of contemporary capitalism is not only "grow or die" but also streamline or die, with frightening implications for both local communities and the planet as a whole. Even staid, mainstream *Newsweek* was moved to comment: "Something is just plain wrong when the stock prices keep rising on Wall Street while Main Street is littered with the bodies of workers discarded by big companies like AT&T and Chase Manhattan and Scott Paper. Once upon a time it was a mark of shame to fire your workers en masse. It meant you had messed up your business. Today, the more people a company fires the more Wall Street loves it, and the higher its stock price goes."[16] The global financial crises of late 1997 and the summer of 1998 showed, however, that even the most herculean efforts at downsizing will not perpetually translate into more dynamic Wall Street stock performances.

As Jeremy Rifkin and others have argued, the precipitous loss of jobs resulting from technological displacement, mergers, and fiercely competitive pressures of the world market cannot be attributed to temporary economic downturns or bad policy but rather stems from a powerful, long-term systemic logic.[17] Worldwide, tens of millions of jobs are expected to disappear in the coming decade, only to be replaced by low-wage service jobs—or nothing at all—swelling the ranks of the marginalized poor (a reality often obscured in the United States by misleading low-unemployment statistics). The plague of joblessness and marginality, when viewed alongside such issues as the global ecological crisis, will confront national governments with seemingly insuperable challenges as we enter the twenty-first century. Indeed, poverty has already been transformed by high levels of unemployment or semiemployment in that work no longer provides the same degree of order and regularity to inner-city community life, thus aggravating the effects of social dislocation.

Yet, public discussion of work and joblessness in the United States has been absurdly narrow—on those few occasions when the subject has been placed on the agenda at all. In general the issue is refocused onto a strictly economistic plane, where positive indicators related to growth, productivity, trade balances, and budgetary deficits are automatically assumed to generate an abundance of good, decent-paying jobs. Politicians seeking votes typically offer little more than platitudes about business expansion, market vitality, and job training; once elected, they usually ignore the problem altogether, fearful of alienating corporate or mainstream interests—unless perhaps there is a plant closing in their own district or state. Legislation that would shape corporations' options in closing plants and laying off workers has not yet seen the light of day. Nor have debates on "Nightline" or similar TV and radio shows devoted much attention to these problems. One searches in vain to find proposals that would limit corporate decisions to relocate or summarily fire workers, or that would stimulate public sources of work in a way that might put millions of unemployed on stable payrolls (while also helping rebuild the social infrastructure). Such proposals, rational as they might appear, run directly against the grain of free-market ideology; they imply a system of "planning" and regulating mechanisms that, assertedly at least, destroys corporate initiative and flexibility. The stubborn reality is that the downward employment cycle cannot be reversed without massive and sustained federal investment in jobs or, more specifically, social programs that will generate new jobs.

Perhaps nowhere is this poverty of discourse more clearly revealed than in the greatest ritual of American politics—presidential campaigns and debates. Minor political differences between the two main contenders are generally blown far out of proportion, while peripheral concerns (trivial malfeasanses or misstatements), contrived and packaged images, and personality issues often take center-stage. Economic disagreements most often revolve around how to reduce the federal budget deficit or how to implement "welfare reform," while debates over corporate investment priorities, for example, remain totally off limits. During the 1996 presidential debates Bill Clinton did make the seemingly straightforward statement that millions of new jobs had been created during his first administration, but he said nothing about the nature of these jobs (or the declining urban infrastructure). Contender Robert Dole argued that the free market would produce new jobs, along with increased levels of prosperity, in the context of continuing growth. Neither offered a developmental program geared to reversing the dark consequences of corporate hegemony. Mainstream economists like Robert Samuelson regularly inform the American public that the issue of "job security," while admittedly serious, can never be amenable to governmental action, for it would violate the sacred tenets of the "free market." The prevailing consensus (shared by Democrats and Republicans alike) is that government can do little more than intervene occasionally to "stimulate growth"—a claim that flies in the face of 60 years of Keynesian state programs in the United States, Europe, and around the world. In the view of economists (and pundits) like Samuelson, politicians should avoid making promises of more jobs and expanded social programs since these promises cannot be fulfilled and therefore can only lead to more popular cynicism and disaffection. Instead, answers are more likely to be found through the ethic of personal responsibility. As for the impact of downsizing, elites are presumably in agreement with the views expressed by former Scott Paper (and Sunbeam) CEO Al ("Chainsaw") Dunlop on the subject: "We're painted as villains, but we're not. We're more like doctors. We know it's painful to operate but it's the only way to keep the patient from dying."[18] And organized labor itself often buys into this message, figuring that it is best to accept a specific number of plant closings, layoffs, and reduced benefits in order to save jobs at a time when labor has lost much of its flexibility and leverage relative to an increasingly mobile capital that can use capital flows and trade liberalization to its endless advantage. The position of labor is of course further weakened by the very culture of antipolitics, which undermines the single most vital mechanism (governmental action) at the disposal of working-class movements.

That there is so little public discourse on the main problems of social conflict constitutes a prime defining feature of contemporary American political culture. Issues that have festered for decades (homelessness, the cancer epidemic, race relations, childcare, military spending) have been either skirted altogether or devalued as urgent policy concerns; they rarely enter the exchanges that occur during presidential campaigns and debates, much less in the format of the (increasingly shrill) talk shows. A host of other social problems—crime, drugs, and education, for example— often enter into the realm of political debate and policy making, but the normal range of "solutions" posed for such problems only winds up exacerbating the underlying conditions. Even the wrenching Los Angeles riots of spring 1992 failed to shake the national inertia with regard to the decay of American cities—a fierce and intensifying challenge that continues to be met with a combination of small-scale economic palliatives, moralizing rhetoric, and coercive institutional practices (expansion of law enforcement, the builder of new prisons, increased privatization of prisons). Democrats have been little better than Republicans on matters of large-scale economic and social policy, the major difference being a stronger Republican commitment to free-market capitalism, the blessings of privatization, and stringent anticrime legislation. None of the four Democratic presidential candidates since McGovern has acknowledged the urban crisis or set forth a systematic agenda for rebuilding the cities—arguably the most important priority now facing the political system. President Clinton has largely ignored the cities with their predominantly working-class, poor, and minority constituencies that, the Democratic strategists recognize, are not likely to vote Republican in any large numbers and thus can be taken for granted. Urban life deteriorates while corporate and governmental elites steadfastly hold to their conservative agendas that cater to largely white suburban constituencies. Both parties currently press for severe cuts in the public sector while at the same time pressing for elevated military, law enforcement, and prison budgets. Both advocate welfare "reform" (i.e., eliminating the bulk of federal entitlements), with Clinton signing a 1996 bill aimed at severely reducing the welfare state, thus in effect putting an end to the Keynesian social contract that was in place since the 1930s. Cutting $55 billion from federal antipoverty programs, Clinton referred to the welfare bill as a "defining moment" of his presidency, a step toward ending the "era of big government." This Reaganesque bill—and, in its wake, dozens of similar ones at the state and municipal levels—condemned millions of urban and rural poor to greater misery, and with only minimal opposition from politicians or the mainstream mass media.

Such a perceptible narrowing of the political terrain holds for race relations, as well. More than three decades after the peak of the civil rights movement, the United States remains sharply divided along racial lines (primarily but not exclusively between whites and blacks), owing in part to increasing urban decline and social polarization.[19] The exacerbation of racial divisions, much like the related issues of joblessness, poverty, and welfare, rarely figures in the elite's calculations. The reality is quite stark: the poverty rate for blacks stands at 44 percent and for Latinos at 42 percent—compared to 17 percent for whites. Nearly 70 percent of jail inmates nationwide (in 1995 figures) were black and Latino, many of them detainees from the war on drugs. Nearly one-third of all black men under 40 are either in jail or on probation, with the number incarcerated annually during the past 15 years nearly tripling. As this predicament worsens year by year, the response of the two major parties has been simply to desert the cities in favor of more upscale, suburban, middle-class constituencies.

While the urban crisis cries out for a renewal of the social infrastructure as the basis of expanded public services and job opportunities, suburban priorities are quite different: lower taxes, fiscal conservatism, social cutbacks, a war against crime and drugs. Clinton-style Democrats, in gravitating toward the mythical "center," have effectively colonized the suburban terrain with its barely concealed neoliberal agenda. Here the recurrent attacks on the "lazy" poor with their supposed lack of personal responsibility, on welfare "dependency," bureaucratic waste, affirmative action, teenaged mothers, criminal deviance, immigrants, and of course "drugs"—attacks waged vigorously by both major parties—contain an element of racial animus (even though many opinion makers insist that American society has conquered its racist demons of the past). It might be argued that this racial animus has been a central factor in the rightward shift in American politics since the early 1980s. Meanwhile, inner-city minorities are registering to vote and going to the ballot box in smaller numbers each year, partially nullifying the historic gains in citizen participation (and other reforms) made by the civil rights movement and the Rainbow Coalition beginning in the late 1950s.

Drug policy occupies a central role in this downward spiral in urban conditions. Since President Richard Nixon launched his "all-out war on drugs" in 1972, the program has turned out to be an extremely costly national fiasco—wasteful, coercive, a threat to civil liberties, a crude approach to health care, and itself a major source of increased crime, violence, substance abuse, and social dislocation. Owing largely to the antidrug crusade, the United States incarcerates more of its citizens—1.6 million in 1997—than any other country in the world. While arrests and ridiculously harsh penalties for both possession and trafficking remain in place, levels of drug use and urban violence have *escalated* during the past two decades. Federal, state, and local prisons are filled with offenders whose "crime" was mere possession of a banned substance (which often turns out to be far less harmful than many legal substances) and whose actions were not especially violent or antisocial. In 1993 nearly 400,000 people were arrested for mere *possession* of marijuana—a drug that never kills, in contrast to tobacco products and alcohol, which annually account for 400,000 and 100,000 deaths, respectively. Drug sentencing in the United States, where just using a substance can bring draconian jail terms, is best described as cruel and unusual punishment. Prison terms for first-time offenders around the country *average* roughly 60 months. The criminal justice system has spent tens of billions of dollars tracking down offenders, arresting them, prosecuting them, and housing them in prisons. The federal government has spent even greater sums in the futile attempt to interdict the flow of drugs from abroad (at a time when most drugs are either grown or manufactured domestically).

The ever widening and costly antidrug campaign, perpetuated by a series of myths about the horrors of illicit substances, serves to deflect our attention from the deeper economic, social, and psychological dimensions of the drug–crime–health nexus. The "war" has developed into a kind of national pathology in which the whole social context of human behavior seems to be forgotten. In his book *Reckoning*, Elliott Currie argues that the drug war confronts nothing more than the *symptoms* of social malaise and decay; all the rest is left untouched, and thus allowed to fester. He writes: "Twenty years of the 'war on drugs' have jammed our jails and prisons, immobilized the criminal justice system in many cities, swollen the ranks of the criminalized and unemployable minority poor, and diverted desperately needed resources from other needs. Yet the drug crisis is still very much with us."[20] Judged on the basis of even its own narrow assumptions, therefore, official drug policy has amounted to one of the greatest fiascos in U.S. history. Meanwhile, the public sphere remains contaminated with the same outmoded and counterproductive rhetoric that gave birth to this policy in the Nixon years.

Consider the following irrefutable facts: (1) with an average of 1.3 million arrests each year and nearly half a million inmates sentenced for drug offenses, the flow of drugs into and throughout the country remains as high as ever; (2) the antidrug campaign devours, directly and indirectly, about $75 billion a year; (3) half of all murders and one-third of all burglaries in U.S. cities are drug-related, resulting from turf wars over underground sales and the desperate struggle for money to support expensive habits owing to inflated black-market prices; (4) the drug war, by perpetuating an outlaw subculture much like that of the prohibition years, fuels gang warfare and street violence in urban areas; (5) the overburdened criminal justice system has given drugs top priority, ahead of all violent offenses except murder; (6) far more people die from legal drugs such as tobacco, alcohol, and pharmaceuticals than from banned substances such as cocaine, heroin, and marijuana; (7) only a small proportion of users (not more than 10 percent, according to most estimates) actually become *addicted* to drugs; (8) government agencies such as the CIA have been shown to be involved in drug peddling; and (9) in countries where drugs have been decriminalized (e.g., the Netherlands) there is a profound drop in both crime and addiction.

To an extent greater than perhaps any other social policy, the war on drugs aggravates the dynamic of inner-city decay, violence, and racism. (Because of foreign interdiction and "eradication" programs, it also helps to legitimate high levels of military spending.) With 550,000 black men in prison as of 1997, the image of young blacks as drug dealers, addicts, and violent criminals resonates throughout the mass media and culture. According to data from the Sentencing Project, while blacks constitute only 13 percent of the total population and 13 percent of regular drug users, they account for 35 percent of those arrested for possession, 55 percent of those convicted, and 74 percent of those jailed. Thus, there is a vast underclass of marginalized inner-city poor, consisting largely of minorities. As Diana Gordon argues, U.S. drug policy is at heart an attack on poor urban minorities—the "dangerous classes"—with the aim (essentially unfulfilled) being governmental and social control over people's daily lives.[21]

This national calamity has provoked some debate, mostly on the fringes of the public sphere, but unfortunately little of it has percolated into the political arena. So much public discourse around drugs, addiction, and crime is emptied of content, framed by the demonizing of sellers and users, hysterical moralizing by the media, politicians, and law enforcement officials, the haranguing scripted testimony of "victims," and pedantic commercials like those sponsored by the Partnership for a Drug-Free America. (Far be it from anyone's intention, however, to speak ill of the *real* killers—tobacco, alcohol, or prescription drugs.) The complexities of social life are drowned out by a cacophony of shrill platitudes. Politicians in each party stumble over each other to urge ever harsher penalties for drug offenders, including even first-time users. In his 1994 crime bill President Clinton introduced several new categories of death penalties for drug peddlers, augmenting the budget for law enforcement and prisons largely with the drug issue in mind. As for candidate Dole in 1996, he would have steeply escalated the war on drugs by, among other things, using the National Guard to seal off borders (an impossibility) while boosting the U.S. military presence in Mexico and South America in order to cut off potential imports (also impossible). Dole's simplistic moralizing outbursts against "drugs" did not, however, apply to the tobacco industry—a far more deadly and profitable network of enterprises, but one that is squarely in the Republican camp. (Clinton, to his credit, has given legitimacy to recent political and legal assaults on Big Tobacco, but his position on the larger drug wars remains unchanged.) The idea of getting tough on crime and building more prisons while giving the state more power over people's daily lives is one of the present era's prime articles of faith. In this milieu rational proposals to legalize drugs, which would end the huge drug profits, black-market prices, and unregulated trade, while alleviating turf wars, street violence, and massive incarceration, do not get very far. Debate is effectively foreclosed in advance despite the obvious benefits of a fundamentally different set of policies. Nowhere is the barrenness of American political discourse more clearly evident than in the area of drug policy.

What passes for debate in the area of foreign and military policy fits essentially the same pattern: "bipartisan consensus" has characterized the postwar U.S. outlook in world politics, with the notable exception of the Vietnam war period, the late 1960s and early 1970s. Democrats and Republicans have fought mainly over the nuances of policy—how many troops to deploy here and there, what anticommunist strategy to follow, how much foreign aid to provide, whether the Pentagon budget should be increased (or reduced) by 1.5 percent versus 3 percent, and so on. Everything since the late 1940s was justified by the imperative of fighting communist aggression; dissent was easily marginalized with simple (but compelling) appeals to "national security," the protection of democratic institutions, and the struggle against "anti-American" subversion. There was only the most trifling of debates over the sustained buildup of a permanent war economy, with the Pentagon overseeing a budget of up to $315 billion annually to meet cold war–defined objectives. During this period, as Robert Aldridge amply documents, the United States consistently took the first step in escalating the arms race, with the Soviet Union always struggling to remain in striking distance of U.S. global military supremacy.[22]

In 1990 the military budget stood at $300 billion, enough to sustain dozens of military bases and naval deployments around the world and to maintain the largest arsenal of nuclear weapons, as well as to design and manufacture high-tech armaments, planes, and ships. Nearly 10 years later the Pentagon was consuming much less (about $260 billion annually), but in 1999 the embattled Clinton proposed massive restorations in outlays (more than $100 billion) to extend over four years. The United States remains the leading purveyor of high-tech weapons to other countries (among them, Indonesia, Pakistan, Guatemala, even Iraq during its war with Iran), however deplorable their human-rights records may be. During the years of the U.S.–Soviet nuclear standoff, American elites could readily legitimate such expenditures, especially since Democrats and Republicans alike shared President Kennedy's depiction of world communism as a "monolithic and ruthless conspiracy" that needed to be stopped at all costs. Critics of this policy were regularly denounced as communists or communist sympathizers—and not just during Sen. Joseph McCarthy's heyday (the early 1950s). Open debate was impossible. Yet, even after the cold war ended in the late 1980s, U.S. military power continued to *expand* as the Pentagon budget hovered near $300 billion a year. The only significant change was in the broadening definition of the enemy: in place of the communist "evil empire" came potentially heightened threats from such "rogue states" as Libya, Iran, Iraq, and North Korea and from worldwide terrorism and drug cartels.

As corporate and governmental elites agitated for increased military outlays throughout the postwar years, they simultaneously renewed their assault on "big government," the welfare state, and public regulation. What set military Keynesianism apart, of course, was its vital role in pump-priming the economy and legitimating high-tech research and development—not to mention its obvious role in aiding the struggle for U.S.

global domination. The system rested on a culture infused with xenophobic self-righteousness, a ready willingness to use military power, and a national sense of historical mission. Postwar American development has always been shaped by a dialectic connecting the militarism of the permanent war economy and the domestic culture of violence, featuring a nearly pathological obsession with guns, world records for street crime and gang violence, and a media fully saturated with images of bloody violence. The Persian Gulf war of 1991 represented a historical moment when this dialectic seemed to reach its peak in a hyperpatriotic, high-tech military onslaught against a rogue state and its demonic leader—all graphically covered by the TV networks.[23] The bonus here was that the first postcold war global encounter could be presented as an object lesson in justifying funds for the U.S. war machine—a vital element of the "new world order" enunciated by President Bush. Debates over the merits of the rationality of such a costly, bloody, and ineffective war were squelched by a media-orchestrated outpouring of patriotic sentiment; voices of dissent preceding the military action were quickly marginalized. The war to keep open Kuwaiti sources of oil killed as many as 200,000 Iraqis (along with additional tens of thousands killed during subsequent U.S.-led international sanctions) but did nothing to remove Saddam Hussein or his regime, build democracy in Kuwait, or restore political stability to the Middle East.

The end of cold-war mobilization might have led to severe reductions in the military–industrial complex, accompanied by an historic conversion from military to socially useful forms of production. Initially, there was indeed much talk of a "peace dividend," but such a dividend never materialized. It was never even seriously discussed by politicians or placed on the national agenda. Local organizations that pressed this issue were routinely dismissed as utopian, naive on matters of "national security," or simply misinformed about the workings of the budgetary process or the "free market." In fact, public input into major investment priorities was no more forthcoming than it was at the height of the anticommunist crusades. "Conversion" was ultimately addressed, but it came to mean nothing more than job retraining for workers laid off in the aerospace sector, along with only modest budget reductions that made little dent in the military apparatus. (Pentagon "cutbacks" turned out to be essentially a euphemism for modernization, or upgrading, of the military infrastructure.) National debate continued to revolve around elite appeals for global military preparedness—rendered all the more urgent in the wake of the Persian Gulf war—and such appeals were just as much "bipartisan" in the 1990s as they had been in the 1950s.

Such erosion of political discourse applies with equal force to environmentalism, despite the sense of urgency it has commanded in important sectors of the society. Themes like "saving the earth," "sustainable development," or "human-scale" community, once considered subversive, have increasingly been assimilated into the domain of corporate liberalism, where ecological renewal is deemed fully compatible with the overriding priorities of material growth, productivity, profits, and the manipulation of nature. Not only the Democrats and Republicans but most established "green" organizations go along with these familiar capitalist imperatives even as they present themselves as tenacious defenders of the environment; debates rarely go so far as to consider the need to regulate big business for the purpose of even minimal environmental planning and controls. Liberals and mainstream environmentalists have mounted lobbying campaigns since the initial, well-publicized Earth Days of the late 1960s, pushing (sometimes quite effectively) for clean air and water legislation, toxic waste cleanup, wilderness and wildlife protection, food and drug regulation, workplace safety, nuclear controls, and expanded consumer information and protection. Conservatives have often, though reluctantly, endorsed such measures but have more recently attacked even modest reforms as harmful to the free market and corporate efficiency, with Democrats frequently caving in to the same system-reinforcing logic. The obsessive hostility to planning and regulation that coincides with the prevailing American mood of antipolitics naturally runs counter to the very mechanism needed to reverse the global crisis, namely, broadened, radical, and urgent governmental intervention.

Instead of embracing the idea of such political action, the main environmental groups and movements have consistently opted for a cosmetic "greening" of institutional (and personal) regimens, which both corporations and the government are eager to propagate as exactly the kind of environmental outlook needed to "save the planet." Even the most notorious multinational polluters (e.g., Dow, Monsanto, Exxon, General Electric) try assiduously to fashion a public image of responsible global "citizen." Corporate executives at IBM, Monsanto, and AT&T, among other companies, earmark funds for conservation purposes, and many urge the public to adopt "green" habits or lifestyles. While corporations fight against public regulation, they proclaim solutions to environmental decay (e.g., voluntarism, more growth, better technology) fully in sync with their traditional profit-maximizing modus operandi. Along with the "greening" of big business and the political establishment has come the predictable flourishing of an "environmental industry" that is lauded as a way to combine sustainability and profitability while it satisfies an international demand for environmental services and equipment anticipated to exceed $300 billion by the year 2000.[24] Meanwhile, of course, the destructive consequences of misguided production and consumption—centered mainly in the industrialized countries—continue apace.

President Bush was hailed as a leading environmental statesman at the 1992 Earth Summit Conference in Rio de Janeiro—at a time when the United States managed to block virtually every serious global reform that was placed on the agenda. Bill Clinton ran as an "environmental candidate" in 1992, and his running mate Albert Gore wrote an influential book, *Earth Out of Balance,* that called attention to the urgency of global ecological problems.[25] By the late 1990s it had become difficult to find a mainstream politician who was not in some way "friendly" to nature and the environment. Yet, few elites, opinion makers, or environmentalists seem willing to address the *systemic* causes of the ecological crisis, much less the need to make rapid and deep changes in the worldwide (but especially North American and European) commitments to unbridled economic growth, which in certain instances lies at the heart of the matter. Reforms usually amount to no more than minimal stopgap regulations here and there, plans that are only partially implemented, or appeals for individual acts of conscience or restitution (tree planting, recycling, organic gardening, and the like), which hardly disturb the overall structure of priorities. With few exceptions, the strongest environmental groups (Sierra Club, World Wildlife Federation, Humane Society) have adopted the same minimalist, conflict-avoiding stance while building their own institutional networks mainly through computerized direct mail and high-tech lobbying efforts.[26] Here is a situation where the public sphere winds up saturated with environmental messages and symbols but where the pressing issue of planetary ecological decline is ignored or trivialized at the national policy level. By placing great hope in some combination of personal solutions, high-tech intervention, and isolated reforms, the seductive "green" culture obscures the complex relationship between a decaying biosphere and such other major problems as a highly fragile ecosystem of food and water supplies, the impending scarcity of certain key natural resources, modern technology's wholesale displacement of human labor power, heightened urban deterioration, and the chronic spread of severe diseases like cancer and immune-system disorders that kill millions of people yearly.

Owing to the decisive role of money, PACs, the media, and interest peddling in American politics, the main currents of environmental thought and action are easily diverted into all-consuming corporate agendas. (Where efforts at genuine debate have indeed been inaugurated, as in the case of the Citizens Party in 1980 and later the Green Party campaigns, they were effectively marginalized by the media and the political system itself.) One unyielding assumption is that political outcomes should not and indeed cannot run counter to market priorities or the hegemonic values of (mostly unplanned) industrial growth, the ongoing quest for profits, property rights, and the human appropriation of nature.

Strictly economistic thinking that focuses on cost–benefit analysis, consumers' rational choice, and the instrumental designs of big business takes unquestioned precedence over ecological modes of thinking tied to distinctly *social* outcomes. Moreover, the capacity of the Environmental Protection Agency (EPA), the Occupational Safety and Health Administration (OSHA), and other governmental agencies to regulate economic activity is often effectively restricted by their symbiotic relations with business and military interests. Various shades of "green" ideology too are commonly influenced by such priorities. For example, when the Clinton administration moved in 1996 to toughen (ever so slightly) regulatory standards on ozone, particulates, and other toxics responsible for thousands of deaths each year, a ferocious counterattack was launched by an alliance of some 500 powerful corporations. Industry leaders and lobbyists argued, as they have in the past, that tightening health standards is far too "costly" and will interfere with economic "growth." Most of these standards, in fact, remain far too low, having remained largely unchanged since the Carter years: particulates alone kill an estimated 60,000 Americans annually. President Clinton's legislation was actually extraordinarily modest; it would allow toxics by the year 2010 to rise to a level of 450 percent of that which scientific research indicates is optimum for human health. The result of this and related cases is that corporations, with their unabashedly global aspirations, have been given more or less free rein to plunder the environment, aided and abetted by a whole stratum of "experts" in government, business, science, the universities, and mass media whose own worldview is distorted by the same instrumental logic.

At the end of the twentieth century it is abundantly clear that the ecological crisis is both systemic and global, reflecting a growing imbalance between human society and nature, between social development and biospheric equilibrium, between the logic of rampant economic growth and that of environmental sanity. We have inherited a world of rapidly shrinking resources, potentially drastic overpopulation, recurrent violence and intense social polarization, and worsening health problems that seem to resist "normal" political solutions. The deterioration of ecological life-support systems has been fueled by a unique congruence of factors: economic globalization, resurgence of neoliberal policies in the United States and elsewhere, the technological revolution, decline of the nation-state, and the absence of worldwide regulatory or planning mechanisms that might curtail corporate plunder. As the flow of capital becomes more fluid, independent of political controls and less accountable to mass publics, all else suffers accordingly—local democratic forms, the condition of labor, consumer rights, and of course the environment. In this context the multinational corporations, assisted by the World Bank, the International Monetary Fund (IMF), and various trade agreements, are presiding over impending ecological catastrophe. To take one example, there is mounting scientific consensus that human-induced world climate changes will bring, sooner or later, massive increases in drought and desertification, an unleashing of more powerful storms, a rise in sea levels, and a crisis in food production. What this might mean for the world's population, and what institutional mechanisms and social policies might be advanced to confront the situation, has been of practically no concern to American elites preoccupied with growth, profitability, and market shares. In other words, arguably the most significant human predicament in the world today—the intensifying ecological crisis—is largely ignored amidst the cacophony of strident voices scoring debater's points in the public sphere.

The contributions of the "expert" strata in business, the military, and academia have turned out to be relatively useless at a time when conventional wisdom has less and less to offer. Cancer, which kills an average of 600,000 people yearly in the United States alone, provides an illustrative case in point. For decades convincing scientific evidence has shown a direct connection between rapidly growing levels of cancer and a host of social and environmental factors—tobacco consumption, diet and nutrition (especially the large intake of animal fat), alcohol, toxics, radiation, pesticides, air and water pollution—yet the "experts" have persisted in the myth that cancer is best understood apart from its social totality, that it must conform to the individual health model that requires technical, surgical, and pharmaceutical remedies. In the medical/scientific establishment the role of social factors has been ignored or downplayed, making it impossible to discover why a disease that killed 120 of every 100,000 Americans in 1950 could kill 174 of every 100,000 in 1990 despite massive improvements in detection and treatment—indeed, why cancer (along with heart disease and diabetes) occurs most frequently in the most highly industrialized countries.

It is one of the great tragedies of the period that a disease that kills so many people, and that is by far the most costly, receives so little attention in the *political* realm. Few election campaigns or debates have even mentioned the cancer scourge in passing, much less confronted it as a social problem with policy implications. Media coverage focuses almost exclusively on conventional medical treatments to the exclusion of social, ecological, and nutritional factors more conducive to preventive medicine, public health concerns, and progressive social policies. This narrow discourse raises even deeper questions regarding the impoverishment of public dialogue around the entire topic of health care. Why do we have drastically worsening health indicators in a country with such unprecedented material growth and prosperity, with the largest medical budget in history, with all the modern improvements in sanitation and hygiene, with all the costly high-tech innovations in health-care treatment? Here it may be possible to establish something of an inverse relationship between levels of economic development and particular social outcomes (health indicators)—a disturbing reality that never enters into national debates and legislative activity, even when the issue of health care or medical policy itself is placed on the agenda—another clear sign of how depoliticized the culture has become.

THE INCORPORATED DEBATES

Perhaps nowhere are depoliticizing trends more visible than in presidential debates, which, like party conventions and election campaigns in general, involve essentially scripted, formulaic, contrived partisan rhetoric (befits a media spectacle). Any true airing of issues, or posing of real alternatives to business-as-usual, would be an extraordinary event indeed. True enough, significant issues are frequently taken up, but they are either submerged by vague symbolic references to family values, personal character, world peace, and the like or are framed in an ethos of narrowly shared premises—who is toughest on crime, who can best balance the budget, who is most prepared to sustain U.S. military preparedness. This state of affairs goes back at least to the first important televised presidential debate, that between John Kennedy and Richard Nixon in 1960, which presented us with the odd specter of the reputedly liberal Democrat (Kennedy) challenging his Republican opponent on foreign policy matters (Cuba, China, the USSR) *from the right*. This was a "debate" that, in TV viewers' opinion, Kennedy won, but not because of the candidates' substantive positions on the issues so much as *how they appeared on camera*—Kennedy seemed crisp and authoritative while Nixon looked tired, nervous, and in need of a shave. (Indeed, radio listeners that were polled concluded that Nixon had won the debate.) Subsequent debates followed this pattern, with form and image winning out over political content (which, in any case, was largely absent or skirted). In 1988 and 1992, respectively, losing candidates Michael Dukakis and George Bush suffered far more from the exceedingly dour images that they projected onscreen than from any failings in political debate.

The 1996 debates between President Clinton and challenger Dole did not depart from this pattern. Clinton took credit, as a Democrat, for reducing the federal work force to its lowest point since 1966; as a fiscal conservative, he was able to slice jobs and programs simultaneously, thus placing himself in a situation to outflank Republicans from the right. Clinton demonstrated beyond doubt that he was willing to dispatch large numbers of American troops to protect overbroadly defined U.S. "interests"—in Bosnia, the Persian Gulf, and Haiti—although questions concerning how to fundamentally reorient American foreign policy in the post-cold war era were never addressed in any forum. Clinton also took credit for being tougher on crime than the Republicans before him and for spending more money to finance the war on drugs (both valid claims). He also called attention to his success in reducing the federal deficit by more than half. In sum, President Clinton exhibited great pride in having cut the operational budget and having downsized the scope of government in order to fit the mood and expectations of a depoliticized, minimalist public. Dole's basic retort was that he could have done these things even more effectively—and that Clinton's drug policies were a case of too little too late, inasmuch as teenagers' drug use rose during Clinton's tenure. He also attacked Clinton (in the second debate) for his flawed ethics and personal character, although the attack lacked vigor and specificity. Dole insisted that, while Clinton as a Democrat still retained faith in "government," his own preference (following Reagan) was to place trust in "the people," in the local communities. Despite more potential viewers than ever, the 1996 presidential debates drew the poorest TV ratings in the history of such debates.

None of this should be viewed as slightly remarkable, given the overriding influence of money, corporations, and the mass media in the whole U.S. electoral ritual. The presidential debates were in fact sponsored by an entity called the Commission of Presidential Debates involving executives from an array of big-business firms—Philip Morris, AT&T, Prudential, IBM, Ford, and General Motors, among others. Such a "commission" would obviously have no desire to see the corporate system challenged in any way, which helps to account not only for the banality of the Clinton–Dole exchanges but also for the unfair exclusion of Ross Perot and Ralph Nader from the debates.

One of the biggest "issues" that candidates bring to these debates, and to the campaign trail in general, is the ever present budget deficit. Yet, this problem is essentially a manufactured one in that the U.S. federal deficit (which totaled 2.3 percent of national income in 1995) is comparatively minuscule on a global scale. In reality the deficit is so small that for the past decade it has been growing far less rapidly than the nation's overall gross domestic product and is now proportionately smaller than at earlier junctures in the 1940s and 1950s. Now, as then, reductions in public spending turn out to be counterproductive to what ought to be central public goals, namely, the generation of new jobs, enhanced social services, redistribution of wealth, even economic growth. In other words, severe attacks on the "deficit"—while perhaps understandable as electoral moves in a depoliticized setting—will have little if any direct impact on overall social well-being. At the same time, however, the "deficit" has emerged as a code word in national political discourse for agendas designed to slash public programs. Ritual arguments that the United States is facing bankruptcy, or that the deficit will destroy the hopes of future generations, are nothing but conservative propaganda. The real issue here is: what are the sources of public revenue and where are government funds presently being allocated? What are the anticipated outcomes in terms of jobs, programs, welfare, the environment, and so forth? Instead of taking up such questions, the packaged debates drag us backward into a mythical past where the "free market" supposedly reigned, the dominant culture was infused with homogeneous values and lifestyles, government (in theory) played a minor role, and social needs were less clearly defined. But the retreat toward such a romanticized laissez-faire paradise—an idea entertained by a majority of Democrats, Republicans, and libertarians alike—only indulges a fantasy that is well removed from today's completely transformed world in which the very underpinnings of production and consumption depend on a greatly enlarged, dynamic public infrastructure. The nostalgic turn backward obscures every major social challenge of the period, which turns out to be convenient enough for elites ever anxious to deflect attention away from the abuses of corporate power.

Republicans historically relied on the cultivated image of a fiscally conservative party that favors personal responsibility over social welfare, getting tough on both crime and foreign policy, and championing traditional values. While this image remains more or less intact, as of the 1990s the Democrats had succeeded in taking over much of that terrain—or at least competing on nearly equal terms with the Republicans over it—especially with the rise to power of "New Democrat" Clinton. Today, perhaps more than ever, policy differences between the two parties on most issues have narrowed beyond recognition. Take the 1996 presidential campaign, for example. Both Clinton and Dole agreed on a welfare "reform" plan that would put millions of poor people in greater jeopardy, meanwhile leaving untouched (and largely *undiscussed*) the hundreds of billions consumed by the Pentagon and various corporate welfare programs (including massive tax loopholes for businesses). Both candidates went along with the idea that health care is best developed and allocated through the supposed automatic adjustments of the free market. Both agreed that billions more should be spent to expand the war on drugs, which would naturally include putting more police on the streets and building more prisons. Both endorsed an outmoded foreign policy that spends $150 billion annually to deploy U.S. troops and weaponry in Europe, South Korea, Japan, the Middle East, and across the world's oceans and seas. Both enshrined the "free trade" agreements tied to GATT (the General Agreement on Tariffs and Trade) and NAFTA above the interests of workers and the environment that suffer when capital becomes more fluid and public regulations are stripped away. Both accepted the idea that a $5.15 minimum wage remained adequate, although that wage failed to lift a family of four above the poverty level. The list could be extended much further.

Any future revival of American politics cannot take place without an open, full-scale debate over the general trajectory of economic development, a debate that does not merely invoke familiar capitalist priorities but rather allows for discussion of alternative models of production and consumption. But this is unimaginable so long as the main political actors (including most interest groups and movements) remain wedded to the logic of sprawling corporate, governmental, and military bureaucracies. It is this logic that the commodified spectacle of politics has not, and will not, begin to challenge. The shallowness of the political spectacle—of politics as part media culture, part marketing venture, part entertainment—is sometimes interrupted by vicious name-calling and character assassinations, which seemed to reach its peak in 1992 with the enhanced visibility of such candidates as Ross Perot and Patrick Buchanan, at the national level. During the 1992 presidential debates one exasperated audience member commented: "The amount of time candidates have spent in the campaign trashing their opponents' character is depressingly large. Why can't your discussions and proposals reflect the genuine complexity and difficulty of the issues?" One result of this impasse, as Tom Schachtman observes, is that fewer and fewer people are taking political language seriously; they see little connection between electoral discourse, for example, and what is actually taking place in the world.[27] And this disconnect in turn only serves to reinforce the pattern of depoliticization that seems to deepen with each passing year.

CHAPTER 3

CORPORATE EXPANSION AND POLITICAL DECLINE

The shrinkage of political discourse and action traced in the preceding chapter has deep roots in U.S. history, making the country somewhat unique in the extent of its depoliticization, even among highly industrialized societies. At the same time, this process has been pushed along even further through a convergence of factors shaped by modern historical development. On the one hand, of course, modernity has given rise to many well-known elements of social progress such as a sophisticated urban life, the diffusion of science and technology, the growth of the knowledge industry and the enhanced role of professional expertise, greater levels of material prosperity, widened social and geographical mobility, and more readily available sources of communication, popular culture, and the mass media. These factors would surely suggest a relatively open, democratized civic culture that could give expression to what is best in the liberal tradition. But that same modernity has generated perhaps even more powerful counterforces: the expansion of state, corporate, and military power (already gargantuan in their scale), the increased bureaucratization of social life, the stifling role of instrumental rationality reinforced by technology, the breakdown of neighborhoods and community with consequent social fragmentation, and, lurking behind all this, the intensifying globalization of the economy.

It is the counterforces that now seem to have the upper hand, imposing a regimen of corporate domination and antipolitics that is certain to strengthen its hold in the near future. The context of this epochal shift is, among other things, the very banality of modern politics itself—the deceit, empty promises, propaganda, fraudulent populism, and corruption that generates so much general revulsion against the entire public sphere. The American political system has become increasingly remote from its legitimating ideals of democracy, freedom, and civic participation, the signs of which are abundantly evident throughout the society. The two-party system disintegrates in the midst of civic withdrawal, judging from the survey evidence and a majority of people feel hopeless and alienated in the face of overwhelming (and often viewed as mysterious) external forces that serve to swallow up local and personal autonomy. Modern bureaucracy—indeed, the whole rationalization of social existence that accompanies high levels of capitalist development—is one example of an "external force" that people experience in most of their activities. As large-scale institutions become more rationalized and integrated, they tend to become more hierarchical driven more by expert knowledge and instrumental success (i.e., accelerated growth, strong profits, and so on). In the Weberian sense, therefore, bureaucracy can be seen not merely as a tool of efficiency enhancing specific goals but also as a mechanism of control throughout society, perpetuating hierarchy, elitism, and discipline in the spheres of work, education, and health care as well as in politics and the military. Thus, insofar as large organizations that govern people's lives rest on strict rules, procedures, specialized expertise, and confining routines, their growth turns out to be antithetical to the idea of a dynamic, active, participatory citizen politics. In other words, bureaucratic power—whatever its ideological rationale—consistently works to reduce the scope of local participation and the capacity of popular assemblies to initiate meaningful change.

THE NEW CORPORATE POLITY

Yet, if the phenomenon of bureaucratization—or mass media, to use another obvious example—contributes so much to the erosion of civic culture, in the American context these factors are best understood in the larger ensemble of forces that help to implement the domestic and global expansion of the corporate economy. While corporate colonization is hardly new, in just the past two decades it has achieved qualitatively new levels of power, accelerated by growing economies of scale, mergers among corporations, the great resilience of the permanent war economy, massive corporate entry into media and popular culture, and, perhaps most significantly, the process of globalization. Every strengthening of corporate colonization weighs strongly against conditions needed for an informed and politicized citizenry. Surely the era of antipolitics closely coincides with that phase of capitalist development in which multinational corporations, in tandem with such international agencies as the World Bank, the International Monetary Fund (IMF), and the World Trade Organization (WTO), have won a strong measure of global hegemony.

Despite significant governmental changes, policy shifts, and evolving social patterns over several decades, one element of continuity in American life remains, namely, the persistent expansion of corporate power. Far from being a simple economic fact of life, this process takes on political, social, and cultural meanings that penetrate into the deepest regions of everyday life. In political terms growing corporate power has worked most of all to hollow out the public sphere, as huge industrial, technical, and financial institutions have won more freedom to mobilize enormous resources for the purpose of shaping public dialogue and social existence. Corporations foster a mood of antipolitics by means of their power to commodify virtually every human activity as well as through their ownership and control of the mass media, their capacity to manipulate electoral and legislative politics toward sought goals, and their key role in globalizing the economy.

Since the 1970s big business in the United States has developed well beyond its traditionally hegemonic status, filling large parts of the void left by weakened labor unions, deradicalized social movements, the waning of broad progressive coalitions, and the growing ennui of the Democratic Party. Today's corporate behemoths (IBM, General Motors, AT&T, Microsoft, General Electric, Disney) depart from their predecessors in that they are generally much larger, more far-flung and diversified, more organizationally streamlined, and far more technologically developed, even as they retain the same profit-driven agendas. At the same time, such giant entities actually begin to constitute a new public sphere of their own by virtue of having taken over many functions of political decision making, including investment and allocation of resources—but in a setting that allows for no internal democratic governance or popular accountability. Corporate networks dominate the state apparatus, own and control the mass media, profoundly shape education and medicine, and penetrate into even the most intimate realms of social life (e.g., the family, sexuality). Societal priorities relating to both domestic and foreign investment, foreign policy, technology, work, and culture are set or overwhelmingly influenced by a narrow stratum of industrial, financial, and technical elites.[1] For the most part, these elites now exercise far more control over the state than the state over the elites. And multinational corporations are relatively unconstrained by the strictures of democratic participation and the open exchange of ideas, being run as disciplined, centralized, and routinized hierarchies in the service of highly instrumental goals such as technical efficiency, material growth, and enhanced market shares. Viewed in this way, corporations function by their very raison d'etre to restrict development of an open, dynamic public sphere in which major issues of the day can be confronted. Much like quasi-feudal institutions, they are set up to guarantee elite domination, rank-and-file obedience, and minimal ac-

countability to outside agencies and constituencies. The post-Fordist corporate system (like the capitalist legacy as a whole) is consciously designed
in myriad ways to undercut citizenship, devalue politics, and resist the pull
of democratic legitimating principles.[2]

The all-consuming "industrial civility" fostered by multinational corporations and Wall Street financial institutions has manifestly depoliticizing effects: not only are these structures themselves rigidly enclosed, but
they exercise enough power to limit political debates and policy choices
and also possess enough wealth to influence the entire field of candidates
in electoral campaigns. Market principles, shaped and redefined by the
modern technocratic apparatus, commodify and instrumentalize virtually
all public discourses, practically everything that takes place in the political
system. The "public good," insofar as it lives on in liberal discourse as a viable construct, does not exist outside of what elites may regard as contributing to efficient, pragmatic, and marketable outcomes; inevitably, economic discourse winds up conquering the public sphere, crowding out
general societal concerns such as collective consumption, social planning,
and ecological sustainability.

The immense growth of corporate power is probably the most fundamental development of the past 20 or 30 years. As economic globalization
proceeds, more than 40,000 multinational companies have moved into a
position to dominate the international and domestic landscape, controlling vast wealth, resources, and institutional power—and with it a greater
capacity than ever to reshape the public sphere. The leading corporations
build power plants, mine and distribute natural resources, control the
flow of the world's oil, gas, and electricity, manage the circulation of
money, manufacture and sell the world's automobiles, electronic goods,
ships, planes, weapons, computers, chemicals, and satellite technology,
and grow most of the world's agricultural goods. They supply the world's
military and police forces with equipment, arms, and munitions. In the
process of doing all this they have maintained control over about 90 percent of all technology, including what goes into the mass media, information systems, and popular culture. From this vantage point the largest corporations are able to dominate virtually every phase of economic,
political, and cultural life; they set the agenda for nearly every dimension
of public policy.

In the United States, huge corporations like Microsoft, AT&T, Time
Warner, Disney/ABC, IBM, and General Electric have assumed unprecedented power to delimit, directly and indirectly, what takes place in the
realm of public discourse. They can shape the images and exchanges that
effectively engage mass audiences, in part by employing sophisticated
opinion-polling, telemarketing, and public relations in order to manipulate discourse toward specific (private) ends, resulting in a subversion of

the public interest (defined in even the loosest sense). The corporations use a wide array of media influences, lobbies, PAC campaigns, experts, and lawyers to undercut the threat from consumer groups, labor, social movements, and community interests.

Intensified corporate colonization of the public sphere took a dramatic turn with passage in February 1996 of the Telecommunications Act. This legislation was ostensibly designed to enhance market competition among rival communications firms, thus stimulating improved services, greater popular access, and technological innovation. It would unleash a new era of heightened deregulation in keeping with the Reaganesque "free market" ethos of the times; indeed, this epochal rewriting of the 1934 Communications Act occurred at the very crest of the deregulatory ideological tide, as Patricia Aufderheide makes clear in her book on this legislation.[3] The result, of course, was precisely the opposite of what the legislation's partisans had claimed: it served mainly to pave the way toward more complete economic control over communications networks by a relatively small number of corporate giants. With the regulatory power of government now minimized, the private interests could more easily take control and set agendas in the entire information realm, including the Internet. Thus, while the Telecommunications Act promised a more interactive, open, even democratic setting, in practice anything resembling the public interest wound up as mere whispering amidst the established players' loud clamor for increased market share and profits. As Aufderheide writes: "It makes the American public, and public life itself, a derivative of the vigor and appetites of large business."[4] In this case the public domain was even further eviscerated by a decision-making process that unfolded largely outside of the public's purview, in a narrow process that received little media attention and involved no input from community groups, labor, consumers, and others left outside the corporate orbit. In Robert W. McChesney's words, "The analysis of the commercialization of the Internet is predicated on the thorough absence of any political debate concerning how best to employ cyberspace."[5] The all-important Telecommunications Act was the product of a closed system in which political "differences"—for example, those between Newt Gingrich and Al Gore—more or less vanished in the powerful field of privileged interests.

One of the hallmarks of a depoliticized society is the largely taken-for-granted character of deeply entrenched forms of domination. Nowadays, the Washington establishment makes certain that oppositional currents are confined to the most limited corridors of debate and participation, where political choices are ultimately instrumentalized, reduced to matters of technique and efficiency. Critical issues that revolve around the undeniably *public* character of corporations—such matters as the structure of authority, what is produced, the rights of labor, trade policies, and so forth—are rarely posed in the political arena. Tobacco production, sales, and advertising are viewed as the prerogative of "private" companies functioning in a "free" market, answerable only to their "stockholders." Similarly, the U.S. military interventions in Iraq during 1991 and later, costing tens of thousands of lives, were undertaken to defend U.S. "security" interests and protect American markets' easy access to oil, to ensure "the American way of life" (in President Bush's language). And continued large-scale worker layoffs and dislocations resulting from corporate downsizing are justified as necessary to keep capitalist firms internationally competitive—examples of that are legion.

Corporate power is reproduced and reinforced in two ways: through the perpetual rationalization of economic structures and through increased atomization of social life outside the confines of the corporation. The rather extreme individualism that has always infused America's liberal tradition, in effect, helps to reproduce corporate power. What needs to be emphasized here is that the celebrated "unity," cohesion, and purposive development of large corporations feeds on a high degree of mass inertia, much of it derived from popular belief in the fiction (again, rooted in liberalism) of a "private" ownership that confers nearly absolute "rights" and "freedoms" on the owners of capital. In this scheme of things "politics" represents an unwelcome challenge to managerial autonomy and flexibility at a time when intensified global competition seems to demand greater adaptation and fluidity. Elites want maximum "freedom" from state intervention that taxes, regulates, influences markets, and otherwise impedes the open flow of resources, goods, and profits. While corporations do not always succeed in fighting off government supervision in certain areas, the legitimating ethos of private firms maximizing their interests in a presumably self-regulating market economy still holds away and has even enjoyed a resurgence in the 1990s. To the extent that politics is devalued in favor of such presumed economic rationality, the main possible counterweight to corporate power—a strong, dynamic public sector—is eviscerated, undermined by an appeal to laissez-faire ideology. By the end of the twentieth century the balance between governmental and corporate power had tipped strongly in favor of the latter, despite continued (and generally unconvincing) protests against the tyranny of "big government by conservatives and neoliberals.

Modern corporations, stronger, more rationalized, more ideologically self-conscious, and increasingly global in scope, have stepped into the political breach; indeed, many nominally "private" firms have for some time performed governing functions normally the purview of the state. Greider describes General Electric as such a company, which not only manufactures light bulbs, jet engines, and nuclear power equipment but also plays a significant role in the mass media (it owns NBC and CNBC), the military, the

environment, foreign trade, and of course the larger expanse of the international economy. It devotes huge resources to advertising, controls important segments of media programming, and influences election campaigns along with legislation, not only through its enormous power and
wealth but through its ubiquitous institutional presence. Few other entities
came close to duplicating such far-reaching activities or exercising such influence in the media. As Greider writes, "Given the failure of the other institutions to adapt and revitalize themselves, corporate politics has become
the organizational core of the political process—the main connective tissue
linking people to their government."[6] The great impact of corporations
like GE, of course, is weighted overwhelmingly on the side of conservatism—in economics if not in social and cultural values. Such quasi-govern-
ing institutions hire large teams of lawyers, lobbyists, public relations
agents, and advertisers to protect their interests and propagate their values,
all the while manufacturing the image of a "responsible corporate citizen"
dedicated to human rights, democracy, environmental protection, Mom,
and apple pie. The economic health of GE is naturally equated with and
might pass for the common good: sustained growth and profits are presented as a necessary link to greater material affluence, proliferation of
jobs, a better environment, a more powerful country. In this schema GE
does maintain an extensive work force, much of it well-paid, with nearly
250,000 employees at 280 plants in the United States and overseas.

The political reality is that General Electric has worked aggressively,
often ruthlessly, for a strong military, a fiercely nationalistic foreign policy, free trade, reductions in taxes and social programs, and loosened environmental regulations. As a major producer of nuclear power equipment it has, not surprisingly, been in the forefront of a pronuclear
agenda. Further, with its multiple internal and external constituencies, GE
has taken on the character of an expanded and updated urban political
machine—though with far less accountability. GE executives and managers
have been found guilty of corruption and criminal fraud, but penalties
have rarely been harsh enough to deter repeated violations. Thus, in 1990
GE was convicted of criminal fraud for cheating the Army on a $254 mil-
lion contract for battlefield computers, for which the corporation paid
$16.1 million in criminal and civil fines—including $11.7 million to settle
roughly 200 other government charges. At GE, as in the rest of the corporate economy, ethics have all too often been bypassed in favor of more instrumental pursuits; while fervently upheld in theory, in practice ethics
have been quietly subordinated to the operational criteria of control, efficiency, and profits. And the influence of workers and consumers on vital
areas of decision making at GE has been minimal, especially at a time
when downsizing and layoffs further erode popular leverage. Managerial
elites want to escape governmental regulations of *any* sort, and—at least

since the later 1970s—there has been a major impetus toward the resurgence of laissez-faire ideology in the United States. By means of a sustained mobilization of professional expertise, moreover, these elites have been able to exercise pervasive influence over the flow of political and cultural information, seeking ever to suppress such tame liberal ideas as the free exchange of ideas, government involvement as needed, and active participation by all citizens in political decision making.

Corporate hegemony is further solidified by the workings of economic globalization, the information revolution, mass media, and the culture industry—all of which are interwoven in a matrix of commodified production. Multinational corporations exercise nearly total control over resource allocation, investment decisions, commerce, and world trade, severely reducing the role of specifically national actors (whether governments or firms).[7] "Global cities" like Tokyo, Mexico City, New York, Singapore, Los Angeles, and Sao Paolo, with no particular regional or national allegiances, become magnetic centers of capital and technology flows that resist the force of territorial boundaries. Working through the World Bank, World Trade Organization (WTO), and the International Monetary Fund (IMF), and aided by such trade arrangements as GATT and NAFTA, multinationals use their financial leverage to push for a market-centered capitalism featuring minimal governmental controls, fiscal austerity, and privatization wherever feasible. Any genuine form of political regulation is regarded as a threat to the "free market," which is glibly passed off as representative of a form of economic "democracy." The deep structural impacts of a highly globalized and interconnected market system have yet to be fully comprehended. On the downside, though, economic upheavals emanating from Asia from late 1997 through most of 1998 (the "Asian contagion" scare) may well offer some clues to the future. The first ripples of economic crisis already reveal momentous forces that are exacerbating class (and possibly racial) divisions in many countries. Meanwhile, globalization has led to a decline of national governmental power and local autonomy to such a degree that many basic economic decisions are being usurped by multinational corporations and allied international organizations. In the absence of effective multinational planning or regulation mechanisms, development will surely have little in common with the utopian vision of elites who see—not chaos and polarization—but only unfettered economic growth, a worldwide strengthening of human freedoms and rights, and the increased technological capacity to solve the world's major problems.

We know that corporate power does in fact translate into dynamic economic development, but the penetration of capital into every region of the world brings with it highly uneven forms of growth, sharpened class divisions, social dislocations, and mounting ecological crises. The process reproduces the same emphasis on privatized modes of production and consumption, market priorities over social goods, technological manipulation of resources and information, and material growth for its own (and profits') sake—leading to the same extreme maldistribution of wealth, authoritarian governance, and familiar coupling of urban decay and violence. With global political instrumentalities lacking sufficient leverage, the public sphere—such as it is—inevitably succumbs to the ceaseless pressures of the economic powers that be, leaving no ethical or governing framework for solving urgent problems. (The failure of the U.N.-sponsored Earth Summit to deal decisively with the global ecological crisis at its meeting in Rio de Janeiro in 1992, among many other such failures, reflects this predicament.) The subordination of politics to the all-powerful commodity underpins the strong corporate drive toward a unified world economy where diversity means little more than capitalist rivalries, where genuine cultural and ideological pluralism are submerged by the homogenizing ethic of market relations.

Economic globalization creates a shrinking world even as markets expand, the flow of capital, technology, material resources, transportation, and telecommunications having generally increased at an accelerating pace since the 1970s. Further, goods and services are no longer produced in only one location but rather enter the market through what Robert Reich dubs the "global web" of producers, computers, and satellites that link designers, engineers, contractors, and distributors worldwide. Resources, knowledge, and customized services are more easily than ever exchanged instantaneously across manufacturing and distribution sectors, across national boundaries. Thus, in an evolving complex global and high-value economy, "fewer products have distinct nationalities. Quantities can be produced efficiently in many different locations, to be combined in all sorts of ways to serve customer needs in many places. Intellectual and financial capital can come from anywhere, and be added instantly."[8] This is just as true for cultural products like film and music as it is for such durable goods as autos, electronic goods, and computers. To be sure, there are still remnants of national economic identity in the multinational system— Japan versus the United States, competition among developing Asian powers for markets, conflict among Latin American countries, and so on— but the entire corporate system, while still tied to specific governments, is becoming more and more disconnected from the nation-state. In Reich's words, "The emerging American company knows no national boundaries, feels no geographic constraint."[9] Moreover, as interdependence weakens nationalism, it also renders national and local politics weaker and more vulnerable to the inexorable pressures of the cosmopolitan market.

We have thus reached what Jean-Marie Guehenno describes as "the twilight of the nation-state," a political construct that has ultimately adapted poorly to the web of economic interdependence and the vast power of global corporations. It follows that a politics organized historically around viable nation-states will be far less today a locus of a mass mobilization, legitimacy, and decision making than it has been for the past 200 years. The result is what Guehenno terms a "crisis of the spatial perception of power," in which the connection between the exercise of power (both economic and political) and territoriality is severely weakened.[10] As politics becomes increasingly subordinated to a mosaic of private interests, governing structures tend to simply follow a variety of short-term, instrumental agendas of the moment, bereft of any larger vision or public sense of purpose that might transcend the pull of corporate power. Globalization undermines the strong historical connection between capitalism and nationalism. As Greider argues: "The obsession with nations in competition misses the point of what is happening: The global economy divides every society into new camps of conflicting economic interests. It undermines every nation's ability to maintain social cohesion. It mocks the assumption of shared political values that supposedly unite people in the nation-state."[11] Here globalism extends and deepens the domestic logic of corporate colonization, making a charade of democracy as it transforms the entire landscape.

With the end of the cold war, the waning of Communist states and socialist politics, and the emergence of the United States as the only military superpower, the capitalist "new world order" proclaimed at the onset of the 1990s would seem to have a relatively unobstructed path toward global hegemony. At the same time, if the multinationals seem poised to dictate terms of development in every region of the globe, the parallel reality is that the postnational, postcommunist milieu is destined to be shaped by intensified class divisions, social polarization, and political uncertainty—even chaos—as the familiar ideological guideposts (including nationalism) give way to a "postmodern" ethos where politics in the most generic sense begins to lose its legitimating (and transformative) powers. The very fluidity and interdependence of the global system, a seemingly positive feature, could wind up subverting the very coherence of established political institutions, ideologies, and strategies. The emergent world economy is rooted more in networks and dispersed horizontal connections, or failed connections, than in discrete national institutions, with territorial sovereignty becoming ever more diffuse and fragile than in the past. The social chaos and upheavals in Russia, Yugoslavia, the Middle East, Indonesia, Colombia, and in several metropolises around the world, while often retaining attachments to established political and ideological symbols, could be harbingers of increasingly depoliticized civil wars in the future.

In Russia, the rapid shift from command to market economy as part of the famous "shock therapy" following the demise of communism opened the country to enormous global pressures that have created massive instabilities in the nascent capitalist system. There has been a dramatic erosion of legitimating institutions and ideologies, not only in Russia but in the Ukraine, Belorussia, and other neighboring countries. In that region, the newly aborning market economies are falling victim to the depredations of nouveau riche robber barons and criminal elements, thus wreaking havoc with the whole society. Grinding poverty, rampant unemployment, unprededented urban violence and social dislocations, and the spread of an underground economy dominated by urban gangs and assorted mafiosi. Capitalism Russian-style has permitted the rise of a new wealthy elite that pursues grandiose entrepreneurial schemes and adventures, thus further exacerbating the gulf between rich and poor, city and countryside, one region and another. Russia, torn by ethnic religious, and territorial conflicts since the dissolution of the Soviet Union in 1991, has seemed perpetually on the verge of collapse despite outward appearances of stable liberal-democratic rule associated with the Westernizing claims of the Yeltsin regime. Russian elites, seduced by images of Western abundance and technological acumen, have scrambled to dismantle or fully privatize factories (which were often running at less than 50 percent capacity); they have also imposed draconian austerity measures in the public sector, gutting most social services. In November 1996 the Russian federal government conceded that it had too few resources to pay workers or to continue to maintain the already depleted social programs. The predictable social consequences have been recurrent strikes, labor sabotage, and, most fearsome of all for the Yeltsin regime, increasing numbers of workers (and the jobless) taking to the streets in a desperate search for new sources of income. Crime both in and outside of the underground economy began to skyrocket, as Russian capitalism took on increasingly semi-anarchic overtones. Since the early 1990s a huge market for illegal guns has appeared, contributing to the emergence of an armed society. In the midst of such turmoil a widespread retreat from politics has been in full swing. Nowadays the public sphere has been largely obliterated by harsh, identity-based rivalries, a sharp decline in the spirit of social or political obligation, and an overall destruction of civic culture—even as the new official ideology champions a transition to liberal democracy, the free market, and consumer society.

The Russian predicament of the 1990s is simply one manifestation of an unraveling of the global order that was set in motion after the end of the cold war. Once the nuclear standoff between the United States and Soviet Union ended, the very specter of an ideologically motivated opposition to capitalism seemed to vanish, at least temporarily, allowing for a resurgence of local conflicts that offered no transformative vision and no exit from the impasse; centrifugal forces gained momentum, but these had little if any connection to the fortunes of particular social classes or political coalitions, much less international movements inspired by some variant of socialism. By the mid-1990s the new post-cold war reality was abundantly evident: mobs, gangs, militias, mafiosi, and warlords began to contest for power, while the traditional Left quickly fell into retreat. This series of developments reinforced the already deepening mood of anti-politics, which above all entailed hostility to *any* oppositional ideology. As Hans Magnus Enzensberger argues in *Civil Wars*, the harsh realities of violence, crime, and local warfare have become everyday experience for tens of millions of people throughout the world. "The most obvious signs of the end of the bipolar order," he writes, "are the 30 or 40 civil wars being waged openly around the globe."[12] Reflecting on the seemingly endless proliferation of local military groups—most of them well armed in a world of readily available, cheap, and sophisticated weapons—Enzensberger aptly points out that modern combatants no longer operate under ideological banners of any sort. Even the time-honored appeals to freedom, socialism, or national liberation have been dropped in a setting where battles over territorial or local identity take precedence. Thus: "What remains is the armed mob. All the self-proclaimed armies of liberation, people's movements and fronts degenerate into marauding bands, indistinguishable from their opponents . . . with no goal, no plans, no idea that binds them together."[13] In this way popular struggles—and ever more frequent expressions of civic violence—are disconnected from the conventional exercise of politics as the struggle to achieve coherent goals, visions, or even immediate policy agendas. In this way the linkage between globalization and antipolitics in the post-cold war system has become solidified.

COMMODIFICATION OF THE PUBLIC SPHERE

As the global market system works to undermine national and local mechanisms of participation, the already waning political influence of legislatures, parties, and social movements is further weakened—a process intersecting with post-Fordist tendencies long at work in the industrialized world. Post-Fordism refers to the economic restructuring of developed capitalist economies, marked by a shift from the manufacturing to the service sector, the rise of temporary and part-time work, growth of the financial sphere and speculative activity, the spread of mass consumerism, and the commodification of practically everything—all fueled by perpetual technological innovation and the internationalization of markets. As the economic power of even the most powerful nation-states begins to fade, so too does the whole apparatus of liberal democracy, which is engulfed by these profound changes, both domestically and globally. Politics itself takes on the character of ritual with the drastic relocation of power centers, not to mention the greatly enhanced role of the mass media, advertising, and marketing in the electoral (and even legislative) realm. The decline of labor and traditional left forces in general coincides with the appearance of dispersed local movements, which for the most part have lacked the ideological and organizational coherence to carry out effective insurgencies against firmly entrenched power structures. The individual too is easily overwhelmed by an imposing social totality that, on the one hand, is so highly amorphous and fragmented and, at the same time, is dominated by remote and threatening global forces that seem well beyond the control of mere mortals. The result is that politics has become thoroughly reconfigured at a time when production, consumption, work, and the entire social structure have been profoundly transformed.

The impact of this reconfiguration is concentrated mainly in the urban areas, especially in the sprawling megalopolis-type world cities where globalization and post-Fordism have converged to produce uniquely and sometimes fiercely antipolitical forces. Beneath the surface of modernity (superhighways, skyscrapers, bustling malls, computer networks) lie urban centers in which turbulence and explosive social contradictions are never far from the surface, reflecting the increased prevalence of poverty, homelessness, environmental blight, violence, and the eclipse of public space. Most "world" cities are rationally organized to meet the imperatives of profit-seeking multinational corporations, often assuming the character of modern fortresses with enclosed spaces, high-rise buildings, technocratic culture, and gated communities. While social problems endemic to the megalopolis often give rise to powerful oppositional tendencies, the difficulty is that so much in urban life militates against the emergence of a thriving public sphere. What this means is that social contradictions cannot readily find political translation. Hence, urban spaces—which we would normally expect to be vital centers of social, cultural, and political life—often degenerate into yet new examples of the Hobbesian nightmare. By the 1990s many of the largest American cities had become caldrons of social pathology, owing to extremely crowded conditions, traffic congestion, noise pollution, the high prevalence of crime and violence, and environmental blight, imposing severe limits to the ways in which people can hope to experience the public realm. Indeed, the modern city seems antithetical to what theorists like Rousseau, Marx, and Peter Kropotkin believed would be necessary for any meaningful form of collective participation. In this fashion too antipolitics feeds into the logic of institutional control and rationalization.

The modern city thus follows a social trajectory that has little in common with the long and rich tradition of the municipality as the site of local community, public space, citizenship, and democratic participation. The

Hobbesian thrust of urban "development" has destroyed the basis of autonomous social, cultural, and political life not only in the city but in its immediate environs. As the urban setting becomes increasingly commodified and atomized, most forms of political activity begin to atrophy and wind up indistinguishable from ordinary exercises in manipulation, with agendas set by and for the privileged interests. Indeed, the citizen of modern states is scarcely encouraged to take political rights very seriously because, as Murray Bookchin puts it, politics amounts to little more than the "efficient, specialized and professional surrogate of 'the public.' "[14] We are left with something resembling the corporate, or entrepreneurial, model of urban life—measured largely by its success as a profitable business enterprise rather than its contribution to community life or citizen participation. In this context elites sharpen their managerial skills in order to build and sustain a particular network of social "constituencies." In the face of such administered control the average person tends toward passivity, or at least quickly concludes that energies devoted to the public sphere are not likely to yield much in the way of visible rewards. As Bookchin observes: "An increasingly disempowered citizen may well become a quietistic and highly-retiring self. A major loss of social power tends to render a person less than human and thereby yields a loss of individuation itself. . . . We thus encounter a twofold development: a world in which growing social power pre-empts concerns that were once largely in the purview of the individual and the community, and the steady erosion of personal power and the individual's capacity for action. In this paralyzing force-field, the individual's self-identity begins to suffer a crucial decline."[15]

In such a transformed American political culture lies another powerful element of post-Fordism: an unprecedented resort to personal consumption, which finds ready expression through the countless images circulated in the spheres of advertising, mass media, popular culture, sports, and fashion. In the age of corporate colonization time-honored values (freedom, democracy, community, even selfhood itself) are more and more subjected to the all-consuming power of the commodity. The shopping mall perhaps best embodies this post-Fordist reality. Although its long-term impact on popular consciousness has yet to be measured, the mall has probably been just as much a source of antipolitics as any of the Hobbesian features mentioned earlier. Yet, if the urban quagmire reproduces social turbulence, alienation, and fear, the consumer mall functions in an altogether different way to induce norms of privatism and passivity, constituting a main linkage between corporate agendas and everyday life.

Throughout the postwar years the individual (and household) desire to acquire personal goods became a central driving force behind the modern social order. While the mall as a sprawling but integrated public space devoted to consumption was initially confined to white suburbia, by the

1970s it had begun to transcend its origins in the middle-class pursuit of happiness through possessive individualism. Even as 1960s radicalism and the counterculture mounted a scathing attack on middle-class material-ism, mall culture was well on its way to becoming a widely celebrated American institution. Soon even people who made up the urban poor could partake of a consumer world made more seductive by a wide array of glittery images, media spectacles, and material inducements of all sorts. As part of the revitalized American dream, sprawling malls and shopping centers became virtual universes unto themselves, escapes from the de-manding regimen of work and everyday life—all fueled by advertising, the credit economy, increased physical mobility, and of course the wonders of sophisticated technology.

Reflecting on how commodification sustains an ethos of privatized withdrawal, Lauren Langman argues that mall culture offers a type of pseudodemocratic experience that gives people a sense of public engage-ment while also discouraging in myriad ways any genuine civic participa-tion. The decline of the public sphere and the subsequent further with-drawal of individuals from it amount to a mutually reinforcing dialectic. Thus: "As the public sphere has become increasingly fragmented and less gratifying, individuals have become more likely to withdraw into their own private realms to seek self-confirmation, gratification, and even ex-press counter-hegemonic practices and contestations. . . . But this with-drawal lets the social order become more powerful with an ever more en-feebled privatized self less likely to contest major issues."[16] Here the mall phenomenon serves as yet another conduit of corporate colonization in that the commodification of social (and political) life can easily generate a false sense of empowerment that works its magic across class, regional, ethnic, gender, and age divisions. As a place where the "public" is reduced to the terms of market relations and material strivings, the mall steadily evolves into a zone of psychological retreat from the civic arena, which, in any case, is permeated with tremendous anxiety and frustration. For adults the mall constitutes a ubiquitous outlet for selfhood through the ac-quisition of clothes, electronics, cosmetics, videos, music CDs, and the like. It should be noted, as well, that other places where people gather—restaurants, cafes, bars, theaters—are also frequently located in or near shopping malls. For young people, in particular, this prime outpost of consumerism offers glitzy alternatives and a constant stream of seductive images and spectacles that provide temporary tangible relief from the mundane world of job insecurity, career anxieties, school, family and per-sonal problems, or simply boredom. Hence, the mall phenomenon, deeply rooted in everyday life, far transcends in its impact the historic presence of the downtown Chamber of Commerce in most American cit-ies. In this way too the commodity as object of worship appropriates both individual and collective subjectivities while short-circuiting any tendencies toward citizen involvement in politics.

Like mall culture, the mass media and the culture industry manifest themselves in every nook and cranny of commercialized public space, probably exerting an even more depoliticizing impact on mass consciousness. The media are situated to both reflect and magnify the converging of forces of corporate colonization, consumerism, informational technology, and the culture industry. Each of these forces has become more potent over time, leading to what Herbert Schiller calls the "corporate capture of public expression."[17] Yet, whereas the malls foster consumer-motivated retreat from the public sphere, the media serve to connect people instantaneously to the fast-moving world of events, spectacles, and cultural phenomena in a way that appears to satisfy peoples' need for information and worldly contact. In truth, however, media culture provides only a false sense of public engagement. In their effects, however, both mall and media cultures amount to mutually reinforcing avenues of privatization, passivity, and escape—with predictably devastating consequences for political life.

Among the various media forms, television remains by far the most popular, and it is clearly the most depoliticizing. Through the medium of TV the entire field of politics emerges as simultaneously spectacle and passive experience, an activity that is equally glamorized and devalued; the ethic of infotainment reshapes politics just as it does news programs, sports events, special features, and the ever present crime sagas. Election campaigns, supposedly the centerpiece of democratic politics, become an occasion for sound-bite advertising, celebrity gossip, staged debates, and computerized calculations. In the guise of high-powered, objective, authoritative reporting, TV news has sunk to the same level. As Todd Gitlin writes, "political news coverage has become at times an accomplice to demagoguery, at times a branch of the sports and entertainment industries, and at times an exercise in cynicism, keeping Americans diverted, perhaps, but failing to help them govern themselves."[18] The "news" itself, depending for its legitimacy on the role of high-paid quasi-celebrity broadcasters, typically serves up false drama about crime ("If it bleeds, it leads" still apparently the operative newsroom imperative) accidents, local human interest stories, sports, and well-known personalities with comparatively little coverage of the international, economic, and social issues that people must understand to exercise real citizenship. One problem is that for TV the visual image captivates viewers' attention so much more readily than any verbal narrative, and the immediate emotional response from viewers is what television producers end up seeking, rather than thoughtful, in-depth reflection (on such issues as plant closings, environmental dangers, corporate abuses, or the causes of cancer).

Yet, the depoliticizing effects of the mass media run even deeper. The very essence of the television medium, which delivers slick, formulaic programming mainly to individual households, is to generate a psychological state of passivity and individual separation. The promise of electronic interaction through media, especially as applied to television, is for this reason illusory in the extreme. With few exceptions TV transmits messages to people in the limits of the household, which means that social "interaction" occurs largely outside the realm of concrete social activity (work, community, politics). Media-driven symbols and discourses circulate well outside the mundane realities of culture and politics, cut off not only from the larger public space but from any sense of geographical or historical terrain, as if floating in some ephemeral "moment." Lacking any sense of history, individual perceptions and experiences come to have little relationship to actual social identities (e.g., of the sort involved in citizen participation or grassroots movements) that could possibly function in such a way as to *reshape* history. Viewed in this way, TV helps to create a kind of independent field of perceptions that has the effect of *separating* people from their actual world even as the medium itself appears, in all its sense of immediacy, to keep them in intimate contact with that world.

The hegemonic functions of mass media take shape in a postmodern milieu where social themes, conflicts, and identities get played out through the emotional impact of shifting images that may be far removed from the material and cultural conditions that actually shape peoples' daily lives. Media representations constitute a series of illusions that can seduce large audiences precisely because of the artificiality of images: they offer *glimpses* of a more attractive world, or at least feelings of empowerment in the present world. The Persian Gulf war of 1991 illustrates this point well, since in virtually every respect what the media labeled a "war" turned out to be a TV spectacle in which the vast majority of Americans could "participate" in the winning of a great patriotic military victory—all from the safe vantage point of their living rooms. That the gulf war would become an epic cause to celebrate was heightened all the more through the miracles of technology (both military and communicative), allowing for a rather quick and devastating outcome along with the comfort of distance, which made the Desert Storm events appear much like a bigger-than-life sports contest. Popular catharsis could thus be experienced without all the normal complications of pain and suffering that normally accompany warfare. The assault on Iraq, in contrast to the Vietnam quagmire, was "surgical" in at least that respect. As Douglas Kellner shows in his analysis of the war, the around-the-clock TV spectacle permitted millions of confused and disempowered Americans to feel as though they were part of a successful military campaign, that they could at least observe the "making of history," that they could be part of a larger community of interests and sense of purpose.[19] The Cable News Network's (CNN) ratings skyrocketed during the period of Desert Shield (the buildup of forces) and, especially, Desert Storm (the air war and brief ground war).

Another example of such media-centered hyperreality was the coverage and popular response to the Clarence Thomas–Anita Hill episode, which played out on viewers' homes screens in 1992 as Judge Thomas appeared before the Senate Judiciary Committee as a justice of the Supreme Court. The confrontation between Thomas and Hill, who accused the nominee of sexual harassment (based on certain actions of Thomas's allegedly committed several years earlier), unfolded in front of TV cameras, and the ongoing drama exploded into a theatrical spectacle that millions of Americans found riveting. Here, as in the Persian Gulf events, media presentations touched the national psyche deeply, in this case involving conflicts over race, gender, and sexuality—all of which was played out on a national stage where conflicting social forces were galvanized, although still viewed from a completely safe distance. The Senate proceedings took on the character of a bizarre, often humorous, media circus where (generally trivial) charges and countercharges tapped into the long-standing social anxieties of many Americans. That the issues in question were comparatively dated and had little to do with Judge Thomas's overall qualifications to serve on the Supreme Court only added to the surreal atmosphere. For a short period the Thomas–Hill confrontation did mobilize certain political constituencies, primarily women's and civil rights groups. In the end, however, this saga too, despite the outward signs of fierce ideological battle, amounted to little more than a media-driven form of artificial politics.

These media events would in time be dwarfed by the most hyperreal spectacle of all—the O. J. Simpson murder case and trials (first criminal and then civil), which monopolized the national media's attention for most of the period of June 1994 through early 1997. Here again a number of powerful social themes, conflicts, and identities were played out in a frenzied media phantasmagoria, but touching on not only race and gender but also class, celebrity, and the very role of mass media in setting social and political agendas. Not only did TV and the print tabloids bring to the public virtually every detail of this macabre crime and practically every murmur that came out of the court proceedings, but the media's hypersensational coverage wound up saturating every popular venue, thus in effect converting a murder case into a highly charged soap opera–spectacle. At the same time, this episode (or, more accurately, series of episodes) provided nothing if not an *escape* from real politics, indeed from the boredom and troubles of daily existence. For many Americans, the celebrities in the case (including the one accused of murder) seemed to be far more interesting than anything in their own daily lives. In the Simpson events, which took on new life during the second (civil) trial, the concrete facts of the case—including the issue of Simpson's guilt for a brutal double murder—seemed at times nearly irrelevant in the context of an entire nation's fixation on celebrity (and celebrities' capacity to hire a legal team perhaps smart enough to outwit the prosecutors team—whatever the facts).

The seductive power of the mass media, especially television, in shaping perceptions of self and social reality points to the precipitous decline in other sources of identity: neighborhood, community, religion, class, political ideology. While media culture in the United States is often touted as a realm of interaction and participation, a more accurate description is one that portrays individuals as relatively passive observers of rituals and spectacles even when such individuals may "feel" integrally to be a part of the public sphere.[20] The point is that "politics" here winds up being sublimated by experiences often viewed as more immediate, sensual, and cathartic—in contrast to the seemingly remote and more confusing elements of the real public sphere. The media constitute a sphere in which the search for meaning, empowerment, and even heroism gets transferred onto larger-than-life characters who, as in the case of Sylvester Stallone's movie persona, John Rambo, can be seen as substituting for the person's own sense of frailty and powerlessness. Viewed thusly, an important dimension of politics in the post-Fordist, postmodern age turns out to be the pursuit of different abstract forms of identity in an increasingly fragmented, shapeless world.[21] Media-shaped perceptions help to reproduce social identities around nationalism, race, ethnicity, gender, and sexuality, which in themselves do not pose the question of corporate domination; when filtered through the prism of the media and popular culture, such identities help perpetuate even more extreme fragmentation. In this context, then, "politics" is reduced to questions of style, ritual, and image where the hyperreal tends to override substantive political debates and concerns. And this aspect of postmodernism in effect parallels the fate of electoral politics, which long ago degenerated into a series of formulaic advertising and marketing campaigns.

THE SOLIDIFICATION OF ELITE POWER

This subversion of politics in late twentieth century America is no simple product of corporate manipulation, media propaganda, and elite-manufactured conspiracies. It is all this, of course, but in a larger sense it is a process that must also be understood as part of the global restructuring process and the aforementioned dynamics of post-Fordism. Traditional modes of governmental control and regulation have been weakened by economic globalization, while the familiar mechanisms of class conciliation rooted in Keynesianism have also broken down, allowing for more direct, brutal, predatory expressions of corporate power. From a political standpoint, one result of this new configuration of forces is a highly evolved form of corporatist interest mediation defined by an institutionalized merging of government, corporate, military, and (to a lesser extent) organized labor interests. Corporatism of this sort inevitably works to narrow the public sphere, closing off the arenas of decision making. The largest corporations business interests do not necessarily have carte blanche in such a setup, but they can more easily bypass the realm of legitimate politics; corporate colonization is faced with fewer and fewer obstacles.[22]

A narrowed and depoliticized public sphere hardly poses a threat to the privileged interests; on the contrary, it is perfectly consonant with the imperatives of domestic elite control and global capitalist hegemony. A relatively barren, eviscerated political terrain coincides with a profound weakening of opposition, where counteragendas to corporate expansion are denied significant institutional leverage and ideological voice. It is no less true today than in the past that the only force powerful enough to challenge (or even regulate) the corporate domain is, for better or worse, large-scale governmental power; local islands of social or political opposition, while surely necessary, are too easily insulated, too cut off from the macro realm of state and economy, to realistically contend for domestic or global power. While the modern state retains essentially bureaucratic features, in a liberal political system with open elections and pluralist interest-group representation there is clearly *some*, at times perhaps extensive, access for popular groups and movements, and there is generally *some* possibility for further democratization where conditions permit. But in a profoundly depoliticized society like the United States where corporatism is so deeply entrenched, a true resurrection of type of old-style politics needed for fundamental social change would, at this point, be too fantastical to conceive. From this viewpoint, too, modernity can be understood as profoundly two-sided: it produces more technology, expertise, and widely dispersed modes of information but also instills more powerlessness and alienation from politics, as we have seen.[23] Individuals feel completely overwhelmed by expanding social and institutional leviathans— the global economy, the state, corporations, the media, bureaucracy—that seem well beyond their reach. Here a generalized retreat from the public sphere, viewed by many as contaminated and impenetrable, may seem normal enough, even desirable. People who are frustrated, angry, and disempowered but who still want drastic change may lack the political language to think or act coherently on the basis of their feelings; they may even want disengagement from the public sphere. In this they remain fully tied to the status quo. Others, pushed to the brink and ready to fight back, will most probably do so in a confining ideological framework that renders most immediate types of action extremely limited and harmless. Still others, possibly the majority, are so devoid of a sense of political efficacy that they cannot see beyond their own (often all-too-pampered) private spheres. Therefore, despite the incessant (and easily available) flows of information made possible by the new technology, the larger picture remains essentially fixed: popular disenfranchisement spreads even in the midst of a modern order replete with all the trappings of liberal democracy.

At the end of the twentieth century the corporate order appears more stable and in control than at any other time in the recent past, despite a series of mounting contradictions that might have been expected to undermine the whole edifice. This is so largely because the system, in its globalized incarnation, has been able to maintain an unprecedented degree of ideological and cultural hegemony over both state and civil society; opposition is subverted before it can fully confront the multiple contradictions of the system. Elites can more easily solidify their position since their claim to rule is rarely questioned enough to place their interests and priorities fundamentally into question. Unlike the popular strata involved with daily struggles and grassroots movements, elites typically do not suffer the well-known "postmodern" malaise of sharply fragmented identities and purposes; despite internal divisions, their overall class orientation is far more unified. As capital becomes more fluid, mobile, and global, as material and technological resources become more concentrated, the multinational corporations begin to enjoy new leverage, qualitatively, vis-à-vis virtually everything that stands before them (including even the most powerful nation-states).[24] And where citizen participation and local sovereignty are already devalued in the domestic society, as in the case of the United States, such leverage expands even further. In the absence of strong global or national counterweights, the worldwide market is much freer to pursue its deadly course of expansionism (and ultimately destruction of the planet). A "new world order" built along these lines—that is, featuring the massive concentration of economic and political power—inevitably conflicts with even the most rudimentary requirements of democratic politics, namely, an open public sphere, a thriving civic culture, broad allocation of material resources, and minimal differences between rich and poor. After all, sustained citizen involvement in community life and political decision making hardly fits the corporate demands for hierarchy, profit maximization, cost cutting, and "market flexibility" in a period of heightened global competition. Whether corporate hegemony can be maintained in a world riven with economic crisis, social polarization, and civil strife—a world ultimately faced with ecological catastrophe—is yet another matter.

What the analysis presented in these pages suggests, however, is that even in the event of the corporate hegemony becoming fragile—that is, even once its contradictions begin to explode—any future revival of politics at the level of mass publics will face tremendous obstacles. The deep, collective sense of empowerment that must catalyze such a political revival runs up against not only the awesome might of global capital but, closer to home, the devastating effects of a hollowed-out public sphere and civic culture. The problem is further complicated once we take into account the disabling limits of those formal liberal-democratic structures that remain from an earlier period; clearly any political rebirth will be forced to reappropriate and transcend that harshly compromised tradition, one that has lately run counter to the creative, empowering psychological energies needed to produce an engaged citizenry.[25] Lacking these energies, even the most ambitious radical-democratic ideals and arrangements, even the most celebrated participatory schemes, will ultimately lose their popular appeal. In an age of corporate colonization, unfortunately, the historical processes at work seem relentless in subverting what is needed for a revival of true participatory politics.

CHAPTER 4

RISE AND DECLINE
OF THE PUBLIC SPHERE

The historic impasse of modern politics is nowhere more clearly reflected than in the mounting global ecological crisis, for which no solution is even remotely in sight. It is a crisis increasingly out of control, with possibly irreversible and horrific consequences in the absence of decisive countermeasures that would require, among other things, durable collective agencies for social change that do not yet exist. Such measures are inconceivable, however, when there is no viable politics; that is, progressive forms of statecraft, widespread citizen participation, a vision and strategy linked to a common set of goals. Politics is the only means by which a transformative project could unfold, for a fundamental restructuring of class and power relations—and it is becoming abundantly clear that such a transformation is required sooner rather than later because so much is clearly at stake. And how this drama unfolds in the United States, which presently controls roughly 25 percent of the world's resources, will be critical to the global outcome.

ECONOMIC GLOBALIZATION: ORDER AND CHAOS

The severity of the global crisis may be far greater than we are generally led to believe. In 1990 the Worldwatch Institute concluded that the major countries of the world had just 40 years to reverse patterns of production and consumption that have long been in place—to initiate a shift toward "environmentally stable societies"—if a major breakdown and attendant chaos were to be avoided. In only a few decades the economic decay, ecological devastation, and social disintegration already visible in the spread of civic turbulence around the globe, will be nearly impossible to reverse.[1] The signs should be menacingly clear to anyone paying attention to the contemporary international situation: rampant deforestation, increasing air, water, and soil pollution, depletion of vital natural resources, global warming, population pressures, extreme poverty and famine, loss of topsoil for food production, and contagious diseases out of control in many places. The implications for economic and social welfare, politics, and military conflict are only beginning to be felt. It is important to emphasize here that ecological problems may not lead necessarily lead to apocalyptic explosion—though such an outcome cannot be dismissed—but rather to a slow, gradual, inexorable, and devastating biospheric and social decline over the next several decades.[2]

The vast implications of economic globalization for human society have yet to be systematically, and deeply, confronted by elites who rule the major industrial countries. This failure is most evident in the United States, despite the growth of environmental consciousness, and adoption of important reforms, during the past 30 years. For reasons that will be explored shortly, we far from an awareness of the kinds of comprehensive and epochal changes taking place. These changes have one underlying impetus: the sustained assault by multinational corporations on national sovereignty, democracy, local cultures, the environment, and (despite increased levels of economic growth) the standard of living of most of the earth's population. The enormous growth of corporate structures, the end of the cold war, the emergence of new industrial powers in Asia and elsewhere, and the solidification of liberal trade arrangements through GATT and NAFTA have given rise to the unprecedented free movement of global capital.

As the crisis steadily worsens, with no effective global mechanisms to regulate economic development and ecological pressures, the destructive cycle of polarization, social and environmental decay, urban violence, and militarism becomes ever more firmly set in place. In Greider's words, "The global system of finance and commerce is in a reckless footrace with history, plunging toward a dreadful reckoning with its own contradictions, pulling everyone along with it."[3] Such a scenario may seem exaggerated at a time of apparent material growth and abundance in some parts of the world; in fact it is a somberly realistic assessment based on terrible and undeniable evidence. As Tom Athanasiou points out, "It is not a matter of opinion but of incessant and terrible fact that we are living in a time of slow biophysical cataclysm."[4]

Of course, the predictable response by the elite strata of corporate managers, politicians, military planners, and academics is one of ritual assurances that the global ecological predicament is really no predicament at all (or is far less grave than the doomsayers argue), that the extent of the crisis has been blown out of proportion by a small nucleus of radical fearmongerers who rely on bogus science, and that the imposing environmental problems that do exist can be solved by some combination of economic growth and technological tinkering. Many who have taken the ecological crisis to heart believe that a move toward large-scale capitalist "greening" (greater corporate responsibility, more frugal energy policies, environmentally sensitive production methods and goods, recycling, and the like) will stave off catastrophe. Others look to an ongoing process of accumulated reforms that lead to vaguely defined outcomes such as "sustainable development" and ecological balance. This type of compelling "realism," however, is simply a form of denial that perpetuates the system of power and privilege responsible for the crisis in the first place. To concede the systemic nature of the crisis, or to emphasize the need for deep structural transformations, would be to carry the discourse well beyond conventional ideological limits.

Public opinion in the United States on the subject of global ecological crisis has reflected largely a sense of confusion and uneasiness. The ordinary person feels unable to register any significant input into the sanitized national "debates" among experts and politicians. Meanwhile, the crisis shows no signs of abating, measured in part by the intensification of chaos and upheaval in such diverse locations as Russia, Mexico, Brazil, Indonesia, Thailand, and Algeria and by the persistent economic weakness in the Pacific Rim—all of which could have explosive consequences for American society. In any case, the relationship between economics and politics, between global realities and national prospects, is destined to become more intricate over time. To quote Greider: "The destructive pressures building up within the global system are leading toward an unbearable chaos that, even without a dramatic collapse, will likely provoke a harsh reactionary politics that can shut down the system."[5] This is indeed the other side of antipolitics.

In the absence of decisive and systematic forms of political intervention, corporate-engineered "growth" and plunder can be expected to continue unabated, its global impact being exacerbated over time. The culture of antipolitics is so deep and so pervasive that reasoned discussions of political strategy to reverse the decline may seem rather arcane, out of fashion, off limits, indeed unfathomable in a public sphere where supposed pragmatism gives free reign to "market" forces (i.e., corporate domination) in allocating social goods and priorities. The inescapable reality is that only some form of global planning and mobilization of resources can correct the present wasteful and debilitating modes of production and consumption, set limits to growth, attack worldwide poverty, narrow the widening gulf between North and South, create an equitable trade system, and lay the basis of an ecological model of development. No small order, to be sure. The point is that very little can happen without the emergence of a rejuvenated, vigorous, democratic politics. Yet, the public sphere in the United States is moving steadfastly *away* from the sorts of political requisites and sensibilities required to carry out even the semblance of a good fight. Where there is such an impoverishment of political culture, should there be any wonder at the precipitous loss of political *capacity*?

A major source of the current drift toward impasse—a central preoccupation of this volume—is that even the most significant movements for change (including the major strands of environmentalism) are deeply afflicted with an antipolitical malaise that is especially widespread in the United States. If something approaching a consensus exists regarding the *reality* of an ecological crisis, there is nonetheless a widespread sense of denial concerning the need for drastic political measures to counteract the problem; issues of class relations and structural power are largely sidestepped all along the ideological spectrum. There are, of course, frequent obligatory nods to the need for policy reforms, but such reforms are not permitted to be other than organic, gradual, moderate, and nonconflictual—that is, painless to the status quo and consonant with corporate operating priorities. This vision of "change," upheld as a sacred belief by elites, has its origins in age-old Enlightenment myths holding that balance, harmony, and progress are the result of unfettered economic growth. In their view, the problem lies not so much in the forms of production and investment but rather in the failure of growth to extend sufficiently to all regions and social groups. Trumpeted as a necessary discourse of pragmatic realism in academia, the political establishment, and mass media, such rational optimism finds added expression in the modern search for technological panaceas. In the optimists' scenario the social crisis can presumably be resolved by greater application of high-tech informational systems, computers, and sophisticated modes of communication—that is, through the enhanced application of data and knowledge in the decision-making apparatus. The pretentious futurism of the Tofflers (articulated in *Creating a New Civilization*) perhaps best embodies this increasingly popular perspective.[6] Whether the focus is on growth and prosperity, or technology, or both, the antipolitical impulse winds up reinforcing the same option, namely, a refusal to address truly urgent issues and challenges that lie at the heart of the current ecological and social predicament.

Retreat from social and political life has become a recurrent feature of American society in the 1990s, extending to all parts of the ideological spectrum. In fact, progressive and community-based groups have been especially vulnerable to the inducements of antipolitics—witness the New Left, the counterculture and its many offshoots, and important currents in the new social movements (including environmentalism) since the 1960s. This includes an array of lifestyle radicals (for example, deep ecologists) who typically seek to prefigure their values and goals by transforming everyday life in the existing social order. Some want to create more or less pristine forms of communal life, generally in rural settings or what is sometimes called "wild nature." Lifestyle radicals hope to establish a closer union with the rhythms and pulses of the ecosystem, distancing themselves from the ugly contaminations of urban industrial life—and, ultimately, from the mundane entanglements of the public sphere itself. A similar dynamic is at work among the mounting ranks of new-age or religious environmentalists whose aim is to establish an organic connection between spiritualism (however defined) and the struggle for ecological renewal, which takes on decidedly metaphysical overtones. A depoliticized outlook also characterizes direct-action groups like Earth First! and the assorted individuals (including the Unabomber) who have embraced Luddism, a type of modern-day antitechnological bias. In each case, the ideal of an ecologically harmonious world is developed largely outside the institutional–political realm, which is viewed as hopelessly corrupt and devoid of any genuine democratic potential.

In the mainstream of the ideological continuum one can find a virtually endless assortment of lobbies, interest groups, and direct-mail organizations located in Washington, DC, as well as many state capitals—all dedicated to winning limited environmental reforms (clean air initiatives, workplace regulations, wilderness preservation acts) through normal electoral, legislative, and bureaucratic intervention. Indeed, the kinds of activities constitute the bulk of what is usually regarded as environmentalism. Some far-reaching reforms have in fact been carried out since the early 1970s, but most of this agenda has been confined to the familiar routines (and frustrations) of normal politics, which has channeled environmental activity in directions compatible with the orderly functioning of government and corporations—and away from the systemic features of the global ecological crisis. Years of elite-centered politicking has given rise to its own brand of antipolitics: vague platitudes and promises, cosmetic designs, pleas for citizens to change personal consumption habits, the "greenwashing" of corporate behavior, and so forth. When everything is taken together, the sad but predictable result is a terrible (and possibly fatal) collapse of political will, strategy, and vision that is the hallmark of a thoroughly depoliticized society. This is especially debilitating in that politics offers a means, perhaps the *only* means, for recovering the ideals of citizenship, democratic participation, and community (not to mention the all-but-forgotten notion of the public good). Such values have fallen increasingly out of fashion in the highly instrumental, economically charged, profit-oriented climate of modern capitalism. Further, politics constitutes arguably the only historical mechanism for achieving the kind of large-scale transformations needed to give substance to fundamental change. In an age that glorifies market values and individual autonomy, politics takes on added meaning in that only a developed form of social governance can furnish the binding power through institutional leverage, resource controls, and planning capacity to initiate and carry out such bold transformations. To imagine that alternatives will somehow magically arrive through corporate undertakings or the work of local volunteer groups, with minimal governmental involvement, amounts to an exercise in utopian naivete. The systemic flow of investments and resources, both nationally and globally, will ultimately have to be routed through a process allowing for both the socialization and democratization of that flow. In the absence of political mechanisms strong enough to counter corporate power, the very prospect for ecological renewal tied to creating a balance between nature and society, sustainable patterns of development, and expanded democracy and equality on a global scale will be nullified even in the midst of legislative reforms. There is no conceivable way that the transformation could unfold spontaneously, according to its own inner logic—as if powerful interests had neither the intention nor the capacity to block serious attempts at change. In point of fact, the profoundly promarket (and antipolitical) mood that has deepened in the United States over the past two decades works incessantly and powerfully against such a transformation.

The growing hostility toward "politics" and "government" in American society cuts across social, regional, ethnic, gender, and ideological differences. While understandable as a profound statement of popular alienation from the power structure, antipolitics obliterates the capacity of people to think and act collectively in order to forge solutions to impending social and ecological crisis. From this standpoint, a full-scale, uncompromising rejection of politics (including conventional politics) leaves many important questions largely unanswered, such as What *kind* of government or politics is being devalued or discarded? Precisely which functions are worthy of being kept or even expanded, which ones in need of being jettisoned as repressive or antidemocratic? When we address the role of the state, do we emphasize its local, regional, or national dimensions, its unitary or federal structures, its centralized or decentralized character? Is the government, at any level, envisioned as a realm in which democratic participation can be more or less maximized? The complete turning-away from government, the state, politicians, and "politics" is far more than a passing fad; it represents a deep, pervasive, secular response to historical conditions that cannot be easily dismissed or sidestepped. In this sense antipolitics can be viewed as one of the defining features of late twentieth century American political culture, one profoundly shared by elites and masses, Republicans and Democrats, conservatives and liberals, defenders of corporate power and populists, by the left, right, and center alike. It is a profoundly *national* malaise that could have a devastating impact on American society and, more ominously, on the future of the entire planet.

THE TRADITION OF POLITICAL DISCOURSE

If we are to speak in any meaningful sense about the contemporary "decline" of politics, or evisceration of the public sphere, we need to address how the legacy of a distinctly political discourse and action has been established, refined, and carried forward over the centuries. While twentieth-century incarnations of politics have frequently given rise to a variety of authoritarian movements, parties, and regimes in the form of fascism, Stalinism, military dictatorships, and ordinary bureaucratic hierarchy, it bears remembering that the special tradition of politics that goes back to the ancient Greeks also embodies much of what is noble, creative, and transformative in the human experience. It encompasses certain ideals and goals that will have to be retrieved if we are to have any hope of confronting, much less reversing, the global crisis. Among these key ideals are: the theme of community and civic participation in what is truly common to all human beings living in a particular society; the notion of individual and collective empowerment through citizen participation; the concern with statecraft and the struggle for general interests by means of social governance; and the commitment to social change made possible in and through the mechanism of popular movements. The complex, interrelated strands of thought and practice that broadly comprise the political tradition remain imperatives as much today as at any time in the past—indeed, given the force of globalization, they might well be more urgent for the present day than for the period of Plato and Aristotle, or Machiavelli and Hobbes, or Rousseau and Marx.

The Greeks upheld the supreme virtue of a uniquely "civic" or "popular" life in which it would be possible to build community and citizenship in a world of evolving shared involvements. For them, it was in the uniquely public realm where the fullest human experiences—social, intellectual, political—could best be realized, where shared meanings and purposes could prevail over the more limited, partial, and fragmented aspects of family, personal life, and work. From this standpoint, the Greeks understood the realization of certain ideals and visions not merely as a matter of individual choices but as the working out of societal concerns, interests, and obligations that can have no parallel elsewhere. Thus Cicero spoke of the *"res publica"* as a peculiarly public realm where the life of political involvements and obligations would impart a sense of commonality rooted in ideals of justice, equality, democracy, and rights extending to all

adult persons residing in the state domain. Aristotle wrote that human beings are, by their very nature, political creatures insofar as the sphere of
political participation inevitably entails higher values—a life of public commitment, a sense of giving and selflessness, a passion for learning, growth,
and enlightenment.[7] In *The Politics* Aristotle observed: "All associations
aim at some good; and the particular association which is the most sovereign of all, and includes all the rest, will pursue this aim most, and will
thus be directed to the most sovereign of all goods. This most sovereign
and inclusive association is the polis, as it is called, or the political association."[8] He added that "the polis belongs to the class of things that exist by
nature, and man is by nature an animal intended to live in a polis."[9] In Aristotelian thought, it follows, all persons were "equally dependent on the
whole" (the polis) and achieve the highest sense of purpose and identity
by means of the fullest possible engagement in it.

In *The Republic*, Plato suggested that "we begin inquiring what justice
means in a state," arguing that such values as justice ultimately pertain far
more to the public than to the individual realm.[10] For Plato, one could
not hope to find a solution to fundamental human problems without a
clear resort to political intervention, which in the end he expected to require an historic merging of political power and philosophy on the same
terrain.[11] There would be no avoiding the reality that, in the end, politics
would have to transcend the whole range of parochial, competing, fragmented, and selfish interests that necessarily clash with the public good.
Here, as in the case of Aristotle, politics decisively contributed to the ele-
vation of social life in a way that no other association was able (or designed) to do.[12] As a defining element of the Greek polis, therefore, politics amounted to the sine qua non of democratic participation and selfless
governance—an ideal that, of course, was realized only in the breach
throughout the turbulent history of the Greek city-states.

This articulation of politics as a form of privileged, enabling discourse in Greek thought found abundant resonance in the much later
work of Rousseau, who believed that individuals could be refashioned exclusively though the intricate workings of the political process. He saw in
the challenge of an untamed natural world little more than expressions of
brute force that favor ascendancy of a corrupt, selfish individualism over
the more enlightened claims of community and public obligation. Rousseau envisioned a scenario in which people come together in a specific
(and clearly delimited) territorial order on the basis of a social compact
that would foster a generalized sense of community; the sphere of governance comes to supersede the very randomness (and destructiveness) of
individual will. In certain ways Rousseau's idealized world was even more
politicized than that of the Greeks, since he anticipated that the collective
force of society embodied in the General Will would eventually prevail

over all manifestations of the egoistic self and parochial attachments—at least where the proper conditions might be found, such as the small scale of community, a premodern type of simplicity, and socialized property relations. The intimate linkage between the community and the politics of local associations and governance meant not only a higher level of citizenship but also an enhanced moral purpose associated with the common life. Thus, "The passage from the state of nature to the civil state produces in man very remarkable change by substituting in his conduct justice for instinct, and by giving his actions moral quality that they previously lacked."[13] Again echoing the Greeks, Rousseau argued that "nothing is more dangerous than the influence of private interests on public affairs."[14]

A second and related dimension of politics extends to the ideal of citizenship itself—of active engagement in the public sphere—which gives individuals, both as discrete persons and as participants in groups, organizations, and whole societies, a broader sense of social identity and historical purpose. While the theme of citizenship (broadly defined) figured prominently in Greek thought, it has taken on special meaning since the French and American revolutions and the development of the modern nation-state. The modern fusion of nationalism and liberalism gave rise to generalized loyalties and commitments beyond the family, village, tribe, city-state, and region. The very notion of citizenship, and with it the historic goals of empowerment through democratic participation, became expanded—gradually and unevenly, to be sure—along with the process of economic modernization.[15] The long-standing but still evolving debate over citizenship rights, obligations, and identities was addressed by such theorists whose work prefigured industrial capitalism as Locke, Rousseau, Paine, Jefferson, J. S. Mill, and by modern writers such as Tocqueville, Weber, Dewey, and Arendt.

Viewed from this angle, politics entails nothing short of the ever broadening capacity of whole populations to be engaged in the vital affairs of public life, to be in a position to make decisions and exercise influence over matters that shape their lives. It is all part of ongoing popular efforts to achieve real, active membership in a political community, enabling ordinary people to make incursions into the authoritarian, oppressive domain of elite rule, bureaucracy, and indeed all forms of social hierarchy. Seen in relief against the old forms of elite manipulation and control associated with the *ancien régime,* the emergence of the nation-state in the late-eighteenth century produced near universal norms of citizenship, consensual governance, political rights, and national identity. While the legal scope of citizen participation was initially and severely limited by the very narrowness of popular access to governing institutions, a constitutional framework was set in place allowing for a further broadening of citizenship as previously excluded groups (workers, minorities, women) struggled to gain a measure of suffrage and representation. Citizenship thus emerged as a vital element in modern discourse, with its emphasis on Enlightenment ideals of scientific and technological rationality, diffusion of education and knowledge, and, of course, the ever increasing material abundance made possible by industrialization.

The gradual expansion of citizenship in economically developed countries over the past two centuries suggests the growth of new social and political space in which freedom, community, and a greater range of human creativity might unfold—as Hannah Arendt has emphasized.[16] As people become more active in the general affairs of society they tend to wind up more fully engaged in various forms of collective life, more capable of intellectual and cultural development, and more adaptive to changing historical circumstances. Following the presuppositions of Rousseau, it is easy enough to see how genuine democracy (not limited to suffrage) must always require an empowered citizenry—one that, sooner or later, begins to push against the boundaries of elite privilege and institutional constraints. The liberal idea that citizens could take their place in civil society as free and independent actors, as essentially sovereign persons, has been upheld and refined in many ways since the time of Locke. The guiding premise was that, while politics had always been the domain of elites, in the era of national citizenship it would now become an increasingly popular and common reality for the masses, owing largely to universal suffrage, constitutional guarantees, and the unfolding of an open and dynamic civil society. Politics would thereby undergo a new phase of democratization as the state system moved to incorporate historically disenfranchised groups and permitted the significant expansion of popular decision making.

Viewed in this historical context, politics can be understood as the realm in which people seek to broaden their forms of identity, their sense of belonging, their capacity to influence the course of events, their ability to make a difference. Citizenship thus gives both substantive and symbolic meaning to the age-old struggle against authoritarian domination, against social hierarchy in its diverse expressions; further, it challenges the very possessive individualism that was at the heart of classical liberalism as forged by Locke, Smith, and Bentham. At the same time, citizenship affirms the search for an authentic self—part of the effort to achieve social individuality—against the encroachments of hierarchical structures that treat human beings as manipulable, atomized objects in the game of power and privilege. Empowerment is unthinkable without a psychology of being that unfolds in relation to the social activity of others, to the larger community of interests, and this in turn requires broad citizen participation in the public sphere.[17]

A third strand of political discourse involves the struggle for social transformation by means of statecraft, the creative use of political institutions on behalf of a historical ideal. Nationalism, for example, has commonly been associated with Jacobin or quasi-Jacobin attempts to build collective identity and purpose through state intervention; a set of values is diffused through the initiatives of a relatively small group of elites who set out to construct a new political order. Such Jacobin impulses are visible in Plato's idea of the philosopher-king, Hobbes's concept of the Leviathan, Machiavelli's vision of a tutelary Italian prince, and of course Rousseau's embrace of a General Will that some have connected to the Bonapartist phase of the French Revolution as well as later incarnations of "totalitarian democracy."[18] In the French Revolution, as in the later Bolshevik Revolution in Russia, Jacobinism emerged as a state-centered protagonist of history in a period of social turbulence and fragmentation; it offered political unity in a context of disorder and breakdown. Here politics became an innovative universalizing force thrown up against narrow parochial interests and strong centrifugal tendencies (e.g., class, religious, and regional divisions) in civil society. It reaffirmed the primacy of politics at a time when the very efficacy of statecraft had been challenged and undermined. Politics alone among all human enterprises was capable of performing these Jacobin functions, of fulfilling epic goals of social transformation.

The Leninist variant of Jacobinism, originating with the rise of Russian Bolshevism just after the turn of the century, can be seen partly as a reaction against the pervasive antipolitics of the nineteenth century. Indeed, Lenin's famous "rediscovery" of politics in an unraveling Russian civil society becomes intelligible against the backdrop of a generalized hostility to politics typical not only of classical liberalism but of the main currents of nineteenth century Marxism and anarchism. Throughout Europe this retreatist mood could be explained to some degree as an outgrowth of the nationalist excesses of the French Revolution, which seemed to obliterate freedom, equality, and democracy in the name of those very ideals enshrined in "The Rights of Man." Liberalism, ever fearful of state tyranny and even relatively limited regulations of the capitalist economy, celebrated the vitality of civil society over the state and trumpeted the ideas of laissez-faire economics and the self-regulating market in opposition to even benign institutional designs and plans. The anarchists, of course, generally rebelled against *all* forms of social and political authority; their hatred of the state, expressed in the ideas of Proudhon, Bakunin, Kropotkin, Malatesta, and Goldman, was deeply visceral and uncompromising—both as to ultimate objectives and as to intermediate methods and strategies. As for Marxism, its view of revolution was shaped by a profoundly anti-Jacobin impulse in that socialism was expected to develop as a lengthy historical process, resulting from the gradual matura-

tion of social and economic forces and the intensification of social contradictions in the capitalist mode of production—not by means of state
intervention (especially of the vanguard or "Blanquist" variety), which
Marx and Engels believed would give rise to authoritarian rule while paying lip service to democratic and egalitarian ideals. In general, classical
Marxism relegated the sphere of politics to the "superstructure," revealing
a theoretical primacy assigned to deeper underlying forces at work in the
material relations of production; politics could be viewed as essentially
epiphenomenal, with no developmental logic of its own and no capacity
to influence the course of events over the long term decisively.

For twentieth century Jacobins like Lenin and Gramsci, however, this
sweeping antagonism toward politics was responsible for a debilitating paralysis of revolutionary will. It indulged the worst forms of spontaneism
and economism which, in the end, rendered any coherent political strategy impossible. If politics as statecraft remained a vital—if always problematic—ingredient of large-scale historical change, then the fashionable renunciation of politics could generate nothing but a sense of futility and
defeat for any group seeking to fundamentally alter class and power relations. By thoroughly "rejecting" politics, insurgent social forces only
wound up ceding the important terrain of state power to those dominant
groups that already laid claim to that power. Lenin thus reversed long-
standing premises of classical Marxism, substituting a primacy of politics
(meaning a decisive role for the vanguard party) for the old orthodox
economism—a shift that Lenin justified in the context of an autocratic
tsarist state and an increasingly globalized economy that brought imperialism to Russia, thus reconfiguring the basic social forces in motion. Politics
for Lenin became an all-powerful instrument in the worldwide struggle
for socialism, an extension of the architectonic impulse found in Plato,
Machiavelli, and the French Bonapartists.

Lenin and the Bolsheviks approached politics as the decisive terrain
on which diverse anticapitalist (and antiimperialist) struggles could be mobilized and united. Statecraft as enshrined in the vanguard party and the
revolutionary state would give strategic and normative direction to movements for change, thus countering the "bourgeois" logic of pluralist fragmentation. Following Lenin, Gramsci conceived of the revolutionary
party (the "modern prince") as a key protagonist of history in much the
same way Machiavelli envisioned a classical Italian nation-state as the
agency of national unity and moral regeneration. While Gramsci shared
Marx's well-founded fear of Bonapartism and emphasized the importance
of social transformation in civil society as the basis for any successful political maneuvers (his "war of movement"), he still held to the dynamic importance of political action. This is one reason why Gramsci, having experienced the bitter defeat of the Turin council movement in 1918–1920,

looked increasingly to the *party* as a central vehicle of change. From 1921 until his incarceration by the fascists in 1926, Gramsci was deeply involved in the leadership of the fledgling Italian Communist Party. And Gramsci's own brand of Jacobinism, inherited from both Machiavelli and Lenin, clearly permeated the pages of the *Prison Notebooks*.

To an extent much greater than any other Marxist of the period, Gramsci insisted on a distinctly political framework of discourse that could not be reducible to any supposedly determinant material conditions. The universalizing thrust of politics could be used to create an entirely new alignment of social forces, to forge a unity of theory and practice, to "make history." Following the Greeks and Machiavelli, Gramsci believed that politics was the guiding mechanism through which human activity could achieve order and meaning. Thus, "Can one not say that the real philosophy of each man is contained in its entirety in his political action?"[19] In other words: "To transform the external world, the general system of relations, is to potentiate oneself." He adds: "One can say that man is essentially 'political' since it is through the activity of transforming and consciously directing other men that man realizes his 'humanity,' his 'human nature.' "[20] For Gramsci, social change achieves its fullest, most coherent expression in and through the medium of politics, since it is politics that best activates a collective sense of identity and loyalty. As it was for Machiavelli before the founding of the Italian nation-state, statecraft emerges as a creative instrument for mobilizing the popular will around a particular historical vision—nationalism in the case of Machiavelli, a fusion of nationalism and revolutionary values in the case of Gramsci. Praising Machiavelli's "original" Jacobinism, Gramsci writes: "But what Machiavelli does do is bring everything back to politics—i.e., to the art of governing men, of securing their permanent consent, and hence of founding 'great states.' "[21] Without politics, no revolution, no forging of a national community, no pursuit of universal objectives, would ever be conceivable.

Gramsci's critique of productivism in the *Prison Notebooks*—his impatience with the familiar Marxist emphasis on unfolding material forces—laid the foundations of his distinctively political theory that refused to see the extensive and complex realm of state power as a mere reflection of class relations. His "philosophy of praxis" was designed to overturn the historical inertia and virtual fatalism prevalent in orthodox Marxism, which dwelled on the logic of capitalist development leading to systemic crisis. He went considerably beyond Lenin's more narrow, organizationally centered Jacobinism in his well-known efforts to theorize a balance between state and civil society, "war of movement" and "war of position," party and local councils (or other popular forms). Moreover, while Gramsci saw in politics a cohesive mechanism strong enough to overcome the dispersive pressures of sectoral, parochial interests, he was also in-

clined to view politics as incorporating a vital pedagogical or "moral–intellectual" dimension; even an organizational vehicle like the revolutionary
party would be designed to perform "collective intellectual" functions. At
this point Gramsci, much like Machiavelli, understood politics as a consensual process rooted in active, informed, socially engaged citizens
rather than manipulated objects to be deployed at the whim of elite pref-
erences. This perspective was essentially a modified Jacobinism, more attuned to the popular, local, democratic energies of counterhegemonic
forces. The vision of statecraft would be linked to the mobilization of oppressed, marginalized groups who would now, for the first time, become
fully enfranchised. Whereas Marx stressed the role of unfolding social
contradictions in shaping political actions while Lenin chose to emphasize
the primacy of politics, Gramsci wanted to merge both of these concerns
into a framework that also incorporated recognition of the great impact
culture and ideology would exercise on politics.

A fourth element of politics flows logically from one side of Gramsci's
conceptual framework: the transformation of (public, collective) consciousness that takes place in the context of social movements—notably
those movements that set out to subvert established institutions and norms
in some fashion. As movements enter into the public sphere, hoping to
transform it as well as the larger society, they become "political" to the extent they are able to mobilize resources against the dominant structures
(class, state, patriarchal, racial) and challenge the discourses that bolster
them. As people join oppositional movements, they typically begin to assert
their claims for justice, equality, or democracy, however partially or unevenly; in this process they are likely to achieve higher levels of efficacy and
empowerment in a setting where prevailing values may no longer be taken
for granted. Collective action becomes politicized as it takes the form of direct action, momentary uprisings, parallel power in counterinstitutions,
organized coalitions, alliances, and parties—all linked to a variety of pedagogical activities. Of course, social movements can rise and fall without
ever moving into the realm of political action, and they have a long history
of retreating from the public sphere into more localized, often spontaneous, modes of engagement once certain goals are achieved (or blocked).
Political outcomes of social struggles are always variable and indetermi-
nate, just as the relationship between movements and the state, between
the social and political realms, is highly idiosyncratic and unpredictable.
Collective resentment and alienation take many forms, as we know from
the complex experiences of popular movements that inevitably call into
question the simplistic premises of rational-choice theory.[22] Those conditions that enter into the translation of social movements into dynamic agencies of political mobilization will be discussed in later chapters.

For the moment it will be helpful to call attention to the distinctly *political* dimension of movements that have historically won some considerable measure of success. Indeed, the very efficacy and dynamism of movements depends on their capacity not only to subvert and delegitimate the power structure but also to build on those other elements of politics just mentioned, namely, solidarity, citizenship, and vision of statecraft. At the same time, this "movement" aspect of politics fills out a dialectical relationship in which politics is more intimately connected to local, democratic struggles and to the process of social transformation; as such, it sheds its conventionally elite definition. While statecraft surely involves the elite realm of architectonics, movement activity forces politics in a different direction, toward a more generalized, diffuse, and popular element in tune with transformative impulses. When viewed thusly, dialectics runs directly against the established universe of discourse and action, against the conventional ways of seeing politics. In Herbert Marcuse's words, "Dialectical logic is critical logic: it reveals modes and contents of thought which transcend the codified pattern of use and validation."[23] Thus, the dialectic embraces a negative opposition insofar as it challenges the very oppressive nature of "reality" and breaks with the governing systems of power and ideology. As Marcuse points out, this negative function of the dialectic is ultimately *political* in nature since it embraces the collective struggle for freedom, and "progress in freedom depends on thought becoming political, in the shape of a theory which demonstrates negation as a political alternative implicit in the historical situation."[24]

Since the 1960s popular movements in the United States have sought to rekindle one or another of these features of political discourse and action, setting out, in one context or another and with highly diverse aims, to broaden a public sphere that has all too often been distorted by market priorities, electoral spectacles, and bureaucratic machinations. Examples of such political revival include the New Left (guided by the participatory spirit of the Port Huron Statement, the Students for a Democratic Society [SDS] founding statement), the civil rights movement, feminism, and the environmental movement. Each of these powerful historical forces, moving according to its own logic, served to extend the boundaries of freedom and democracy, carving out new spheres of personal and social autonomy, rights, and decision-making power. And each, in its own way, aimed to extend and broaden the ideal of citizenship, which has deep (however flawed) roots in American political history.[25]

A strong impulse to revitalize citizen participation, as both a strategic goal and an existential vision, gave historical meaning to the New Left, countercultures, and new social movements from the early 1960s through the 1980s. Port Huron embodied the time-honored values of participation, community, and citizenship inherited from previous traditions: liberalism, progressivism, populism, socialism, the labor movement. It was a document, forged at the beginning of the 1960s, that uncompromisingly affirmed the capacity of ordinary people to decide their own fate, to resist institutional limits, to make history, to carry the ideals of democracy into every sphere of life.[26] Activists of the period hoped to reclaim and rejuvenate politics by purging it of corruption, interest-group bargaining, and electoral narrowness, borrowing ideas from the legacies of Rousseau, Jefferson, and Thoreau along with the more contemporary thought of Paul Goodman, Jean-Paul Sartre, Albert Camus, and C. Wright Mills. The American New Left grew out of a historical milieu laden with problems and challenges: the growth of bureaucracy and political authoritarianism, a conformist culture, poverty, racism, and imperialism. Its participatory ideals, however distorted they would become in the heat of actual popular struggles, shaped an entire era in which the Vietnam war was waged and then ended, a myriad of popular movements was spawned, the South was largely desegregated, and historic barriers to racial and gender equality were broken down. These ideals surely contributed to a mood that helped to topple two presidents, Nixon and Carter. They gave rise to an emergent culture that sustained at least the outlines of a freer, more diverse social, cultural, and sexual milieu, that encouraged one of the most explosive periods of human adventure and experimentation in American history. They posed a new range of issues, challenged widely held myths about social reality, and greatly expanded the realm of cultural and political freedom. Perhaps most significantly, they offered the glimpse of a broadened citizenship, sense of community, and oppositional politics that seemed to offer hope and optimism for the future. They empowered millions of people in groups, organizations, and movements that began to counter stale formulas inherited from the past: consumerism, the work ethic, a self-centered individualism, a view of politics that went no further than the ballot box.

The civil rights insurgency originated in the late 1950s as a series of black struggles, catalyzed by organizations such as the Southern Christian Leadership Conference (led by Reverend Martin Luther King, Jr.), the Student Nonviolent Coordinating Committee (led during the mid-1960s by Stokely Carmichael), and the Congress of Racial Equality, which collectively sought to integrate southern society and achieve formal legal and political rights denied to most African-Americans throughout U.S. history. This movement quickly won mass support and then, during the 1960s, spread to most regions outside the South. Over a period of two decades the movement made great inroads into the political culture, extending the realm of participation and rights far beyond the established limits, winning significant social and economic reforms, and forcing new terms of debate over race relations in a country that had long been in denial over

the horrible legacy of racism. It led to a virtually unprecedented mobilization of poor and disenfranchised groups, often by means of direct action
that included boycotts, marches, demonstrations, sit-ins, and civil disobe-
dience. Without question the civil rights movement exerted a dramatic
moral and political influence that continues to the present day, arousing
antiracist opinion in all regions and at all levels of society. It was a powerful force in the early development of the New Left and student movements, feminism, peace and anti-intervention mobilizations, and later politically defined mobilizations such as the Rainbow Coalition. It fueled the
urban insurrections of the 1960s and the rise of the Black Panther Party,
concentrated mainly in the north. Whatever the ultimate limits of its legislative and policy gains—some of which, like affirmative action, have been
subsequently eroded—the civil rights movement did create an enormous
public space in which not only blacks but other minorities and sectors of
the population could secure a beachhead in the political arena as a means
to securing new forms of identity, recognition, and civic involvement.

These struggles found additional resonance in the women's movement that appeared as both an outgrowth and *critique* of 1960s radicalism,
which, in its New-Left manifestation at least, was dominated largely by
white male activists. Affirming an organic connection between the personal or "private" realm and the public sphere, feminism (particularly its
earlier, more radical, variant) brought forth a deep critical analysis of
what had previously been viewed as peripheral areas of social life: the family, personal relationships, sexuality, popular culture, work, health care,
education. (These concerns had not been entirely ignored, either in the
mainstream or among progressives, but they had generally been excluded
from serious *political* discussion before the rise of contemporary feminism.) Following the New Left, feminism reaffirmed the human capacities
of freedom, participation, and community—the very capacities that were
being blocked by patriarchy with its historically rigid system of gender
stratification. Citizenship here meant a progressive expansion of women's
involvement in social life, in the public sphere from which they had been
traditionally excluded. Areas of contention involved demands and interests previously denied public or explicitly "political" status; they would be
pursued, as in the civil rights movement, by creative methods ranging
from small encounter groups to mass demonstrations, legal actions, electoral campaigns, and the building of local institutions (rape-crisis centers,
health clinics, bookstores, media productions, cafes, and so on). Following
its civil rights precursor, feminism opened up new areas of discourse and
debate, challenging the received wisdom about social roles, rights, obligations, and even the very definition of citizenship itself. It likewise mobilized millions of people, though with considerably less enthusiasm for
electoral contests and normal politics, and it helped refocus general un-

derstanding of the common good, the nature of power, and the role of governance while asserting the centrality of collective forms of self-determination.

What these two great postwar social movements accomplished, more than anything else, was a broadening and deepening of the public sphere, even if neither movement could sustain a deep oppositional presence over time. They were vehicles for a long overdue revitalization of politics, bringing new groups into a political arena that had always been the stronghold of elites. Both movements struggled mightily, albeit in different ways, to counter the corrosive processes of institutional manipulation and objectification that always seemed to transform human beings into malleable pawns, and both managed to elevate the very scope and meaning of public discourse. Moreover, both validated the notion, following Port Huron, "that politics has the function of bringing people out of isolation and into community."[27] They embodied a rebirth of politics at a time when the vast majority of people were alienated from the entire orbit of governmental activity. Yet, the relationship between these movements and the political realm was ultimately more problematic and even conflicted, especially when the broader legacy of the New Left is taken into account. As Frances Fox Piven and Richard Cloward argue, the disruptive logic of the civil rights movement eventually gave way to the blandishments of electoral politics and routine legal in-fighting, thus undermining its capacity for prolonged insurgency and opposition; as with the labor movement of the 1930s and beyond, the process of incorporating the civil rights movement into the political system led to a number of important gains but in the end turned out to be a mixed blessing. Politicization in this sense always entailed sacrifice and compromise, a loss of militancy, and a tendency to retreat from the most radical of the original goals.[28] As for feminism, it has carried forward an enduring New-Left flavored element of antipolitics: a focus on local, or "micro," concerns, a preoccupation with consciousness over "structures," a quasi-anarchist rejection of all forms of authority, and an inclination to dismiss the utility of normal politics.

The extremely tense relationship between modern popular movements and the political realm is easily detected in their strong hostility toward the fourth dimension of politics, statecraft, a hostility that has been a hallmark of civil rights struggles, the New Left, feminism, and most strains of environmentalism. Indeed, the New Left was born more or less as a reaction against what was seen as an obsolete "Old Left," against the bureaucratic deformations of both Socialism and Communism. Of course, the entire record of statecraft in the twentieth century, both on the left and the right, was one of authoritarian domination—from the rise of fascism in countries like Germany, Italy, Spain, and Japan to the diffusion of Leninist regimes in Russia, China, Vietnam, Cuba, and elsewhere, not to mention the persistence of military dictatorships in dozens of countries around the world. Jacobinism on the left has produced various versions of bureaucratic centralism, defined by single-party states, leadership cults, systematic ideological controls, coercive state policies, and command economies. This was hardly a legacy that might inspire a Jacobin rediscovery of politics in the advanced capitalist societies where at least partial expressions of democracy and citizenship have taken root over the past two centuries. On the contrary, bureaucratic centralism, like fascism on the right, generated a widespread fear of politics insofar as the generalized search for "politics" activated through strong leadership could so readily be associated with what Erich Fromm described (in the case of Nazi Germany) as an "escape from freedom"—an extreme manifestation of political will that, during periods of extreme social crisis and breakdown, may annihilate collective subjectivity and with it the prospect for democratic renewal.[29]

The new social movements of the 1970s and 1980s shared a nearly obsessive desire to avoid this authoritarian logic, reflected in their familiar recycling of well-known 1960s New-Left themes: citizen participation, grassroots activism, consciousness transformation, cultural renewal, and of course personal politics. It was these very themes, however, that fed into a deeply visceral antipolitics, even as the new movements sometimes pushed up against the limits of the public sphere. The historic collapse of Communism in the late 1980s and early 1990s, which only further dramatizes the bankruptcy of the Soviet model and the Jacobinism that underpinned it, served to reinforce this mood of antipolitics. At the same time, the retreat from the possibilities of statecraft of any kind, essentially abandoning the creative, sometimes Promethean, discourse of the Greeks, Machiavelli, Rousseau, and Gramsci, would leave its mark of futility on the contemporary trajectory of popular movements, the Left, and indeed the whole scope of American political culture at the end of the century. The revolt against authoritarian models of statecraft, against the notion of politics as architectonics, has been understandable enough; predictably, progressive movements and parties have been unwilling to champion the Jacobin example under *any* ideological banner. At the same time, we have witnessed a growing retreat from politics in a more general sense—as a refusal to meet the challenges of governance, or to employ mechanisms of political power in behalf of particular goals and interests. Equality, justice, community, even democracy—these historic ideals ultimately depend on the strong leverage made possible by public governance, since only such governance can provide an effective counterweight to the narrow, parochial, self-interested designs of huge private interests. This logic applies even more forcefully in the case of ecological movements with goals that necessitate deep, permanent, structural changes in the political economy.

The depoliticization of social movements in the context of a growing popular retreat from the public sphere involves loss of collective agency that is debilitating for long-term transformation insofar as the whole terrain of governance, state power, and political initiative is inevitably ceded to the ruling elites. It follows that any historic recovery of politics would not so much *jettison* the statecraft tradition as help to *redefine* it to fit new conditions and imperatives: Jacobinism would give way to more democratized forms of governance rooted in those dimensions of politics mentioned above (a view of the common interest, revitalized citizenship, social agency linked to grassroots popular movements).

MODERNITY: A DUAL LEGACY

The concept of a "public sphere" incorporates those modes of discourse and action that have a bearing on politics as we have defined it, namely, the exercise of state power, governance, citizen participation, a sense of civic community, and so forth. Without an open and vigorous public sphere the realization of anything resembling authentic democracy (or "radical" democracy, in the contemporary parlance) is out of the question, as the Greeks knew full well; "politics" in this sense is therefore no stronger than the public sphere that nourishes it and gives it life. According to Jurgen Habermas in his familiar discussion of this topic, the public sphere historically evolved in the context of a distinctly expressed public *opinion,* which arose for the first time in the eighteenth century and achieved fuller expression with the mature development of liberal capitalism. In effect, the public sphere serves to "mediate" between society and the state where "the public organizes itself as the bearer of public opinion—that principle of public information which once had to be fought for against the arcane politics of monarchies and which since that time made possible the democratic control of state activities."[30] As Habermas observes, general and open debates about the exercise of institutional political power grew out of a specific phase of capitalist development. Thus: "Citizens behave as a public body when they confer in an unrestricted fashion—that is, with the guarantee and freedom of assembly and association and the freedom to express and publish their opinions—about matters of general interest. In a large public body, this kind of communication requires specific means for transmitting information and influencing those who receive it."[31]

Habermas follows a long line of theorists—Aristotle, Rousseau, Jefferson, J. S. Mill, and Dewey, among them—who affirmed the centrality of a dynamic public sphere for human development and social progress. A democratic realm characterized by the open exchange of ideas, a high threshold of political and intellectual tolerance, and a milieu of trust and reciprocity would furnish the basis upon which critical self-reflection, broad societal identities, and democratic self-directed activity could be realized; it would constitute, in Rousseauian terms, the essence of freedom in community. As the Greeks insisted, the common realm (polis) allows for the development of community as part of a sense of belonging to a larger public arena or body politic that stands mainly outside the local, parochial sphere of the household (oikos), family, and kinship networks. The classic ideal of a fully engaged public citizen stood in contrast to the more limited and provincial concerns of everyday life, for it was in the activity of such a citizen that universal values could best be realized. A dynamic public sphere presupposed a constant and relatively open flow of communications, allowing for far-reaching debate, dissent, and critical response to major issues of the day. Divergent social backgrounds, experiences, interests, values, and goals enter into the complex flow of public discourse and action, reshaping visions of the general interest in constantly unfolding dynamics of interaction, conflict, and change. The very idea of an *ascribed* political unity or consensus grounded in a specific universal ideology stands diametrically opposed to this understanding of the public sphere.

Throughout most human history societies were typically organized around kinship or local (e.g., tribal) relations, but during the past two centuries modernity has eroded that foundation of community. The culturally integrative role of the household has probably been lost forever, at least in the most advanced industrial societies.[32] Social hierarchy rooted in blood ties and territoriality has been replaced by an expanded public sphere, transformed civil societies, diversification of social structures, and great advances in social and geographical mobility. Large-scale institutions (corporations, the state, the military, universities) have come to dominate the social landscape, undermining the old parochial ties and identities that, however, may today seem appealing to people who have lost any real sense of group belonging or identification. In many ways the public sphere came to prevail over private life in an age of urbanization, a broadened role for science and technology, more universal aspirations, and growing citizen participation.[33] Modern history has witnessed a series of efforts designed to erect and consolidate a public sphere in which roles, loyalties, rights, and obligations might be firmly established, most notably in the early fusion of nationalism and liberal capitalism that found fertile terrain in countries like France, England, the United States, and Italy. Despite the stubborn persistence of racial and patriarchal forms of domination, along with the emergence of far-flung corporations and state bureaucracies, this renewed public sphere offered the glimpse of an epochal "great transformation" where market and democratic values might coexist. Proclamations, constitutions, legal charters, and political legislation all codified a wide range of basic human freedoms and rights, and on a much wider scale than ever before.

With advancing modernization, the public sphere in most Western countries came to be shaped by an emergent participatory culture both galvanized and restricted by the underlying precepts of the nation-state. A new era of mass mobilization gave shape to an enormous variety of democratic and quasi-democratic forms: parties, labor unions, interest groups, civic associations, political machines, social movements, ad hoc expressions of political initiative. The appearance of *homo politicus* on a large scale required far greater dissemination of, and access to, knowledge and information of various sorts. Thus, as pre-industrial society gradually gave way to modernity, politics was transformed in one country after another from the realm of elite control and manipulation into a more broadened and democratized public sphere, imperfect as it was. The rise of the nation-state in the aftermath of the first bourgeois revolutions generated universal norms of consent, citizenship, participation, rights, and national identity. The principles of freedom, community, and democracy, however partial and flawed in their definition and implementation, corresponded to a new era of mass involvement and opinion formation that inevitably conflicted with the hierarchical imperatives of modern capitalism and the authoritarian state. An energized citizenry, more informed and dedicated while struggling to transcend its own (liberal-capitalist) parochial immediacy, thrived on the novel discourse of empowerment made possible by the guiding ideals of Enlightenment rationality.

The main characteristics of any public sphere are crystallized through the evolution of a political culture over time; central beliefs, values, and symbols furnish critical subjective responses to objective circumstances, to events and developments that in some way demand popular as well as elite interventions. Political culture can be defined as a general outlook, among both masses and elites, regarding issues of power, governance, allocation of resources, identity, social change, and so forth. It fluctuates in response to elements of complexity, rapid change, and unpredictability in the modern world, making precise statements about political outcomes profoundly hazardous where they are not completely misleading. There is no way to establish a clear correspondence between political culture and *specific* modes of political action, even if one can always refer to contextual factors that contribute to specific outcomes. Dimensions of political culture span the range of attitudes toward trust and distrust in governmental authority, local or parochial versus national forms of identity, sense of fatalism or passivity versus a feeling of mastery over the course of events, optimism about the future versus fear of change, engagement in the public sphere versus privatized modes of retreat, and the pursuit of grassroots as opposed to state-centered forms of intervention. Political culture influences what people may expect from government, what issues are seen as most salient, and what modes or styles of participation may be viewed as legitimate in pursuit of ultimate objectives.

In most of the industrialized world the public sphere was somewhat broadened and democratized beginning in the late nineteenth century—a process that deepened after 1945 with the defeat of fascism and the decline of kindred authoritarian regimes. Universal suffrage became a reality that now sought to enact earlier proclamations and formal commitments, multiparty systems flourished, constitutional and legal rights became widely legitimated, labor and allied movements were able to build unprecedented strength, and diverse sources of knowledge and information became far more widely accessible. Citizenship took on new meaning, including greater popular participation and democratic input into governmental decision-making machinery. Expansion of the public sphere appeared to reach its zenith in the 1960s and 1970s, with the explosive (and generally democratizing) impact of civil rights struggles, New-Left radicalism, and new social movements that, all taken together, seemed to burst through ideological boundaries set by liberalism and Marxism alike. During at least the past two decades, however, important historical trends have been moving in just the opposite direction: we are seeing more pronounced disaffection from government, mass depoliticization, and shrinking of the public sphere—an epochal shift that cuts across national, social, and ideological divisions. Probably nowhere is this phenomenon more deeply established than in the United States, where elites continue to trumpet the virtues of democracy and citizenship but where all the signs point toward a collapse of such values.[34] This festering mood of antipolitics is fueled by economic globalization, which tends to subvert national and local political autonomy, along with the corporate and state colonization of social life. While elections and other types of popular involvement are increasingly reduced to the status of empty and passive spectacles, the real forms of governance become all the more oligarchic—controlled by massive private structures and their empires made up of lobbyists, PACs, media networks, financial services conglomerates, experts, and a multiplicity of intricate global trading arrangements. In such an institutional setting Republicans and Democrats, conservatives and liberals, look more alike with each passing year; presumed ideological differences blur, then largely disappear. The mass media itself has become little more than an extension of corporate agendas, with the much celebrated diversity of information sources barely masking a pervasive and conformist homogeneity. In both education and politics, as in the media, the myth of professionalized knowledge, expertise, and specialized discourses continues to hold sway, with powerfully disenfranchising consequences.

It is hardly surprising, therefore, to find a public sphere in which major issues wind up ignored or trivialized, their "solutions" often relegated to a mythical self-regulating "free market" or to technological panaceas. What generally passes for public debate takes place in the context of largely meaningless electoral campaigns defined by media sound-bites, advertising blitzes costing millions of dollars, personality assassinations, pedantic posturing over "family values," "deficit reduction," personal morality, and kindred issues having little to do with actual policy choices. One eminently predictable mass response to such trivialized discourse is to turn away from distinctly public concerns toward more privatized lifestyles and to indulge in greater cynicism, passivity, or a deep sense of pessimism concerning the political enterprise as such. The signs of retreat are indeed many, among them, the famous "taxpayers' rebellion," growth of paramilitary militias and an urban gang culture, the spread of domestic terrorism, the increased popularity of identity-based movements, widespread new-age and therapeutic fads, and an ethos of nihilism that has permeated the popular culture. And the universities have hardly been immune to such antipolitical trends, as reflected in the strong appeal of postmodernism and its numerous offshoots. Postmodern theory often explores themes of chaos, fragmentation, local knowledge, and, by extension, finds futility in political action tied to macro societal institutions and processes. During the 1990s postmodern intellectual culture moved well beyond the confines of higher education into the realms of mass media, popular culture, and even social-movement activity itself.

Such a redefinition of the public sphere is hardly unique to the American experience—it was, in fact, a defining feature of many preindustrial systems, where politics remained the province of elites, and it surely applies to other industrialized societies (e.g., Japan, Scandinavia) even if not to quite the same extent. At the same time, it is probably safe to conclude that a widespread manifestation of antipolitics in the United States makes abundant sense for a population fed up with false promises, politicians' lies, legislative ineptness, and the unending corruptions of power. But it is nonetheless a highly problematic, even frightening development for at least three reasons. First, we live in a society where all the trappings (and claims) of democratic participation have been well established for at least several decades, made credible by virtue of our Constitution, Bill of Rights, universal suffrage, party system with open elections, legislative bodies, judicial review, and civic associations. In whatever guise, "democracy" in the 1990s remains a vital legitimating ideology in the United States, and it continues to have genuine (if more truncated) political significance. Second, U.S. citizens today have greater access to sources of information and communication, by far, than can be said for any other citizenry in history. American society possesses a vast (and extraordinarily expensive) network of institutions and services in the form of an educational system, universities, libraries, bookstores, technology and media outlets, and cultural activities. An increasingly accessible computer technology enables not only elites but ordinary persons to process and (ideally) transmit enormous amounts of data—far more than any individual, group, or even institution could possibly find useful in a lifetime. Third, key social problems in the United States have (with only a few exceptions) persisted with each passing year; thus, civic violence, urban deterioration, substance abuse, erosion of public services, declines in job security, and environmental crisis remain among our most persistent social problems. Insofar as direct forms of public intervention are needed to confront these problems, the atrophy of politics gravely undermines the capacity of society to seriously *address*, much less solve, its most urgent challenges.

If depoliticization therefore cuts short prospects for social transformation, then the only hope lies in fundamental renewal of the public sphere. Any renovated politics of the future would require a break with hegemonic patterns that for so long have confined public discourse in narrow, system-reproducing boundaries. If we can still speak of the perpetuation of a bourgeois public sphere at the end of the twentieth century, this is because discourse and action remain colonized by powerful interests, not least of all by mammoth transnational corporations that have hundreds of billions of dollars at stake in future developmental outcomes. While power unquestionably resides in fewer and fewer hands and is now more concentrated than ever, it remains true that the vast majority of American citizens is still psychologically immersed in the dominant structures and values (even where there is deep skepticism or cynicism). An historic reopening of the public sphere, therefore, would necessitate more fluid, critical, and ultimately subversive modes of communication of the sort one might expect to find among a more enlightened, active (i.e., politicized) citizenry. Groups and constituencies on the periphery of the main centers of power would have enlarged space in which to articulate a counterhegemonic opposition, create new rules of discourse, press for popular initiatives, and lay the groundwork for self-governance. A dynamic clash of ideas and social forces is the sine qua non of a repoliticized citizenry, of a grassroots activism that works against the privatizing, localizing, fragmenting tendencies that presently engulf civil society.

As Nancy Fraser points out, the situation calls out for something akin to a "postbourgeois" model of the public sphere—beyond the concept put forth by Habermas and others—that constitutes an arena not only for discursive opinion but also for the formation of social identities and actual decision making. To speak of equal access to the public sphere, therefore, is to affirm the requisite of (increasing) social and economic parity among political actors, which of course is far from the case under a regime of corporate colonization. And to guarantee real discursive openness the main realms of social life (including, above all, economics) will have to be repoliticized in some fashion. In Fraser's words: "The rhetoric of economic privacy . . . seeks to exclude some issues and interests from public debate by economizing; the issues in question here are cast as impersonal market imperatives or as 'private' ownership prerogatives or as technical problems for managers and planners, all in contradistinction to public, political matters."[35]

A thoroughly democratized public sphere gives substance to one of the most basic of all human needs—entering into and being part of the *res publica*, which enables people to forge community and struggle for social change in ways that make the world a more livable place. In classical Aristotelian terms, a revived public sphere flows from recognition of what is an inescapable fact of life, namely, that human beings are all socially and politically interdependent, living as they do in a complex, rapidly changing, and in many ways fearsome world. Today the process of globalization—and with it the globalization of human problems—merely carries this time-honored imperative further. If a broadened public sphere signifies an historic shift toward both the culture and the institutional forms of self-governance, then it simultaneously requires an all-out assault on the bastions of economic and political power that have so devastatingly colonized civil society and taken decision making out of the hands of the general population. For such an explosive dialectic to become manifest, however, the system will have to undergo a profound (probably unprecedented) crisis of legitimation, made possible by a wide diffusion of critical ideas, values, and attitudes. This in turn will demand a fundamental rethinking of the political enterprise itself in a social universe that poses new challenges literally every day. Statism, authoritarian rule, bureaucracy, social hierarchy—all these debilitating legacies historically associated with "politics" would have to give way to revitalized notions of social governance grounded in popular struggles for universal goals (e.g., democracy, racial and gender equality, ecological sustainability) in the common realm. A democratized public sphere thus allows for (but hardly guarantees) a vital linkage between social movements and transformative politics, between civic discourse and an engaged citizenry, between emancipatory vision and emergent forms of self-governance.

LIBERALISM, MARXISM, AND BEYOND

The great historical legacies of the past few hundred years, which derived their powerful impact from Enlightenment ideals of social progress linked to modernization, affirmed in the most uncompromising terms the values of human freedom, popular sovereignty, and community that, sooner or later, would depend on an ever widening diffusion of such civic virtues as citizenship, democratic participation, consensual governance, and an open and dynamic public sphere. With advancing levels of industrialization politics did, of course, become more democratized than it had been during the reign of the more rigidly authoritarian *ancien regime*. At the same time, these legacies contained strong and recurrent elements of antipolitics, despite their enormous ideological differences, and these elements remain a durable part of the modern political heritage. Indeed, it is difficult to find any modern discourse that is completely impervious to the deep ethos of antipolitics that so often finds its expression in a generalized hostility to state power. Thus in the nineteenth century liberals, Marxists, and anarchists of all stripes hoped to reduce the scope of governmental power even as they upheld the Promethean visions of human progress summoned up by the French and American Revolutions. For partisans of each of these traditions the state was regarded as little more than a form of alienated social life, cut off from the rhythm and flow of real human existence; popular struggles, citizenship, the quest for communal solidarity were mainly relegated to the realm of civil society—a realm uncontaminated by the incursions of a coercive, homogenizing state system.

Politics was indeed one of the driving forces in classical liberalism, from the work of John Locke through Adam Smith, the American Federalists, and the English Utilitarians. A critical dimension of the liberal-capitalist outlook was the vision of a society whose members could enter into more or less free exchange with one another and who could thereby maximize their economic and political capabilities. Classical liberalism embraced the norms of consent, civic participation, self-directed activity, and the "rights of man" measured before a system of laws. Tyrannical, capricious rule was rejected as antithetical to social progress, which required the subversion of traditional institutions and roles associated with the church, the monarchy, and the landholding aristocracy. Simultaneously, however, liberal ideology gave full sway to capitalist market values, which encouraged the most competitive, predatory forms of human activity in a way that tended precisely to undermine those democratizing values. The Utilitarianism of James Mill and Jeremy Bentham, for example, upheld a view of human beings as simple maximizers of economic utility in a market model that allowed, in fact strongly encouraged, people to impose their will over and against that of others, sometimes by any means at their disposal. The liberal ideal was none other than *homo economicus*, or economic man, in search primarily of material gain or private property—distinctly different from what might be called "political man," as envisioned by such radical democrats as Paine and Jefferson and later by such Jacobins as Lenin and Gramsci. In the liberal scheme of things, freedom amounted to a form of escape from the outmoded, arbitrary rule of the *ancien regime* rather than collective participation for the purpose of achieving popular goals and, ultimately, a democratic citizenry.

What politics meant in this context, as Macpherson observes, was a kind of "protective democracy" in which elites would be relatively unencumbered to go about their business, with few restrictions placed on their economic behavior and without the meddlesome intrusions of propertyless, unwashed mobs.[36] The very concept of "laissez-faire" suggested a definitely impoverished view of the public realm, one where the state would be limited to essentially custodial or "night-watchman" functions. This variant of antipolitics was given impetus by the widespread acceptance of a form of social Darwinism, that is, championing fierce individualism while rejecting public or collective priorities. Such a worldview conveniently devalued at least three components of any developed political vision: community, emphasis on some ideal of the public good, and social governance. In Burkean fashion, it simply assumed that society could always be held together by means of organic formations such as kinship and family; large-scale social and political structures were generally met with suspicion and thus received little attention as *positive* vehicles of social progress.

In spite of its well-known emphasis on consent, rights, and participation, therefore, classical liberalism ended up devaluing politics while simultaneously affirming the primacy of civil society along with the centrality of economic interests in human motivation. As a result, that component of politics that incorporates what is distinctively common and public is inevitably eviscerated in favor of an ethos stressing individual strivings over the general interest, material aims over ethical vision. There is little theoretical substance in the liberal tradition on which to build any ideal of community or any criteria for sustaining a democratized public sphere. All modes of behavior wind up as largely matters of calculation linked to individual rational choice or, in modern parlance, cost-benefit analysis rooted in material concerns.[37]

Moving from entirely different premises, classical Marxism too, whatever its undeniably powerful revolutionary ambitions, erected and carried forward a discourse of antipolitics that extended well into the twentieth century. While it is true enough that neither Marx nor Engels were able to arrive at a full theoretical elaboration of the role of the state or politics in history, the crucial problem was not so much the unfinished nature of their theory but rather the consistently epiphenomenal status they assigned to politics in the historical process. From the very outset, Marxism typically approached politics as derivative of presumably underlying material and class forces, as a function of changes in the mode of production; in class society politics could have no autonomous power or logic. For

Marx and Engels, as for most later Marxists, capitalism was doomed on the basis of its own inherent developmental logic, which propelled it toward crisis and breakdown. Their antipolitics accordingly assumed three propositions: that the state was an expression of dominant class interests; that fundamental economic shifts in civil society, not political intervention, were decisive in the transition to socialism; and that the state would wither away in the postrevolutionary order since it would no longer be needed as a tool of class domination.

The overwhelming optimism that permeated classical Marxism depended on an unwavering sense of certitude about the future—a quasi-scientific certitude grounded in the power of objective historical forces and, in those forces, the unfolding dynamic of class struggle. In fact, the state apparatus, coercive as it might be, was a phenomenon to be confronted (and overthrown) only at the end of a protracted historical process, when material conditions and class relations in civil society had already been transformed enough to pave the way toward socialism; the actual contest for state power would come largely as an afterthought, when the main class battles had been fought and won. Distinctly political concerns—forms and practices of governance, strategies of change, conceptions of democratic participation—were either ignored or relegated into the distant future on the assumption that they would be "resolved" in the context of class struggle. In fact, the Marxian scenario of crisis and breakdown of the capitalist system amounted to a fatalistic, perhaps even metaphysical, view of history that pushed the theory toward a naive, depoliticized faith in the laws of historical development. From this standpoint, politics could easily be understood as operating strictly in the immanent logic of capitalist production itself, with change emerging out of dialectical necessity rather than through conscious political intervention that, in turn, required creative human will. Thus, despite its inspiring radical visions, classical Marxism—much like the liberalism it so harshly denounced—was always far more an *economic* than a political discourse.

Anarchism was yet another matter. As a belief system that often affirmed the notion of a "perpetual state of revolt," it carried the ethos of antipolitics even further than liberalism or Marxism. If liberalism sought to clear the social terrain in order to create space for the freest possible ascendancy of capitalism, and Marxism looked to the primacy of class forces beneath the whole superstructure of governmental institutions and laws, anarchism generally adhered to a more uncompromising antiauthoritarian stance in which the state was always and everywhere regarded as the deadly enemy of freedom and community. For classical anarchists like Proudhon, Bakunin, Kropotkin, and Malatesta, this state of affairs held sway whatever the formal institutional or ideological character of a particular state system. In contrast to both liberalism and Marxism, however, anarchism (especially in the more communal ideas of Kropotkin) did at least generally hold out prospects for a kind of *alternative politics* embedded in small-scale communities, local assemblies, and perpetual forms of direct action.

This nineteenth-century retreat from politics, which in different ways has shaped so much of social theory and institutional practice since the time of the American Revolution, has, ironically, contributed to the very growth of centralized, authoritarian structures that were so feared and derided. The narrowing (and in some cases collapse) of the public sphere, largely vacated by movements of revolt and change, served to create an immense void into which the powerful interests could move and solidify their hegemony with minimum interference. Thus, even in the relatively democratized European context, the state, big business, and the military were able to establish their domination over civil society—often with minimal resistance. Antipolitics generated its own antithesis in the embodiment of a strong authoritarian state. Indeed, even fascist movements and regimes were often able to win popular support by masquerading as populist or quasi-anarchist forces. Referring to this antipolitical current in modern social and political theory, Wolin writes: "To reject the state meant denying the central referent of the political, abandoning a whole range of notions and practices to which they pointed—citizenship, obligation, general authority—without pausing to consider that the strategy of withdrawal might further advance state power."[38] Hence, the deep strains of antipolitics in modern thought were often compatible with the re-emergence of politics in an even more coercive and authoritarian guise. At the same time, while the political realm was affirmed more energetically than ever at the onset of the twentieth century—witness the Leninist turn in Marxism, the emergence of an influential group of "elite" theorists (Michels, Mosca, Pareto), and the rise of fascism along with kindred right-wing authoritarian parties or regimes—certain vital elements of the political experience such as rights, citizenship, and consent were either devalued or crushed. The result was an impoverishment of the public sphere and political discourse that lingers on in many parts of the world even today.

The early twentieth-century decline of the public sphere was not immediately accompanied by the disappearance of popular movements or vigorous political debate, but these consequences would be felt, with a vengeance, in the later emergence of fascism and Stalinism. Much of this was anticipated in the work of Weber and the elite theorists and then further analyzed by a new generation of neo-Marxists and Critical Theorists tied to the Frankfurt School. They all shared a deep pessimism and cynicism that grew out of their penetrating critique of modernity, especially the tendencies toward bureaucratization and elite control that seemed to be the hallmark of the new period. From this standpoint, the well-known democratic pretensions of the liberal-capitalist order were met with skepticism; such pretensions were easily overtaken by rationalizing trends toward ever greater concentration of economic and political power, which reduced most elections and legislative activity to a sham. Bureaucracy, the intensifying social and intellectual division of labor, the growth of scientific and professional expertise, the innate drive toward oligarchical control on the part of elites—all this functioned to separate controlling elements of the power structure from the general population. It even gave rise, as Michels argued, to an "iron law of oligarchy" in the most progressive and ostensibly democratic organizations such as trade unions and left-wing political parties.[39] With the consolidation of hierarchical authority relations in all realms of society, the very idea of popular decision making or individual participation turned out to be little more than a sad hoax.

These insights pointed to a crucial historical trend, namely, that the new source of order and stability in a rapidly developing capitalist system was not so much religion or nationalism (though both continued to play a role) but rather the emergent rationalized economic and administrative structures made possible by modernization. Guided by scientific and technological principles, new modes of control and planning were designed to place limits on the harshly competitive, sometimes chaotic and centrifugal, tendencies of advanced capitalism. As Weber observed, bureaucratic regulation was needed in a complex industrial society insofar as it allowed for a more streamlined network of control and efficiency. In a world inclined toward social turbulence, the logic of economic rationality and political control might break down without forms of administrative regulation and coordination.[40] For capitalism to stabilize itself under conditions of fierce market competition and severe business cycles, mechanisms would be required to tame the always explosive forces at work in civil society (and in nature itself). The result was a highly rationalized framework of domination that would militate against the spread of critical thinking, oppositional movements, and transformative politics. Mussolini's idea of the "corporate state," introduced in Italy during the 1920s, already carried this tendency to quasi-totalitarian conclusions even as he cloaked it in populist verbiage. The myriad forms of localism, spontaneity, and romanticism characteristic of preindustrial society would now be contained and superseded by the new authoritarian regime, which, despite its rhetoric, viewed civic participation with great fear and suspicion. For Weber, as for Michels, Mosca, Pareto, and of course Lenin, politics in modern society had become a supremely important realm of activity, a driving force of history. But it was conceived largely in terms of *elite* action, as competing strategies for power, control, and domination, even in cases where constitutions might have furnished the basis of legality and broad citizenship.

Power might serve to corrupt or to ennoble, but there was no getting around the fact that power in modern society was increasingly concentrated, rationalized, and destructive of civic political culture. It was precisely the reverse side of the coin of the antipolitics celebrated by classical liberalism and its various offshoots.

If large-scale organization and elite initiatives became the essence of modern rationality for Weberian discourse, Lenin's vanguardist definition of Marxism carried forward many of the same premises in a party-centered communist model of politics initially designed for a relatively underdeveloped Russian setting. In a sense Lenin turned Marx's emphasis on class struggle and the transformation of civil society on its head: the revolutionary party of professional cadres, geared to the insurrectionary overthrow of the old order, would emerge as the main protagonist of history. For Lenin and the Bolsheviks politics amounted to the art of large-scale societal transformation, demanding all the elements of organizational cohesion, discipline, total commitment, and of course flexible leadership. As far as the workers and allied groupings were concerned, theirs was a world of ideological subordination to the ruling class; left to their own unmediated strivings, they could hope to achieve little more than a parochial, economistic, reformist consciousness, given the limits of their social existence. A vanguard party was needed to furnish true (revolutionary) class consciousness of the sort that could bring workers out of their social immediacy and ideologically empower them to mount assaults on the status quo.[41] Thus, Lenin's Jacobinism provided strategic focus, a combat vehicle, prospects for stable governance, leverage for economic development, and a vision of common objectives that would transcend local or provincial interests.

Yet, Lenin's famous primacy of politics, while assigning the party-state (or "dictatorship of the proletariat") a decisive historical role, ironically gave rise to its own brand of antipolitics by virtue of its effort to obliterate conflict in the public sphere and its devaluing of popular participation. Thus can be explained the ban on open dissent in the party, the crackdown on political opposition and "factions," the subordination of soviets and local committees to party controls, and the general rise of bureaucratic centralism in the Soviet Union after 1920. Statism ultimately annihilated politics as a *mass* phenomenon, because collective subjectivity had no legitimacy outside the realm of the party-state. Indeed, Lenin never offered a theory that could begin to accommodate such a possibility. Analyzing the thematic motif of Lenin's key text *State and Revolution*, A. J. Polan concludes that the model "demands a situation devoid of all political conflicts, of all economic problems, of all social contradictions, of all inadequate, selfish, or simply human emotions and motivations . . . It demands, in short, for Lenin's political structures to work that there be an absence of politics."[42] (This abolition of politics was actually less extreme in the case of fascism, at least in its inception. For example, Mussolini's concept of the corporate state, which sought to institutionalize social conflict in a clearly established hierarchical framework, set definite limits to the public sphere and relegated politics to bargaining arrangements among elites but did not jettison the idea of competing groups or interests altogether.)

The pervasive influence of Weber and the elite theorists on intellectual discourse after the turn of the century, along with the subsequent rapid growth of bureaucratic centralism in the Soviet Union and the diffusion of fascist ideas and movements throughout Europe, seemed to illuminate deep authoritarian but nonetheless antipolitical tendencies at work in modern society. If social and political forms of power became increasingly concentrated, the image of a strong, all-consuming politics in fact concealed the opposite reality, namely, a public sphere more and more bereft of meaningful debate and popular input. The early Frankfurt School, notably in the seminal work of Max Horkheimer and Theodor Adorno, carried an understanding of these bureaucratizing yet depoliticizing tendencies even further, laying the groundwork for a Critical Theory tradition that culminated in Herbert Marcuse's landmark *One-Dimensional Man* and the later work of Jürgen Habermas.[43] In *Dialectic of Enlightenment*, Horkheimer and Adorno explored the ways in which the Enlightenment legacy, rooted in the norms of scientific and technological rationality, leads inexorably to modern forms of domination that begin to engulf the most remote reaches of everyday life. Departing from the elite theorists, the Frankfurt School devoted the bulk of its attention to largely *ideological* forms of authority that were unique to modern capitalist society. The principles of order, control, manipulation, the domination of nature, the fetishism of technique, the obsession with instrumental rationality—all these were a product of industrialism and gave rise to a "totally administered society" beneath the facade of parliamentary democracy.[44] In this rationalizing process the vast majority of human beings became material resources, passive objects, for ruling elites to manipulate for purposes of their own privilege and power. Here Critical Theory incorporated significant elements of Weberian theory but gave it a more critical, dialectical twist made possible by the adoption of other currents such as *Lebensphilosophie* and neo-Marxism.

In the view of Horkheimer and Adorno, the rationalization of society overcomes the massive social contradictions and dysfunctions inherent in liberal capitalism. Economic development surely enough gives rise to material growth, prosperity, formal democracy, and some forms of social progress, but there is a dark side that paves the way toward new modes of elite control and domination, including terror. The Enlightenment bequeathed a legacy favoring the diffusion of knowledge and more open forms of communication, but it simultaneously produced ideologically closed, instrumental systems of thought that in fact narrowed the range of critical discourse and, ultimately, oppositional politics; in destroying the vestiges of the past, modernity upheld the ideal of a mechanistic, administratively integrated social order. As modernity began to permeate every facet of human life, people were increasingly assimilated into the very logic of administrative rationality with its universalistic rules, procedures, and laws. At the same time, people were manipulated and pacified by such diversions as consumerism, the mass media, the emergent culture industry, and a variety of spectacles (including electoral politics). The result was more or less the epochal collapse of politics as a dynamic, participatory, transformatve enterprise. As Adorno wrote regarding the impact of the culture industry: "It impedes the development of autonomous, independent individuals who judge and decide consciously for themselves."[45] Higher levels of industrialization and commodity production would inevitably exacerbate this entire developmental process.

As Marcuse observed, the decline of freedom and opposition was not a matter simply of moral or intellectual corruption, but was rather an objective societal process insofar as the production and distribution of an increasing quantity of goods and services made popular compliance an essentially rational technological attitude. In the end the Frankfurt School came to accept the most cynical and pessimistic view of politics even as it held to the dialectical philosophy that it embraced at the very outset. The fact is that modernity turned out to be a treacherous phenomenon, subverting the claims and pretensions of both liberalism (e.g., parliamentary democracy) and Marxism (class struggle leading to revolution) as elements of a broadened, democratized public sphere. It appeared that the dark side of modernization had triumphed.

CHAPTER 5

ANTIPOLITICS
LEFT AND RIGHT

The ever intensifying globalization of corporate capitalism has brought, on the one hand, greater economic, technological, and cultural integration while, on the other hand, giving rise to sharpened social polarization, urban decay, ecological crisis, and the proliferation of local and regional wars. This epochal process unfolds at a time when the cold war has become a distant memory, when the majority of communist regimes have imploded, when the whole terrain of international politics has been thoroughly reconfigured. It has meant, among other things, freer rein for multinational corporations and greater latitude for market forces to gain ascendancy in a new global order. The major ideologies of the recent past (liberalism, nationalism, communism, social democracy) have verged on obsolescence in the face of dramatically altered historical conditions, marked by growing political turbulence and uncertainty. As I have argued earlier in this volume, the very environment in which politics gets defined and played out in the 1990s has been fundamentally reconfigured.

It might be suggested that, in the contemporary setting, the role of the state among even the most powerful nations has become more intimately tied to the vagaries of the world economy; the once taken-for-granted autonomy of governments has been severely constricted, whether in North America, Europe, Japan, or the third world. The ideological discourses of the world's governing elites have been rendered far less meaningful, less relevant to policy formation—witness the harsh neoliberal economic policies adopted by nominally socialist French and Spanish governments in the 1980s or the incessant drift toward privatization and deregulation in the few remaining communist systems (such as in China). One consequence of these trends is that political opposition to capitalist hegemony has been profoundly weakened or at least thrown into disarray, in part owing to the solidification of conservative ideas over the past 20 years and in part resulting from the *internal* erosion of antisystem movements around the world. The eclipse of Marxism, at least in its most politically organized forms, is reflected in the increasing deradicalization of labor as a social force in virtually all industrialized societies. Opposition has been further undermined by the deep colonization of civil society by behemoth economic and political institutions made all the more powerful and mobile by globalization.

This transformed international situation, however, is hardly a picture of simple "order" and equilibrium either globally or domestically: on the contrary, it is rife with explosive contradictions and tensions. The degree to which these contradictions and tensions have been, or are likely to be, translated into strong *political* opposition is precisely the crucial question of the coming period. In the United States, as I have argued earlier, the dominant trend is toward antipolitics, which effectively solidifies elite rule. At the same time, some forms of antigovernment mobilization, as well as the widely expressed visceral revolt against politics in general, could have profoundly destabilizing implications for the status quo. Throughout the 1990s popular support for antigovernment mobilization has been reinforced by the manipulation, corruption, interest peddling, and electoral charades that people in liberal-capitalist societies have come to associate with ordinary politics. The state system is widely perceived, accurately enough, as increasingly removed from the domain of citizen influence, despite the well-known populist rhetoric of government leaders and right-wing politicians and despite all the democratic myths upheld daily by the mass media.

Economic globalization is to some extent clearly *designed* by the engineers of multinational capitalism to neutralize political intervention as an agency of counterhegemonic insurgency. As Benjamin Barber writes, "The economic totalism of unleashed market economics seems now to be trying (at costs yet to be fully reckoned) to subordinate politics, society, and culture to the demands of an overarching market."[1] There can be little doubt that commodity production and exchange in an internationalized economy imposes a severely limited range of choices—personal, social, national—that can only work against the emergence of oppositional agencies in the public sphere, typically pushing popular dissent and revolt in manifestly nonpolitical directions.

THE 1960s: POLITICS AFFIRMED AND SUBLIMATED

American history is replete with events suggesting the theme of antipolitics, beginning with the founding principles of a republic established on strict constitutional limits to suffrage, citizenship, and democratic participation—principles based on the twin fears of both tyrannical government and too much popular mobilization (reflecting much of the classical liberal theorizing of the period). The guiding motif of classical liberalism was anything but democratic. A strong aversion to politics was indeed central to the entire national experience, which, filtered through an ascendant liberal-capitalist ethos, consistently upheld the primacy of civil society over the state. Powerful strains of nineteenth century antipolitical liberalism worked their influence in many areas, among them, laissez-faire market ideology, the celebration of local civic virtues, a social Darwinian hostility to social definitions of welfare, and the frontier ethic of rugged individualism. Later forms of liberal antistatism, reformulated in more broadly positive tones, were taken up by dynamic Populist and Progressive movements around the turn of the twentieth century. A hegemonic liberalism, embracing deep faith in the vitality of a self-regulating market economy, persisted throughout the twentieth century, setting the United States apart from other industrialized countries in certain respects.

The much-discussed phenomenon of 1960s radicalism can be viewed as still another expression of this uniquely American strain of antipolitics.[2] Of course, the antipolitical tendency was present in only one aspect of the 1960s—the counterculture, which consistently affirmed personal and cultural over political modes of identity and often was opposed to those more highly politicized struggles of the New Left. In fact, dominant currents in the New Left, going back to the manifesto-like Port Huron Statement of 1962 by Tom Hayden and other Students for a Democratic Society (SDS) radicals, mark a significant breakthrough in long-standing attempts to *revitalize* American politics, to give substance to the most progressive traditions, to broaden and democratize the public sphere. Many partisans of the New Left saw this process as recovering the best elements of liberalism, consonant with the time-honored struggles for equality and democracy; others believed liberalism would have to be transcended by an ideological commitment (inspired perhaps by anarchism or democratic socialism) fully in alignment with a radical politics. In either case, the ideal was that of a rejuvenated citizenship grounded in distinctly American experiences, discourses, and traditions. The New Left hoped for, and in some measure achieved, a rekindling of politics articulated through a culture of activism and protest, secured by means of the fullest possible citizen engagement in the public arena—from the civil rights movement to antiwar mobilizations to campus-based struggles for educational reform, all eventually part of what Marcuse called the "Great Refusal."[3] As is well known, the New Left was infused with deep antiauthoritarian sensibilities framed by a virulent opposition to bureaucracy, social conformism, and centralized government, but such opposition followed the logic not so much of antipolitics purely and simply as it did the ideal of a more democratized politics grounded in new forms of grassroots collective action.

In its effort to subvert the whole spectrum of rules and regulations underpinning a repressive social order, the New Left contributed to a broadening of public discourse, in the process challenging a number of sacred conventions about work, authority, the family, sexuality, U.S. foreign policy—indeed, the very manner of conducting politics itself. The idea of a Great Refusal implied radical new perspectives on race and gender relations, culture, and education along with a move to create new rules of participation and accountability, both in and outside the political system. Taken-for-granted assumptions were questioned and, more often than not, were rejected or countered on the political terrain. Electoral politics itself was widely viewed as bankrupt; the puritan work ethic was dismissed as self-abnegating and repressive; the U.S. role in international affairs was viewed as Machiavellian and destructive; the dominant culture was contemptuously rejected as little more than an expression of commercialized emptiness; and so forth. Through its sweeping indictment of the "system," the "power structure," and the "war machine," 1960s radicalism adopted a rather consistent political modus operandi linked to a series of concrete demands—desegregation and racial justice, an end to the war in Vietnam, a severing of university ties with the military, far-reaching educational reforms, and a full-scale democratization of the political system, among others. To these ends the New Left carried out literally thousands of marches, demonstrations, and sit-ins, initiated spontaneous forms of direct action, sponsored public debates and teach-ins, built organizations and coalitions, produced books and pamphlets, and set up community institutions such as bookstores, cooperatives, and free clinics. It created a social milieu in which hundreds of alternative, or "underground," newspapers and periodicals thrived. Despite an uneasiness over electoral campaigns, it supported candidates for office and otherwise sought to influence the outcome of political contests or, where it seemed appropriate, the content of governmental policies. Following the injunctions of the Port Huron Statement, it produced a whole generation of "community organizers" in the tradition of Saul Alinsky's famous model of grassroots politics. If the New Left rejected the banalities of politics-as-usual, it never considered abandoning politics altogether but rather set out to construct an *alternative* politics—one that would be far more participatory, lively, and relevant to the task of solving urgent social problems.

To call attention to this manifestly *political* dimension of 1960s radicalism is not to ignore the spontaneous impulses, fragmented groups, and internal divisions that served to block development of a coherent organized politics at the time. To be sure, New-Left movements were locally dispersed and often drawn toward bizarre expressions of spontaneity, adventurism, and purely symbolic or theatrical gestures and actions. Diffuseness and fragmentation, along with the familiar American revulsion against concentrated governmental power, stood in the way of a coherent political agenda that could unify the myriad groups amid occasional skirmishes with the establishment and among themselves.[4] Then, too, the very scope of emancipatory vision tended to outrun the political capacity of human agents to achieve such a vision. Of course, the very turbulence of the period helped to nourish many hopes, fantasies, and dreams that, for the most part, were never tied to concrete possibilities. As Theodore Roszak has observed: "Out of that [New Left] dissent grew the most ambitious agenda for the reappraisal of cultural values any society has ever produced."[5] At issue here was not whether the New Left was able to achieve political definition—it clearly did—but whether its immensely utopian goals could be assimilated, concretized, and even partially realized in such a brief time span.

The bulk of commentary on 1960s radicalism obscures its enduring political impact—first, by insisting on a disjuncture, or sudden break, between the New Left and what came later in the 1970s and after, and second, by failing to distinguish between the New Left and countercultural tendencies of the period. As I have argued elsewhere, neither the collapse of SDS nor any other signal event spelled the "end" of oppositional movements associated with the period; in fact, such movements simply went off in new (and sometimes more explosive) directions, giving rise to more coherent organizational forms.[6] In fact, one can locate a continuous line of development from the New Left to later new social movements, which carried forward many central themes of 1960s radicalism—collective empowerment, the struggle for self-actualization, direct action, the critique of technocratic values—in a more strategic paradigm. From this standpoint one can speak unequivocally of a New Left's political legacy.

The countercultural ethos, on the other hand, was essentially anarchistic in the most antiauthoritarian, spontaneous, and unplanned embodiment of that tradition. Though impatient with "theories" and conceptual schemata, visionary figures in the counterculture looked toward psychological and social transformation tied to epochal shifts of consciousness and lifestyles going much deeper that mere institutional struggles or contests for power.[7] Genuine, durable change would have to be extrapolitical, moving through the subterranean depths beneath the corrupt (and ultimately meaningless) temples of institutional power. It would be unleashed through the medium of an enlightened human spirit capable of fighting social oppression, inspired by the "cunning of art" (to use Charles Reich's apt phrase); in Reich's words, "To describe a new way of life is to describe fully the society that is coming. For the locus of that society is not politics or economics but in how and for what ends we live."[8] This proposition seemed to apply whether one was talking about theatrical modes of protest (as with the Yippies), communal living and its "back-to-the-country" ethos, the psychedelic consciousness of an alternative drug culture, the hedonistic self-actualization of the rock and sexual revolutions, or what later came to be known as "postmaterialist" ideology in general. Articulated in its most blatant utopian form, the counterculture was embraced by many as the harbinger of a new world that many believed would unfold rapidly and more or less peacefully, much like the "new paradigm" thinking of later new-age theorists like Fritjof Capra.[9] In any event, world-historical changes were expected largely without the intervention of such mundane forces as movements, parties, and states, and presumably without the need for struggles over economic interests and political power. (In fact, such activity was roundly dismissed as part of the anachronistic "old" paradigm.) In the counterculture scheme of things changes move quite simply, if also mysteriously, through the mechanism of an ever expanding consciousness powerful enough to prevail over even the most intractible material processes and conditions.

Drawing on such wide-ranging influences as William Blake, Alan Watts, Aldous Huxley, Eastern mysticism, Allen Ginsberg, Gary Snyder, Timothy Leary, Ken Kesey, and R. D. Laing, the counterculture privileged the discourse of "experience" over reason, subjectivity over objective circumstances, and was motivated by a fierce and uncompromising hostility to the whole Enlightenment tradition. In this panoply of ideas and goals—the counterculture always lent more respect to intellect than its image conveyed—there was a celebration of mystical doctrines and existential philosophies, an eclectic outlook connected to the most unbridled individualism, a rejection of conformist rules and inhibitions, a search for unbounded fantasies and utopias, and upheld a lifestyle radicalism that often knew no limits. It was all energized by an odd mix of impulsive responses and glorification of direct action that would never be compatible with sustained political mobilization; it was, in fact, a substitute for such mobilization. Countercultural motifs worked powerfully, and for the most part self-consciously, against such normal requirements of political action as organization, discipline, planning, strategy, and immersion in the public sphere. On the facile assumption that more developed forms of consciousness and emancipatory lifestyles would inexorably triumph over a fading, corrupt social order, it was easy to ignore or downplay the role of large corporations, the state, and the military in sustaining a power structure designed precisely to neutralize fundamental social change. The counterculture always preferred gestures, stylistic flourishes, and theatrical displays over political realism, or realpolitik, which was dismissed as the relic of a decaying society. This misjudgment was hardly just a matter of tactical methods, since it was precisely such lack of *political* conscious-ness that turned out to be fatal to whatever oppositional agendas the counterculture hoped to advance.

The counterculture emerged not only as a distinctive American phe-nomenon but also as yet another expression of a feeble leftist tradition. Perhaps above all it helped to nurture an ideological milieu in which ther-apeutic and new-age movements of the 1970s and beyond could flourish. The motifs of consciousness transformation, the pleasure principle, psy-chic renewal, and individual self-realization took shape, expressed in such forms as encounter groups, health fads, and spiritual awakenings that Christopher Lasch, Allan Bloom, Thomas Frank, and others conceptual-ized as a turn toward narcissism or hedonistic individualism, a "revolu-tionary" change made possible by a series of reflective encounters with the self. Despite some weak disclaimers that a retreat from public life was not intended, this fixation on self was inevitably accompanied by a retreat from civic life and a devaluation of citizenship; too much preoccupation with societal or institutional concerns would distract from the more press-ing existential realm, or so the refrain went. Politics was little more than a superficial imposition, an enterprise that could not generate a sense of ei-ther obligation or purpose. Hence, although the counterculture gave pri-macy to the immediacy of passions, desires, and needs, this resulted in re-jection of the need to have a view of history, an orientation to the past or the future, a political compass. In Lasch's words, "Having displaced reli-gion as the organizing framework of American culture, the therapeutic outlook threatened to displace politics as well."[10]

The post-1960s shift to therapeutic concerns in American culture is covered later in this book, but it is in part driven by the popular will to overcome alienation by nonpolitical means, which may itself be condi-tioned by deeply ingrained feelings of cynicism, despair, and powerless-ness, especially regarding the role of government and political action. Thus, it is an alienated solution to the problem of alienation. Ironically, countercultural antipolitics was in part an extension of the minimalist side of American liberalism that, as we have seen, encourages withdrawal from the civic domain. The legacy of cold war anticommunism cannot have failed to reinforce such national antipathy toward active government and mass mobilization, themes that were commonly equated with "totalitarian-ism" and Soviet expansionism. Then, too, the debacles of Vietnam, Water-gate, the Iran–Contra scandal, and other events intensified the mood of antipolitics across the whole social and ideological spectrum. Feelings of insecurity and pessimism about the future would scarcely be conducive to the notion of employing the state as an agency for positive social out-comes. When plagued by anxiety and fearful of chaos, people may choose to avoid the public arena, especially when the mood of antipolitics is already present. The result was a strong convergence of two disparate lega-cies—minimalist liberalism and 1960s-inspired counterculture—which fed into the cycle of depoliticization.

Added to these two ideological influences was yet another element, the all-powerful commodity. In breaking through the stifling boundaries of a conformist mass society, the counterculture rediscovered a familiar American concern with self and subjectivity that was eventually commer-cialized and turned, to some extent, into the very negation of espoused 1960s values. Lacking political articulation, the counterculture easily de-generated into manifestations of individualistic self-absorption that were all too easily marketable in a corporate system eager to integrate every-thing before it, whether in the venerated rock culture, open sexuality, therapy fads, psychedelic art, or clothing styles. By the early 1970s what passed for youth culture has already been transformed into a hip consum-erism advertised and marketed in the mainstream as a sign of authenticity and difference, even rebellion. Thus, the youth revolt that was so central to the counterculture wound up being appropriated by the corporate sec-tors even as it often proclaimed its continued independence and radical-ism. Dissent, too, was co-opted by a highly resilient capitalist system, a pro-cess made all the easier by virtue of a "movement" that sought to escape politics. However progressive many of its impulses may have been, the counterculture rather quickly turned on itself, giving rise to a libertarian-ism that nourished a type of antistatism that became a magnet for a vari-ety of neoconservatives, free marketers, right-wing militias, and religious fundamentalists whose main agenda was to consolidate the power of American capitalism.

THE REBELLION AGAINST "BIG GOVERNMENT"

If the post-1970s trend toward antistatism was the product of converging historical factors along with a revisiting of earlier legacies, it was further pushed along and given fuller definition by popular movements that cre-atively seized upon the ethos of the period. One important catalyst was the renewed assault on the Keynesian welfare state that picked up steam with what is known as the taxpayers' revolt of the late 1970s and gained added momentum during the Reagan–Bush years, culminating in the Re-publicans' ambitious (but short-lived) "Contract with America" in 1994. Partly a backlash against the progressive inroads of the 1960s and 1970s, this revitalized form of antistatism echoed themes that have deep roots in American history, such as personal over collective modes of consump-tion, a preoccupation with the marketplace, populist distrust of elites and bureaucracy, and frontier-style individualism. The familiar revolt against

"big government" was often couched in libertarian discourse where freedom was defined simply as individual autonomy outside of—and in some
ways *against*—the public sphere. It typically upheld the primacy of "civil
society" grounded in the laissez-faire principles of the free market, minimal government, and local self-reliance, involving the full-scale reversal
of commitments to an expanded public sector that had been in place
since the New Deal.

One early launching pad of this revolt was the famous Proposition 13
campaign that began to sweep California in 1978. A consumer-based rebellion that was populist in ideology, the campaign appealed mainly to
middle-class homeowners and small-business interests angered not only by
high taxes (and declining real income) but by the bureaucratic aloofness
and indifference evident at all levels of government. The main targets,
however, were local jurisdictions that derived the bulk of their revenues
from property taxes. At the time, prices and tax valuations were skyrocket-
ing, and the anti-big government movement gathered strength from a variety of grassroots conservative groups opposed to other state policies
such as school bussing. The passage of Proposition 13 was a historic victory, but this achievement took several years of sustained local organizing
inspired by movement leaders Howard Jarvis and Robert Gann.[11] Millions
of Californians responded to the message of lower taxes and smaller government;, yet the militant antistatism that infused the campaign never
generated much in the way of popular hostility to (or avoidance of) the
public sphere. To the contrary, the taxpayer revolt depended for its success on a full panoply of political initiatives, ranging from educational forums to referenda to ordinary electoral campaigns. Its antipolitics was
thus linked to the specific ends of movement activity rather than the prevailing modus operandi that involved retreat from the political terrain.

A crucial ideological appeal of Proposition 13 was its manifest glorification of the home—as both a safe haven from a turbulent world and as cul-
mination of the American dream. The household readily took on greater
private meaning in a society where the very sense of "public" had been corrupted, where "politics" had become associated with scandals and false
promises (i.e., as in American elections) or bureaucratic nightmares (i.e., as
in Soviet-style communism). In this context the home, especially the suburban home, emerged as the symbolic realm of local neighborhood and community life pitted against a faceless, cold, oppressive state. In the words of
Jarvis: "I have always believed that private ownership of property and the
idea that a man's home was his castle made the U.S. the greatest and freest
country the world has ever known."[12] Thus, the struggle over taxation
struck directly at the heart of the white, middle-class, suburban lifestyle,
tapping the fear that one's home and one's entire style of consumption
might be subverted by a parasitical external force. At the same time, Jarvis

and the antitax crusaders added still another element: a strongly belliger-
ent posture toward (liberal) "elites," who were attacked for being completely out of touch with the lives of ordinary people. The charismatic nature of Jarvis's leadership stemmed largely from his hell-bent,
uncompromising bellicosity, his no-holds-barred approach to fighting
vested interests. A majority of consumers and small business owners could
respond emotionally to his proconsumer-flavored populist rhetoric.

Despite its professed hatred of politicians and opposition to governmental controls, the Proposition 13 campaign benefited from highly effective organization, financing, and leadership; it pursued a well-conceived
alliance strategy that sought to link tax concerns to other pressing issues
(including welfare and education). Its vision was far-reaching and seductive, its facility with political tactics shrewd and decisive, its capacity to attract media attention undeniably powerful. Once the grassroots victory in
California was achieved, the clear message burst across the country, taking
hold in such diverse states as Michigan, Idaho, Massachusetts, and Oregon. All told, 37 states eventually voted to reduce property taxes, 28 of
them also supporting income tax cuts, just in the decade of the 1980s. Initially attuned solely to the issue of big government, the taxpayer revolt
quickly enveloped other targets, including developers, realtors, school
boards, and city councils, although it usually managed to ignore the role
of large corporations. The Reagan and Bush administrations were able to
channel this explosive movement to their own electoral advantage, since a
significant plank in the Republican's platform was the privatization of
functions that once were performed by the public sector.

The period of Proposition-13-type campaigns turned out to be a watershed phase in modern U.S. political history in that the campaigns
helped to crystallize a growing consensus against the welfare state, that began to reshape the discourse of both the Republican and Democratic
Parties. The entrenched Keynesian synthesis that assigned a critical role to
government in job creation, social programs, economic regulation, and income redistribution was now thoroughly debunked and subverted. The
rise in neoliberal, as well as libertarian, sentiment in the 1980s was ush-
ered along by a number of misguided priorities that both major parties
contributed to, including increasingly regressive taxation policies, the cur-
tailment of certain federal government functions, and a declared intention (albeit more rhetorical than real) to balance the budget and achieve
deficit reduction. Reagan–Bush partisans thrived on the familiar political
myth that "welfare spending" constitutes the greatest drain of all on federal revenues, unnecessarily precipitating under-class dependency
through overly patronizing state handouts. Of course, the reality was
something altogether different: annual spending on welfare entitlements
comprised little more than 2 percent of the federal budget, a pittance

compared to more than 10 percent consumed by military expenditures (about $300 billion annually throughout the 1980s). Still, a virulent antiwelfare mood persisted into the 1990s, laying the basis for the Republicans' social Darwinian "contract" that inspired their 1994 congressional triumph. The goals of this "revolution," articulated by then Congressman Newt Gingrich and others, far transcended the concerns of taxation and welfare; indeed, these goals, if translated into social policy, would lead to a systematic dismantling of long accepted public, environmental, and health regulations. Republican efforts to enact the contract soon wound up being frustrated, however, as it became increasingly clear that the anticipated popular majority for such programs was rapidly dissipating before their very eyes.

Still, the themes of privatization, reduced government, and fiscal austerity remained very much alive in the political culture, even if it did not always get translated into specific programs or policies. Laissez-faire proposals were researched and advocated by a wide range of foundations and think tanks both in and outside of the universities, including the Hoover Institute, the Heritage Foundation, and the Cato Institute. Another example was the Progress and Freedom Foundation, based in Washington, DC, which spent tens of millions of dollars in support of antiwelfare initiatives and governmental deregulation—goals always dear to the hearts of the corporations. Right-wing organizations gathered financial support from a variety of medical, pharmaceutical, and telecommunications companies that desperately want lessened state controls and federal taxes, the right-wing organizations' stated goal being to minimize government intervention in order to give impetus to a theoretically self-regulating marketplace. Dozens of state and municipal governments moved to downsize, and in some instances privatize, their operations on the assumption that the public sector can do little more than produce endless bureaucratic waste and inefficiency, that social planning is necessarily authoritarian and counterproductive. In California, in 1996, Governor Pete Wilson unveiled a scheme whereby more than one-third of the state's activities would be transferred to the private sector; indeed, no aspect of state operations would escape thorough scrutiny as potentially worth privatizing. This scheme, had it been even partially set into motion, would have translated into the layoff of tens of thousands of public employees along with a severe reduction in many social services. In some cases the intended privatization would have even violated provisions of the state constitution, but Governor Wilson hoped to bypass that obstacle by putting his own "reform" measure on the ballot, a measure that—had it passed—would have fundamentally altered the role of state government in California. In keeping with the national consensus, both Democrats and Republicans seemed prepared to go along with *some* privatization as a cost-cutting move, whatever its devastating implications for social programs, jobs, and the public weal. Similar aggressive cost-cutting agendas were taken up by several other states (e.g., Arizona and New York) in the late 1990s.

The wave of antigovernment campaigns and movements that swept the United States during the 1980s served to energize other, more militant grassroots groups on the right, including movements aligned with Christian fundamentalism. One consequence of this shift was the growing popularity of more ideologically self-conscious libertarian organizations that attacked the very legitimacy of modern government. A major beneficiary of the new mood was the Libertarian Party, founded in 1971 but only nominally a political presence until the mid-1980s. The party stood resolutely opposed to all forms of "collectivism," a theme carried over from Ayn Rand, Friedrich Hayek, and more recently Murray Rothbard, who upheld the ideals of individual freedom and social autonomy against any form of institutional constraints.[13] Their vision was that of a society grounded in natural harmony, tied to the workings of a self-regulated market, allowing for the fullest expression of human self-actualization. In their view, government should do little more than provide for military defense and social order, much in keeping with the tenets of nineteenth-century liberalism and the celebrated night-watchman state. As Rothbard argued, beyond these basic functions the state was nothing other than a mechanism of robbery, murder, and oppression. Following this ideology, the U.S. Libertarian Party rejected virtually all institutional arrangements and social programs, insisting that even the most well-intentioned regulations and controls, even the most intelligent planning regimens, were anathema to human freedom.

The long-term objectives included in various Libertarian manifestoes focused on the abolition of such public agencies as the Food and Drug Administration (FDA), OSHA, and EPA, the elimination of public funding for schools, the privatization of social services, and the abolition of the income tax. The party, in accordance with its foreign-policy ideal of nonintervention, also advocated withdrawal of the United States from the United Nations, World Bank, and other international organizations. At the same time, despite its hard-line opposition to practically all government initiatives, the party refrained from confronting the even more gargantuan power of corporations and banks in American society—a power that, with fewer governmental controls, would become even more bureaucratic and unaccountable, with predictably horrifying consequences. Perhaps sensing this, the U.S. electorate has never responded in large numbers to Libertarian appeals; the party has won a few local elections but has never able to garner more than 5 percent of the vote in any major contest.[14] Still, the impact of Libertarian ideas remained strong in influential cultural and intellectual circles throughout the 1990s.

Whether the revolt against big government could ever be politically meaningful in an era of increased global interdependence, deep integration of state and economy, and worsening social crises raises yet another set of issues. Here it may be useful to point out that right-wing and neoliberal attacks on big government have been, and continue to be, highly selective insofar as history clearly shows that the privileged interests work assiduously to *strengthen* some of the most authoritarian and oppressive features of the state (the military, police, prison system, controls over personal life) while tearing down only those *social* programs that account for a relatively small proportion of the federal budget and that hardly can be seen as a threat to personal freedom. Nor can one find on the right the slightest inclination to question the most powerful institutions of all—the multinational corporations, huge financial networks, and their global extensions in the World Bank and IMF, and of course the entire military–industrial complex. Somehow these massive fortresses of power and wealth escape the conservative reaction against "bigness," bureaucracy, waste, and lack of accountability. The reality is that the modern state and corporations are thoroughly interwoven, and both for many years have been integrated into the permanent war economy.[15] In Roszak's words: "When we talk about 'big government' in America, this ought to be the meat of the discussion. It is big war that created and sanctioned the big corporations. It is the big corporations that undergird big government. Big government is quite simply the American economy as the local extension of global industrialism."[16]

The idea of dismantling the welfare state (itself a misnomer) is essentially a code for lowered taxes, deep cuts in social programs, deregulation, and the freeing of more resources for private modes of consumption. (The Libertarians are more consistent in their blanket rejection of government, but, as we have seen, they have little to say about corporate power.) Values associated with citizen participation, much less a recovery of the public sphere, receive at best only lip service in this Libertarian agenda. Thus, the Reagan presidency, having derived great momentum from its avowed opposition to entrenched governmental power, in effect contributed to the expansion of that very power year by year. Resources were poured into the military, intelligence activity, and law enforcement at record levels while taxes were increased, administrative corruption spread, and bureaucracy showed no signs of dissolving. Reagan also concocted the "Star Wars" defense scheme that, had it been fully adopted, would have been the most expensive (and surely most wasteful) federal government program in history—and which we may still get (in some form) in a Democratic administration, should President Clinton get his way!

The intensifying war on drugs is yet another case in point. The very same Republicans who claim to defend small government and personal freedoms are the most vociferous proponents of bigger, more ambitious, and more costly antidrug campaigns—all on the assumption (proven historically false) that greater military interdiction, more arrests and more prisons, and broader surveillance and controls over personal life will solve the problem of illicit drug use (or abuse). The collective wisdom of such antidrug crusaders as former "drug czar" William Bennett is to give big government vastly expanded power over people's lives—all without the slightest evidence that the strategy could work even on its own terms. By any measure, their approach it has been one of the most dismal and costly failures in American history. Many Republicans, including presidential candidate Dole in 1996, argued for harsher prison sentences, for both users and traffickers alike, and for the militarization of interdiction efforts. Meanwhile, as conservatives become more obsessed with the flow of drugs from countries like Mexico and Colombia, looking to tighten further the failed prohibition policies, they ignore the larger context of drug use (both legal and illegal) in a society riven with deep social problems, civilian urban violence, and personal alienation. The result is that antigovernment platitudes, along with familiar pleas for individual responsibility, become the stuff of campaign oratory without any real implications for policy improvements. Right-wing populism in the end is antistatist only where social programs are concerned or where corporate interests are being regulated; elsewhere, it is even more draconian than those "liberal" policies it decries.

Still, Republicans and other conservatives have persisted in their (ofttimes libertarian) rhetoric about the evils of state power, about the need to transfer federal functions to localities, about their desire to eliminate bureaucracy, always invoking "free market" principles that, in fact, have little relevance to the actual workings of an economy already suffused with massive governmental, military, and corporate controls—controls that in fact turn out to be essential to capitalist priorities. In fact, the much heralded shift back to an autonomous market, family values, local neighborhoods, and individual sovereignty could never occur without at the same time destroying the very material foundations of state-integrated corporate capitalism, a system the Right has been vigorously defending all along. Moreover, the theme of decentralization—that is, transferring power to local government as the main site of popular decision making—which is so central to the libertarian vision, turns out to be even more misleading. Surely, there is no iron law suggesting that smaller jurisdictions will necessarily provide needed services in a more efficient and humane way than they would without at least some guidance as to minimal national standards to which all citizens should be entitled. On the whole, the record of state and municipal governments in providing for their citizens' needs equitably is a history replete with *inequities*—ones that a more solicitous federal government eventually felt compelled to correct.

Conservative antistatism since the late 1970s thus hardly represents an attempt to strengthen democracy or citizenship, or to rejuvenate the public sphere; rather, it more closely resembles a strategy for restructuring the corporate economy and political system in order to win back the social gains that labor and other movements achieved between the 1930s and 1970s. That is, conservatives' apparent aim is not to abolish or curtail concentrated power but instead to *reconsolidate* that power in a way that would give elites even more social and institutional autonomy than they presently have. The real thrust behind appeals for smaller government is to severely weaken the social and popular side of the state and to legitimate an assault on "welfare," popular constituencies (women, minorities), and "special interests" (labor) that might impede the global developmental objectives of corporate planners. In these instances, conservatives actually seek to insulate government from the fearsome incursions of citizen input, from what some mainstream observers have decried as an "excess of democracy,"[17] or simply from the unsettling effects of civic turbulence. Ironically, the conservatives' approach would lead to broadened state control over potentially insurgent groups at precisely the time when the Right continues to agitate for an all-out assault against "big government." The flourishing of an ideology of antipolitics in contemporary American political culture is best understood in this context.

Although deeply flawed in its highly selective application, antistatist populism shows no signs of disappearing. One reason is that everyday life in the 1990s remains fraught with anxieties and fears about the future—many of these result of intensifying social crisis grounded mainly (but not only) in economic disequilibrium and social dislocation. Feelings of uncertainty and despair about what political action is or could be—about the very efficacy of governmental intervention—often get translated into ever more privatized lifestyles or the pursuit of therapeutic solutions, as we have seen. Sometimes these feelings are accompanied by deep hostility toward the public sphere in general. In such a milieu people can easily move to withdraw from civic participation of *any* sort, or they may choose to join or support movements of engaged citizenry, such as the Proposition 13 proponents, for example, who had have the objective of "getting government off our backs." As I have already argued, however, rarely does the typical contemporary response involve a systematic challenge to governmental power; the main focus is generally more parochial and ideologically charged, whittling away at the social functions of the state while readily accepting, and perhaps even seeking to enlarge, the more intrusive and repressive functions of the state that go hand in hand with expanded corporate domination—along with a romantic attachment to traditional values.

WARRIOR DREAMS—AND NIGHTMARES

The widespread appearance of right-wing populism in the United States stems from the activism not only of free marketers, antitax partisans, and libertarians but also of a bizarre variety of cults, sects, militias, and enclave groups, often galvanized by the familiar "angry white male" caught up in a backlash against social movements and disruptive change. Many resisters see themselves as engaged in an all-out war against an evil and oppressive federal government that taxes and regulates American citizens against their will. Others see the national state apparatus as an agency or repository of international conspiracies, frequently involving the United Nations or other global organizations. Inevitably, violent confrontations between these groups and the state have occurred—the FBI assault at Ruby Ridge, the Waco standoff and conflagration at the Branch Davidian compound, the Oklahoma City bombing, and the siege of the Montana Freemen, among others. In most of these episodes the very legitimacy of the U.S. government was being called into question. In hundreds of other lesser confrontations, generally in the west and Midwest, federal agents and employees have been subjected to threats, intimidation, and verbal attack. A Gallup poll taken in May 1995 revealed that about 39 percent of Americans believe the federal government is "an enemy of human rights." In the first 10 days following the Oklahoma City bombing, dozens of federal agencies received a total of 140 bomb threats. There were two incidents, in San Francisco and Puerto Rico (1994 and 1995, respectively), where individuals became so aggravated at red tape and mistreatment at the hands of agency officials that they took government employees hostage. Public officials at all levels have often been the target of name-calling, threats, and harassment.

Such expressions of public outrage can hardly be dismissed as the irrational response of people on the margins and crazies, though clearly that is part of the picture; far more common is the visceral lashing-out of ordinary people who feel powerless and think, sometimes justifiably, that government officials and politicians are totally indifferent to their needs and demands, or corrupt and untrustworthy, or simply incompetent. Here again the historical context must be taken into account. With the near disintegration of communism worldwide and the end of the cold war, conservatives in the United States have suddenly been forced to seek out new enemies, whether in the form of all-powerful institutions or of remote, mysterious external forces. Then, too, there is the mounting public anxiety over the social chaos evident in most American cities, reinforced by a visceral hostility to bureaucracy but also to progressive movements that are thought to embody principles destructive to traditional values.

The phenomenon of cults and sects has taken off in American culture since the 1970s—most recently dramatized by the organized suicide of 38 Heaven's Gate cult members in San Diego in early 1997. The impact of cults and sects (whose members may number as many as several hundred thousand) is far greater than total membership numbers might suggest. Recent U.S. history is replete with numerous examples of cultlike groups on both the left and the right, ranging from the Weather Underground (of the early 1970s), the Symbionese Liberation Army, the People's Temple and Jonestown, the Moonies of Reverend Sun Myung Moon, and the various Hare Krishna sects everywhere, to the Rajneesh colony in Oregon and various communes associated with the Guru Maharaj Ji, to name some of the most visible. What these cults and sects share is an intensely millenarian vision of the future, a strong attachment to charismatic leaders, and a manifest contempt for politics. Often overlooked is the fact that popular belief in prophesies and mystical ideals, as well as a fascination with conspiracy theories, has a long tradition in American culture. Such millenarianism dovetails with the widespread populist conviction that life entails a perpetual struggle against hated outside enemies and that there can be no escape from the miseries of everyday life through either conventional religion or normal politics. Given this outlook, a presumably corrupt public sphere can never be the arena for genuine human involvement or emancipation (however defined). Insecure about the future and cut off from the past, people responding to an atmosphere of change and crisis are especially vulnerable to highly seductive messages about promises of an entirely new life, especially when those messages are conveyed by strong, articulate leaders who offer the "true" path to empowerment.[18]

The search for an idyllic separate kingdom, made up of a community of believers standing firm against an oppressive world, motivated David Koresh and the Branch Davidians in their quest for religious transcendence. Their legacy had roots in the Millerite Christian movement founded by William Miller in the 1830s and inspired by Old Testament prophecies about the coming apocalypse. The Millerites were able to build a following of close to 100,000 believers dedicated to the renunciation of material possessions; members spent much of their time praying on hilltops, waiting for the second coming of Christ. This cult gave birth to the Seventh Day Adventists, who later produced a split-off group called the Davidians, out of which the Branch Davidians were formed under the stewardship of Ben Roden. Following Roden's death in 1978 his wife Lois formed the Mount Carmel Commune and entered into a relationship with Vernon Howell, who soon changed his name to David Koresh and then proclaimed himself the new Messiah, using his charisma to take over the organization in the early 1980s.[19] Taken to quoting long biblical verses, Koresh placed himself above any earthly criticism, talking incessantly about the future liberation and how it was destined to come about. He envisioned a strictly religious process confined to the Davidian faithful. Eventually the group came to embrace a series of wild prophecies, most of them linked to the idea of inevitable and perpetual conflict with a corrupt and hated outside world. In the context of this overall mindset, the Davidians established a specific target of fear and hatred, namely, the U.S. government.

The Davidian siege mentality perpetuated a manicheistic and paranoid view of social reality that lent itself to a form of militarism that soon gripped the membership which totaled only a few hundred by 1990. This belief system further helped to solidify the leader's control over the organization; not only was Koresh's word held sacred, it also embraced a line of defense against the incursions of sinister external threats. By the early 1990s the Davidians had amassed a substantial arsenal of weapons at their compound in Waco, Texas, including a large assortment of grenades and automatic rifles. Following a series of law enforcement inquiries into the cult's activities, there came to be a number of confrontations and skirmishes, both violent and nonviolent, eventually leading to a 51-day standoff in 1993 that ended when federal authorities moved in force against the compound. The resulting inferno cost the lives of 84 members (including Koresh), most of whom apparently preferred total annihilation to surrender. To the very end, the Davidians remained implacably hostile to the federal government, rejecting any compromise with its agents and refusing to extend legitimacy to it during negotiations. Beyond this fierce antigovernment stance, the Davidians—true to the long heritage of prepolitical revolt—never articulated a coherent view of either their goals or a strategy for building a movement.

The Davidian cult thus bore striking resemblance to comparable religious and quasi-religious groups analyzed by Eric Hobsbawm in *Primitive Rebels*.[20] One case study explored by Hobsbawm was the millenarian cult founded in Italy by David Lazzaretti in 1875, which appealed to hundreds of poor, marginalized, and uneducated people lured by images of quasi-religious salvation. Like Koresh, Lazzaretti set himself up as an earthly messiah whose mission was to perform miracles in order to end human suffering. Many peasants, especially in southern Italy, were convinced by the power of a message that could challenge the hegemony of both the Catholic Church and the much despised political system. While Lazzaretti did inspire an ethos of resistance by encouraging peasants to refuse to honor any tax assessments, he offered neither a specific program nor a method for carrying out even minimal social reforms; the "ideology" consisted of little more than unwavering belief in imminent miracles, a search for divine intervention. In 1878 Lazzaretti and most of his followers were killed during combat with the carabinieri, having chosen—as the Davidians would later—violent death to capitulation.[21]

The search for apocalyptic deliverance likewise motivated members of the Heaven's Gate Commune near San Diego, 38 of whom decided to commit suicide together in May 1997 in the belief that their spiritual departure from spaceship Earth at the coming of the Hale–Bopp comet would enable them to reach the "next level." Their millenarian ideology amounted to a severe and total escape from politics or, perhaps more appropriately, a complete exit from society. What is most interesting about the Heaven's Gate phenomenon is how the members, followers of Marshall Applegate, incorporated into their thinking some mainstream beliefs (about such matters as the science fiction mania, new-age transcendence, and fascination with UFOs and alien beings) while carrying their own commitments to apocalyptic extremes. In this respect Heaven's Gate represents a quintessential end-of-the-century millenarian cult that, hardly by accident, was located in one of the most affluent San Diego suburbs (Rancho Santa Fe) and attracted members (overwhelmingly white and middle-class) who had worked mostly in a variety of high-tech jobs. Their sense of alienation and powerlessness, their feelings of being under siege, could be overcome only through the ultimate apocalyptic act: departure from the mundane existence of inept, disabled sentient beings.

In contrast to the Davidians and Heaven's Gate devotees, for whom apocalyptic belief was everything, contemporary skinheads—part of the growing (but still relatively small) bands of right-wing or neo-Nazi youth—are more closely linked to elements of urban gang culture. Like most millenarian cults, however, the skinheads have attracted members largely from the poor, marginalized, and uneducated sectors, including above all young males who have yet to establish strong roots in work and family. While generally not overtly ideological, the skinheads often adopted the rhetoric of a racist, sexist, xenophobic subculture bent on reproducing the division between initiates and outsiders, between the (usually homogeneous) youth groups and various stereotyped "others." In many cases they took on the symbolic paraphernalia of historical fascism, adorning themselves with swastikas, German eagle medals, and tattoos, listening to German marching music, and so forth. In most instances, however, skinhead groups expressed little interest in political ideology or in changing the world. As with most gangs, there was a strong attachment to turf and a swaggering, macho cult of violence that could easily be directed against scapegoats: rival gangs, feared or despised ethnic groups, and other "enemies."[22]

The skinheads have their origin in the Teddy Boys, a youth subculture that spawned the rival Mods and Rockers groups in England during the early 1960s. They came together around dispersed gangs of young males who felt alienated from social convention, hopeless about the future, and often looked for scapegoats to attack as the source of their economic hardship and social powerlessness. Their targets were mainly immigrants and racial minorities. Hence, their deep sense of collective solidarity derived more from this insular ethos of pitting members against a corrupt and oppressive world—and from their passion for music—than from any coherent belief system. Skinheads first built a presence in the United States during the late 1970s, when they came to be associated with punk rock, "screwdriver music," episodic acts of violence, and advocacy of white supremacy. On the whole they were inclined toward neither religious nor political ideology; as in England, it was more a case of poor young white males confronting a hostile conformist society. Many held low-paying jobs, for example in the service sector—part of the emerging "Burger King" economy in which manufacturing work historically carried out by white men was rapidly vanishing.[23] At a time when few good jobs and careers seemed available to poor youth, when the family had deteriorated as a source of cohesion and identity, and when politics was viewed as a boring, meaningless exercise, skinheads came to epitomize the alienation and nihilistic outlook of urban youth in general. Much like cults and sects, youth-based gangs of this sort can furnish solidarity where it is otherwise absent. But it is an emphatically *antipolitical* solidarity that views any kind of routine institutional life (especially involving government) with total contempt.

By the early 1990s the skinheads totaled an estimated 3,000 members across 31 states, concentrated largely in the west; their social impact, like that of the cults, has been greater than the numbers alone might suggest. As with social bandits of an earlier era, skinheads tend to be nomadic and relish occasional violent encounters with targeted groups or the police. And much like urban gangs, they constitute a strongly fraternal (if even more marginalized) subculture without aspirations toward any real public influence. The milieu is one mostly of drifters and outsiders who feel uncomfortable with the discourse of elections, campaigns, and institutional concerns; there is no vision of grassroots politics. Even with all their Nazi symbols and culture of rebellion, therefore, skinheads have come to embrace an ethos of cynicism and nihilism that self-consciously refuses the duties and challenges of citizenship, that debunks the idea of winning (or influencing) political power, that looks with deep skepticism on anything resembling official discourse.

Such retreat from the public sphere is, in a territorial sense, even more pronounced among the growing ranks of survivalists than among cults, sects, and skinhead groups. Survivalists generally seek refuge in the wilderness, forming tightly knit, isolated groups intent on preserving self-sufficient and (in most cases) traditional lifestyles. Unlike the millenarial cults, they have no single-minded religious or utopian mission; unlike the skinheads, their escape from society takes them into more insular rural enclaves; and, unlike both, they adhere to relatively coherent beliefs (usually some variant of fascism).[24] At the same time, survivalists typically appeal to the same constituency of marginalized, poorly educated, lower-class white males. More significantly, they view politics with much the same degree of hostility. Thus, while many participants may reject en toto the existing social order, leaders seem to have little interest in framing alternative visions or strategies, even along fascistic lines.

The term "survivalist" was first coined by Kurt Saxon in the early 1960s—a reference to self-assertedly superior beings who, bonded to one another in the remote wilderness, were prepared to endure some cataclysmic event such as nuclear war. Initially they were mainly consumed with the idea of self-protection from hostile intrusions, whether from urban elites, police, the United Nations, minorities, or communist aggressors. Over time, as survivalist ranks grew to the tens of thousands, organizational and ideological coherence followed. Their élan was boosted by the ideas contained in certain racist, neo-Nazi texts such as William Pierce's *The Turner Diaries*. Eventually the survivalist rebirth gave rise to such dispersed groups as the Aryan Nations, The Order, the Posse Comitatus, and numerous militias, which together claimed as many as 60,000 members scattered around the country.[25] Inspired by the Civil War Posse Comitatus Act, which prohibited federal troops from intervening in local disputes, the Posse formations refused to obey any government officials higher than those at the county level; all other jurisdictions were scorned as corrupt and implicated in a conspiratorial world-governing body. The Posse groups of the 1990s include tax resisters, home schoolers, religious fundamentalists, gun enthusiasts, and others who see their life as a perpetual struggle against an implacably corrupt and hostile world. Some leaders and activists predict an imminent race war that could threaten the survival of the white population. In this ideological subculture many groups have taken on the veneer of a militarylike structure, replete with uniforms, chains of command, large arms caches, shooting ranges, and the entire lingo of an army outfit.

As with other kindred groups, survivalists face the daunting challenge of retaining their organizational dynamism over time—that is, of sustaining high levels of commitment in a situation where members are so often thoroughly removed from normal routines of work and family life. As participants age and mature, there is always the question as to how long even the most strongly dedicated activists can remain in such an isolated, paranoid, and hostile atmosphere where conspiratorial tales abound. (At times survivalists have seemed ready to believe in virtually any outlandish scenario—indeed the more far-fetched, often the more credible.) Moreover, without any presence as a genuine social movement or hope of achieving specific goals, members are hard put to point to actual or even potential worldly successes. In these circumstances insular groups will frequently turn more and more inward; in the process they may wind up fighting among themselves, splitting off, perhaps disintegrating as a result of the ever mounting levels of frustration. Destructive patterns of this sort have become one of the modern legacies of primitive rebellion—witness the fate of the Weather Underground, the Symbionese Liberation Army, the Rajneesh commune, the People's Temple, and more recently the Heaven's Gate cult. As the disillusioned survivalist founder Saxon remarked about these groups in the late 1980s, "Leave them to their own devices and they'll wipe each other out."[26] Even in the absence of such an implosion, however, it would seem that these groups are condemned to political irrelevance, owing, at least in part, to their militantly isolationist stance.

Among all extreme right-wing groups operating on the fringes of the political system, by far the largest, most dispersed, most well-known, and probably most ominous have been the militias, which by 1996 had an estimated membership of 250,000 with a sprawling base of support totaling between 3 million and 5 million people across at least 30 states. Theirs is a thriving (and growing) nativist, antiurban subculture that, like the cultists, skinheads, and survivalists, views government and politicians of all stripes as objects of ridicule. In fact, the paramilitary organizations have evolved in such a way during the 1990s as to incorporate the main thrust of these other groups, including much of their modus operandi and espoused aims but with a clearer focus on the idea of armed mobilization. It seems clear from the evidence to date that the militias attract typically poor and working-class white males who are the most amenable to the whole panoply of racist, xenophobic, militarist, and conspiratorial messages.

What its members like to call the patriot movement gained its biggest notoriety at the time of the Oklahoma City federal building bombing in April 1995, but the militia presence goes back much further—probably as far back as the emergence of survivalists and kindred groups in the early 1960s. The movement is generally formed through networks of small, relatively autonomous, "leaderless" cells that can move swiftly, flexibly, and secretly if necessary. They are inclined to stockpile weapons, dress in army fatigues, conduct periodic quasi-military "maneuvers," and hold "intelligence-briefing" sessions, typically in remote rural areas. Both active members and supporters often come out of a military background; they are mostly white, male, Christian, have little if any college education, and live in rural or semirural regions. They come together under such banners as the "Colorado Free Militias," the "Florida State Militia," "Christian Identity," the "Militias of Montana," and the "Viper Militia." Oddly enough, support for the paramilitary movement actually *increased*, in some cases dramatically, in the period immediately following the Oklahoma City carnage, presumably reflecting widespread fascination on the part of the public with matters of intense violence.

If the names and images of the U.S. militias convey a worldview thoroughly cut off from social reality, the groups nonetheless have an ideological rationale, however murky, behind their pretensions and actions. They see the ordinary person (again mostly white and Christian) as politically disenfranchised, struggling for survival and identity under circumstances made more difficult by the actions and designs of a governmental behemoth, hoping to restore basic individual rights and freedoms. Crucial to that struggle is the ownership of weapons that the federal government is viewed as illegitimately trying to deny to law-abiding citizens. A popular refrain is "What will you do when they come for your guns?" Militia partisans are fond of apocalyptic scenarios—for example, the one where UN forces, assisted by the CIA, FBI, and perhaps the IRS, have mobilized to occupy the American heartland with the aim of delivering the country over to agents of a sinister (but never clearly defined) "New World Order." Taking as their inspiration the Minutemen of America's revolutionary period, militia groups follow a myth of rugged individualism and frontier heroism in which guns appear larger than life—symbols of a disappearing sense of historical mission.[27] Members harken back to a simpler, far more homogeneous world of rural harmony, religion, family values, and ethnic solidarity—a world in which outsiders, foreigners, and government agents are regarded as personae non grata. Aside from books like *The Turner Diaries*, a major conduit of propaganda for the militias has been the bourgeoning ranks of extreme right-wing talk radio hosts (like Chuck Harder in Michigan) who urge listeners to resist—violently, if need be—those global demonic forces that seem hell-bent on disarming and enslaving American citizens.

A highly celebrated case of patriot action was the protracted standoff between the Freemen and federal agents in Jordan, Montana during the spring of 1996. Engaged in a long-standing conflict with agents of the FBI and the IRS, the Freemen—a group of less than 100 resisters led by Leroy Schusasinger—hoped to create their own republic (called Justus Township) with its own legal territory, constitution, currency, and armed units. Their overriding goal was local governance, but strictly in the framework of a white, patriarchal, rural Christian order. For several years Freemen activists carried out a series of antigovernment actions, often inundating local courts with bogus documents and claims, refusing to pay taxes, and making payments to creditors of up to $30 million in counterfeit checks. They issued death threats to federal officials who, in the Freemen ideology, were denied the credibility to regulate, control, or tax individuals who, in any case, should not be required to pledge allegiance to the outlaw U.S. state. Federal arrest warrants were issued against several Freemen members in March 1996, leading to the prolonged encounter and eventually culminating several months later in the arrest of two leaders.

Another paramilitary group, the Phoenix-based Viper Militia, seemed to be preparing for an extended violent confrontation with the federal government—largely, as it turns out, without the knowledge of any local residents. In July 1996 agents from the Alcohol, Tobacco, and Firearms (AFT) office, following a nine-month investigation, arrested 12 people involved in the Vipers and found a large arsenal of machine guns, rifles, 56 boxes of ammunition, and hundreds of pounds of chemicals that could be used to manufacture bombs. Agents also found a videotape in which militia members provided detailed instructions for blowing up government buildings. Operating underground, the Vipers were a dispersed, loosely organized network that was able to move about without attracting much public attention. Their nucleus was made up of mostly ordinary working-class people, including housewives and a fairly large percentage of women. Relaxed gun-control laws in Arizona enabled the militias to go about their normal daily activities, with members often dressed in fatigues with weapons visible, more or less above suspicion. Based on their literature and videotapes, the Vipers apparently believed that "urban warfare" and "race wars" were imminent and that it was the duty of citizens to mobilize for this imminent Armageddon. At the same time, militia partisans and spokespersons liked to embroider an image of simple folks just out for fun and games in the woods or desert.

THE NEW OUTLAW HERO

As an expanding and potentially ominous national presence, the militias carry forward—in quasi-militarized form—the familiar American idea of disenfranchised outsiders fighting for identity, recognition, and local democratic control against a distant, impersonal, and bureaucratic government. The vast majority see themselves as bearers of a renewed citizenship that must be won by vigorous battle in the midst of a harsh and ever threatening world. Their obsession with conspiracies, their fascination with mysterious schemes and plots, and their glorification of gun culture can easily draw them into the zone of domestic terrorism. The much celebrated cult of violence, however, does not seem to detract from the populist image that the militias have so patiently sought to cultivate. Of course, the militia is a reactionary form of populism, but its anti-government zeal does inspire the semblance of a grassroots activism that shares some of the symbols and even aims of progressive populism. Indeed, the militias' hostility to state power is deep, visceral, and generalized, going well beyond the targeting of specific officeholders or legislators or the familiar conservative assault on bureaucracy. Such grassroots sympathies are compromised, however, by their undeniably shadowy element, which often features a virulent white racism or, at the very least, an ethos of intolerance. More tellingly, their populist critique never extends to the power of multinational corporations; the struggle for local control is strangely directed against only the national state, not big business or the military. Furthermore, the militias rarely mobilize popular support on the basis of some positive vision of the future—even a vaguely anarchistic one—but focus instead on people's fear of change, their insecurity about material and social dislocation, and a scapegoating of minorities, immigrants, and outsiders. The result is a kind of Rambo syndrome, a macho defiance of elites by any means necessary, along lines of the traditional American outlaw hero and frontier ethos of rugged individualism.

This last point demands further elaboration. The importance for the militias of a weapons subculture, of preparation for armed combat, of everyday people locked in mortal struggle against a wicked federal bureaucracy, cannot be stressed enough. The new rebels are, after all, simply carrying to extremes the worship of guns and violence, the attachment to rugged individualism, that is historically embedded in American culture. There are an estimated 220 million guns in civilian hands in the United States, including several million automatic weapons belonging to people who for the most part are able to roam freely across the rural and urban terrain. It is the hard-fought and well-financed lobbying campaigns of the National Rifle Association that have done so much to legitimate the gun culture. Add to this mix a mass media and popular culture saturated with images of violence, along with an increasingly atomized civil society that feeds into a variety of angry and paranoid responses, and the resonance of messages predicting warfare involving ordinary citizens (as in Larry Pratt's widely read *Armed People Victorious*) becomes all the more fathomable.

As Bill Gibson observes in *Warrior Dreams*, guns and violence have become a powerful male obsession in the United States since the Vietnam war.[28] This weapons fetish has spread rapidly, across class and ethnic lines, with more than three million assault rifles having been purchased in just the past two decades. Manifestations of male violence have been on the upswing since the 1960s, from street crime to domestic violence to serial murders. Films devoting seemingly inordinate attention to mass killings—or just regular mayhem—like *Silence of the Lambs, Reservoir Dogs, Pulp Fiction*, and *Natural Born Killers*, have become the object of cultlike fascination. The immense popularity of the televised coverage of the Persian Gulf war, much of it graphically depicting bloody carnage, is well known.[29] Reflecting on this trend, Gibson points to the emergence of a "new warrior hero" in American society that mirrors a shifting masculine ethos—one less focused on soldiers and cops and more attuned to an everyday warrior life that encourages common individuals to take up arms, join quasi-military groups, and "prepare for heroic battle against the enemies of society."[30] So the modern male warrior, whether in the guise of the Freemen, patriot organizations, marauding bandits, gangs, or skinheads—or even a hermetic figure like the Unabomber—becomes the archetype of the renegade hero who in earlier days tamed the frontier, robbed trains and banks, or simply took the law into his own hands to fight commies and other alien intruders.

The recurrent search for the American male warrior identity goes back to the Minutemen, frontier settlers, and foreign adventurers like Teddy Roosevelt's "Roughriders," which attracted men looking to conquer the world, or at least hoping to defend their own territory, with a powerful sense of adventurism. That imprecise warrior identity also runs through the myths and rituals of the Mafia and organized crime as well as urban street gangs. During the 1990s it has appealed far more to white men than to any other social category—to men who feel threatened by a heartless and encroaching urban world and often driven by feelings of racial superiority, sexism, male bonding, and the familiar ultranationalism of fascist ideology. Writes Gibson: "American men—lacking confidence in the government and the economy, troubled by changing relations between the sexes, uncertain of their identity or their future—began to dream, to fantasize about the powers and features of another kind of man who could retake and reorder the world."[31]

The new paramilitary culture was shaped in part by a national mood of defeat and pessimism stemming from the aftermath of the Vietnam war. As Gibson points out, the Indochina debacle was a great blow to the collective American psyche, representing the end to a long U.S. tradition of military victories; it eclipsed the national doctrine of manifest destiny that had such deep roots in the imperial designs of American ruling elites going back to the early nineteenth century. U.S. military hegemony was challenged and smashed, at least in one geographical locale and for one historical moment. The result was a massive social-psychological disruption leading to a "crisis of self-image" in the general culture but which seemed most disorienting for the military subculture. During a period of intense and rapid change, including the strong impact of feminism and the erosion of long-established gender roles, a large number of men felt driven to recapture the patriarchal ethos of a simpler era. In this context many sought out images of violent power, which they found validated in the popular culture. But for such fantasies to make sense, to have credibility, they would have to be directed against purported enemies: communists, foreign terrorists, drug dealers, illegal aliens, nebulous conspirators, even the U.S. government itself, which in fact was often seen as behind these other forces. In this fashion the national crisis intersected with a variety of identity crises (and perhaps economic hardships) that for good reasons seemed impervious to normal political initiative.

Take the case of Timothy McVeigh, brought to trial and convicted for his role in the Oklahoma City bombing. Whether McVeigh acted alone or not, it is known that he had close ties to various militia groups based in the Southwest. According to FBI interviews with previous friend and co-worker Carl Lebron released in January 1997, McVeigh expressed a strong dislike of the federal government, politicians, and especially liberals. He went out of his way to proselytize friends and acquaintances into paramilitary circles, expressed outrage over the Waco events (he personally visited the site of the raid), and sometimes came to work with literature from right-wing groups, cults, and secret organizations including the Ku Klux Klan. He expressed kinship with Randy Weaver, whose wife and son were shot to death by the FBI during the 1992 Ruby Ridge siege. McVeigh talked endlessly about "unidentified flying objects," according to Lebron, and suggested at one point that the U.S. government was deeply involved in shipping drugs into the country through a river on a miniature submarine. When McVeigh quit his job in Buffalo in 1994, he told friends that "people were coming after him" and that it was time to prepare for a long period of armed mobilization.[32]

This type of siege mentality characterizes angry right-wing extremists who form the backbone of rural groups such as the Aryan Nations, Christian Identity, The Order, and The Order-2, many of them based in the west, in Idaho, Utah, Montana, and eastern Washington. Richard Butler, long a fixture in the white supremacist organization the Aryan Nations, has set up a 20-acre enclave surrounded by barbed-wire fences in northern Idaho where members can meet, practice target-shooting, and generally vent their rage at a country that has sold out white people. Butler's goal is a "ten percent solution" that would set aside one-tenth of the United States as a "white homeland" while letting the rest of the country rot in its own corruption and decay. Funded in part by Silicon Valley high-tech money, Butler and his followers rejected the Klan and the John Birch Society as being "too liberal"; as of 1998, they retained close contacts with Aryan Nations chapters in at least 12 states and with a variety of neo-Nazi groups worldwide. Referring to the Bible as a "book of separation," displaying photos of Hitler, and fascinated with both punk rock and German marching music, the Aryans look to a protracted "war of freedom"—a "war," however, that lacks any coherent political definition.

Like survivalists, skinheads, and some cultists, militia members comprise a diffuse subculture—more an alternative way of life than an explicit ideology or political grouping. In this respect militias parallel earlier proto-fascist groups that in countries like Italy, Germany, and Spain eventually fed into full-blown fascist movements, parties, and regimes. Like these older phenomena, contemporary right-wing groups oppose some sectors of the power structure and rail against cultural decadence that they view as an outgrowth of modernity. The struggle is understood, for the moment at least, as essentially *cultural*—part of a historical battle to regain lost values and social structures (community, family, religion, and so on). As with earlier embodiments of reactionary populism, however, the *Kulturkampf* of today's rebels combines elements of xenophobia, racism, and militarism. Theirs is nothing less than a "struggle for the soul of America," as some militia leaders are fond of repeating. So far this is quite remote from the more developed ideologies of classical European fascism on the road to political power: the antistatist outlook of the militias and allied groupings is infused with such utter contempt for the public sphere—indeed, for any generalized mode of civic participation—that translation of their populist energy into movements for social change will be extremely difficult. This defect is compounded by an ethos of dispersion and secrecy, by an intense commitment to localism, that is viewed as necessary to the "leaderless resistance." Here the paramilitary groups are doubly antipolitical: they have an aversion to the whole realm of social governance and statecraft, and they reject the public arena *in principle* as a site of collective action. Dedicated and solidary as they might be, therefore, the militias—like the millenarial cults and skinheads—are not likely to amount to anything more than hotbeds of primitive rebellion: fragmented, local, insular, and lacking the capacity for political definition and expansion. They have little in the way of political language or methods that could give worldly substance to their undeniably militant beliefs or connect their actions to social processes and historical possibilities. For the near future, at least, theirs is likely to be nothing more than a protofascist form of cathartic activity built around their own unique brand of antipolitics.

TERRORISM AS SOCIAL CATHARSIS

Our understanding of contemporary political terrorism has been largely associated with random acts of violence, usually carried out by small underground groups, mainly in Europe, Japan, the Middle East, and certain regions of the third world. Only recently, beginning in the 1990s, has ideologically motivated violence become a fairly widespread *domestic* phenomenon in the United States. While both the Left and the Right have resorted to terrorism, in the 1990s it has been the product mainly of either disgruntled individuals or extreme right-wing groups like the militias. (It should be emphasized here that, while many such groups may discuss the imminent prospect of armed combat, few so far have actually followed through.) The rise of domestic terrorism is a historically significant development, not only because of what it might portend for American politics but because it reflects powerful trends at work in the society as a whole. Protofascist acts of violence directed at public targets may be less deviant or exceptional than is commonly believed; on the contrary, they are the work of mostly ordinary people taking a few very ordinary ideas (freedom, rugged individualism, patriotism, the right to bear arms) to fanatical excesses. As earlier noted, the cult of violence resonates throughout American society in the form of the gun lobby, images in the mass media, urban gang subcultures, astronomical rates of violent crime, and of course the war economy itself (which, though downsized, still devours more than $270 billion yearly).

In this social milieu the problem of right-wing terrorism cannot be dismissed as the isolated shenanigans of fringe crazies. Indeed, local incidents of such violence have been surprisingly common during the 1990s: according to the ATF, there were no less than 2,400 bombings in the United States during 1993 alone, leading to 70 deaths and 1,375 injuries. Reportedly, hundreds of other planned actions were intercepted by the FBI and police agencies. Throughout the 1990s more than 35,000 people in the United States were reportedly injured by acts of terrorism and physical violence waged by dozens of groups. A heightened fascination with bombs and guns, including sophisticated assault weapons, is fueled by mail-order companies that cater to paramilitary enthusiasts, not to mention Internet transmissions, short-wave radio, fax systems, and the omnipresent talk radio programs (some of them hosted by militia sympathizers). Aided by the Internet and alarmed about the coming of the new millennium, "hate" groups around the country have multiplied rapidly in just the late 1990s. In 1998 observers from Klanwatch and the Militia Task Force documented an all-time high of 474 hate groups in the United States—an increase of 20 percent from 1996. Activists in such groups, many of them biblical doomsayers and many fascinated with violent rock lyrics, are increasingly drawn to domestic terrorism; they collect high-powered weapons, build bombs and chemical weapons from easy-to-obtain ingredients, and set up websites (163 all told, as of early 1999) as intricate networks of communication. Their main target is an evil, tyrannical federal government. No longer confined to the South and Far West, such groups (they hardly constitute movements) now have the kind of nationwide presence that enables them to avoid social and geographical isolation.

Right-wing terrorism thus goes much deeper than the bombing of federal buildings and occasional acts of sabotage: there are the frequent assaults on women's health clinics, along with a tremendous increase in hate crimes directed against minorities and gays. Outside this quasi-fascist subculture there have been recurrent Luddite efforts to smash the artifacts of modern technology—witness the Unabomber's mail bombings to those he thought to be agents of the industrial order during the 1980s and 1990s. Viewed in this context, terrorist episodes involving the World Trade Center, Oklahoma City, the 1994 Amtrak derailing, and the 1996 Olympics bombing in Atlanta, to name only the most publicized, could be a prelude to mounting domestic insurgency that might eventually spill beyond reactionary populist boundaries. The violent mood is nourished by a popular cynicism and frustration over the meaningless of normal politics—measured by the precipitous loss of efficacy that pervades any depoliticized society—and by the rapid spread of paranoid, conspiratorial beliefs often tied to some future apocalypse or fear of conquest by (undefined) intruders from afar. Militia members' paranoid references to black helicopters, alien creatures, drug cartels, and secret military missions—all supposedly leading to a tyrannical New World Order—are best understood in this context. Such beliefs add up to a demonology that, for the Right, offers a substitute for the familiar cold-war images of the communist devil.

The spread of domestic terrorism in the United States can be interpreted as a particularly dramatic manifestation of antipolitics during the 1990s. The appearance of groups that place violence at the center of their agenda has the effect of closing off public space for open dialogue and collective action. They generate a heightened degree of police and military vigilance, which may soon produce government repression, crackdowns on basic political freedoms, and is detrimental (in some cases even fatal) to progressive social forces. A good case in point is Italy, where the once thriving radical Left was decimated by the end of the 1970s in the wake of the abduction and murder of Aldo Moro by the Red Brigades. Random and widespread acts of violence generate fear and suspicion far beyond their points of origin, endowing the state security apparatus with geometrically more power, both institutionally and psychologically. Terrorist episodes can also spread the flames of racism and scapegoating that may already be present in the culture, weakening the public sphere.

Given the complexity of modern society and the critical role played by the mass media and popular culture, civil unsettling can result from just a few acts of terrorist violence—as the deadly work of the Red Brigades, Baader-Meinhof in Germany, Supreme Truth in Japan, and even the Unabomber in the United States has already demonstrated. Where this occurs, politics itself shrinks beyond recognition. On the one hand, the state becomes more authoritarian while, on the other, oppositional groups and movements are thrown on the defensive; that is, democratic participation at the society-wide level is readily blocked or crushed. And, while reactionary populists may welcome any disaster that may befall liberals and progressives, and may derive short-term benefits from a state of emergency, their own long-term fate will almost certainly be the same, namely, political oblivion. In any case, it should come as no surprise to find that proponents of terrorist methods are usually quite explicit about their contempt for politics. Thus, writing in his *Manifesto*, the Unabomber was quite clear "This is not to be a political revolution."[33] It follows that terrorism by its very nature can never amount to a viable political strategy; it cannot lead to social transformation. At the same time, if right-wing violence fails in pursuit of its own goals, it can nonetheless achieve victories of a sort insofar as it helps to perpetuate an ideological milieu in which social change is stymied. A Hobbesian world constitutes the pinnacle of antipolitics in a double sense—neither the turbulence of civil warfare nor the repressive Leviathan that is almost certain to result are consonant with a vital, open, democratic public sphere.

POLITICS AND ANTIPOLITICS ON THE RIGHT

American society since the 1960s has, of course, hardly been devoid of political activity—nor of sustained oppositional activity in the form of grassroots social movements. As in any national setting, the trend toward depoliticization has been less than monolithic, with citizen participation of one form or another across the ideological spectrum.

It is important to remember that strong divisions exist on the right between the antipolitics of parochial, localist, quasi-combat-oriented militias, cults, and terrorist groups and those organizations with different modus operandi. A case in point is James Dobson's ambitious, well-organized, and media-savvy efforts to "take America back for Christ." According to Dobson and his nationwide legion of followers, the historical struggle between forces of good and evil in the United States—more sharply posed today than ever—must take a profoundly political direction if the Christian (good) side is to emerge triumphant. The ethos of retreat that typifies the cults and militias, for example, can only be self-defeating. Dobson's group shares many ideals with other right-wing groups—Christianity, free market, patriotism, traditional values—but these ideals are not paired with an interest in conspiracies, paramilitary operations, global scenarios, and the like. Rather, Dobson's aim is nothing less than to reclaim politics for a deeply conservative agenda by more conventional means: organizing, agitating, educating, and propagandizing as part of a "civil war of values" throughout civil society. Thus Dobson has taken his place at the center of a huge media network that features daily radio programs, magazines, books, seminars, conferences, and videos designed for the edification of a broad population. Instead of apocalyptic theories, paranoid tales, and military posturing, he offers practical solutions to everyday problems in the realm of family life, relationships, health, and education. As for the political arena itself, the Dobson organization works tirelessly to achieve concrete reforms, including legislation outlawing pornography and legalizing school prayer, to influence the Republican Party, and to shape the outcome of electoral campaigns. Moreover, there are continuous local and national efforts to build institutions that could leave a durable imprint on public consciousness and social life. In this respect Dobson and some of his allied movements have made remarkable gains in a relatively brief time span, both in gaining attention to their work and in molding public opinion.

Another (though less successful) case of right-wing political mobilization has been the Unification Church of Reverend Sun Myung Moon. More cultish than Dobson's groups, the Moonies too set out to create a "God-centered universe"—in this instance, combining Korean shamanism, numerology, and scientism with Christianity. The Moonies appeal mainly to conservative youth who want to be part of a clean-cut, patriarchal, God-fearing community. While the Reverend Moon has been championed as an earthly messiah, the Church has for the most part dispensed with millenarial visions and scenarios, opting instead to build a dynamic secular movement that pursues its goals openly in the public sphere.[34] Believers are expected to be not only devout believers in the faith but also politically active—as they were, for example, in the Presidential campaigns of Richard Nixon and Ronald Reagan. Over the past two decades they have conducted hundreds of canvassing drives in behalf of a wide variety of (conservative) issues and candidates. Using his own vast wealth, Reverend Moon founded the conservative daily *Washington Times* as well as the weekly periodical *Insight* and Paragon House publishers. As with the Dobson organization, his approach merges politics and culture in a multifaceted agenda that targets academia, the media, the arts, and of course politicians—all regarded as caldrons of liberalism and socialism. Moon financing also went into the founding of the Universal Ballet Academy along with several symphony orchestras, revealing a strong preference for "high" as opposed to mainstream or popular culture. The Unification Church has also sponsored seminars and workshops on dozens of topics around the country. Yet, despite these and other ambitious efforts, the Church ultimately failed to win the kind of popular support that Dobson's groups were able to mobilize, owing in part to a rigid sectarianism, in part to the irrelevance of its continued fanatical anticommunism. In fact, the Moonies were never more than a tiny (if loud) fringe group on the right, despite their considerable resources and their keen sense of political strategy.

A far more successful enterprise has been the Promise Keepers, a rapidly expanding organization founded in the early 1990s by former University of Colorado football coach Bill McCartney that, like other conservative groups, is deeply committed to restoring religious and family values. A special élan infuses the Promise Keepers, a product not only of McCartney's charismatic leadership but of the massive involvement of evangelical Christians who help to fill huge stadium venues with as many as 50,000 people. At such mass meetings one finds a quasi-ritual devotion to spectacle and highly emotional encounters that exhort men to reclaim their role as true patriarchal leaders of the nuclear family—a message (directed here mostly to whites) that parallels that of the Reverend Louis Farrakhan's Million Man March in 1995 that made similar demands on black males. Starting with a membership of only 70, the Promise Keepers was able to build a flourishing organization with an enrollment of 725,000 and a yearly budget of $115 million by 1996.[35] One key to its unique popular appeal is abundant references to sports and military imagery mixed with symbols of traditional innocence lost; adherents typically express feelings of pride and belonging after having joined this self-declared "Wartime Army of God." The Promise Keepers upholds a vision inspired by a new era of "prophets and disciples," when religious faith will no longer be split into rival denominations. While such traditional ideals are officially defined as "nonpolitical," they are disseminated with the aim of galvanizing a protracted cultural revolution linked to creative forms of public intervention, distinctly contrasting with the more insular modus operandi of the cults and militias. Replete with its own rock music and artifacts of modern technological society, the Promise Keepers is self-consciously oriented toward the mainstream even as it retains a strong presence in the right-wing Christian subculture, following the pattern of Jerry Falwell's Moral Majority during the Reagan–Bush years. Much as with Falwell, McCartney is determined to construct for himself a noncontroversial image of the devoutly religious traditional family man as model citizen.

As these examples reveal, reactionary populist tendencies in the United States are sharply divided between antipolitical formations like the cults and militias and more politically defined organizations like the fundamentalists and Promise Keepers. Even among the latter groups, however, there is a tension between emphatically political *methods* (that is, actively operating in the public sphere) and their own stated *objectives* (typically, a free market, reduced government, lesser roles for politicians). With regard to the former groups, there is always the provocative question as to whether they could ever make the transition from "primitive" to "modern" forms of activity—that is, whether they might eventually become politicized in some fashion. Since historical conditions can change virtually overnight, firm generalizations at this point about the fate of such tendencies would be quite premature. Hobsbawm writes that certain prepolitical groups (bandits, urban mobs, millenarial sects) did historically make this shift, with some of them being absorbed, for example, in the orbit of the Italian Communist Party (PCI) during the mass-based Resistance struggles of the mid-1940s. This transition could occur because antifascist mobilization cast such a wide, popular, nationwide net,[36] and the PCI was the main catalyst behind this powerful social bloc. For American cults, skinheads, gangs. and militias to be politicized along these lines would require a similar historical transformation implying even higher levels of social crisis and political upheaval where choosing sides would be seen as critical to one's survival. Even in such a scenario, however, reactionary populist tendencies would have to be so transformed that the ethos of retreat from true political involvement could finally be broken. But the deeply ingrained features of a highly depoliticized society would seem to work inexorably against just such a transformation.

A PRELUDE TO FASCISM?

A related and even more provocative question is whether reactionary populist groups might anticipate the emergence of a more mature fascist ideology and organization—whether, in fact, they could eventually mobilize large constituencies around a broader (and more politicized) fascist agenda. After all, fascism originated in Italy and a few other countries in a similar manner, first appearing in the form of paramilitary, messianic, and extreme nationalist groups, that, on the whole, lacked a coherent political design; these groups, then, movements, had many of the characteristics of modern reactionary populism.

European fascism was above all a virulent type of nationalism that, in most countries where it achieved success, strove for a maximum degree of social and political integration from above. Fueled by a collective sense of heroic, transcendent values that were expected to overcome the decadence and alienation that had previously corrupted civil society, fascism took shape as a distinctly populist ideology with a sprinkling of transformative impulses, but it was eventually driven by elites as the doctrine (such as it was) became incorporated into the organized realm of movements, parties, and regimes. What began as a highly diffuse *Volkgeist* associated with local interests and struggles was ultimately appropriated as a legitimating ideology for dictatorial elites.[37] It became the self-assigned task of these elites to forge a new national community that, in Italy and elsewhere, would be supported by broad sectors of masses who felt atomized and disenfranchised by the corrosive effects of modernity and the impotence of an archaic political system (a mixture of the old regime and liberalism). As Roger Griffin rightly stresses, fascism in this sense involved a complex dialectic of national rebirth and renewal growing out of the ashes of social decay—what he calls a "palingenetic form of populist nationalism" that was the "mythic core" of a new heroic patriotic worldview. In Griffin's words: "At the heart of the palingenetic political myth lies the belief that contemporaries are living through or about to live through a 'sea change,' a 'watershed,' or 'turning point' in the historical process."[38] Historical fascism thus appears as means to subvert not only those destructive forces associated with modernity, but also corruption, bureaucratic despotism, anarchism, social and cultural decline, weak political statecraft, and of course the ever present threat of the Left. It would be a thoroughly redemptive force—a theme that could easily be fastened to visions of national and racial supremacy, militarism, and rapid economic development. From there it was but a short leap to the idea that some form of authoritarian regime would be the logical outcome of fascist culture and ideology.

In the case of Italy, a thriving right-wing populist subculture, emboldened by flourishing *squadrista* (local militia) groups around the country, was able to develop into a mass movement and then the dictatorial regime headed by Benito Mussolini in a decade; a similar process took place in Spain, parts of Eastern Europe, and Germany. The emotional appeals to national rebirth cut across class lines, winning over a large percentage of workers and peasants as well as elements of the petty bourgeoisie, veterans, and elite sectors (the Church, big business, the military, the aristocracy). Fascism was a truly multiclass ideology—even if it wound up serving the interests only of the privileged groups. The capacity of strong charismatic leaders to unify such diverse groups around a common national banner was central to the political breakthrough of fascist movements and regimes. In Italy Mussolini was able to ride the crest of *ducismo* for 20 years. Yet, if charisma and the search for national purity were the order of the day, paving the way toward ideological fanaticism among many activists, the reality was that fascist organizations were intensely pragmatic in the way they conducted political business: they formed loose and temporary alliances, made compromises, and shifted positions (as necessary) on significant issues. All the while, of course, they remained faithful to the "palingenetic core" of beliefs that furnished their élan, their legitimacy, and their modernizing drive. In each case, moreover, fascist elites were adept at drawing on a wide variety of cultural and ideological themes, including irrational beliefs and romantic folkish yearnings that would probably be put under the heading "new-age mysticism" today. Such themes were crucial to the initial fascist assault on rationalism and modernity, which, however, was largely forgotten once the regimes consolidated power and set out on a path of rapid economic development. Folkish appeals were directed toward overcoming the growing psychological and spiritual void created by the familiar crisis of traditional values, notably religion; the masses had become available to new sources of meaning and authority.[39] Fascist ideas historically spread at times when traditional values and social relations were undergoing severe challenge—witness the situation in Italy after World War I, when a nearly successful revolutionary upsurge gave rise to massive chaos and breakdown. The palingenetic ideology upheld the vision of an entirely new kind of community that would modernize while at the same time restore important features of the old order, among them, religion, patriarchy, a strong nation, the family.

Striking parallels between the present-day American extreme Right and European fascism of the 1920s and 1930s clearly exist and deserve further analysis. Now (as then) growing sectors of the population feel threatened by forces beyond their control: the global economy, rapid technological change, massive bureaucracy, the mass media, and so forth. And now, as then, conspiratorial theories and millenarian prophecies are on the upswing, often inspired by deep-seated racial, ethnic, and religious identities as well as by media-induced fantasies. Each period too has been marked by intense backlash against progressive change—against the Left, "liberals," "socialists," and various popular movements. No comparison would be complete without mention of the gun culture, or *squadrista* mentality, that permeated Europe then as it does the United States today. Beneath all this is a growing popular disenchantment with the facade of normal politics, reflected today more than before by a generalized disgust with anything having to do with ordinary politicians, bureaucracy, and official discourse. European fascism culminated in a series of powerful reactionary movements and regimes attached to perhaps the most virulent ultranationalism in modern history, always enshrined in traditional verities and the sanctity of the common person. Today in the United States the scattered militias, cults, and fundamentalist groups are undoubtedly a long way from seizing state power, and there is probably no Mussolini, Hitler, or Franco on the horizon. Yet, the ideological affinity of such groups with earlier incarnations of fascism and neofascism, along with certain undeniable similarities in the historical context, cannot be overlooked.

At the same time, there are a number of critical and perhaps telling differences. First, Mussolini, Hitler, and Franco focused their attention on the realm of state power, in stark contrast to the insular, turf-oriented, localist antipolitics of modern reactionary populist groups. The fascist party-state set out to either destroy or incorporate autonomous groups and subcultures, albeit with mixed results. The state assumed primacy, if not in theory then at least in practice, becoming the repository of legitimacy and development; in most cases (Italy, Germany, Spain) the party actually wound up subordinated to the state system. As Mussolini once stated: "Everything for the state, nothing against the state, no one outside the state." Although such monolithic rule always remained outside the grasp, and probably the intentions, of fascist regimes, Mussolini's dictat nonetheless reflects the essence of fascist ideology. The very genius of fascist leadership in Europe resided in its capacity to forge a coherent social bloc of forces among widely dispersed and often conflicting groups; it was able to translate *social* insurgency into *political* action, which would have been impossible in the absence of a strategic preoccupation with state power.

Second, present-day reactionary populist groups lack a coherent, future-directed ideology that could give political shape to their vast assortment of antistatist beliefs and irrational fantasies. Their ethos is of retreat, it is not an aggressive plan to transform the order of things, to create new social and authority relations, to build an entirely new state. Mussolini insisted on a thoroughgoing revolution, a total rebirth of Italy in the spirit of a new "eternal Rome" that would rejuvenate the country "from top to bottom." National socialism at the time represented a kind of secular religion that, once accepted and internalized, would produce an entirely reborn human being. "Believe, obey, and fight for a new country"—that was Il Duce's injunction to the Italian masses.[40] The fact that such psychological regeneration was never fully realized does not detract from its immense influence during the early stages of fascist mobilization.

Finally, fascist movements and parties were able to seize state power in Europe because large sectors of the power structure—the aristocracy, the Catholic Church, big business, the military—swung over to the fascist side at decisive moments. The social bloc that empowered fascism in Italy and elsewhere was grounded in an uneasy but explosive coalition of elites and masses, traditional and modernizing groups, urban and rural constituencies. Such alliances were a major ingredient in the success of historical fascism. In the United States today, however, there are few signs of such a critical alignment: corporations, Wall Street, the Pentagon, and the bulk of the political establishment are all lined up resolutely against the extreme Right, particularly where destabilizing forms of insurgency or domestic terrorism enter the picture. The *squadrista* mentality of the armed groups is anathema to the elites; so too is the xenophobia, racism, and fervent localism that extends throughout the whole reactionary populist subculture, for it runs against the historical grain of economic globalization. Meanwhile the cults, fundamentalist groups, and militias, for their part, generally want nothing to do with the elites, nothing to do with politics.

Any modern authoritarian system that would go beyond the highly concentrated economic and political power that already exists must adopt an extreme corporatism. Elites would push for structures to more firmly regulate interest representation and popular involvement and would seek even more effective mechanisms to control public opinion. Such a corporatist scenario would eventually require vast mobilization of human, material, and technological resources from above, thus severely undercutting those pluralist-democratic norms now in place. For the extreme Right to engineer such an outcome seems rather implausible, for it would have to work in tandem with big capital, the military, and a whole spectrum of governing elites whose agenda is already rationalized. Clearly, the localized militarism and deep, often irrational, antipolitics of the extreme Right clashes with the globalizing priorities of elites, who remain committed to economic rationalization and political order on a large scale. In fact, the social and political alignments that made European fascism a viable option hardly seem conceivable in any of the advanced industrial countries today.

Protofascist or not, therefore, the contemporary extreme Right in the United States seems to be devoid of real transformative potential—even granting that this is part of their larger design (or would sooner or later become so). The classic European pattern does not appear ready to duplicate itself in the modern sociopolitical setting. As John Kautsky writes in his seminal analysis of the phenomenon: "Fascist *movements* have come to power only with the support of non-fascist elements, namely big capitalists and the aristocracy with its strongholds in the military and the bureaucracy, and frequently with its allies in the higher clergy." He adds: "Our analysis indicates that fascist totalitarianism is a product of some degree of underdevelopment and is not likely to appear in advanced industrial countries because for it to develop the aristocracy must have retained some positions of strength."[41] It is true, of course, that highly developed capitalist societies give rise to expanded sectors of the population capable of entering politics, to more diverse social interests, and to greater complexity of civil society, meaning that any highly integrated fascist regime would be virtually impossible to erect, or sustain. This is even truer in the United States, where—despite recent depoliticizing trends—traditions of pluralism, civic involvement, and even "limited government" remain largely intact.

Historical fascism appeared in nations like Italy, Japan, Germany, and Spain as a response to the ineptness or breakdown of the political system: grave social problems had been met with governmental paralysis. It would not be too far-fetched to suggest that precisely such a condition prevails in 1990s America, although it has not yet led to widespread upheavals as in 1920s Italy or 1930s Germany. Still, fascism as a form of palingenetic ultranationalism requires broad multiclass legitimation—a state ideology that stands above specific interests, above fragmented and parochial loyalties of reactionary populist groups like cults and militias. Its idolatry of the state would be a far remove from the militant antistatism of these groups. And the state itself would embody an even more hierarchical, centralized, perhaps militarized model of economic and political order. A shift of this magnitude would have to involve deep ideological and cultural transformations at all levels of American society. The critical question here is, from what sources, and under what conditions, could such total commitment to an all-powerful state by the majority of citizens arise? In the absence of this commitment, efforts to impose a right-wing authoritarian regime on a recalcitrant civil society would inevitably result in utter chaos.

It is often forgotten that historical fascism, even where it won mass support and conquered state power, ultimately failed on its own terms—and not simply because it was dismantled by war and its aftermath. The regimes either disintegrated from their own inner contradictions (Spain, Portugal) or clearly would have even had World War II not provided the final push (Italy, Germany, Japan). One of the fatal shortcomings of fascist elites, skilled though they were at mass mobilization, was their lack of any coherent, long-term strategy for economic development. Their ultranationalism and grandiose posturing could rouse patriotic passions and generate an initial modernizing upswing, but their plans were inevitably tentative and reactive, their goals unfocused and ephemeral; still tied to traditional, antiurban interests, they had no vision of how to create a truly modern economic order—quite in contrast to liberal capitalism, social democracy, or Soviet communism. Nor in all likelihood could the fascists ever had *administered* a modern system even if they had managed to build one. As Griffin argues, nationalism as a core ideology, reliant on folkish myths, cannot furnish an agenda for sustained modernization beyond short-term (and probably futile) forays into military adventure.[42] Thus, while Nazi Germany did create the world's first behemoth war economy, it was sustained for less than a decade, and that long only through recourse to wartime emergency footing. Moreover, the very modernizing forces that fascism set in motion would sooner or later have undermined the very foundations of the authoritarian system, much along the lines of what happened later in Soviet-style dictatorships. When viewed in the context of already modernized economies like the United States, fascism would have less viability as an alternative to even the most crisis-ridden corporate capitalist system.

THE AUTHORITARIAN IMPASSE

The spread of reactionary populist groups in a highly modernized setting raises questions about the future of American politics that go beyond the issue of fascism (or neofascism) as such. Assuming such groups will persist and even flourish, there are two possible scenarios: either further social polarization, leading to a downward cycle involving local retreat and further growth of an authoritarian state, or slow but steady evolution toward greater concentration of power in the rationalized state-capitalism system that we now have.

The Hobbesian solution to increased fragmentation and chaos in civil society evokes a familiar pattern throughout modern history: the huge Leviathan imposes order at a time of rapid change and sharpening conflict, when society appears increasingly "ungovernable." The protofascist tendencies that swept Italy, Germany, and Spain, for example, fed off the breakdown of established traditions and norms; Mussolini probably never would have come to power during 1922–1926 if not for the postwar insurrectionary tumult, and the deepening chaos and upheavals of the Weimar Republic preceding the Nazi rise to power are well known. In these cases, as in more ordinary authoritarian takeovers, the dictatorial state came into being as a Bonapartist reaction to the collapse of social order and political legitimacy, under conditions where effective governance had largely vanished. From this standpoint, while groups in the United States on the extreme right have to date mostly withdrawn from the public sphere, the resulting vacuum could precipitate conditions favoring a Leviathan: extreme localism, social fragmentation, civic violence, more maneuvering room for authoritarian elites. Such a Leviathan, of course, would not be likely to embrace overt fascist goals or symbols, at least not those associated with Nazism or classical fascism, since the residues of a "liberal" political culture in the United States would still be much too pervasive. We have already seen the rise of reactionary authoritarian regimes in countries such as Chile, Argentina, South Korea, Pakistan, Indonesia, and the Philippines—surely one manifestation of intensified civil wars and tribal conflict analyzed by Hans Enzensberger and others.[43] So far, however, this outcome has not been the fate of any highly industrialized nation.

The reality is that, today as before, the growth of a depoliticized culture and the threat of an authoritarian politics develop as opposite sides of the same coin, each tending to reinforce the other. Conditions favoring this dialectic are exacerbated by the process of economic globalization insofar as local populations feel increasingly disempowered by forces beyond their control. In this milieu, social polarization is less rooted in class struggle, or even conflict over rival political agendas and worldviews; rather, it is primarily a struggle between what Benjamin Barber calls "Jihad"—fierce, often violent, assertion of parochial identities—and "McWorld," the rationalized universe of multinational corporations and international finance. This struggle operates on two levels: to fan the flames of chaos and erode democratic participation in civil society, and to reinforce elite control in the state system.[44] Centrifugal tendencies deny or repress outcomes that might contribute to progressive social change.

It follows that the more intense the polarizing dynamic between Jihad and McWorld, the more difficult it will be to avoid the antinomies of chaos/anarchy and right-wing authoritarianism. Such a dialectic seems to have taken hold in late-1990s Russia. Further, as the global system expands, we encounter the erosion of historical and geographical boundaries (with Russia again offering a good example), thus reshaping our view of space in which politics gets defined and carried out.[45] In reality the commodified market dynamics of McWorld has no particular need for physical boundaries, no need for citizen loyalties beyond a willingness of people to work, pay obeisance to the governing symbols, and stick to their own turf. Here the very capacity to frame, let alone implement, some vision of the common good vanishes in an atmosphere of unbridled self-interest. For this reason the popular reaction against McWorld in the affirmation of local identities and terrain, in the escape from politics, makes a certain tortured sense. If such conditions do not necessarily make for a rebirth of classical fascism, they are surely compatible with the rise of a new Leviathan. As Barber writes: "In the tumult of this confrontation the virtues of the democratic nation are lost."[46] And herein lies one of the great dilemmas, and possible tragedies, of the current period.

As the corporate-state system further destroys local communities that make genuine participation, belonging, and autonomy possible, larger numbers of people are driven into privatized retreat and new forms of local solidarity—or into the arms of huge centralized institutions. The forces of economic and bureaucratic rationalization, reinforced by global pressures, seem to offer disenfranchised individuals only the most extreme alternatives: withdrawal or capitulation. In the words of William Ophuls: "Lonely, anxious, frustrated, powerless, and despairing individuals thrown back upon themselves alone are wide open to ideological and fundamentalist persuasion and defenseless against state power; fearful and lacking a firm sense of identity, they hunger for security and a sense of belonging; and to the extent they do not get them, they long for escape."[47] Such a trajectory, in Ophuls's view, could easily generate new modes of authoritarian power that might turn out to be functionally equivalent to historical fascism, in that it would aspire to higher levels of social and political integration. Ophuls fails to take into account the possibility of other outcomes. Even so, this more "totalitarian" version of the Leviathan would probably not share many features of classical fascism, for reasons outlined earlier. Concentration of power, even in reactionary hands, is much less likely to be monolithic, and it probably would not have to be. In a highly rationalized global system, moreover, there would be scarcely any justification for the more heinous elements of fascism: widespread terror, concentration camps, overt forms of racism and ultranationalism, wars of aggression.

A far more plausible outcome than any despotic Leviathan is the second one—steady growth of concentrated economic and political power in the framework of already existing rationalized state capitalism. Even if the reactionary populist groups continue to proliferate, they are unlikely to achieve enough social leverage and ideological clout to overthrow a deeply entrenched power structure that is so closely interwoven with the global market system. Further, any authoritarian (or even antistatist) impulses in civil society that embrace traditional values can easily be short-circuited by elites pressing for all-consuming forms of administrative control. As rationalizing pressures intensify economic globalization, we can expect a further diminution of both civic traditions and democratic participation as pluralist institutions and electoral politics remain more or less intact, offering a convenient facade for authoritarian rule.

Ironically, historical fascism achieved its greatest success in those societies where conventional right-wing interests were *weakest*, or were in disarray—as in Italy, Germany, and Spain. A political vacuum on the right enabled protofascists and fascists to maneuver more freely than in settings where the old Right remained a dominant force (as in Russia and China). In the contemporary United States, of course, reactionary authoritarian movements or parties with dictatorial ambitions have very little presence; the extreme-Right groups, as we have seen, are essentially localist and antipolitical. Nor is there a powerful established Church or aristocracy, or other preindustrial forces (peasantry, petty bourgeoisie), that are ready to support a fiercely conservative alternative to the status quo. It follows that the terrain on which protofascism might hope to develop into full-blown fascism is hardly fertile, at least in the United States. Such terrain is further muddied by persistence of a liberal-democratic legacy, however compromised. A more critical factor yet, however, is the steady buildup of centralized power in the United States, facilitated by a technocapitalism with authoritarian features that are already well known: war economy and security state, technological rationality, mass media, bureaucratization of social life, growing scope of executive power, and so forth. In this setting an administered order reproduces itself easily beneath the facade of liberal-democratic institutions, rendering the more fearsome version of a Leviathan obsolete if not dysfunctional. At the same time, even while such an authoritarian system dispenses with classical fascist trappings—ultranationalism, xenophobia, racism, folkish romanticism—it could even more effectively pursue similar goals, including expansion of the security state, spheres of global hegemony, and the taming of political opposition.[48] To the extent this trajectory holds, technocapitalism might well neutralize the power of reactionary populist groups, since what these groups augur—in contrast to historical fascism—is less a new rationalized order than it is heightened chaos or instability. This scenario, while perhaps appealing to members of various gangs, cults, militias, and survivalist groups, is hardly an attractive one to mass publics.

Surely corporate colonization in early twenty-first century America will depend far more on the workings of ideological hegemony than on the tools of institutional coercion or terror. If the "new world order" means anything, it refers to an administered system in which popular consciousness is shaped and contained by the media spectacle, the culture industry, the shopping malls, and the charade of democratic politics—all inducing privatized retreat, depoliticization, and withdrawal from the public sphere, against a backdrop of reinforced state–corporate networks of surveillance and controls. (Fascism, on the other hand, always set out to *mobilize* the masses, hoping to instill new modes of active participation—however narrow these turned out to be.) In such a rationalized, high-tech, globalized universe there seems to be little role for a Mussolini, Hitler, or Franco; instead of charismatic passions and adventurous schemes, what the system requires is more the routinized managerial intervention of market-oriented CEOs who reside at places like IBM, Bank of America, Mitsubishi, General Motors, and Walt Disney/ABC. Hence, the menacing incursions of reactionary populist groups in the United States represent not so much the harbinger of a coming fascist nightmare as the localized, defensive, antipolitical, and ultimately impotent response to globalizing forces that seem outside the purview of active human control.

CHAPTER 6

POLITICAL POWER
AND ITS DISCONTENTS

Popular hostility to government has been and continues to be far more than a phenomenon of the Right—or even a more generalized reflection of apathy, cynicism, and civil privatism in American political culture as a whole. It also extends, albeit in profoundly different ways, to the Left and to the multitude of progressive movements that have entered the public arena during the past two or three decades. Indeed, antipolitics of the "Left," while perhaps less widespread, offers a more fascinating topic of study in that its implications for future social change may be even more far-reaching. For both the Right and the Left, of course, we have in mind the development of manifestly depoliticized expressions of alienation that may or may not emanate from the margins of public life. The dramatic rise of antistatism in the United States since the late 1970s extends not only to the militias, skinheads, and cults but also to various identity-based movements, new-age and therapeutic approaches, local enclave cultures, urban gangs and insurrections, deep ecology, and other diverse expressions of postmodern intellectual life. While anything but homogeneous in outlooks, methods, constituencies, and long-term historical impact, these tendencies share an often self-conscious flight from politics that could, if sustained, be corrosive to positive social transformation. The Left too has been infected by contagious antipolitics.

The contemporary decline of leftist politics in most of the industrialized countries can be understood as one response to a drastic weakening of the public sector at a time when global capitalist hegemony appears to be increasingly solidified. Globalization creates the conditions favoring not only weakened national sovereignty but also fierce economic competition among actors in the world market, thus diminishing the scope of local politics. Antistatism gained added momentum from the crisis and then collapse of communism, which fed into the triumphal celebration of free-market capitalism and privatized consumption in Europe and North America that found its most poignant expression in Francis Fukuyama's "end of history" thesis.[1] When the eclipse of European Social Democracies is taken into account after the sad performances of the French, Spanish, and Italian socialist parties during the 1980s, the waning of a long and rich socialist tradition emerges as a watershed event that has been evoked to justify the most extreme (even utopian) forms of anti-statism. In this historical milieu the much ballyhooed "death of socialism"—and with it the discrediting of virtually any state regulation of the economy—has been widely interpreted to mean that state power is inherently corrupt, inefficient, and authoritarian. When coupled with the failures of the New Left, the predictable result is the growth of depoliticizing pressures in a Left that has always depended on various forms of political intervention to achieve transformative goals. Meanwhile, the time-honored concept of "left opposition" has atrophied as popular movements for change have become increasingly personalized, local, and fragmented.

UTOPIANISM IN THE NEW AGE

Since the 1960s, groups and tendencies that might loosely be called "new age" have flourished in the United States, attracting millions of people interested in spiritualism, astrology, goddess worship, crystal healing, Eastern philosophy, reincarnation, and related pursuits. As a kind of metaphysical, romantic escape from the murky secular world of politics, it embraces but goes considerably beyond what E. J. Hobsbawm means by "millenarianism."[2] The new-age revival has roots in the 1960s counterculture, which in its time drew from many sources both ancient and modern, as we have seen. Like the utopianism of early prophets, mystics, healers, and religious missionaries, metaphysical thinking encourages a search for empowerment, identity, personal renewal, even divine intervention in a society overwhelmed by change and uncertainty. It affirms the struggle for individuality, self, and autonomy in a situation where planned, collective action may seem altogether hopeless. And it seeks out transcendent values and sources of authority in a world where external forces may appear fixed, awesome, and irreversible. Significantly, too, its gaze lies essentially outside the public sphere, far removed from the difficult and brutal terrain of actual day-to-day politics.

The New Left, the counterculture, and later new-age movements all included struggles to recover a sense of self—to articulate and carry forward processes of consciousness transformation that were seen as resist-

ing the harsh regimen of technocratic capitalism. Advanced industrial society gives rise to massively powerful structures that, however, cannot be
overthrown until forms of personal autonomy are recaptured as part of
an ongoing cultural revolution that touches every area of social existence,
including work, culture, the family, sexuality, politics, and the entire flow
of everyday life. If structures of domination are embodied in a wide array
of hierarchical institutions, the commodification of society, and the social
repression of human needs, then only a deep, far-ranging process of
change could succeed in overturning this overburdening totality, beginning with efforts to subvert the multiple forms of ideological hegemony.
For 1960s radicalism (and later similar tendencies) the overriding problem was that the power structure could easily reproduce itself through the
intricate but often subtle workings of system-regenerating values, attitudes, myths, habits, and traditions that shape virtually every facet of popular consciousness. Hence, not merely the workplace but to arenas of education, mass media, and popular culture were regarded by the Left, as
vital zones of contestation. To one degree or another, this priority was
taken up by important offshoots of 1960s radicalism such as the ecology
and feminist movements, and by kindred theoretical traditions such as Critical Theory, humanistic Marxism, anarchism, and postmodernism. It was a
priority that countered not only the technocratic conformism of advanced
capitalist society but the main thrust of the Old Left, social politics, and
the conventional form of Marxism that was seen as overly economistic.

As Gramsci had predicted several decades before the 1960s, higher
levels of industrial development would elevate the "war of position" (ideological struggle) over the "war of movement," or the realm of political-
institutional maneuver.[3] This is so because modernity generates a far
more differentiated class structure, more refined modes of economic rationalization, a greater interweaving of state and economy, and the increasing role of ideas in holding power structures together. While such
trends were visible earlier in the century, they became more decisive after
the 1960s with the steadily broadening scope of state power, technology,
mass media, and higher education—above all in the United States. In this
post-Fordist setting it was natural enough for progressive movements to
address the role of lifestyle or consciousness transformation (Gramsci's
"counter-hegemonic" politics) in social change. Departures of this sort
were positive enough and ultimately necessary to break the historical impasse. After all, throughout the twentieth century, socialist parties—in and
out of power—have generally run up against the limits of their own
economism and statism, while the myriad reform efforts never made a serious dent in the powerful capitalist armor. One reason for this paralysis,
as Critical Theorists and humanistic Marxists emphasized as early as the
1920s, was the failure of socialists to systematically confront questions of

culture, ideology, and everyday life, including the dynamics of individual character structure (as Wilhelm Reich had already begun to theorize about in the late 1920s). As Reich, Erich Fromm, and others argued at the time, it was precisely this creative intervention into the sphere of popular consciousness that enabled to fascists to wrestle power from the Left in Europe between the wars. The long-anticipated breakdown of capitalism was thus resolved, in one country after another, to the advantage of right-wing dictatorships galvanized by a novel and virulent reactionary populism.[4]

What theorists like Gramsci, Reich, and Herbert Marcuse recognized was that far-reaching social transformation required deep changes in popular consciousness, which in turn meant that an assault on the power structure would have to be grounded in ideological shifts already well underway in everyday life, personality formation, and so forth. A commitment to cultural revolution of this sort was lacking in both the Leninist and social-democratic variants of the Marxist tradition. What this early Critical Theory or humanistic Marxism emphasized was a balance between macro and micro dimensions of struggle, between the strategic concerns of institutions and consciousness, between state and civil society; the sphere of politics was not to be jettisoned but was simply reincorporated into a more general transformational matrix. The war of position was never devalued or ignored. A few decades later, the New Left and derivative social movements—and even more emphatically the counterculture—fastened onto this radical departure from conventional socialist ideology, the terrain in the United States having been cleared by the special frailty of the Marxist tradition itself. Yet, the new tendencies embraced just one side of this equation: consciousness over structures, civil society over state, the cultural over the political. This dramatic turn was more pronounced, as we have seen, in the counterculture than in the New Left, which immersed itself in the public sphere. With the later emergence of new-age and therapeutic fads in the 1970s, the political side of the equation was lost altogether as the quest for self took increasingly metaphysical and spiritual directions. The search for meaning, the need to be part of something larger, now implied an escape from politics if not from society as a whole.

In the myriad articulations of new-age ideology that have surfaced in American society since the 1970s, through literature, cultural motifs, and lifestyle shifts, one overriding thematic stands out: the path to social change lies not in tampering with large-scale institutions but in transforming consciousness, demanding a renewal of everyday life, personal character, and spiritual values. Not the material or social conditions of existence but rather one's psychological state is decisive in this process; macro struggles in the absence of an underlying cultural revolution will be illusory or even destructive from the standpoint of individual well-being. Borrowing from Eastern religions and earlier forms of spiritual traditions while also building on countercultural motifs, new-age ideology presented an image of the world in which individuals are fully responsible for their own fate, can take control of their lives through the simple exercise of willpower, and can set out to achieve unlimited goals so long as such goals are in alignment with some definition of spirituality. Extreme subjectivity of this sort appealed to many white middle-class youth who felt alienated from the dominant materialist values, were insecure about the future, and were disinterested in conventional religion. It offered a source of hope and vision in an otherwise difficult and chaotic universe.

The idea that people could readily gain control of their lives without having to participate in the slow, frustrating work of collective organizing or messy politics was seductive to those weaned on the blandishments of liberal individualism. And of course the idea contained a few truths about the importance of psychological or even spiritual renewal in the dismal world of politics—truths that were never grasped by partisans of the "Old" Left. Thus, new-age guru Louise Hay's injunction that "we are 100 percent responsible for all our experiences"—a lesson contained in her classic *You Can Heal Your Life*—resonated among millions of people frustrated with politics-as-usual but nonetheless anxious to see fundamental changes in their lives.[5] The endless proliferation of such individual changes would presumably be enough to trigger desirable macro transformations that would in time galvanize the whole society. A paradigm shift in mass consciousness might help to pave the way toward solving previously intractible problems such as crime, poverty, environmental degradation, and illness. Popular spiritualists such as Hay, Marilyn Ferguson (*The Aquarian Conspiracy*), Marianne Williamson (*A Return to Love*), and later James Redfield (*The Celestine Prophecy*) were able to appeal to mass audiences as they moved into the ideological vacuum produced by the dominant instrumental rationality and effectively tapped people's hunger for a deeper sense of purpose.[6] The new age played on the quest for novelty too in its excursions along such paths as astrology, shamanism, crystal healing, goddess worship, reincarnation, and channeling.

The most ambitious effort to fashion a new-age manifesto was Mark Satin's comprehensive but quite readable *New Age Politics*, which appeared in 1978 just as multiple strains of the counterculture began to converge as part of an identifiable if not yet coherent "movement."[7] More historically grounded than the bulk of new-age literature, Satin's book found transformative significance in the feminist and ecology struggles of the period, which, however, he tried mightily to fit into the new paradigmatic shift; these movements were important precisely insofar as they transcended "politics" and could be integrated into a spiritual outlook. Satin conceded that efforts by movements and parties to win reforms might be useful here and there, but they could never be the heart of the matter. The all-important challenge was for people to recover a sense of self in opposition to the totalizing, repressive features of the industrial system. Satin was convinced that, in the end, the desired aim of a new harmonious world comprised of people fully in touch with nature and their inner selves would have to be realized outside of and against a hopelessly corrupt and dehumanizing institutional system.

From the 1970s through the 1990s new-age metaphysics has taken on many guises, sustaining a multi-billion-dollar industry with millions of adherents consumed by primal screaming techniques, channeling, rebirthing, psychic readings, dream therapy, UFO sightings, and so forth. While some of those explorations may have short-term psychological benefits, the very idea of consciousness transformation suggests a deeper long-term potential for both individuals and society as a whole. Many new-age advocates speak of the emergence of a new historical era in which new forms of cosmic unity and harmony would be generated. Beneath any differences in focus or methodology lies a binding perspective: reality is conceived in highly subjective terms, shaped by experience and intuition rather than logic and reason. Here it takes on those characteristics of liberal individualism that hold that people live essentially through and for themselves as more or less autonomous producers, consumers, and partakers of everyday life; as such, it reproduces important strains of the dominant ideology despite the familiar spiritualized rhetoric of "transcendence." As Michael Parenti observes: "New-age self-centeredness resembles the hyper-individualism of the free-market society in which it flourishes."[8] From this standpoint "society" appears as a complex of atomized subjects all independently seeking self-affirmation, all living in an objectless world where norms of social interaction and community—not to mention collective action for public goals—have little meaning.

If human beings are indeed architects of their own fate, achieving purpose and identity only through individual psychological or spiritual renewal, then social reality is bereft of any historical or political substance; it becomes essentially indecipherable. The ideological motifs advanced by Reich, Hay, Ferguson, Williamson, Satin, and their generation of metaphysical theorists contain the notion that the social realm amounts to nothing other than an arbitrary, perhaps irrelevant, construct in people's lives. Thus, the hundreds of millions around the world who suffer from abject poverty, sickness, racism, civic violence, and war are categorized as victims of "spiritual malaise" who can, with the requisite willpower and spiritual outlook, overcome the limits of their harsh circumstances. They can be makers of history (at least their *own* history) without having to confront obstacles imposed by class relations and power structures, without for the most part, needing to be "political."

Probably the most widely read new-age treatise is James Redfield's *The Celestine Prophecy* (1993), which sold more than eight million copies and was a bestseller two years in a row.[9] Redfield's main argument (presented in his baroque narrative style) is that the great "irrational conflicts" of the modern world have little if anything to do with external social reality and everything to do with problems of the inner self, the overriding issues of human life being preeminently psychological or spiritual. If at present human beings tend to be controlling, selfish, manipulative, and violent, the new millennium—owing above all to the great emancipatory potential of technology and changes in the nature of work—promises to bring equality, a sharing of power and resources. Such a historical shift, however, can take place only as people on a global scale begin to evolve toward new forms of "mystical consciousness," at which point "guided by their intuitions, everyone will know precisely what to do and when to do it, and this will fit harmoniously with the actions of others."[10] The new millennium will thus be one of "synchronicity," where people will be free to connect with "God's source of energy and direction."[11] The vagueness of Redfield's prescription is matched only by his failure to confront the intractible reality of economic and political power.

One of the most thorough and balanced presentations of new-age ideology is contained in the volume *Spiritual Politics: Changing the World from the Inside Out,* written by Corinne McLaughlin and Gordon Davidson with the intention of covering and situating all dimensions of the ideology. Their account is based on a personal odyssey spanning three decades and sets out to address the complex issues related to psychological transformation during a period of unprecedented change and upheaval. "Politics became all-consuming for us as activists in the 1960s," they write. "Finally, after much soul-searching, we each in our own way took time out for a retreat, realizing we had to turn in. We had to begin the inner journey and confront our own shadows, our own darkness—instead of seeing evil only outside ourselves and blaming the government and big corporations for all our problems."[12]

In the view of McLaughlin and Davidson, these problems cannot be solved until a critical mass of people begins the momentous search for an "Ageless Wisdom" they are convinced has been part of planetary life for millions of years. If the world is to be made better, it will have to take place "from the inside out," starting with demanding effort to find "karmic causes of global crises" such as poverty and ecological decay. Social change is energized by a "transmission of spiritual energy" that gives people the capacity to construct their own reality by aligning themselves with a mystical entity called the "Divine Will."[13] Only at this juncture will it be possible to replace "conflict" with "harmony." Thus: "The old approach to politics as a dirty business dealing merely with the exercise of power is transformed into a new one that elevates governance to a science of synthesis. When the underlying inner unity of humanity is honored, it is then possible to create harmony out of apparent diversity and conflict."[14] McLaughlin and Davidson conceptualize society as a global entity defined by process, interconnection, and a web of relationships that follows the lines of systems theory; there is a "constant circulation of human, planetary, and solar life forces" imparting content to all social activity. These forces, in the end, are governed by the Divine Will, which opens up new vistas and brings profound new insights into the "mystery" of world events.[15] In concluding, the authors suggest that "the underlying objective of the Divine Plan is to unify humanity into a subjective whole [and provide] a regular and rhythmic progression toward unity and synthesis in all areas of life." From this observation it is but a short step to claim that it is possible to interpret U.S. history itself as having been shaped by "Divine Guidance" of a higher power.[16] The governing themes of *Spiritual Politics* are broadly representative of the entire new-age tradition—from systems theory to Eastern philosophy, from astrology to goddess worship, from ecospiritualism to crystal healing. They also intersect with underlying currents of other forms like Gaia theology, deep ecology, and humanistic psychology since, as McLaughlin and Davidson argue, the great problems of our epoch stem from the fact that people are out of touch with the "heartbeat of the Earth." Social transformation, including ecological renewal on a global level, can be realized only in congruence with the "hidden spiritual causes of world events."[17]

As well-intentioned as advocates of metaphysical politics might be, their agenda marks a profound withdrawal from the public sphere, whatever their self-defined status as architects of a "new" (and more radical) paradigm. Despite its great infatuation with emancipatory ideals, new-age ideology represents a turning away from political discourse, methods, and strategies, a scornful disinterest in any belief system that addresses the importance of class forces and governmental power. The solution to worldly problems is left to the (always vaguely defined) intervention of transcendental forces or agents. It is surely no accident that, in the United States at least, the popularity of new-age theories arose just as the new social movements began to lose their momentum.

As Theodor Adorno found from studying the mass appeal of astrology in the 1950s, the flight into metaphysics often makes sense for people longing for comfort and stability in circumstances where the "anonymous totality of the social process" is so overwhelming that the very prospect of changing one's situation by political means appears self-defeating, a waste of time and resources. Metaphysical escape from pressing everyday concerns enables people to adapt more painlessly to the frequently over-whelming challenges and hardships of work, family, and everyday life. In the case of astrology there is also the search for higher sources of author-ity, the pursuit of cosmic significance in a remote, seemingly unintelligible universe while conceding that human will cannot hope to change the ma-terial conditions of worldly existence.[18] The result, according to Adorno, is "submission to unbridled strength of the absolute power"—a power that is no longer human but is ultimately stable in its distant and supposedly fixed character. Thus, the external authority of astrology serves to com-pensate for the individual's own feelings of weakness and futility, a sense of powerlessness in the face of unfathomable obstacles.[19] Adorno believed that such modes of retreat have a stronger pull in a social context where the liberal ideals of freedom, rights, and individualism have been sub-verted by the growing imperatives of hierarchical organization and mass culture.

What Adorno discovered on the basis of his exhaustive review of astro-logical literature was that metaphysical discourse, while presenting itself as an alternative paradigm, in fact turned out to be perfectly compatible with the dominant ideology—for example, in its nearly obsessive attention de-voted to money, achievement, status, and material gain. Thus: "The stars seem to be in complete agreement with the established ways of life and the habits and institutions circumscribed by our age."[20] Readers of astrological columns were typically addressed as being anxious and frustrated, often desperately in need of solutions to their personal problems. (Such prob-lems, of course, were never contextualized or explained in relation to social or historical conditions.) A common piece of advice was to "be happy," though happiness was generally viewed as behavior or a state of mind more or less consonant with established social patterns; the universal logic of the stars allowed for individualism but simultaneously enforced conformity. More specifically, astrology catered to subjective experience and intuition but never pushed this experience and intuition beyond the confines of a highly rationalized hierarchical world. In this fashion the illusion of free choice was attached to a pseudoscientific belief system that appeared to em-brace universal properties.[21] In Adorno's view, the seductive power of metaphysics lies in the profound reluctance of most people to recognize their human frailty—their strong feelings of dependency and impotence—in an environment where power and wealth may seem close at hand but where in fact such power and wealth is quite concentrated and remote. Herein lies the "scientific" value of astrology that, like spiritualism, pro-vides self-confidence born of certitude.

Adorno's thesis on the depoliticizing role of astrological thinking had much in common with Erich Fromm's thesis in his seminal *Escape from Freedom* written some two decades earlier. Fromm wrote that the growth of individual autonomy in modern society enhances freedom but can also lead to loss of identity and security—a loss that is often resolved by means of flight from individual self-oriented activity into submission to a higher power.[22] A dynamic of this sort was at work in the rise of European fascism, where formal political freedoms were reduced to shreds once an authoritarian, xenophobic mass psychology took hold of large populations; in some cases people chose the strength and clarity of a Führer or Duce over their own fragile, anxiety-ridden individuality. Psychological mechanisms of escape, of course, do not always point to a fascist dictatorship or even to authoritarian politics. Quite the contrary: the search for millenarian or spiritual outlets, as Adorno observed, can have an even greater resonance in societies where liberal values are more deeply ingrained. Under these circumstances, instead of a fascist dictator, the "higher power" could just as easily turn out to be a cult, guru, therapeutic movement, brotherhood of militias, or the worshipping of a Divine Plan.

Fromm believed that certain psychological impulses toward escape would intensify as impersonal forces in bureaucratic mass society came to overwhelm the individual (giving rise to even more widespread loneliness, anxiety, and fear), and would most likely surface at times of economic crisis. Personal empowerment would be strengthened through identification with a Promethean external force, as Adorno suggested in the case of astrology. But this "submission to extra-personal ends," while offering a sense of historical purpose in the short term, produces retreat from active engagement in anything resembling a democratic public realm insofar as subjectivity is now transferred elsewhere.[23] Here the self achieves a (false) sense of independence and power, lacking in the worldly domain in which there are enormous material and psychological hurdles. Metaphysics, in common with authoritarian ideologies, elicits a feeling of catharsis that comes from submitting to the unfathomable power of "anonymous totality" mentioned by Adorno. But the active self, the self of citizenship and collective solidarity, winds up submerged in the process.

Much the same logic applies to a phenomenon such as goddess worship, an expression of spiritual politics grounded in the convergence of feminism and ecology that first gained a wide following in the early 1980s. A strong component of ecofeminism, it reveals women's supposedly unique relationship to nature by glorifying the early Neolithic period. Drawing on various metaphysical traditions, it sees women's connection to nature as "divinely immanent," but without linking such a cosmology to specific historical conditions or social forces. Spiritual concerns are so overwhelming that they tend to crowd out space for collective pursuit of concrete feminist and environmental goals in the public sphere. As Janet Biehl argues, "the more radical feminists who initiated that movement recognized that the full equality of women could not be achieved without far-reaching changes in all structures of society. By contrast, ecofeminism's sweeping but highly confused cosmology introduces magic, goddesses, witchcraft, privileged quasi-biological traits, irrationalities . . . and mysticism into a movement that once tried to gain the best benefits of the Enlightenment and the most valuable features of civilization for women."[24]

Ecofeminist denigration of politics comes across most clearly in the role assigned to the household, or domestic sphere, as the main source of women's identity and self-oriented activity. Biehl shows that the eco-feminist idea of community does not really go much beyond the *oikos* (household), which takes clear precedence over the *polis*; indeed "women's values" gain expression almost exclusively in boundaries of the *oikos*. While a vibrant domestic life can be a strong bulwark of community, a stubborn truth has persisted, namely, that it is only in the public sphere that human interaction and decision making have distinctly society-wide implications. In romanticizing the household, therefore, goddess worship puts forth a parochial vision of social life in which politics is either dissolved into the *oikos* or relegated to a male-dominated *polis*. In either case, the ideal of citizenship is ultimately broken up and destroyed.[25] This "feminist" withdrawal from politics constitutes a form of inverted statism insofar as it allows the patriarchal state apparatus to wield power with relatively few impediments.

While the search for spiritual wholeness and universal togetherness, along with quick panaceas for multilayered social problems, has been a constant feature of human history, never has this search given rise to such a large and influential subculture as in the United States since the 1960s. For millions of Americans it has become the defining motif of the times. New-age ideas in many guises proliferate in a society dominated by inaccessible bureaucratic organizations and dispirited by the crumbling of traditional belief systems—including not only religion but the core liberal ideology itself. As Jürgen Habermas argues, a system held together mainly by instrumental rationality is bound to generate repeated crises of legitimization;[26] the current popularity of metaphysical options is unquestionably a reflection of such crises. Individual attachment to new-age thinking is both convenient and reassuring in its promise of security and transcendence. It may be comforting to believe that social or institutional change cannot take place until requisite personal changes are achieved, that there is no distinction between victim and victimizer (which means no target has to be confronted), that historical analysis of actual, living, concrete social forces is unnecessary, and that political activity is destined to be just a waste of time. The rationale for privatized withdrawal into the realm of "self-development" and personal consumption is thus fully established. This is hardly coincidental since, as Parenti aptly points out, beneath all the spiritual rhetoric of "transcendence" and "harmony"—beneath the lofty critiques and disavowals of "politics"—lies the age-old pursuit of material gain in a society that fetishizes possessive individualism.[27]

Spiritual politics therefore amounts not so much to a new politics as an end of politics, where authoritarian rule, social hierarchy, and the capitalist market coexist with a growing devaluation of the public sphere. New-age millenarianism represents a false overcoming of alienation in which "opposition" to existing values and institutions masks a profound cynicism or fatalism regarding prospects for social change. As Dana Cloud suggests, metaphysical pursuits inevitably add up to a concession that the capitalist system is stable and bound to last indefinitely.[28] Even granting its professed transformative intent, however, utopianism of this sort indulges the same low sense of political efficacy that is so widespread in the culture as a whole. One function of such ideas is that they frequently nurture dreams of a flight from society *in toto*—dreams that, as Harold Bloom writes, have become particularly strong in the United States with the emergence of a "post-Christian" ethos.[29] The perpetual search for harmony, spiritual oneness, and divine intervention—realizable largely outside the public sphere—marks a profound turning away from politics that, by the 1990s, had made a deep imprint on American society.

THE THERAPEUTIC REVOLUTION: ALIENATION DEPOLITICIZED

The yearning for spiritual self-affirmation in a turbulent society has its parallel in the sustained popularity of therapeutic approaches, methods, and ideologies since the early 1970s. Like new-age mysticism, the human-potential movement and its various offshoots has deep roots in the 1960s counterculture, but it traverses quite different (though sometimes overlapping) paths.[30] These paths cover a seemingly endless array of psychological solutions: transactional analysis, humanistic therapy, bioenergetics, Est, family systems, encounter groups, and self-help methods, not even considering all the recovery movements inspired by Alcoholics Anonymous. This emergent therapeutic culture thrives on popular efforts to understand and overcome alienation at a time when the consequences of social dislocation and political retreat are increasingly visible. Much like new-age ideology, this culture frequently speaks the language of consciousness transformation, human liberation, and global harmony. Yet, it also absorbs and helps reproduce the same powerful depoliticizing trends discussed elsewhere.

The vital role of ideological and cultural work in social transformation today is no longer really debatable, as we have learned from the contributions of humanistic Marxism, Critical Theory, the New Left, and more recently, the feminist and ecological movements. In this legacy the concerns of psychological renewal and self-actualization always loom large, giving added depth and meaning to collective action; the personal and the political are intricately connected. One problem with the contemporary reassertion of the self, even when embedded in the rhetoric of social change, is that individual subjectivity is so often pitted *against* the public sphere and *against* the ideals of citizen participation and political obligation. As Tocqueville and subsequent observers of the American scene have found, individualism can be a highly problematic notion given the perpetual tension between the personal and social realms, between self and society—a tension aggravated by the extreme capitalist emphasis on economic self-interest, competition, laissez-faire, social Darwinism, and so forth. Extreme forms of possessive individualism tend to corrode democratic politics insofar as they devalue efforts to formulate a general interest.

Historically, liberal definitions of worthwhile or fulfilling activities for individuals have conflicted with the norms of planning, regulation, and community action—not to mention the prevailing organizational culture of the twentieth century. Predictably enough, individual desires to break free of external restraints, to pursue immediate wants and aspirations with little regard for the common good, has intensified with the blockage of those very wants and aspirations by corporate and bureaucratic domination. If individual self-expression assumes either economic or psychological forms in the wake of declining religious identities, the psychological side has increasingly come to the fore with the growth of corporate and state power along with social disintegration of communities, neighborhoods, and families. Deepening personal alienation is revealed by a long list of symptoms: crime, violence, substance abuse, suicides, high divorce rates, mental illness, and an enormous variety of medical problems. This persistent reality underlies the emergence of a therapeutic culture that, for many, provides a mechanism for breaking free of conventional moral and institutional restraints.

As writers like Philip Rieff and Christopher Lasch pointed out long ago, therapeutic culture is built upon a wide range of character disorders, anxieties, fears, phobias, and dysfunctions—geared mainly toward progressive middle-class whites. Although personal-growth techniques address genuine issues, their one-sidedness has inevitably pushed the conflict between the individual and society, private and public, emphatically in favor of the former. Whereas popular movements (civil rights, feminism, ecology, and so on) generally affirm collective values and action, the therapeutic shift tends to focus on the self in a way that detaches individuals from their social context. This phenomenon is understandable enough, problematic as it might be for the development of transformational politics. After all, as Paul Wachtel argues, the instrumental rationality endemic to capitalism works mightily against the personal struggle for identity and purpose, reproducing instead a manipulated, objectified population.[31] Attempts to recover a sense of subjectivity, however confined, under these circumstances cannot be dismissed as mere self-indulgence or escapism. The "economic" persona of possessive individualism has been privileged throughout the history of modern capitalism, allowing little room for creative expression in noneconomic realms; business culture has been thoroughly hegemonic.[32] This situation is exacerbated by the growth of both large-scale organization and technology over the past few decades. Reassertion of the "psychological" (or even "religious") persona offers prospects for restoring a vision of self defined according to noneconomic or more purely expressive criteria. The problem with the new therapeutic culture is not so much its focus on the inner self but rather its obsession with a self-contained psychic world cut off from relationships grounded in work, family, social life, and of course politics. What emerges from this is an artificial, one-dimensional construct of self that lacks important social referents.

A heightened preoccupation with the self, while perhaps unavoidable in modern society, tends to produce modes of self-absorption that readily coexist with everyday cynicism and political withdrawal. As Russell Jacoby observes, once the psychological realm is understood as an autonomous, self-enclosed bundle of forces, the individual ultimately winds up disempowered, losing the capacity to act on external reality; the person becomes an "objectless subject," permitting himself/herself only the most hollow and abstract forms of subjectivity. In his critique of the humanistic tradition of Abraham Maslow, Rollo May, and others, Jacoby sees profoundly depoliticizing implications: the almost frenetic search for inner freedom produces a kind of pseudoself trapped in a confining emotional immediacy.[33] In such a paradigm there is no way to distinguish between social reality and psychological illusion, between the active subject and the agent of history. The cult of pure subjectivity represents an abstract negation, and thus a conformist replication, of existing class and power relations. Jacoby writes: "The more the development of late capitalism renders obsolete or at least suspect the real possibilities of self, self-fulfillment, and actualization, the more they are emphasized as if they could spring to life through an act of will alone."[34] Instead of leading to a supposed recovery of self, the therapeutic process, in short, may reflect the modern individual in advanced stages of disintegration. What Jacoby argued in the mid-1970s would appear to be even truer in the late 1990s.

The proliferation of countercultural therapies and human-awareness programs has been accompanied by an ever more elaborate society of the spectacle, which encourages diverse kinds of ersatz subjectivity as refracted through media images and symbols. Much like new-age mysticism and humanistic psychology, the "self" of a media-saturated world of TV, radio, and other forms of popular culture unfolds in the absence of a viable object. In a society where pursuit of identity so often moves in the world of media-driven images, where public voicing of opinions and feelings (a staple of the omnipresent talk shows) is common fare, it is extremely difficult to find connections between individual self-directed activity and collective action in the public sphere. Where the spectacle reigns supreme, as it has for so many years in the United States, so too does the hegemonic pattern of discourses. The quest for self-renewal is simultaneously celebrated and denied in the absence of ongoing *structures* of social interaction, giving rise to a diffuse, "postmodern" subjectivity expressed in and through the spectacle. As Guy Debord put it in *Comments on The Society of the Spectacle* (1988, on his own 1983 work) the incessant flow of images in the culture consumes virtually everything in its wake, leaving a world of "impartial and total logic" toward which the individual feels utterly powerless. Without space for response, or "room for reply," the public sphere inevitably atrophies; the spectacle thus impoverishes all social and political life.[35]

In such an environment the words, gestures, and symbols expressed by ordinary people easily take on a reactive and hyperbolic character, feeding into what we have come to experience as a "complaint" or "victimizing" culture along the lines depicted by Robert Hughes and Richard Sykes, where personal grievances, dysfunctions, addictions, codependencies, and family conflicts are aired openly, regularly, and vigorously.[36] Where subjectivity is so extensively shaped by media culture, replete with rapidly shifting and often confusing or distorting frames of reference, it often becomes refocused away from the public realm, which now becomes increasingly blurry and remote. In the case of the Persian Gulf war, for example, a massive upsurge of (superpatriotic) ideological outpourings provided an ephemeral sense of American identity but turned out to have relatively little lasting substance. After a quick and bloody military campaign, the war ended, little changed, and the popular catharsis evaporated. Much the same could be said of the O. J. Simpson murder trials: the spectacle mobilized identities around race and gender, but it did anything but channel these identities into something politically meaningful; compelling social issues were mystified and deflected while "identity" consciousness encompassed everything that transpired. Somewhere in this morass the very subjectivity that surfaces so dramatically gets lost in the inflated totality of media hyperrealism while politics vanishes into an ideological haze.[37] Where political discourse is so corrupted, the concept of the public ends up similarly corrupted and devalued. It is hardly a coincidence that the great popularity of therapy-oriented talk shows on radio and TV has come in the wake of the therapeutic shift in American society.

By reinvigorating the ideology of individualism in a highly impersonal world of mass media, bureaucracy, and corporate colonization, therapeutic culture offers predictably formulaic (and thus conformist) solutions to intricate personal problems, often in the garb of progressive values. These solutions are marketed by an impressive array of therapists, counselors, medical doctors, media pundits, and talk show hosts whose task is to help people arrive at a sense of identity and empowerment with respect to a host of threatening phobias, anxieties, fears, abuses, disorders, and illnesses. From this standpoint it is relatively easy to view crucial social problems (the environment, military conflict, civic violence) as little more than derivative of personal ones, so that a micro transformation of attitudes and perceptions ("visualize world peace," get in touch with your body or with nature) on a large scale becomes the foundation of macro changes.

Here it is easy to see that discourse stressing the influence of social factors on individual behavior can be easily dismissed as an escape from personal responsibility—a view shared by new-age and therapeutic ideology alike.[38] Hence, an ordinary interest in therapeutic treatment leads to an excessive psychologization of politics.[39] This indeed may have been the implicit message of humanist intellectuals such as Carl Rogers, Abraham Maslow, Rollo May, and (to a lesser extent) R. D. Laing. The fact is that the new psychology did little to refurbish a sense of citizen obligation and democratic participation, above all because the subjectivity it celebrated was largely detached from its social and political milieu. The communitarian ideals of Rousseau, Marx, the anarchists, liberals like J. S. Mill, and even the New Left simply disappeared in this therapeutic ethos, which did, however, contribute significantly to the development of new social movements in the 1970s.[40] Change was generally oriented toward individual agents, not collectivities, or it was placed in the hands of experts and leaders. Where people are reduced to a "bundle of impulses and traumas," as Sykes observes, then all semblance of social individuality disappears along with the very notion of historical actors.[41]

By far the most popular (and most lucrative) form of therapeutic culture has followed the self-help model, which is designed to address issues of codependency, dysfunction, addiction, and abuse, relying largely on the "disease" paradigm made legitimate by Alcoholics Anonymous. While this model has been in vogue since the early 1960s and in fact goes back as far as the 1930s, it became a fad in pop psychology during the 1980s with the rapid spread of 12-step programs, the influence of "recovery" experts like John Bradshaw, and the attention devoted to struggles of victims, addicts, and the abused on such TV talk shows as those hosted by Oprah Winfrey and Geraldo Rivera. This "movement" has been energized by the appearance of thousands of books, seminars, videos, and lectures on how to resist and overcome "toxic" influences in one's life—from bad relationships, to work problems, to a wide range of mental and physical illness. Decisive to the recovery process is the capacity for self-affirmation: writing one's own script, breaking free of codependencies, finding one's "inner child," getting in touch with one's own feelings and one's own body, moving closer to nature, and so forth. It is a discourse strongly influenced by Jungian psychology, which has consistently dwelled on the importance of rediscovering the pure, innocent, powerful inner self that lies just beneath the frail, corrupted, disempowered individual presence of everyday life. It also connects with the traditional American motif of puritan self-improvement, where economic and religious modes of participation converge. More recently, the AA groups have built on these ideas in their development of a methodology to combat alcoholism and drug abuse, linking self-help techniques with reliance on a "higher power."

While the main trajectory of the self-help movement may seem innocuous or even positive enough, its definition of self nonetheless remains problematic, largely because individual affirmation or recovery is understood as taking place in its own self-contained sphere, far removed from the difficult vagaries and temptations of social life. In such a closed therapeutic universe virtually anything the recovering individual wills is thinkable and possible, but the will is isolated and atomized just as it is in new-age mysticism and humanistic psychology; the possibility of any collective or public will is ignored or, more likely, denigrated.[42]

Yet, the fate of the victimized but struggling self is far more complicated. Turning to the immensely popular 12-step programs, victims become quickly immersed in "disease" theory, which the groups invoke to explain and treat many types of destructive habits, addictions, and dysfunctions, ranging from drugs and alcohol to gambling, sex, eating, and even shopping. The onset of "disease," of course, requires some type of expert analysis and intervention, much as it does in more conventional medical and psychological approaches; where there are experts, of course, there are followers and believers. In the case of AA, moreover, there is also the ritual of recovery meetings, the processes, steps, and jargon of self-help, and the frequently invoked "higher power." In reality, therefore, what the self wills is considerably less than what might be regarded as free and open; on the contrary, it is perpetually mediated and restricted—by experts, by the rules of process, by the "higher power"—giving rise to a psychology of surrender rather than one of affirmation.

The 12-step emphasis on surrender to the "disease" model and the higher power is infused with quasi-religious premises that undermine independent thinking, skepticism, and making connections between the problem of addiction and the social conditions surrounding it. Of course,

the "disease" approach functions to render such connections superflu-
ous—the addictions are strongly influenced by biological conditions. It is
an approach where human beings, reduced to their endemic frailties and
sicknesses, are afforded nothing more than day-by-day resistance against
their darkest impulses. Self-help therapies rarely entertain genuine debate
over the way drugs and addictions are defined in American society; what
policies, methods, and treatments actually work; what social and environmental factors need to be brought into the equation; or even whether invoking a "higher power" actually works. People who want to restore their
health and lives follow a well-developed script laid down by the program,
forever compelled to avoid the dangers of a toxic world and its myriad diseases and temptations. In such a controlled (but always fearsome) milieu
there is little space for new empirical insights, policy debates, or questioning of mainstream values.

The disease model coincides with general intellectual trends that seek
to translate human problems into biological, genetic, or medical ones and
that, therefore, effectively denigrate the social context of behavior, that is,
the material conditions, the environment, what goods people consume. In
the dialectic between human willpower and the environment in which it
must assert itself, willpower is losing. For all the emphasis on subjectivity,
the self remains overwhelmingly passive, an inert receiver of external influences—in this case, the mysterious "disease" agents that, though presumably rampant in society, have never been proven as a principal cause
of alcoholism, much less out-of-control gambling or shopping. People
emerge as hopeless victims of their addictions and dysfunctions that, once
detected, will likely persist for life, thereby necessitating eternal vigilance. As Stanton Peele argues, this medical conception of self-development is both scientifically bogus and ideologically conformist—in other
words, hardly consistent with any enlarged vision of citizenship or social
change.[43]

It follows that, contrary to all claims, the self-help and 12-step programs are above all disempowering: in a world composed of abusers, victims and "recovering" victims, disease agents and the afflicted, the very
idea of social movements comprised of active, creative, free-thinking subjects becomes untenable. The only possibility is individual recognition of
necessity, or adaptation to a prestructured recovery agenda that, as we
have seen, is shaped by exceedingly narrow premises. In Peele's words:
"Because internal (psychological) and external (environmental) factors are
given short shrift in disease views, we lose hope of changing our
worlds."[44] If the new-age mode of self-absorption was excessively optimistic in its millenarian view of a harmonious future, here we have a far more
pessimistic, resigned view of self in which alcoholics, for example, likely
face an irreversible lifetime affliction, condemned forever to be victims of

ill-defined biological factors. Without any supportive evidence, the act of consuming particular substances (drugs, alcohol, glue fumes) is set apart from the rest of life, from the social totality—from all that the individual thinks and does. Fixed labels imprison the self in an objectifying, fatalistic worldview.

The idea that collective activity might qualitatively improve the situation of *both* the individual and the group, both the person and the society, is never seriously entertained. In its place we get moralizing sermons, hysterical attacks on "drugs" (ignoring the fact that we already live in a well-established and highly profitable drug culture), implausible scare scenarios, and ritual accusations of "denial" against those who do not or cannot recognize their "disease." In the end recovery theory serves to justify a massive retreat from an enormous range of social and political issues that must be confronted if lasting solutions are to be achieved. Peele writes: "The disease theory of alcoholism and addiction is an elaborate defense mechanism to prevent us from examining those things that—individually and as a society— we fear too much and do not believe we can deal with."[45] What Peele has in mind here is one of the greatest of all human fears, the fear of change.

Meanwhile, as the self-help and addiction industry becomes more popular and lucrative, the magnitude of substance abuse in the United States—one of the great mechanisms of privatized escape from alienation— continues to grow apace. And the capacity for citizen participation is further undermined by the spread of addictions and medicalized, expert-driven recovery programs alike, which perpetuate a condition of powerlessness. Subjectivity is obliterated either in the haze of habitual excess or in the highly rationalized, controlled world that lies outside the self. Any transformative politics requires the capacity to act—not simply by and for individuals but also by and for the whole. Effective action in turn demands more or less open communication, widely dispersed information, and organizational leverage. The therapeutic culture embraces the first of these but denies or minimizes the other two as *distractions* from the basic aim of self-affirmation. Even in the framework of self-help groups, therefore, the quest for personal liberation amounts to yet another, in this case quite virulent, rejection of politics.[46]

The antipolitics of the recovery movement flows logically from the disease model and the related cult of victimhood, as both Peele and Wendy Kaminer have persuasively argued.[47] The 12-step formula, ostensibly the sine qua non of empowerment, winds up as one of the most powerful rationales for disengagement from the public sphere. As Kaminer observes, such programs entail no vision of citizenship, no understanding of collective action, no guide to worldy social involvement beyond "recovery."[48] It might be argued that the recovery function alone is adequate so long as it can bring people out of their self-destructive cycle. But there is no evidence to support such inflated claims—in societal terms or even at the level of individual substance abuse. While individual treatment obviously has an important place, more general, lasting solutions will have to be found elsewhere, in the complex dialectic between self and society where the concerns of joblessness, poverty, crime, urban crisis, and social dislocation are taken more fully into account, where "solutions" are largely removed from the punitive criminal justice domain.

There is no universal law dictating a separation between the private and the public, between the tasks of therapy and the imperatives of social change; on the contrary, these disparate realms must be reunited if either aim—personal liberation or social change—is to be fully realized. In Paul Wachtel's words: "Only a false understanding of the nature of individual fullfillment pits concern with personal psychological development against a commitment to a better society." He adds: "It is not psychology that is our problem; it is the wrong psychology."[49] While it is an article of faith in the therapeutic enterprise that social concerns merely serve to muddy and compromise individual pursuits, the reality is just the opposite. An explicitly socialized therapy process *enhances* self-affirmation along severed poles: it addresses the causes of alienation, establishes a collective basis of interaction and sharing of problems, broadens the notion of (social) individuality, and permits individuals to embrace larger, more positive, more change-oriented visions of the future. Therapy grounded in fear, anxiety, and insecurity, in the fetishization of the pure inner self, is inevitably regressive and also thoroughly depoliticized. There have been glimpses of alternative models in the recent past, including Wilhelm Reich's famous Sex-Pol movement in Germany toward the end of the Weimar Republic, where a mixture of neo-Marxian and neo-Freudian insights was employed at dozens of local clinics around the country. Politicized forms of therapy later found expression in some New-Left encounter groups, feminist consciousness-raising projects, and a multitude of radical, movement-oriented, and psychoanalytic models that, in one way or another, affirmed the nexus between personal and political, between self and society. But these forms remain on the margins of a far more extensive depoliticized therapeutic culture.

LOCALISM AND THE ENCLAVE CULTURE

As Tocqueville observed, civic associations and multiple expressions of local democracy were integral to American political life from the earliest days of the Republic. However compromised by slavery and limited suffrage, the system did represent a model that departed from the European *ancien régime,* enabling citizen participation to exist and eventually flourish. The Jeffersonian tradition grew out of a vision of local self-directed activity and ongoing governmental renewal that demanded a vigilant and informed citizenry. Both the abolitionist and women's suffrage campaigns drew from this inspiration, as did the earliest Populist and Progressive movements, which sought to redraw the boundaries of both national and local governance. The themes of democratic revitalization still resonate today—the challenge to centralized economic and political power, the fight against corruption and injustice, the integration of marginalized groups into the political process, the struggle to make government more broadly accessible. It was the late-nineteenth-century Populists who most fiercely championed the ideal of participatory democracy built on a thriving local community—a project enlisting some of the best ideas of Rousseau, Paine, Thoreau, and Jefferson.[50]

More recently, beginning in the 1970s, urban community-based groups influenced by Saul Alinsky's ideas have appeared by the hundreds throughout the United States, fueled by diverse constituencies and issues but all riding the crest of a populist revival. Going back to the 1930s, Alinsky had departed from conventional left-wing organizing that emphasized socialist ideology, class struggle, and mass-based organization, choosing instead to mobilize around specific issues in a *community* framework devoid of any clearly defined ideology. His priority was to work for the empowerment of urban groups previously marginalized or in some way disaffected from the power structure. From World War II into the 1970s, Alinsky's organizing schema coincided with the prevailing mood of a political culture in which Marxism seemed to have little relevance to the major popular movements of the time, class was declining as a factor in popular consciousness, and the cold war had made Americans suspicious of "imported" or "alien" ideologies. In the postwar milieu adopting an "ideological" stance typically meant identification with authoritarian or statist models derived mainly from the Soviet experience. In its place Alinsky pushed a hard-nosed, pragmatic, but also confrontational style more in sync with American traditions, including classical populism; his aim was to develop, above all, a stratum of skilled and trained organizers who could take on the power structure.[51]

Since the 1970s new populist theorists like Harry Boyte, Sara Evans, Derek Shearer, and Lawrence Goodwin have championed local urban-based movements as the basis of a potential "backyard revolution" (Boyte's phrase), while radicals like Kirkpatrick Sale and E. F. Schumacher envision such forms as the framework of a decentralized, human-scale politics.[52] Inspired as much by 1960s movements as by Alinsky's remarkable legacy, grassroots activism was seen as the essence of a new politics, extending and redefining our historical sense of citizenship, participation, neighborhood—and perhaps radical change. Community movements were in fact able to mobilize often broad constituencies around issues of urban space, tenants' rights, health care, the environment, plant closings, and violence against women, exhibiting great resiliency through cycles of ebb and flow. New populist groups and coalitions worked to defend the integrity of neighborhoods, win social reforms, and build local institutions such as medical clinics, rent-control boards, rape-crisis centers, alternative newspapers and radio stations, public-interest and research groups, and bookstores. They sometimes created or entered into electoral alliances—a strategy Alinsky himself and some new populists viewed with suspicion, believing it would drain resources from community organizing. By the mid-1980s new populists were able, alone or in coalitions, to win municipal power in small cities like Burlington, Vermont; Madison, Wisconsin; and Santa Monica, California.[53]

By the early 1980s there were reportedly at least 500,000 local change-oriented organizations scattered across the United States, with an estimated membership of more than five million—numbers that may have actually grown during the 1990s.[54] A number of such groups have established a national presence or influence: the various Committee on Public Safety (COPS) groups based on the San Antonio model, Association of Community Organization for Reform Now, Friends of the Earth, disparate public interest and research forums, tenants' rights organizations influenced by the successes of Santa Monicans for Renters Rights in Santa Monica, Citizens Against Toxic Waste, Massachusetts Fair Share, and many others. Most of these groups survived intact through the conservative 1980s and 1990s, but generally only after adopting more modest goals and/or strategies. For Boyte, the new populist turn amounted to a new phase of democratization, affirming a recovery of civic spirit rooted in the long American "citizen advocacy" tradition. That spirit contains a strong "populist sensibility" tied to a

> renewed vision of direct democracy coupled with a mistrust of large institutions, both public and private. Such a democratic vision [entails] a rekindled faith in citizenry itself, a conviction that, given the means and the information, people can make decisions about the course of their lives [and] a belief that people can develop a conception of the public interest that does not deny—but rather is nourished by—specific interests. In turn, the building blocks for a revitalized ethos of citizenship are to be found in the voluntary structures of all kinds at the base of American society.[55]

Boyte and others were convinced that new populist initiatives, in order to be successful, would have to maneuver in the orbit of established American traditions—liberalism, religious values, the family, and the neighborhood—in a way that could build on the most active, progressive side of those traditions. It would be a rebirth of Jeffersonian democracy in the modern setting. The premise was that a vast majority of citizens can readily identify with such values, in contrast to imported ideologies like socialism, communism, or anarchism, which never established deep roots in the political culture. Community empowerment was viewed as a process directed against the colonizing power of bureaucracy (the state) and the commodity (corporations); only the "people" could furnish the necessary ingredients of both democracy and community, only the people could revive an otherwise decaying public sphere. Thus, new populism was not only about voicing grievances, winning social reforms, or even taking over local governmental power—as significant as these goals were. The movement was also about building *community*. Further, it was not enough merely to enter the political arena; the idea was to give it renewed *definition*, in terms of both new institutions and social solidarity. Here was a recognition that politics was far more than a simple instrumental exercise in the winning of elections and the exercising of power, but must carry forward the pursuit of egalitarian personal and social relations without which politics rapidly degenerates into crass manipulation.

This model of a renovated politics, along the lines of the West German Greens during roughly the same period, gained some popular currency at a time of mounting dissatisfaction with conventional politics, with party systems in decline and electoral campaigns degenerating into media-driven spectacles. It pointed toward an alternative route to social identity and democratic participation, galvanized in part by the energies of new social movements. Not only did new populism make inroads into the political culture, it also contributed to rejuvenation of the public sphere at a time when general levels of civic involvement were deteriorating.

For all their undeniable achievements, however, the Alinsky and new populist strategies have been forced to confront a number of powerful structural and ideological obstacles; deradicalizing pressures have proven virtually impossible to avoid. As a result, this legacy has been more one of localist inertia than oppositional politics, more one of retreat from than transformation of the public sphere. New forms of empowerment and identity have been carved out here and there, but mostly in the confines of neighborhood and locale where issues commonly become narrowed and struggles are turned inward, depoliticized. This dynamic has prevailed even where new populist coalitions have won municipal power.[56] Where power has not been won, as in the vast majority of cases, efforts to revive citizenship typically wound up even more insular, attuned to a defense of turf and material interests consonant with the "consumer ethic" described by Allan Heskin in his analysis of the tenants' rights movement in Santa Monica during the 1980s.[57] Instead of a broadened public sphere leading to a "new politics," localism of this sort tends to reinforce the prevailing ethos of fragmentation and privatism. The quest for community empowerment and human-scale democracy, motivated by even the most progressive ideals, moves in a defensive and parochial direction, often laying bare a process of conservative retreat beneath the facile rhetoric of grassroots activism. Where local gains fail to achieve a revitalized political translation, they inevitably lose their transformative capacity—a limitation built into the very logic of the strategy. As Joseph Kling and Prudence Posner observe: "Democratic efficacy is experienced at the local level, yet in the world of corporate capitalism, the power necessary to achieve democratic and egalitarian goals exists, if anywhere, only at the level of the bureaucratic national state."[58]

The result of much (though clearly not all) local organizing in the United States thus follows the pattern of what Sidney Plotkin calls "enclave consciousness," the typical pattern being that the struggle for community space and identity normally turns inward and defensive in a world dominated by powerful interests. In an urban milieu filled with menacing outside forces, people readily come to "see their neighborhood as home territory, a familiar environment of people, buildings and space, surrounded by alien threats. Enclave consciousness is first of all a political orientation to the defense of such a place. . . . Thus, while celebrating community, neighborhood households that embody the enclave consciousness also regularly strive to preserve privacy and social distance between themselves to retain their otherwise individual apolitical character."[59] Plotkin writes that modern urban protest employs collective action not so much to gain power or fight for social change as to enlarge the space for local autonomy. As with the spiritual and therapeutic models, one finds here a self-conscious attempt to maneuver *around* the public sphere: "Buttressed by beliefs in its hard-earned independence, members of the enclave feel they owe little to the larger society."[60]

True to their new populist origins, many enclaves contain a subculture that resists expansion of corporate and state power; local movements often make demands that can be disruptive of the status quo. But the general trajectory has been toward the more insular enclave, regardless of strategy employed. In Plotkin's words:

> Spirited by moral outrage against elite manipulation, . . . enclave consciousness channels the political activism and resistance of ordinary people mainly into demands to "leave us alone." With its characteristically defensive, exclusionary, and reactive character, the resulting politics is a "geopolitics of local community," in which "deterrence, counterforce, holding ground, securing borders, flanking maneuvers, and standing fast are central organizing concepts." Each enclave becomes a mini-fortress.[61]

What we have in such cases, according to Plotkin, is a cultivated image of radicalism that in reality masks a social and political conservatism. The very fact of organizational success itself in the local enclave can breed conservatism.

Such an example of enclave localism is described by Allan Heskin in *The Struggle for Community*, which looks at the protracted mobilization of low-income residents in Los Angeles against a freeway project that, if carried out, would have obliterated their neighborhood. More than 500 households created an alliance called the Route 2 Project, which took shape in the late 1970s.[62] A multiethnic organization, the Route 2 Project set up an informal "war council" responsible for developing strategy and tactics. Mass meetings, some of them chaotic, stormy, and counterproductive, were regular occurrences in the life of a movement where solidary but nonetheless combative interactive styles prevailed. As mobilization began to peak in the early 1980s, participants were able to create what Heskin (following Benjamin Barber) refers to as a form of "public talk"—a type of discourse through which the entire community could articulate its shared values, goals, and culture. In part because of this integrated culture, residents won major victories in the 1980s: they held off powerful forces such as Caltrans (the state transportation agency), saved their homes, built housing cooperatives, and in the process established a community of struggle. Each stage of the process, from initial mobilization to setting up and then managing co-ops, brought participants face-to-face with the pressing concerns of power, housing, class relations, and ethnicity. Beneath the drama of grassroots struggles were some persistent, binding elements: direct democracy as a means of empowerment, the struggle for community, and vision of a common good. To capture this process Heskin invokes the legacy not only of Rousseau but of Martin Buber, Paulo Freire, and Gramsci as theorists who established a dialectic between participation (self-oriented activity) and consciousness transformation.

By the late 1980s, however, a crucial question inevitably came to the fore, namely, How far can a local transformative process be extended where the groups involved are so at odds with surrounding institutions and values? To what degree can a viable counterhegemonic politics be sustained against the immense force of corporate colonization and state bureaucracy? Indeed, how in such a context is "success" ultimately defined? Heskin found that the most significant gains of the Route 2 Project were the product of a quasi-anarchistic celebration of locale that, in effect, detached the movement from its larger urban milieu and from prospects of entering into political coalitions that could give the local groups much-needed broader leverage. Empowerment for the Route 2 Project was confined mainly to housing issues, linked to the overriding concerns of family, neighborhood, and ethnic identity (a majority of residents were Latino). As

Heskin shows, these limitations meant that a language appropriate to collective action in the larger public sphere was never created.[63] The movement, in other words, was unable to reproduce itself in political terms; it followed the logic of enclave consciousness outlined by Plotkin.

A related but quite different illustration of this localist predicament is furnished by Plotkin and his collaborator Robert Scheuerman, who analyzed workers' ill-fated efforts to fight plant closings in the Monongahela Valley area of Pennsylvania.[64] Two grassroots organizations were created in the early 1980s to fight massive layoffs and disruptions to the community resulting from corporate decisions to close down steel factories—part of the general decline of the steel industry and manufacturing as a whole in the U.S. economy. These local groups carried out militant and confrontational, but mostly defensive, battles to hold corporations like Bethlehem Steel legally and morally responsible for the social devastation that came in the wake of their unilateral economic decisions. The situation posed difficult challenges from the beginning: surely it would be a daunting task to mobilize sufficient resources to fight corporations on their own terrain. Despite the intense buildup of anger and militancy among most workers, neither the DMS (Denominational Ministry Strategy) nor the SVA (Steel Valley Authority) could generate effective opposition, and leaders made serious attempts to politicize the struggles; anticorporate consciousness, powerful though it was, could not transcend its local immediacy. Thus, "these organizations engaged in futile, self-destructive actions that had no impact on the political understanding or class consciousness of workers, except perhaps to reinforce their sense of alienation and helplessness against corporate power."[65] Their plant-centered activity never escaped the enclave, never confronted larger issues of corporate control or political governance. Everything was fully immersed in the realm of immediate experience so that, in the end, the capacity to act, to win even limited concessions or reforms, was fatally muted.

Grassroots movements, of course, remain an inescapable part of any transformative agenda. At the same time, while there are no rigid causal patterns favoring an enclave outcome, in a highly depoliticized culture such an outcome will be all the more difficult to avoid. In fact, the enormous dilemmas of local activism have a long history in American politics, in part because the system was designed to provide space for local participation apart from federal apparatus, making it difficult for even the most sustained grassroots insurgency to destabilize the national governing structures. Even where oppositional groups were able to achieve some measure of local presence, as in the case of both the Populists and the Socialists roughly a century ago, their influence on national government was bound to be severely restricted owing to the complex maze of checks and balances, multiple levels of representation, cumbersome legislative practices, and a winner-take-all electoral system that pushes the two main parties toward the "center." Over time, too, the federal government grew stronger and more bureaucratized, further reducing the scope of local decision making and rendering the domain of grassroots empowerment less and less promising. Meanwhile, the federal government, with its expanded role in the military, foreign policy, and global economy, assumed ever greater control over people's lives—at least until globalization began to usurp some of that power. Such realities, along with constitutional and legal obstacles that make it virtually impossible for local movements to gain national leverage, have forced progressive groups (in the Alinsky mold) to pursue strictly grassroots organizing. At the same time, as Mark Kann argues, community-based radicalism might in some cases actually help to solidify elite interests by localizing discontent and deflecting oppositional energies away from the real centers of power.[66]

An analysis of new populist experience since the late 1970s suggests that the typically parochial focus of community-based struggles can be indeed difficult to get beyond: groups readily become inner-directed and insular, with each constituency or interest group going its own way. In his assessment of local organizing efforts in the United States, Robert Fischer writes: "The commitment to diversity encourages each constituency, each identity, or issue group to identify its own struggles, develop its own voice, and engage in its own empowerment."[67] This pattern is familiar to students of the European Left, where historically movements linked to anarchism, syndicalism, and council communism—all ideologically localist and antistatist—wound up similarly trapped in their own localism. The crucial point here is that grassroots mobilization, when left to its own resources, eventually loses its capacity to challenge state power—locally or nationally—a defect that is more fatal today because of economic globalization. And this logic is all the more likely to take hold in the absence of a consensual ideology that can incorporate local groups into a more universal *political* schema (as with socialism or the Green parties). Hence, the sometimes frenetic search for local autonomy in the contemporary world appears destined to have sharply depoliticizing consequences.

Parochialism of this sort has yet another side: the pursuit of identity generally leads to the most exclusive sense of community—around strict definitions of locality or ethnicity, for example—which seems to empower but actually does just the opposite. Thus, a shrinking view of community can be stifling in its overpowering conformism, which often gives rise to the kind of "tyranny of the majority" that was perhaps best pilloried by J. S. Mill.[68] In an intensely communitarian milieu individual participation runs up against a number of barriers—often more cultural than legal or political—as Mill stressed. Thus, our very understanding of the public realm should be broad enough to allow for ethnic, social, and (most emphatically) ideological divergences in the same overarching rubric of citizenship. In cases where citizen participation implies conformist ideas and practices, the very concept of empowerment becomes hollow. But this is precisely what new populism tends to reproduce as it struggles to navigate in and through the hegemonic ideological and cultural traditions.

As seductive therefore as the agenda of community organizing might be, in a world of increasingly concentrated economic and political power it will always be inadequate—and could turn out to be counterproductive. Whatever the undeniably significant gains of grassroots movements, the stubborn reality is that necessary institutional leverage for deep structural change ultimately lies on the terrain of national government. But so much new-populist theory is designed to avoid precisely that reality. The massive scope of economic and political power today works to the detriment of localist models. Further, where grassroots organizing fails to make a dent in the power structure or even win limited reforms—as is generally the case—even the most dedicated activists may become disillusioned and sour on "politics." Even where important inroads have been made, as we have seen in the case of the Route 2 Project, the frustration of arriving at an impasse typically feeds into an ethos that favors neighborhood maintenance over wider political activism.

Of course, there are no ready-made formulas for resolving the perpetual dilemmas of local organizing. The point is that powerful depoliticizing tendencies are built into the very logic of new populist organizing initiatives, especially those closest to the Alinsky model. And the problems of localism do not stem merely from a refusal to confront the imperatives of governmental power; the question of *ideology* being equally crucial. Alinsky's strategy, as we have seen, consciously disavowed "ideology," while in fact insisting on the need for oppositional groups to appropriate traditional American values and redirect them toward progressive ends. He believed, in other words, that for organizing work to be effective it would have to dispense with "extraneous" or imported belief systems (socialism, anarchism, and so on) in favor of a home-grown, more easily digestible liberalism. But herein lies the fatal predicament: an *alternative* ideology, along with uncritical acceptance of "common sense" and familiar worldviews helps explain how the logic of enclave localism could so easily prevail.

Alinsky, Boyte, and others have looked to the efficacy of self-interest, pragmatic organizing tactics, and traditional values, but this entire schema is ultimately compelled to make peace with the status quo; the relevant maxim here is, No alternative vision, no transformative politics. A model that accepts, even celebrates, the need for local adaptation cannot seriously confront issues of class and power in a world where the main centers of decision making are increasingly global. In psychological as well as political terms a coherent ideology empowers people to see beyond the present, to connect seemingly disparate issues, and to view the travails of everyday life as part of a larger global totality. As Fischer puts it: "Without ideological challenges, those in power continue to set the agenda and activists continue to respond to it."[69] The historic crisis of socialism and the failure of nascent green alternatives to mount a viable challenge only sharpens this dilemma. In any event, the unpleasant truth remains that enclave consciousness, tied to a defensive protection of local turf, constitutes yet another instance of the shrinking public sphere. Contrary to its surface claims, therefore, new populism marks a significant turning away from vital elements of the political enterprise—the transformative side of power, the role of social governance, and the ideal of citizen participation—that extend to the larger society. This is one of the hallmarks of a depoliticized society.

THE URBAN REBELLION: BEYOND POLITICS?

Since the mid-1960s the United States has experienced numerous urban upheavals of varying scope and intensity, from Los Angeles to Detroit, Newark, Chicago, and Miami, and then back to Los Angeles again in 1992, when the Rodney King jury verdict triggered the most violent rebellion in modern American history. As a convergence of class and ethnic revolt, the upheaval was fueled by mounting joblessness, poverty, racial divisions, and generalized social polarization of the sort that has come to define the modern urban landscape. By the 1990s these conditions had worsened in the wake of intensified corporate and government "restructuring," which drastically altered the employment structure and further squeezed social programs, exacerbating the process of inner-city deterioration, which in the case of Los Angeles hit people of color (blacks and Latinos) by far the hardest. Capital flight away from the metropolitan centers, stemming partly from the effects of economic globalization, has fed into the downward spiral of urban decay, social conflict, and everyday violence.[70] When the ingredients of urban crisis include a phony drug war that criminalizes large sectors of the population, the alienation of inner-city groups (especially youth) from the political system, and the failure of elites to even acknowledge the crisis, the mixture becomes even more highly flammable. Yet, while revolt may be explicable and even predictable, its outcome has been a classic instance of antipolitics.

Hobsbawm's seminal analysis of the urban mob focused on the Lumpen upheavals of early industrial Europe that were, among other things, protests against social marginalization. Mob revolts were typically sparked by cataclysmic events such as drastic increases in food prices, the step up of police repression, or even some natural catastrophe. Cities like Naples, Milan, Liverpool, and Paris were populated by thousands of street people living on the edge of survival. In such an environment direct action tended to be more emotionally cathartic than politically effective, however, since in its very worship of spontaneity it inevitably devalued the role of ideology, organization, and strategy—all essential ingredients of modern politics, as Hobsbawm emphasizes. Outlaw countercultures that nourished the spirit of rebellion had a strong presence in cities, where the Lumpen strata reviled all manifestations of state power as an infringement on their local space, as a negation of their very social existence. Finding itself trapped in a vortex of misery and powerlessness, the urban mob looked to militant direct action but in the end found that this could never abolish or even mitigate the institutional sources of its oppression. Nor, of course, could it alter the balance of social and political power. Since the participants lacked a universal belief system such as socialism, the upheavals were inchoate and dispersed, cut off from prospects of winning reforms or making inroads into the power structure. Once the carnage of mass disruption was swept away, the status quo returned intact—often more deeply entrenched than before—condemning the city Lumpen to a life of poverty and despair.[71]

The Los Angeles riots of April–May 1992 were set in motion by not-guilty verdicts for police officers accused of beating Rodney King. The verdicts were a shock to the city of Los Angeles, especially to blacks, who comprise nearly 40 percent of the inner-city population and who had experienced decades of tense relations with the Los Angeles Police Department. Evidence in this case included a videotape showing the beating (which lasted for more than one minute) in graphic detail; the guilt of the police officers, tried in the largely white suburban town of Simi Valley, seemed obvious to many, based on the videotape. The violent response began immediately after the verdicts, spreading from the epicenter of Normandie and Florence avenues in the Watts area and rippling outward. Young males, mostly black and Latino, smashed windows, torched cars, pulled motorists from vehicles, and generally went on a rampage in south-central neighborhoods, later spilling over into other areas: Koreatown, Hollywood, downtown, Culver City. With the LAPD in a state of confusion and retreat, flames engulfed whole neighborhoods, including stores, homes, cars, and even large multiunit structures. Looters ran wildly through the torched areas of the city, targeting especially Korean-owned markets, liquor stores, and shops. Urban violence over a two-day period left huge portions of the city in shambles; merchants, residents, police, and others were caught up in a maelstrom of burnings, shootings, beatings, and random street actions that was allowed to run its course. The

National Guard mobilization ordered by Governor Pete Wilson took effect only after the upheaval had partially exhausted itself.

When the fires were finally extinguished, Los Angeles was left with 57 dead, nearly 3,000 injured, and 15,000 arrested for crimes ranging from murder and arson to looting; property damage totaled well over $1 billion. Contrary to what was believed at the time, blacks made up less than half of those most directly involved in the rebellion—42 percent of the total, compared with 44 percent Latinos, 9 percent whites, and 2 percent from other groups. Also, the arson that was done was not entirely unsystematic in that 90 percent of Korean-owned stores in the affected areas were torched, reflecting the buildup of animosity of blacks in particular toward Korean entrepreneurs. Indeed, the explosion was fueled by long-festering anger that engulfed many inner-city groups, including not only gangs but ordinary blacks, Latinos, Asians, and poor whites. The King verdict, of course, was simply a catalyst, just as a heated argument between a black motorist and an LAPD officer was the spark that set off the flames of the Watts riot in 1965. As one commentator remarked about the 1992 events: "Whatever happened in Los Angeles—police brutality, the unjust verdict, the angry response—are part of an ancient spiral. The spiral will continue in the absence of fundamental change."[72]

In contrast to the Watts events, the 1992 violence extended well beyond the black community both socially and geographically, even though the jury verdict had great symbolic meaning for blacks. As for the inner city itself, social conditions had actually worsened in many areas since 1965: the gulf between rich and poor, between the affluent Westside and Valley sectors of Los Angeles and south central, had widened. Unemployment among blacks and Latinos in Los Angeles stood at 19.5 percent—a predicament exacerbated by large-scale social and military cutbacks since the late 1980s. While hardly unique to Los Angeles, the deteriorating public sector further aggravated the desperate straits of people needing improved health care, education, housing, welfare, and of course jobs, thus worsening the conditions of interethnic conflict. Some inner-city neighborhoods were devastated by poverty and blight. For Latinos, including immigrants from many countries south of the border, the predicament was often even more desperate than it was for blacks. Many tens of thousands of Latinos found themselves in the nightmare world of a (mere) survival economy, with its sweatshops, crowded living conditions, virtual lack of social services and education, and the horrors of daily repression at the hands of employers, landlords, policemen, and occasionally gang members. Extreme social and political marginalization of Latinos was the rule: not only immigrants but many indigenous Latinos were excluded from legal and voting rights. Although they made up nearly 40 percent of the city's population, Latino political representation—in the mayor's office, city council, county board of supervisors, and school board—had always been nearly invisible.

The urban crisis was intensified further by the sustained indifference and neglect of both corporations and government. Politicians of both parties were preoccupied with winning back the loyalties of middle-class voters who had fled the inner city, or who simply wanted to preserve their suburban lifestyle. No broad-based program for rebuilding the urban centers was forthcoming at any level—federal, state, or municipal—before and even *after* the 1992 uprising. No plans were set in motion to counter the deadly effects of capital flight and social cutbacks. As Mike Davis put it: "In the face of unemployment and homelessness on scales not seen since 1938, a bipartisan consensus insists that the budget must be balanced and entitlements reduced. Refusing to make any further public investment in the remediation of underlying social conditions, we are forced instead to make increasing private investments in physical security. The rhetoric of urban reform persists, but the substance is extinct."[73]

Befitting the logic of a depoliticized society, elite debates and proposals in Los Angeles seemed almost entirely removed from those urgent problems that simply refused to go away; the public sphere could not have been more disconnected from the everyday social existence of millions of people. Social programs had been declining for many years, not to mention erosion of the public infrastructure in general, but nothing was done. In the aftermath of the rebellion, elites were forced to pay lip service to the idea of urban redevelopment and a rebuilding Los Angeles agency was established with hopes (misplaced as it turned out) of success dependent on a mixture of corporate initiative and community "volunteerism." With little infusion of public resources Rebuild Los Angeles predictably stagnated and, more significantly, so too did long-term prospects for genuine urban reconstruction. Scores of small businesses were soon rebuilt, especially in Koreatown, but burnt-out and blighted areas of south central Los Angeles remained untouched many months and even years after the riots. Meanwhile, it was politics as usual for the Los Angeles power structure: instead of far-reaching proposals for increased publicly funded jobs and social services, Angelenos were treated to furious debates over how best to put more cops on the streets, develop more effective riot-control techniques, build more prisons, and carry out the drug war more expeditiously. Among more than 20 Los Angeles mayoral candidates in 1993, not one came forward with a bold or imaginative plan for reversing an urban crisis the explosive and deadly consequences of which were a recent bitter memory.

From this standpoint the Los Angeles uprising can be viewed as a manifestation of both class and racial protest against the harsh inequalities of a social order that the political system seems almost bound and determined not to fix. One can detect a certain fatal logic to the spontaneous outbursts of inner-city poor and working-class youth. In Haki Madhubuti's words, this was more than anything a "going to the streets of the unheard."[74] Had the Rodney King verdict been guilty for the LAPD cops involved, some other outrage would likely have triggered a comparable explosion months or years later. But, above all, such massive outpourings of anger signaled the degree to which the urban poor and minorities have essentially given up on politics as a means of escaping the morass. The King verdict deepened that mood even further, especially among blacks. It is easy enough to understand why many urban youth have chosen to act on their alienation by turning to the streets—to gangs, drug culture, violent outbursts, and even riots. Surely the realm of normal politics such as voting, party campaigns, and interest lobbying held out little appeal for people who felt excluded from the system of representation, who are fully convinced they can never be treated fairly in the criminal justice system.[75] The absence of a strong civil rights movement on the national scene made this society-wide failing all the more painfully obvious.

Once the riots were over, it was painfully obvious that, a with the urban Lumpen mobs described by Hobsbawm, the Los Angeles uprising had left behind nothing of a *political* legacy—"politics" here referring to far more than simple electoral activity. With no articulated vision or program, no organization or strategy, no perspective on issues of power or governance, the catharsis of rebellion quickly vanished. The two days of rioting seemed to be a time of spontaneous but deeply passionate antipolitics, as if the assembled masses could not be bothered with the trivia of strategies, tactics, and programs, much less long-range goals. In this highly charged but amorphous environment, no ideology, no universal values or beliefs, would have seemed relevant; the collective participation of the mainly black and Latino youth was far too momentary, spontaneous, and dispersed. Other urban upheavals followed, in such scattered cities as Miami, San Francisco, Washington DC, and Detroit, but with less explosive outcomes. Even apart from the fragmented character of participating gangs, these spontaneous uprisings similarly involved no effort to create an oppositional discourse and no struggle to build an organization or develop a strategy of change. Indeed, such questions were never really addressed, even among leaders of community and movement groups.

Reflecting on the prepolitical aura of the Los Angeles protests, bell hooks wrote a seething critique in which she puzzled over why blacks and others had been unable to arrive at even a tentative strategic orientation in advance. "Our collective failure to predict the outcome and organize meaningful responses prior to the announcement of the verdict was deeply disturbing. It suggested that black Americans ceased to be politically vigilant." The images of rebellion, she observed, were "tragic expressions of powerlessness and not strategic confrontations with the white supremacist power structure."[76] In hooks's view, the indications were that minorities had essentially given up on progressive movements and that, even more tragically, their struggle for rights and identity was tied more than anything else to the desire for material goods, as shown by the endless looting. There was, of course, the ample and predictable denunciation of the police, the criminal justice system, and the entrenched political elites. But the only semblance of cultural and organizational coherence was furnished by the growth of extensive gang networks. As Mike Davis observed: "If the riot had a broad social base, it was the participation of the gangs—or rather, their cooperation—that gave it constant momentum and direction."[77] In Los Angeles, as in many other U.S. cities, gangs have emerged in part of a growing outlaw subculture composed mainly of male youth driven by concerns of turf and identity. Street gangs have become an all-consuming way of life and death, a vehicle for survival in the Hobbesian world of the inner city. Some gangs have established a vast geographical presence in the urban setting: the 18th Street gang in Los Angeles, with at one point a reported membership of 20,000, has taken over large sections of the city with a membership that is well armed, financially entrenched, and technologically sophisticated. The gang rents out street corners for purposes of drug peddling, enabling members to earn between $400 and $1,000 a day for territorial "collections." According to LAPD statistics, the gang was responsible for at least 20 killings in 1996—one reason why those areas most influenced by the 18th Street gang were ruled by local networks of power.[78]

An intricate and quasi-underground gang structure gives expression to the deep alienation of youth, especially those from poor or marginalized families who often feel hopeless about a future in which jobs, education, careers, and status seem completely out of reach. This is a localized world delimited by neighborhood, ethnicity, intense male bonding, and territorial warfare, in which personal and social struggles are universally defined as "us" versus "them"—the "them" being rival gangs rather than the power structure or class enemies. In this milieu violence is often the preferred (and sometimes glorified) mode of combat. As Dwight Conquergood writes, on the basis of his own lengthy involvement with Chicago gangs, everything revolves around a clearly defined sense of space, which the members endow with an emotional, aesthetic, and moral power. All the symbols and codes refer to spatial values. In these circumstances "the space of the other is attacked in order to clarify identity and clear more space for self-representation."[79] While gangs do not generally embark on community organizing projects, the parallel between this turf-obsessed ethos and the enclave consciousness described earlier is rather obvious.

In addition to the sprawling 18th Street gang, there are hundreds of other street gangs scattered throughout Los Angeles, the vast majority of them established along both ethnic and territorial lines. They are partly an expression of long-standing interethnic rivalries involving blacks, Latinos, Asians, and whites, and many joined the 1992 uprising, helping to give it energy and incendiary power. Some gang networks—the best known being the Bloods and Crips—set aside their differences during and after the riots, presumably in order to forge a common protest against the King verdict. There were brief glimpses of this deep anger becoming politicized, as when some gang leaders denounced the criminal justice system, the LAPD, and even the "white power structure," but no organizational or strategic definition of the events developed beyond the highly fragmentary, local nuclei of gang structures. Moreover, although often well armed and prepared for battle, the Los Angeles gangs refused to initiate any kind of guerrilla warfare; in fact, not a single LAPD officer was killed during the riots. What the Bloods and Crips did (later) was to issue a brief proposal for rebuilding the city along lines of a series of ambitious reforms that would require $3.7 billion in public funds (their estimate).[80] But this proposal was never given any organizational leverage and thus contained no realistic political substance; nor was it connected to any larger vision of change. Nothing ever came of this initiative, and in the period following the urban upheaval most Los Angeles gangs settled back into their previous modus operandi characterized by the same brutal and thoroughly nonpolitical turf wars.

The Los Angeles rebellion symbolizes in many ways the altered nature of social conflict in American cities—and around the world—in the 1990s. Enzensberger's definition of "civil wars" as detached from class interests or political ideology, discussed in Chapter 3 (page 78), seems applicable here; we have a situation where conflict is shaped mainly by local identities, bonds, and rivalries. What happened in Los Angeles was triggered by an event that brought to the surface class and racial animosities, but the ensuing violence followed the pulse and rhythm of the urban mob: spontaneous, chaotic, and essentially prepolitical. Once the uprising exhausted itself, the harsh conditions of urban life, interwoven with the web of corporate and governmental power, returned just as before. Indeed, the social chaos not only produces more of the same, it serves to reinforce those authoritarian elements of state power (more police, more prisons, more draconian laws, and so on) that will surely exacerbate the urban crisis over time. In this way the Hobbesian features of civil society and the rationalizing features of the state apparatus become dialectically intertwined. One result of this deadly vicious cycle is that all the trappings of democracy are weakened precisely as the power structure is strengthened, an unfortunate developmental logic, but typical of the era of antipolitics.

DEEP ECOLOGY: FROM POLITICS TO NATURE

The worsening ecological crisis has spawned hundreds of environmental groups and movements in the United States since the late 1960s, ranging from lobbies such as the World Wildlife Federation and Sierra Club to radical protest organizations like Greenpeace and Earth First! to the more politically focused Greens. One of the most novel and pervasive tendencies is deep ecology, a broad arc of ideas inspired by the writings of Dave Foreman, George Sessions, Arne Naess, and Fritjof Capra, among others, which calls for a radical transformation of human consciousness grounded in an organic relationship between human beings and nature. Deep ecology provides the basis of an imaginative social practice for many local groups in typically small towns and rural areas, as part of the (generally white and middle-class) revolt against urban and suburban culture. It has often been associated with the rise of "lifestyle" environmentalism and its myriad concerns: tree planting, recycling, organic gardening, wildlife preservation, and so forth. In contrast to most other expressions of antipolitics, it is possible to find in deep ecology a fusion of theory and action, consciousness and practical work, enriched by three decades of environmental activism.

As a more or less coherent social philosophy, deep ecology insists on a massive and sustained reconstruction of values, attitudes, and lifestyles needed to subvert the destructive power of "modern industrial growth societies." Defining itself as radically "biocentric" in outlook, it rejects the old Cartesian mechanistic paradigm rooted in anthropocentrism, human domination of nature, material growth, and fetishism of modernity, and looks instead toward new forms of ecological thinking, or "ecocentrism," consistent with an organic, holistic worldview shaped by an understanding of systems theory articulated by Capra and others. Repulsed by the hierarchy, violence, and social disintegration of modern urban society, the movement—diffuse in both its organizational presence and ideological presence—looks toward an ideal of harmony with nature that can best be realized in the countryside or wilderness.

In some ways an outgrowth of the 1960s counterculture, deep ecology draws on much of the same metaphysical tradition: Thoreau, Huxley, the work of Lewis Mumford and Alan Watts, Eastern philosophy, the poetry of Gary Snyder. This tradition holds that the modern crisis stems from forces even more profound than capitalism or bureaucracy or patriarchy; to fully understand the ecological predicament, we must go back to the Enlightenment legacy and its glorification of rational knowledge, science, and technology that produced a conflicted dualism between human existence and the natural environment. Here deep ecology looks beyond the "anthropocentric survival environmentalism" of such figures as Rachel Carson, Barry Commoner, and Ralph Nader, who have worked tirelessly for reforms to improve urban life in the cities but go no further than a technocratic fine-tuning of what has become a deadly growth economy. The deep ecology view is that humanity must scale down its consumption, its materialistic lifestyles, indeed its population levels in order to restore worldwide ecosystems and avoid environmental catastrophe. These goals will never be achieved, as George Sessions puts it, without a global paradigm shift "from an anthropocentric to a spiritual/ecocentric value orientation."[81]

Ecological crisis, according to Arne Naess, strikes at the very heart of modern culture, especially in the United States, "because of our inability to question deeply what is and what is not worthwhile in life."[82] The main challenge is to mount a thoroughgoing cultural revolution since, in Naess' words, "Our culture is the only one in the history of mankind in which the culture has adjusted itself to the technology, rather than vice-versa." The emphasis on normal politics in conventional environmentalism fails to see this, and yet ends up with, a kind of "computerized cost–benefit analysis designed to benefit only humans."[83]

In Capra's view, cultural revolution depends on a systems outlook that, consistent with deep ecology premises, sees human beings and nature as bound together in a network of connected and interdependent relations, with "nature" being the ultimate source of transformative values. Basic to this understanding of the systems model is the "recognition of value inherent in all living nature." Thus: "The reason why most of old-paradigm ethics cannot deal with the underlying problems is that, like shallow ecology, it is anthropocentric." The ethical framework derived from Enlightenment rationality simply cannot deal with the underlying problems of modern civilization, which inevitably "involve threats to non-human forms of life."[84] Capra believes that, as the social crisis intensifies, the ethos of domination and control will necessarily have to give way to a more holistic outlook "grounded in the experience of oneness of all living forms" and consonant with "Native American spirituality, Taoism, and other life-affirming, Earth-oriented spiritual traditions."[85]

The immediate significance of all this, according to partisans of the wilderness lifestyle such as the poet Gary Snyder, is the turn toward a social life carved out of the fabric of the countryside—what is referred to as a "practice of the wild." To fully embrace the concept of wilderness, human beings must decide to incorporate it into their person, take residence in it, and live in it as part of a larger ecosystem of plant and animal communities governed by sharing and reciprocity. As Snyder argues: "Grassroots politics is local, the politics of locale. To take up residence in a wild system is a political act."[86] In this context one can see how deep ecology, with its abiding concern for local experience, social immediacy, and spiritualism, closely intersects with elements of the enclave consciousness and new-age mysticism as well as some aspects of postmodernism. Indeed, at one point Sessions even chooses to characterize the new paradigm as a "postmodern, spiritual worldview."[87] In contrast to postmodernism, however, deep ecology envisions the unfolding of a universal "planetary consciousness" that will someday be achieved through a process of global unification.

These ideals have an enormously seductive appeal, in part because they insist on a profound renewal of democracy, citizenship, and public space that rekindles the spirit of thinkers like Rousseau, Paine, Jefferson, Charles Fourier, and Peter Kropotkin, all of whom formulated a premodern vision of community. Many of the parallels between deep ecology and distinctly urban populist movements are striking. Without doubt both have exerted a powerful influence on grassroots activism in both urban and rural settings. On the whole, however, their trajectory has been more inward than expansive, more parochial than public in their reach—which in the case of deep ecology leads to a kind of back-to-the-country enclave consciousness. The political value of deep ecology is ultimately weakened by a theory that fetishizes "nature" and turns it into something detached from the real, ever changing, conditions of social existence. The very idea of a wilderness or ecological totality separate from human life has no basis in history and in fact blinds us to a social reality that is being vastly altered by intensifying corporate colonization. The theory affirms a reified view of nature that defines ecology as something quite apart from social structure and processes, thus rendering theoretical critique and political intervention virtually impossible. Even the most compelling philosophical vision is severed from its historical and social context, eroding the capacity of theoretical critique to grasp the dynamics of industrialism, domination, and alienation, which lie at the core of the modern crisis. The search in deep ecology for a "new paradigm" of human consciousness instills flight not only from politics but from society itself. As Murray Bookchin has argued, the human subjectivity required to fully understand and change the world must transcend the simple awareness that strives to detach itself from the accumulated knowledge associated with "first nature."[88]

This fatal theoretical cul-de-sac can be detected in the important anthology *Deep Ecology for the Twenty-First Century*, edited by Sessions with contributions from 25 other leading proponents of "new paradigm" thinking. Nowhere in the roughly 500 pages of text does one find any significant mention of capitalism or class relations, corporations, the global economy, or even bureaucracy, and nowhere is there any discussion of political methods and strategies beyond vague references to consciousness transformation. Despite the undeniably radical vision of deep ecology, it contains no language of political engagement, no effort to specify how epochal transformations might be expected to unfold in real time and space. With alienated individuals pitted against huge (but largely incomprehensible) structures of domination, deep ecology simply assumes that an outmoded system propped up by Enlightenment values will gradually be replaced by an entirely new civilization rooted in the equilibrium between humans and nature. The change, as far-reaching as it might be, would presumably be rather peaceful and painless—a simple end-run around the ugly realities of government, big business, the military, and so forth. Such institutions would apparently wither away under the onslaught of new-paradigm values that are expected to spread rapidly throughout civil society, much as Charles Reich imagined for urban society 20 years ago in *The Greening of America*.[89]

If deep ecologists were able to frame a powerful critique of Western rationalism and its norms of possessive individualism, instrumentalism, and domination of nature, their fetishized view of nature disconnects that critique from the social world in which people live and work. This observation suggests a number of intriguing questions, such as, How can the development of nature be separated from historically evolved processes of human intervention—or domination? How can definitive boundaries between the social and the natural be established? To what extent would it be possible to dismantle a complex modern urban society, and at what price? How can we hope to achieve an unmediated form of local communal life, in or outside of the "wild"? Turning to the critical issue of popular consciousness, how could the vast majority of people whose lives are so thoroughly interwoven with the industrialized world ever be convinced to move toward a simple Rousseauian lifestyle, with all of its material hardships and sacrifices? As Peter Dickens argues, the "deep greens" conception of an abstract, idealized nature inevitably gives rise to a utopian, defensive, and reactive outlook that stands firmly against modernity in all its aspects—in other words, it erects an antipolitics that refuses to operate in the public sphere.[90]

The ecocentric worldview of deep ecology harks back to ideals long ago obliterated by modern industrialism: local community, human-scale interaction, regional autonomy, an organic relationship between humans and nature. Even apart the unfeasibility of such a project, the theory fails to confront difficult questions about class and power relations, gender and racial divisions—about social hierarchy in general. Such questions are dismissed or sidestepped as if they would simply no longer apply to smaller locales immersed in the rhythm and pulse of Mother Earth. Commenting on both deep ecology and ecofeminism, Cecile Jackson writes: "Like the broader tradition of populism they offer little analysis of conflicting interests and inequality within the community."[91] Moreover, on the premise that everything local and indigenous is good, deep ecology upholds an untenably innocent view of the family and household, not to mention neighborhood and community, in a society where idealized notions of harmony and cooperation are obliterated by the harsh actuality of material struggles, social hierarchy, and everyday violence—most of it bound up with those macro economic and political forces that the theory ignores. The local cannot be separated from the national or global, nor does it automatically take on a more democratic or egalitarian character simply because of its smaller terrain. The parallel here with the urban enclave is once again obvious for, as Jackson notes, ecological communalism in the name of radical change often turns out to be profoundly insular and conservative.[92] Moreover, as Bookchin points out, deep ecology—by virtue of its nature worship, its simplistic new-age platitudes, and its vague identification of "humanity" as the source of crisis—expresses a profoundly antiurban, nativistic impulse that readily accommodates itself to some of the worst features of the dominant order.[93]

The systems theory that underpins deep ecology rests on the belief that harmony and equilibrium are the guiding principles of both nature and society. As a statement about ultimate ideals this may not be especially objectionable. The problem comes with the effort to apply this philosophy to a social reality that is anything but harmonious, that is permeated with hierarchy, exploitation, and conflict. Such a disjuncture works against historical analysis and political vision grounded in actual social forces or possibilities, and coincides with an ideological style that vacillates between adventurism and quietism. In Timothy Luke's words: "All that deep ecology seems to offer are new symbolic rituals of sacralization instead of substantive rational criteria for choosing between alternatives." The result is that "political action is displaced into the realm of ethical ideals, making it every individual's moral duty to change himself or herself in advancing cultural change."[94] Thus, even where local defenders of wilderness culture initiate militant action from time to time, these initiatives do not lead to transformative politics. Relocating to the countryside might well be viewed as a desire to "exit" from industrial society, to use Rudolf Bahro's term,[95] which also suggests the most extreme withdrawal from the public sphere that is possible. Such withdrawal converges with a nearly obsessive pursuit of local, communal, domestic lifestyles uncontaminated by the oppressive power of large-scale institutions. The communal bond achieved in the rural setting is likely to be purchased at the same price as the pursuit of community in the urban enclave—an escape from politics.

NEITHER MOVEMENT NOR PARTY

The multiple expressions of social critique and protest explored in this chapter—new-age spiritualism, the therapeutic culture, local enclaves, urban eruptions, deep ecology—all have one thing in common despite their obvious differences, namely, a thoroughly depoliticized approach to social change. In some cases these modalities intersect with and reinforce one another, often drawing from the same influences and energies. By no means are these forms meant to account for everything that in American society might be described as an escape from politics; we know that many variants of religion in general, simple everyday diversions, and episodic spectacles like sex scandals, celebrity trials, the Superbowl, and rock extravaganzas also help reproduce a mood of antipolitics. The emphasis in this chapter has been on some rather common responses to felt resentment among widely diverse populations—resentment that extends across class, ethnic, and regional divisions. The crucial point is that in such instances no viable *movements* for social change could be created or sustained, that is, the movements had little of a transformative presence in the public sphere. They did not construct a specifically political discourse because the very relevance of such a discourse was either "transcended" or rejected out of hand—or it was abandoned out of feelings of despair and hopelessness.

It would be misleading, however, to suggest that antipolitics can never give expression to any positive social or personal goals. We have seen how it can provide an element of catharsis and a sense of identity, even strong feelings of empowerment and an optimistic view of the future—ephemeral as those goals might be. Moreover, as Hobsbawm shows in *Primitive Rebels*, various diffuse and fragmented forms of protest (e.g., millenarianism and social banditry) can be a prelude to more developed types of political involvement, as where the Italian Communist Party was able to politicize such local stirrings at the time of partisan struggles during the mid-1940s. It is clearly possible for limited, prepolitical groups to enter into a larger "social bloc" of forces (to use Gramsci's phrase) that might give them greater political leverage and historical impact. For such a breakthrough to occur, however, two preconditions must be met: social crisis and well-established political opposition.

Looking at the contemporary American situation, a crisis of perhaps explosive dimensions is not out of the question, but the second precondition—strong oppositional parties and movements—is precisely what cannot be found in a depoliticized society. Indeed, the intricate structural and ideological mechanisms of American society work ceaselessly to block such opposition, so that even the most far-reaching sentiments for change will be extremely difficult to translate into struggles over class domination and state power. Such eclipse of the public sphere would thus seem to be virtually guaranteed by certain key developments: sense of powerlessness among those most likely to want change, a deeply visceral hatred of "politics" and all that it represents that extends throughout society, and the absence of an oppositional political culture where transformative visions could take hold. Each of these developments is at work in late twentieth-century American society. Viewed from this angle, it is easy to see how the phenomenon of antipolitics is increasingly detached from the great political traditions we have inherited—socialism, communism, social democracy, even liberalism and nationalism. These preeminently "modern" traditions helped to keep alive collective struggles for community, justice, and equality, broadened notions of citizenship and identity, and promoted democratization of state power and governance—all in the national public sphere. More than anything else, the steady disintegration of socialist politics over the past two decades has left an ideological void that no alternative has yet filled; aside from the momentary breakthrough of the European Greens in the 1980s, there has been no universal ideology, no pole of attraction, no widely shared critique of the established order, and few popular struggles that could rise above the local, often spontaneous, and dispersed modes of thought and action just now discussed. As this ideological quagmire worsens, urgent problems of a national and global character go unsolved, perhaps even unrecognized, only to fester more ominously into the future. In such a "postmodern" milieu, where the familiar alternatives vanish but are replaced only with confusion and pessimism, we are left to encounter the great political dilemmas of our time.

CHAPTER 7

THE POSTMODERN IMPASSE

In the preceding chapter we explored the myriad, widely scattered, and typically localized modes of escape from politics in contemporary American society—expressions of antipolitics that by now have become deeply rooted in the political culture. The present discussion shifts the focus toward the more insular but nonetheless vital terrain of intellectual and cultural work, where the turn toward postmodernism has exerted a similarly depoliticizing influence. The diffusion of loosely defined postmodern ideas has its origins in the late 1970s, a time of dashed hopes for the New Left and the sharpening crisis of Marxism. Postmodernism took on an added dimension with the emergence of strong popular movements (feminism, ecology, peace, citizens' initiatives, and so on), and gained resonance for other reasons, among them: the widespread revulsion against bureaucracy; the growing importance of mass media and popular culture; the ascendancy of conservative ideology, along with the seeming stabilization of capitalism; the weakening of the labor movement; and the immense appeal of therapeutic solutions in the wake of a declining 1960s radicalism. From this standpoint, postmodernism can be understood as an inevitable intellectual and cultural reaction to the collapse of established ideological paradigms, especially those associated with liberalism and socialism.

The major theoretical articulation of European (mostly French) post-Marxism, associated with such thinkers as Michel Foucault, Jacques Derrida, Jean Baudrillard, and Jean-François Lyotard, postmodernism (or poststructuralism) initially embraced a mood of revolt and experimentation, a sense of questioning sacred texts and received truths rooted in decaying (but still influential) paradigms. More a broad framework for theorizing than a coherent social theory as such, the postmodern approach opened up new vistas on a world of social fragmentation and political confusion, where reality could be viewed as infinitely more complex, transitional, and ambiguous than had been true of Marxist currents—notably those identified with communism, the Soviet model, and in deed most variants of academic Marxism. In a world drastically reshaped by rapidly changing economic, social, and cultural forces, the arrogant certitude of grand theories, with their pretentious historical sweep, totalizing claims, and grandiose visions of progress, could no long hold up when subjected to close scrutiny. Nor could the idea, epitomized by Marxism–Leninism, that social change must be the outcome of actions by a privileged single agency (class, party) or must follow the logic of a single set of interests or goals. In its most extreme form—and there can of course be diverse readings—postmodernism has refocused attention, away from the macro realm (the global system, or the national state, or economy), toward a "micro politics" grounded in the immediate, local, and more tangible elements of everyday life. It is precisely this dimension of postmodernism that overlaps with the rhythm and flow of new social movements, the rise of identity politics, and the pattern of depoliticized retreat addressed in Chapter 6. And this same dimension has made postmodern discourse appealing to an academic culture that, by the 1980s, had grown increasingly disillusioned with grand theoretical systems and had, at the same time, become more detached from the sphere of politics.

THE CRISIS OF MODERNITY

Postmodernism and its various offshoots (semiotics, difference feminism, new-social-movement theory, some areas of cultural criticism) have indeed transformed much of academia, particularly the humanities and social sciences, giving rise to a vast outpouring of literature that has revitalized discourses in several important fields of study. In its debunking of sweeping, ambitious historical narratives, postmodernism affirms a kind of antiparadigm paradigm where no body of truth or knowledge is regarded as stable or given, where notions of causality, determinism, and structural analysis are viewed with deep suspicion. It celebrates a "post" orientation with reference primarily to a post-Fordist order shaped by the commodification of all social life, the fragmentation of identities, a media-dominated world of consumed and consuming images, dispersion of sites of conflict and resistance, and the ultimate loss of faith in conventional ideologies and politics. While it would be misleading to suggest that postmodernism has become a hegemonic intellectual outlook in any but a couple academic disciplines, it has contributed to the development of a scholarly framework in which debates—most notably, around feminism and various cultural thematics—have been given free expression.[1]

Although a few postmodern currents seek a revitalized oppositional politics grounded in the marriage of elements in both postmodernism and Marxism,[2] and therefore have not rejected Marxism entirely, in the university more extreme, quasi-anarchistic "post" tendencies have flourished. Such tendencies see modernity as having reached its apogee in the mounting dysfunctions of a system built on the logic of domination, bureaucratic regulation, growth-oriented economic development, and manipulation of nature—dysfunctions rooted not only in liberal capitalism but also in prevailing socialist alternatives including above all, the Soviet model. Modernity is fraught with contradictions because it embodies Weberian norms of economic and bureaucratic rationalization and because it always seems to generate imposing new obstacles for itself—the one-sided preeminence of technology and the media spectacle, the ecological crisis, loss of sense of agency, and so forth. The modern world is one characterized by a pervasive crisis of faith, by alienation from the public sphere, by erosion of the belief that knowledge (however constructed) can be used in the service of general societal interests. It is also a world in which political parties, unions, interest groups, even social movements are subverted, to serve state realpolitik and a productivist economic system. The Enlightenment rationality that once so supremely governed the modern world, with its unshakeable conviction that science and technology would be the engine of social progress, has finally been overthrown.

The crisis of modernity that has been so central to the emergence of postmodern theory—what some call the postmodern "condition"—reflects above all a deep sense of pessimism and cynicism about the future, about the very efficacy of collective social action. Postmodernism takes hold at a time of intensifying urban and ecological crisis that for many seems to be impervious to political problem solving; the great oppositional currents of the twentieth century (socialism, communism, even social democracy) have failed at a time when "free-market" capitalism has solidified its hold, both globally and nationally. This two-sided developmental logic points toward a more complex reading of what postmodernism addresses than one finds in the bulk of postmodern literature: all the chaos, fragmentation, and indeterminacy that is seen as a defining feature of the crisis of modernity in fact refers only to the fate of oppositional forces in civil society—rather than being a crisis of the monolithic forces working at the level of the power structure. Here it is interesting to note that the entire apparatus of domination, including the global economy, political institutions, and the system of media and communications, is generally viewed by postmodern writers since Foucault as more pervasive and colonizing than ever. Though rarely theorized as such, at least implicit in their ruminations is the idea that social and ideological consolidation in effect neutralizes potential agencies of change. So the crisis of modernity expresses itself only partially and unevenly, coinciding with the distinction made earlier between the process of rationalization (and globalization) in the macro realm and the dynamic of social decomposition that occurs throughout society as a whole. Such a distinction, while hardly mentioned in the postmodern literature, has enormous implications for the conduct of politics since it suggests that the splintering of public life reinforced by postmodernism applies only to tendencies. The Hobbesian theme of civil disintegration does not extend, so far at least, to the power structure, which continues to be organized more along Weberian lines of institutional rationalization. The famous postmodern "malaise" thus hardly applies to the structures of domination, where economic and political power is concentrated in fewer hands and where the mass media and popular culture exert an unprecedented, ever deepening influence on mass consciousness. Clearly the postmodern age is also the era of corporate colonization.

From this standpoint, it is easy to see that the postmodern challenge to Enlightenment rationality extends to Marxism and the socialist tradition—the main belief system defining political opposition for nearly a century—but *not* to liberal capitalism, as is commonly supposed. With Marxism having disintegrated as the guiding (radical) philosophy of the epoch, the legitimating components of liberalism (such as individualism and the free-market emphasis) have been globally strengthened even while liberal ideology itself is now detached from contemporary social reality. Historically, Marxism always embraced a transformative project that would go beyond capitalism, but that project has essentially collapsed— and with it the entire discourse of collective agency (labor) and political strategy linked to a systematic critique of political economy. Further, the visionary and optimistic sense of the future that Marxism once imparted to millions of people has likewise disappeared. As the most grandiose of all historical narratives, Marxism wound up being subverted by the convergence of certain factors, among them, the increased economic and cultural diversity of post-Fordist society, the decline of the manufacturing sector, the challenge of the New Left and new social movements, and the bureaucratization of regimes and parties labeled "socialist." While no socialist current ever established any deep popular presence in American society, its disintegration *globally*, coinciding with the end of the cold war, had far-reaching negative consequences for the public sphere in most advanced industrial countries. Liberal capitalism in a period of flourishing multinational corporate power now had greater ideological room for maneuver.

As a product of the Enlightenment, Marxism carried forward a vision of social progress connected to economic growth and technological innovation, going beyond liberal capitalism in its commitment to egalitarian values. Although Marxism took more nuanced trajectories in the form of humanistic and critical Marxism during the twentieth century, it never escaped its productivist and determinist foundations; issues of bureaucratic power, culture, gender, and race relations were either sidestepped or subordinated to a class-based paradigm. This void was occupied by the new social movements of the 1960s and beyond, when such issues came to the forefront of progressive struggles. The new-movement celebration of plural sites of power and resistance fed into the postmodern "mood," which first began to influence academic circles in the late 1970s. The idea that Marxism (or any other grand theory) could provide a total, comprehensive view of history was more and more regarded as obsolete. More specifically, time-honored concepts such as the class struggle and revolution—not to mention Lenin's vanguard party—were treated as increasingly problematic. From this standpoint, efforts to unify a dispersed opposition were destined to fail or, if successful, would probably lead to some form of totalitarianism. As Ronald Aronson points out, the collapse of Communism (along with the globalization of the market economy) means that "the world of states and societies is without an alternative vision of social life for the first time since the birth of capitalism."[3]

As the world system becomes more rationalized at the top owing to the enhanced fluidity and mobility of capital—and to the integrative power of the technological and informational revolutions—transforming it seems more and more impossible. The centers of power have become more remote and inaccessible, seemingly beyond the scope of tangible political opposition. The splintering of meaning, so celebrated in the postmodern age, is also a splintering of the public sphere, and only serves to aggravate this historical impasse, helping to account for deep cynicism and pessimism among intellectuals and ordinary citizens alike. By the end of the twentieth century, no empowering master discourse has supplanted Marxism—rather, there is only a mixture of dispersed local identities, ideologies, and movements that are roughly consonant with the postmodern ethos. This is independent of the postmodern theoretical legacy of Baudrillard, Foucault, and others. Indeed, the modest ambitions of the New Left and new social movements easily predates the influence of theoretical currents associated with postmodernism, which did not gain wide acceptance until the 1980s. Meanwhile, as the multinationals establish a firmer hold over global power and wealth, the public sphere in which oppositional politics must flourish continues to be narrowed and localized, as we have seen. The only all-consuming universal discourse that remains is governed by the language of commodities, the spectacle, and instrumental rationality—a language that reproduces a definite uniformity and homogeneity even as postmodernism continues to herald the primacy of difference and chaos.

THE POSTMODERN AS POSTPOLITICAL

When viewed in some contexts, postmodernism is a rather healthy break from the past.[4] Surely it has helped to revitalize many aspects of intellectual and cultural life. The problem is that the main contours of its outlook, beginning with Baudrillard and Foucault and extending into a variety of contemporary feminist debates, tend to devalue the general realms of power, governance, and economy. Because the overwhelming reality of corporate, state, and military power is submerged in the amorphous discourse of postmodernism, the very effort to analyze social forces and locate agencies (or strategies) of change is nullified. In its reaction against the grand historical scope of Marxism and Leninism, the new approach—oriented mainly toward the micro politics of everyday life—tends to dismiss *in toto* the realm of macro politics and with it an indispensable locus of any large-scale project of social transformation. This exaggerated micro focus is most visible in the work of Baudrillard and some postmodern feminists who, as Steven Best and Douglas Kellner put it, in effect "announce the end of the political project and the end of history and society"—a stance of a radically depoliticized culture.[5]

It is probably not too far-fetched to argue that postmodernism, with a few important exceptions, helps reproduce antipolitics in the academy, fully in line with the mood of defeat that has permeated the Left in industrialized countries since the early 1980s.[6] In this way, academic fashion coincides with broader historical trends: the strata that had been the backbone of New-Left politics turned in larger numbers toward professional careers and affluent, suburban lifestyles. Radicalism in the academy, after the late 1970s, often is an "aesthetic pose," or its ideas are submerged in unintelligible jargon. The working class was jettisoned as a political subject, the notion of *any* collective action grounded in *any* social constituency was increasingly viewed with contempt or scorn: oppositional forces were likely to become assimilated into the irresistible logic of the commodity and media spectacle, the victims of a hegemonic discourse over which they have little control. Thus, at a time of mounting pessimism and retreat, the rhetorical question posed by Alex Callinicos becomes "What political subject does the idea of a postmodern epoch help constitute?"[7] By the 1990s any serious discussion of political subjectivity or agency among leftist academics would seem hopelessly passé, hardly worthy of intellectual energies.[8] A great deal of postmodern theorizing seemed inclined to close off debate altogether, especially regarding the precarious linkage of theory and politics, what Barbara Epstein referred to as a "subcultural sect" with its own rigidly enforced codes of discourse.[9]

One of the compelling aspects of postmodernism, however, has been its congruence with contemporary historical trends—including the process of depoliticization itself. It also reflects the quagmire of post-Fordist oppositional discourses and practices. Thus, Foucault's emphasis on the ways in which domination is reproduced through discourses in every area of society, from health care to popular culture, the family, and sexuality as well as politics and the workplace, makes sense. So too does the attention he devoted to the diffusion of power in modern society and to the manner in which such power enters into virtually every mode of communication. It has become abundantly clear that Enlightenment rationality itself embodies various codes of domination. It is a critical problem, however, that discourse ends up being privileged over institutional life to the extent that macro economic and political structures disappear from view, with power becoming so diffuse that it loses all concrete referents. In a conceptual scheme where power is regarded as so pervasive and anonymous, it is impossible to envision concrete *struggles* for power that would involve a range of specific interests and constituencies. Resistance to power winds up dispersed in the generalized ethos of domination, which, at best, allows for limited popular incursions in the micro sphere. While Foucault raised important concerns about the diffusion of power outside the institutional realm, the intimate link between ideas and domination, and the failure of Marxism to address such issues, Foucault's theories in the end amount to a recipe for antipolitics. He furnishes no social grounding for his critique of domination or for potential modes of resistance to that domination.

Turning to Baudrillard, the antipolitical predicament takes on an added dimension insofar as Baudrillard dismisses the possibility of any oppositional politics in a media-centered world that transforms everything into commodities and spectacles. In such a society the very foundations of reason, science, and truth—foundations that allow for the development of objective knowledge—are fully mystified because ideas in this context are the product of cultural distortions and political manipulation in an all-embracing system of commodification. In an age of "hyperreal" networks of fleeting images, symbols, and codes, the market system is able to assimilate virtually any thought or activity and convert it to its advantage, including struggles for social change. Lacking the capacity to sustain antisystem mass consciousness, oppositional politics is inevitably subverted by the overwhelming influence of postmodern culture before it can make significant headway. Reinforced by the hegemonic influences of technology and consumerism, the media obliterates all distinctions between public and private, external and internal reality, truth and fiction—indeed, between the status quo and alternatives to it. Popular consciousness is formed increasingly through the workings of the spectacle, through the medium of entertainment, diversion, and fantasy, with TV always in the forefront. Lacking even the basic avenues for achieving awareness, the ordinary person is reduced to a passive impotent object with no hope of changing the world; where the spectacle takes command and absorbs human subjectivity, as in Baudrillard's scheme, the public sphere loses all meaning. With the commodified media and culture industry retaining such ideological supremacy, politics ends up as nothing other than narrow institutional maneuvering at the elite level, largely detached from competing economic interests and rival visions of the future.

For Baudrillard, then, the postmodern milieu is one of simulated meanings and experiences where oppositional ideas, movements, and parties wind up neutralized by the immense power of the spectacle, just as Guy Debord anticipated in his *Society of the Spectacle* and Herbert Marcuse concluded (with greater emphasis on technological rationality) in *One-Dimensional Man.*[10] Given the highly superficial and fluid character of media images, simulated reality always lacks stability and permanence, whether one is referring to social conditions or institutions or even discourses. Such fluctuation—not to mention, possible confusion or chaos— is hardly compatible with the requirements of sustained, reflective political action. From this position it is no giant leap to anticipate a universe filled with nihilism and absurdity, where the individual stands alone in an ideological void, and where the very idea of social change is dismissed as futile. For Baudillard as for Foucault, the construct of a political economy that takes fully into account the role of government, corporations, banks, and global institutions is dissolved into a labyrinthine mélange of fictitious meanings. And, like Foucault, Baudrillard constructed a theoretical edifice that questions even the *discourse* of political subjectivity. No amount of knowledge or information at the disposal of the public can possibly change this historic impasse. Thus: "Instead of transforming the mass into energy, information produces even more mass. Instead of informing as it claims, instead of giving form and structure, information neutralizes even further the 'social field'; more and more it creates an inert mass impermeable to the classical institutions of the social and to the very contents of information."[11] In effect, the more people become overloaded with images, signs, and "data," the more cynical they become about how to sort out this unmanageable array of inputs and apply them to the dictates of social change.

The postmodernism that has become most fashionable in American intellectual discourse is a product of this manifestly antipolitical current associated with the work of Foucault and Baudrillard; the contributions of Lyotard, Derrida, Rorty, and early "difference" feminists like Carol Gilligan have carried forward this outlook.[12] Indeed Foucault, well before his death in 1986, had achieved legendary status among scholars from a wide range of disciplines in the United States. Others, including Frederic Jameson, Ernesto Laclau and Chantal Mouffe, and theorists of new social

movements like Alain Touraine approached postmodernism as an opening toward either a reconstituted Marxism or a radical–democratic alternative to failed socialist models of the past.[13] Many in this tradition sought
to theorize collective subjectivity and a politics of transformation on new
grounding. Whether labeled "post-Marxism" or yet another alternative,
this departure assumed a definite continuity from modernity to postmodernism, from Marxism to a revitalized democratic radicalism, that avoided
the more extreme antipolitics of that form of academic postmodernism
first inspired by Foucault and Baudrillard. While critical of Enlightenment
values, the post-Marxist turn affirmed some of the best elements of modernity (including what was most progressive in both Marxism and liberalism).

    Since my overriding concern here is with the problem of depoliticiza-
tion, I will not dwell on this more politically oriented side of postmodernism except to call attention to different strains of postmodern theory.
Still, while the work of Jameson, Laclau and Mouffe, Touraine, and others
in this tradition has opened up important new theoretical terrain, it too
has become vulnerable to flaws in the general postmodern discourse. In
the view of Laclau and Mouffe, postmodernism is useful as a vehicle for
moving from the restrictive, mechanistic premises of Marxism to a post-
Marxian conception of radical democracy—a shift that goes beyond a singular emphasis on class conflict to a focus on multiple sites of struggle
(and power) appropriate to the era of new social movements. The uniqueness of this approach lies in its incorporation of both Marxist and postmodern ideas while dispensing with the reductionist and productivist elements of Marxism and debunking its scientific pretensions.[14]

    Rejecting a view of advanced capitalist society as divided by class pat-
terns, Laclau and Mouffe project an unstable, perpetually changing system of differences that do not correspond to fixed material or objective
referents. This abandonment of the concept of Marxist totality opens the
social terrain to a more plural, open-ended, discursive view of change,
where radical democracy involves multiple "nodal points" of change but
no clear revolutionary break with the past. Theirs is a vision of change
that would "deepen and expand" liberal democracy while at the same
time advancing goals historically associated with socialism (social equality,
collective ownership, full democratic participation, and so on). So far as
this argument goes, Laclau and Mouffe achieve an important and probably necessary break with dated theoretical assumptions inherited from the
traditional Left. Even their Foucaultian attention to discourse—the pursuit
of "discursive conditions of collective action"—is far less debilitating than
some critics claim, since emphasis on discourse does not in itself negate
the importance of material conditions.[15] Nor does their project suggest a
flight from politics in the fashion of extreme postmodernism; on the con-

trary, their departure from reductionist Marxism and their embrace of multiple sites of resistance suggests creative, multifaceted politics. There are two problems: privileging the "discursive field" over structural factors and preoccupation with localized micro concerns in such a way that the macro realm of state governance, corporate power, and global economy is diminished. It is hardly coincidental that the macro level receives little attention in their otherwise insightful analysis of social movements or their assessment of counterhegemonic forces.[16]

This emphasis on a dispersed micro terrain of power and struggle in Laclau and Mouffe—surely a needed corrective for the overly totalizing legacy of Marxist politics—contains its own disabling antipolitical logic when carried to extremes. The social totality must be reconceptualized, rather than jettisoned, in the context of drastically altered historical conditions. What Laclau and Mouffe write in this regard is the following: "The incomplete character of every totality necessarily leads us to abandon, as a terrain of analysis, the promise of 'society' as a sutured and self-defined totality. 'Society' is not a valid object of discourse. There is no single unifying principle fixing—and hence constituting—the whole field of differences."[17] Herein lies the major difficulty: the perfectly valid observation that society may not be "self-defined" or held together by a "single unifying principle" does not thereby logically justify abandoning it (or *any* macro sphere) as an object of analysis or strategic transformation. To establish this continuum is to undermine our very capacity to theorize the social and the political. Discarded here is the capacity to view macro institutional forces according to a logic quite distinct from what is appropriate to the micro realm—as different as the global economy is from the family or the state is from gender relations. Further, and equally problematic, is the extent to which the Laclau–Mouffe framework *severs* the vital and complex linkage between global and local, macro and micro, the systemic and dispersed. Not only does this approach devalue the role of macro forces, it effectively subverts full understanding of larger influences at work in people's daily lives. Indeed, radical-democratic politics is *inconceivable* in the absence of such interconnections. These complex linkages can be seen graphically, for example, in the documentary film *Roger and Me*, which depicts the accumulated economic, cultural, and psychological consequences that General Motors plant closings have had on community life in Flint, Michigan—closings that were clearly the product of global economic pressures. Thus, while Laclau and Mouffe correctly argue for a new radical-democratic paradigm and manage to avoid the cynicism and pessimism typical of most postmodernism, they end up trapped in much the same depoliticizing impasse.

The translation of poststructural thematics into academic discourse in the United States during the 1980s and 1990s placed such dilemmas in even starker relief. Whether by design or not, fashionable variants of "post-Marxist" theory have become a refuge for career-minded professional scholars who seem anxious to skirt or ignore the political terrain even as they uphold a radical faith. Much of this theorizing, notably among film and literary critics, feminists, and postmodern social scientists, has degenerated into an insular, self-referential ideology fitting of intellectual cults with their own esoteric jargon. Grounded in an academic subculture and yet attached to norms of difference and fragmentation, scholastic postmodernism generally upholds a contempt for the public realm that could be appropriated directly from Baudrillard. In Barbara Epstein's words: "The implicit values of poststructuralism, its celebration of difference and its hostility to unity, make it particularly inappropriate as an intellectual framework for movements that need to make positive assertions about how society could be better organized and that need to incorporate difference in a collective unity for social change."[18] A close reading of texts shows that most postmodern academics have little interest in confronting or changing the status quo, preferring to couch their critiques in the safe framework of relatively obscure texts and narratives. As Russell Jacoby writes: "At the end of the radical theorizing project is a surprise: a celebration of academic hierarchy, professions, and success. Never has so much criticism yielded so much affirmation. From Foucault the professor learned that power and institutions saturate everything. Power is universal; complicity with power is universal, and this means university practices and malpractices are no better or worse than anything else."[19]

Perhaps nowhere has the influence of postmodern scholarship been so pervasive, and so corrosive, as in contemporary academic feminism, which achieved its fullest expression in the "difference" or "identity" motifs of such theorists as Carol Gilligan, Donna Harraway, Judith Butler, and Drucilla Cornell, and in the pages of such journals as *Feminist Studies*.[20] As in the seminal work of Baudrillard and Foucault, the point of departure here can be appreciated as a necessary leap forward: a break with productivist and class-defined Marxism, emphasis on multiple locations of power and conflict, a renewed emphasis on the micro concerns of everyday life, attention devoted to dispersed meanings and truths (including gender-based forms of knowledge), an embrace of "cultural politics." Indeed, the basic contours of this work flowed from a theorization of positions already established in both feminism and the new social movements, following the insights of Foucault, Baudrillard, Touraine, and others. Over time, however, postmodern feminism came to more extreme articulations of these motifs, to the extent that issues related to patriarchy, gender, and the family were situated in a more strictly discursive, localized terrain, often removed from the flow of concrete social movements and smothered by arcane, frequently incomprehensible jargon. In its most developed forms, exemplified by what Teresa Ebert calls "ludic feminism," postmodern feminism wound up associated with a certain playful or trivializing quality that seemed to view politics in almost contemptuous terms—often dismissing the public sphere as a bastion of male domination.[21]

In Ebert's conception, postmodern feminism serves to transplant politics onto the terrain of culture and aesthetics, the inevitable outcome of a theory that displaces the central reality of material forces with discursive practices. Oriented toward a kind of irreverent but largely superficial focus on texts, codes, and identities, ludic theory questions the prevalent social science notion of durable structures and social relations, conflating an immense range of practices (including politics) into a postmodern mélange of highly fluid discursive expressions. Thus: "As a result, any transformative or materialist politics—any emancipatory politics—based on the struggle against hierarchies of differences (such as class struggle . . .) are seen as foundationless."[22] Leaving aside here problems raised by what exactly constitutes a "materialist politics," the implications of ludic feminism for the theory and practice of social movements (much less "class struggle") are, in Ebert's view, simply devastating. Moving from a deep suspicion of any preoccupation with macro concerns, postmodern theory in the form of ludic feminism sidesteps the realm of power (both economic and political) beyond its local, everyday manifestations. Thus Foucault, for example, insists that domination is so pervasive, so diffusely spread throughout everyday life, that efforts to root it in specific institutions are doomed to failure. And for Laclau and Mouffe, the ludic dimension separates micro from macro realms, leaving them unconnected and without adequate theorization—and feminism without any coherent foundation. The ludic call for the subversion of hegemonic discourses apparently does not extend to the zones of state and corporate power. Postmodern feminism in its most avant-garde forms therefore winds up indulging some of the most extreme antipolitical tendencies at work in the university and in society as a whole.

Postmodern feminism, like other subgenres, frequently clings to a language of transformation even as it reduces the field of struggle to mainly discursive practices—or to narrowly localized forms of rebellion against male-dominated public space. One example of the latter is Leslie Gotfrit's exploration of nightclub dancing as an arena of social contestation where gendered meanings can be confronted and emancipatory possibilities developed.[23] Writing on the basis of her visits to the Big Bop Club in Toronto, Gotfrit analyzes the way in which feminist values can be affirmed through expressions of bodily desire, sensuality, and freedom on the dance floor, in this instance by virtue of women dancing together or in small groups. The "active mobilization of desire" and the "realization of fantasy" can lead to a challenging of power relations in everyday life. Gotfrit looks at "how dancing can be understood as a site where dominant ideologies are both reproduced and resisted through women's accessing the powers of desire and their appropriation of pleasure and space for themselves."[24] Openly expressed desire, especially if manifest in the form of "unsanctioned sexuality," can fuel defiance and resistance. Thus: "The more we express desire and sexuality in public space, the less willing we are to accept powerlessness."[25] Inspired by such Reichian insights, she concludes that the body becomes "crucial to any oppositional politics," especially where rules are broken or where there is a "transgression of normal practices."[26] Especially for women, the dance floor allows for a "certain pleasure of subversion, of defiance, and of rejection."[27] The result is that in one significant area of everyday life it is possible to imagine the realization of alternative social spaces that can allow for the overthrow of hegemonic norms and practices.

Here we have a fascinating case study illustrating just how far postmodernism can take us into a theoretical and political cul-de-sac. Of course, dancing can indeed be a source of pleasure and sensuality, and it can surely convey feelings of bodily freedom in public (or quasi-public) spaces. Dance clubs of the sort described by Gotfrit can be areas of powerfully intense social interaction inspired by music, physical gyrations, and natural exchanges of sexual energy. And this can be very empowering—at least for the moment. But how far can such claims be legitimately pushed? How seriously can we regard pretenses of subversion, defiance, and rejection in a nightclub setting designed for little more than spontaneous, momentary expressions of pleasure? What does it mean to speak of "oppositional politics" in this context? Power relations are scarcely transformed in any meaningful sense in the club setting; a night's dancing, however exuberant and satisfying, leaves behind nothing that is durable; there is no linkage established (or even claimed) by Gotfrit between these micro practices—even conceding their emancipatory character—and what takes place in the community, work, politics, and so forth. We are left with nothing in the way of structured alternative spaces or practices and no "empowerment" that can be extended to actual social relations—any more than pleasurable lovemaking (even if it "breaks the rules") can be a prelude to oppositional movements. In this instance the micro realm becomes so fetishized and overtheorized that the observer gets lost in a maze of exaggerated and mystifying discourses.

While multiple forms of power and resistance need to be more clearly theorized than in the past, and while Marxian fixation on production and class factors has been too conceptually restrictive, the postmodern subversion of the macro sphere—of the very notion of political economy—leads to an artificial separation of the micro and the macro, reducing the force of any critique. Moreover, as postmodernism upholds a concept of subjectivity that is perpetually decentered and fragmented, or even obliterated altogether, the theme of citizenship gets necessarily obscured. As Philip Wexler points out, the social, legal, and political requirements of citizenship were historically erected on universal norms of democracy, rights, and equality, but postmodernism, which blurs social reality and dissolves politics into the sphere of culture and everyday life, destroys this foundation. Once the subject melts into a murky cultural diffuseness, into an ever-changing world of images and spectacles, the elements of public life constituted through citizenship simply evaporate.[28] Civic ideals may be kept alive in the official ideology and political science texts, mainly for the purpose of legitimating the electoral ritual, but they become increasingly detached from social conditions. As Wexler concludes: "For now, citizenship will remain the appropriate sign of postmodernism and semiotic society—a restored sign artifact that may be recycled and used so long as it does not disturb contemporary society's newfound need for superficiality."[29]

In the splintered, discontinuous universe theorized by Foucault, Baudrillard, Richard Rorty, and kindred writers, social coherence is weakened and the linkage between personal and public, micro and macro, and local and global is fractured—a devastating turn for politics, especially radical politics, in an age of globalization. Further, where truth, language, and social referents are so tenaciously contested as to dissolve into limitless interpretations of what constitutes basic social trends in the world, where nothing is ever settled, no strategy for change is even thinkable. While this perspective may correspond well to a milieu in which greater attention is devoted (perhaps rightly) to local knowledge and concerns, it is nonetheless depoliticizing insofar as it tends to obscure what in fact needs to be retheorized—that is, macro levels of economic and political power. Where the state system, for example, is devalued or broken down into a mosaic of dispersed and partial entities, politics too ends up obliterated. Oddly enough for a discourse that embodies such radical pretensions, the whole realm of symbols and images—central to what Norman Denzin describes as the "cinematic age"[30]—becomes far more important than concrete struggles around rival claims to power, economic interests, and visions of a better society.[31]

Despite its critical and oppositional language, therefore, postmodernism is actually system-reproducing in its celebration of fragmented, localized, and (occasionally) privatized discourses; it fits the imperatives of corporate colonization, partly because it reflects an ethos of public disintegration and partly because, in its extreme formulations, it gives rise to a disempowering nihilism. The virtues of the local enclave, the therapeutic culture, the most insular and separatist of identity movements—

even the market system itself—can easily coexist with the main postmodernism currents. The much-needed critique of "progress" as a vision grounded in Enlightenment rationality soon degenerates into a more pervasive disaffection with the public sphere that is simply reinforced by the growing cynical and nihilistic attitudes in American society as a whole. The collapse of hope, so frequently pinned to the gains of economic and technological development, can only serve to reduce the scope and vitality of citizen participation—a sure recipe sharpening bybles of despair and retreat in the future. Murray Bookchin, who believes that postmodernism embraces an inherent nihilism, comments on this point, noting that "the more one feels disempowered about the human condition and bereft of social commitment, the more one becomes cynical and thereby captive to the prevailing social order."[32] In the ever tempting flight from rationality one finds a mounting sense of weariness and futility that postmodernism appears to share with the larger political culture.

In a social order where media-perpetuated symbols and images dominate mass consciousness, the splintering of local identities coincides with a drastic (and perhaps historically unprecedented) weakening of political opposition—a development anticipated long ago by Marcuse, who, however, concluded that the "one-dimensionality" of his day could be more strictly attributed to the influence of technological rationality.[33] It should hardly need to be emphasized that corporate colonization has never been effectively subverted through the proliferation of micro centers of resistance or the extreme affirmation of diversity and multiculturalism that has become so central to American public discourse over the past two decades. Dispersed movements and identities, while no doubt inevitable in the present social and ideological climate, are all too easily assimilated into the orbit of the all-powerful commodity. As communities begin to take on what Zygmunt Bauman calls an "imaginary character,"[34] identities have less and less resonance with the public sphere, thus freeing politics to descend even further into the morass of the spectacle. As Bauman observes: "Postmodern politics is mostly about the reallocation of attention. Public attention is the most important—coveted and struggled for—among the scarce commodities in the focus of political struggle."[35] From this standpoint, the eclipse of collective subjectivity and the atrophy of political language—one of the more significant legacies of postmodern theory—converges more and more with the stubborn reality of corporate domination.

THE PREDICAMENT OF SOCIAL MOVEMENTS

The proliferation of new social movements in the 1970s and 1980s opened up new ways of understanding the processes of change in advanced industrial society; beyond the antinomies of revolution and reform, change was expected to follow a disruptive but nonetheless peaceful and molecular pattern rooted in disparate popular struggles. The idea of a unitary class-based movement or party is increasingly seen as obsolete—a relic of the traditional Left—even more so in the wake of political upheavals that brought down the Soviet-bloc regimes. One important theme associated with the new movements was the neo-Gramscian project of a counterhegemonic transformation of civil society, building toward an overturning of the institutional fortresses of class and state power. This possibility was at least the more radical interpretation of new-movement prospects at a time when the crisis of Marxism had sharpened and labor movements seemed moribund. Whether overtly radical or not, emergent popular movements—community-organizing feminism, gay rights, ecology, youth culture, and peace campaigns—could be situated in the phase of post-Fordist capitalism and the spread of "postmaterialist" consciousness. Such movements gave expression to particular meanings, identities, and solidarities as part of what could be seen as the historic struggle to broaden empowerment and reshape the public sphere. In some cases (for example, the Green parties) new movements entered coalitions and translated their energies onto the political terrain with hopes of altering power relations or at least influencing government policies.[36] On the whole, however, such energies were confined to the sphere of civil society consistent with much theorizing along the lines of Gramsci's "war of position" (discussed in Chapter 4); the "war of movement" (for state power) was either diminished or forgotten. Like postmodern theory, which accompanied it, this one-sided Gramscian model essentially sidestepped the critical imperatives of economic and political power.

Following nearly three decades of new-movement experience in Europe, North America, and elsewhere, oppositional struggles in virtually every area of activity have wound up at a strategic impasse; in some cases significant reforms have been won, but ideological backlash and conservative institutional retrenchment since the early 1980s have revealed the imposing limits of dispersed movements. The failure of the Left to take advantage of new political space opened up with the end of the old war reflects this deep predicament. Oddly enough, at a time of socialist defeat combined with intensified social crisis resulting from economic globalization, antisystem mobilization has probably been more feeble than ever—especially in the United States, where the tide of depoliticization has engulfed new-movement forces too. By the 1990s, local grassroots movements, though still present in large numbers, were increasingly situated on the margins of the political system and were just as likely to swing ideologically to the *right* as to the left in a period when identities rooted in localism, ethnicity, and religion had come to the forefront.

The predicament of local movements was accentuated clearly during the Persian Gulf war in the early 1990s. Legitimating its actions as a global military initiative sanctioned by the UN, the Bush administration was able to push through its interventionist policies in a climate of frenzied war hysteria. Ideological components of the strong prowar consensus are by now familiar: superpatriotism, anti-Arab xenophobia, worship of high-tech military power, glorification of violence in the service of (presumed) American global interests. By the time the U.S. military finished its rapid but bloody (air and land) campaign, fully 90 percent of the American people were in support of President Bush's policies. More than a year later, in August 1992, surveys revealed that nearly 70 percent of Americans would go along with yet *another* military action against Iraq, this time with the goal of overthrowing Saddam Hussein. This continued endorsement of such military agendas, well after the crumbling of Soviet power, could have profound implications for the scope and efficacy of social movements in the United States. Even at a time of ongoing postmodern celebration of dispersed sites of micro resistance, the massive fortresses of the war economy and security state remain firmly entrenched. Further, the expansion of transnational capital along with continued global militarization could give rise to what John Stockwell calls the "new world security complex" designed to contain antisystem movements in the United States and throughout the world.[37] Although the Persian Gulf war's conclusion failed to satisfy U.S. policy makers' grandest expectations, the enormity of the military mobilization and the ease with which it was ideologically legitimated both have tremendous import for the future.

A major impediment to oppositional movements—one too rarely emphasized—is the long-standing popular support for the war economy and foreign military intervention, revealed most recently during and after the Persian Gulf encounter.[38] However it is legitimated, militarism helps to solidify the power structure by, among other things, mobilizing nationalist sentiment and undercutting those social movements that challenge established priorities. In the United States such movements have included a variety of peace, anti-intervention, and citizen-action groups that opposed military ventures in southeast Asia and, later, in Central America. Pentagon campaigns to extirpate the well-known residues of the "Vietnam syndrome" (i.e., skepticism toward the efficacy of sending troops abroad) can be understood in this context. The Persian Gulf events in fact bolstered the perceived efficacy of military intervention at a time when the legitimacy of Pentagon power was being increasingly called into question. Even leaving aside the "Vietnam syndrome," the end of the cold war might expected to give rise to a milieu in which popular demands for significant reductions in military spending could be effectively voiced. While some limited cuts were pushed through (against Pentagon resistance), the decline of Soviet power actually removed an important counterforce to U.S. global hegemony; that is, the nearly simultaneous *end* of the communist threat gave considerable impetus to full-scale military intervention during the Gulf crisis.

These events illustrate the degree to which the military–industrial apparatus has so thoroughly transformed the economy, system of governance, and larger culture in ways that may be extremely difficult to reverse. The Pentagon has been central not only to the reproduction of the war economy but to the maintenance of concentrated power, a huge intelligence network, and the prolific (and highly profitable) weapons trade around the world. It also contributes mightily to shrinkage of the public sphere to the degree that vast resources are devoted to surveillance, social control, propaganda, and of course war making. Concurrently, the war economy thrives on norms of regimentation that, as in all quasi-garrison states, demand maximum popular obedience, which helps solidify the networks of state and corporate rule. From this standpoint, the Gulf war was less a case of economic imperialism pure and simple (though oil markets were surely a critical factor) than a move to further consolidate U.S. global power. Indeed, the United States remains, in the 1990s, a militarized form of state capitalism where military, political, and economic decision making is the province of a narrow stratum of elites, streamlining the already rigid hierarchies of a multilayered system of domination.[39] It is a system guaranteed to reinforce the devastating effects of corporate colonization. If the war economy persists as a linchpin of capitalist development, it also imposes limitations on what can be spent to sustain the domestic infrastructure. While the Pentagon has consumed nearly $8 trillion since 1950 and now devours almost $300 billion annually to support U.S. global power, vital social programs deteriorate more rapidly with each passing year.[40] Pentagon tanks, missiles, and ships can easily triumph over the Iraqi armed forces, but the domestic economy is so bereft of public resources that it cannot solve basic problems of housing, education, health care, the environment, and urban violence.

The war economy also has drastic consequences for the political culture in general. Of course it is well known that actions intended to inspire mass outpourings of xenophobic anger serve to bolster power by deflecting popular attention away from pressing domestic problems and needs. The deeper problem, however, is that warfare—and preparation for warfare—requires by its very nature subordination of the masses to norms of patriotism, loyalty, order, and violence that, in time, become constitutive of the general culture. Moreover, the celebration of war making as a mass spectacle has deep roots in the national psyche. And this phenomenon has recently been given added meaning with the advent of the information revolution and the cult of technology that play such a powerful role in post-Fordist capitalism. In this setting military adventures can help relegitimate the system at a time of growing social dislocation and individual anomie. The great U.S. battlefield successes against Iraq served to rationalize Pentagon faith in expensive high-tech weaponry while also offering the American public a deep sense of patriotic identity and achievement—revealing, perhaps, the scope of collective angst and insecurity in the culture as a whole. If even for a brief interlude, popular consciousness seemed infinitely manipulable at the hands of political elites and the electronic media. The war and its aftermath showed that a virulent nativism remained deeply embedded in the political culture, even well after the eclipse of Soviet power. The main point here is that perpetuation of such a highly militarized culture poses serious questions for the future of civic involvement—not to mention oppositional movements—in the United States.[41]

When military power becomes such a dominant force in economic and cultural life, as in the United States, the forms of ideological hegemony are inevitably reconfigured. Elites can more easily legitimate their rule by invoking the need to defend "national interests." Foreign enemies of various sorts are readily manufactured: rogue states, terrorists, international drug traffickers, possible resurgent Communist regimes such as China and North Korea. At the same time, military vigilance encourages a compulsive national trend toward ever greater routinization of bureaucratic power, technical efficiency, order, and conformity, a trend hardly consonant with the requirements of maximum democratic participation. War-making consensus depends on a high degree of patriotic or nonpartisan agreement, where doubts and ambiguities at both the elite and popular levels can be resolved or downplayed. In the case of the Persian Gulf conflict, military options were embraced quickly and justified as a moral imperative (fighting Saddam Hussein's "Hitlerite" regime); beneath the familiar myths of democracy and tolerance a large percentage of Americans seemed to view the conflict as an opportunity for revenge in a fantasy world perpetuated by the security state and mass media. In this frenzied situation many people looked to the aggressive deployment of military power as a source of national identity and power, lending the ordeal of human suffering an almost surreal character. The impact of this phenomenon on American political culture is far more corrosive than has generally been recognized.

The lingering presence of a war economy in the age of corporate colonization raises critical questions about the relationship between social movements and the prospects for oppositional politics in the United States. First and foremost, it challenges the validity of a postmodern culture that dwells on micro spheres of resistance and the extreme pluralization of movement identities and goals. The issue here is not so much the solidity or historical importance of the movements themselves—they are clearly a durable feature of post-Fordist society—but rather their ultimate *political* significance.

New social movements have often been grounded in modes of personal involvement tied to specific discourses (feminism, ecology) that have origins in 1960s radicalism: an emphasis on local participation, community, cultural renewal, psychological or spiritual transformation, and (in some cases) social forms of consumption. At the same time, these movements have been ambivalent if not hostile toward the sphere of normal politics, largely rejecting sustained involvement in the major parties, elections, lobbying, legislative work, and so forth. Here it might be useful to conceptualize the *radical* side of new-movement practice as a form of localism in search of autonomy. While certain local movements were able to create a somewhat durable community and even institutional presence, in the arena of politics they were hobbled by limits that had paralyzed the New Left, mainly related to fragmentation, excessive localism, and a retreatist attitude toward issues of power and governance. They failed to translate their energies onto the terrain of political organization and strategy except in those cases where citizens' groups coalesced to form Green parties, as in West Germany. To speak of politics here means simply a linkage of immediate struggles to long-range goals, the development of a conscious, planned framework of action connected to *societal* issues and priorities, to a broadening of social governance. Historically popular movements have rarely carried out strategic self-transformation of this sort since, in contrast to parties, they usually remain confined to local, partial realms of activity. Many community-based groups, as we have seen, have actually embraced an ethos of antipolitics, where defense of space and identity was always a more pressing concern than social change. New movements that look to the ideals of local autonomy, personal politics, and consciousness transformation have been especially vulnerable to the seductions of a nonpolitical, extrainstitutional, civil society–oriented strategy.

Antipolitical tendencies have probably been most visible in the peace movement—or at least the multiple expressions of U.S. peace that can be traced back to the anti-Vietnam war mobilizations of the 1960s. Grounded in universalistic ideals (opposition to war and military intervention, support for disarmament and test bans, and so on), such activism never achieved political coherence despite its capacity to inspire huge turnouts for marches and demonstrations and generate creative forms of direct action.[42] Beginning with the first broad-based protests against the Vietnam war in 1965 and extending to the Persian Gulf events in the early 1990s, antiwar movements revolved mainly around contesting U.S. actions abroad (in southern Asia, Central America, the Middle East). Of course, other issues and priorities entered the picture from time to time: pacifism, antinuclear protests, the lobby for arms control, campaigns to reduce Pentagon spending and waste. In most cases a discourse of moral witness shaped the "peace" vernacular, whether from test bans, to nuclear reactors, to the bombing of foreign countries. It was a discourse that helped to raise popular consciousness about the threats of militarism and war—and to a more limited extent about the dangers of Pentagon power—but it has fallen short of calling attention to structural aspects of the war economy and the security state. The institutional apparatus responsible for the continuing U.S. global presence, with all of its predictable foreign adventures, remains completely unchallenged; protests against one intervention are followed by yet the next wave of protests, to continue indefinitely. Peace groups and social movements that remain immersed in this modus operandi wind up trapped in a strategic impasse characterized by relative ineffectuality.[43]

This impasse, of course, cannot be attributed to the internal flaws of new social movements alone; activists have been forced to advance their goals in a milieu that, as I have argued, serves to impede any political definition of local struggles. For example, in the months preceding the Persian Gulf war, a revitalized peace movement did appear in the United States, often projecting broader aims than most previous anti-interventionist campaigns in that there were significant efforts to link domestic and international issues. Once President Bush's military campaign started, however, the rapid pace of events along with the triumphs of propaganda and the dramatic results of the campaign itself quickly neutralized and silenced most of the opposition. Even mild criticisms of the war were drowned out in an orgy of self-congratulatory patriotism, reflected most obviously in the widespread media celebration of Desert Storm and the public's massive display of flags and yellow ribbons. Most critics were silenced. It would have been difficult for any peace movement to effectively challenge the prowar consensus of 1991, much less to carry out sustained organizational activity—yet another illustration of how deep conformism runs in a society that celebrates pluralism and diversity.

By the 1990s it had become obvious that social movements alone, however expansive their scope and definition, cannot serve as transformative vehicles, at least in societal terms. The main locus of new movements has been in civil society, outside of or peripheral to the routine elements of the political system, consistent with the postmodern emphasis on micro, localized, and dispersed zones of resistance. When such groups have chosen to enter the political arena, along lines of the Sierra Club, the National Organization for Women (NOW), and various tenants' rights movements, they have typically done so as agencies of modest reforms or as old-fashioned interest lobbies; their politicization, while real has been very narrow. For any popular movement this raises the familiar strategic dilemma of autonomy versus effectiveness, transformative agendas versus instrumental goals. As Claus Offe argues, social movements by nature are ill equipped to deal with long-term requirements of planning and time because they are so fragile, diffuse, and confined to their immediate milieu. Thus: "In their demands, new movements do not anticipate a lengthy process of transition, gradual reform, or slow improvement, but an immediate sudden change."[44] Continuity, on the other hand, depends on the capacity of movements to evolve into viable organizational forms that can supply leadership, funding, discipline, and planning. Such a transition inevitably brings movements into the realm of "normal" politics where, as the example of peace groups and the record of European Green parties have shown, the logic of deradicalization can be overpowering; that is, the autonomy of grassroots struggles and the spirit of direct action are easily lost in the trade-off involved in winning elections and a share of governance. Adaptation to institutional politics can give rise to moderating pressures of the sort that historically transformed the U.S. labor movement (as well as socialist and communist parties around the world) into a tame loyal opposition preoccupied simply with fine-tuning liberal-capitalist institutions.[45] This danger of embourgeoisiement will never be countered by means of the simple flight from politics that seems to be at the core of postmodern culture. And the stubborn presence of a war economy and security state, along with intensified globalizing pressures, only illuminates this predicament more clearly.

THE IDENTITY MAZE

The post-Fordist stage of capitalism is one where several important trends have converged, among them the social fragmentation of civil society, the diffusion of postmodern culture, and cult of identity—all filtered through the reality of corporate colonization. Heightened attention paid to issues of multiculturalism, subjectivity, identity, and the self can be understood, at least in part, as a visceral reaction against a rationalizing, commodified system bent on the reproduction of an integrated global order that subverts those very interests and needs. Popular struggles to recover a sense of culture, roots, or identity are redoubled precisely at a time when the very foundations of identity seem to be evaporating, when traditional constructions of identity—whether through religion, nationalism, class affiliation, or some kind of universal political ideology—have lost much of their strengths. Efforts to locate one's identity today, refocused around immediate categories of ethnicity, gender, sexual preference, and locale, may also be viewed as a mode of psychological adaptation to an environment in flux, with a great deal of mobility, insecurity, and alienation. If the essence of modern society is to be found in universalizing pressures of the market and commodity, reinforced by the power of bureaucracy and mass media, then their antithesis is the growing obsession with plurality and "differences." While this dialectic has given rise to awareness of multiple forms of domination, its long-term implications for a transformative politics (or any revitalization of the public sphere) are problematic in that identity-based groups and movements seem to inevitably contain highly corrosive forms of antipolitics.

The preoccupation with self, subjectivity, and identity has taken on new meaning in post-Fordist society since the 1960s. In the wake of the New Left, some movements gave expression to the idea of multiple subject positions, or identities, constructed by individuals and groups in the process of "making history" and forged in rapidly changing social and political circumstances. The civil rights, feminist, and gay movements carved out new collective consciousness as part of challenging dominant, stereotypical notions of social experience, thus moving beyond long-established identities built exclusively on religion, nation, class, and family. At the same time, new movements went against the inherited wisdom of socialism and the traditional Left, which linked identity to class relations and posited a more or less automatic relationship between social being and consciousness, class position, and politics. Such relationships are now viewed as mediated and problematic. As Derrida and a whole generation of postmodern theorists stressed, a determined connection between material conditions and social or political consciousness could no longer be sustained; the linkages are always variable and mediated in a world characterized by openness and indeterminacy.[46] The idea of any singular "class consciousness"—much less a "transition to socialism" or "world revolution"—was no longer tenable in the advanced capitalist era. Identity (much like the fields of culture and politics through which it gets expressed) is a product of historical definition (and redefinition) over time. The sense of belonging to certain religious or national traditions or being a member of certain ethnic, kinship, or gender groups grows out of lived history rather than predefined, inherited, or "natural" formations that are generally rooted in hegemonic discourses. If the subject is now increasingly "decentered," it can be no other way under circumstances where the discourses and frameworks are inescapably multiple and crosscutting—a reality embedded not just in theory but in history.[47]

Taking shape in the emergent paradigm of new social movements and postmodernism, this renewed focus on identity made sense and in certain ways reflected the vitality of popular struggles (especially feminism) and the legitimization of previously excluded or marginalized voices. Identity concerns did in fact coincide with the maturation of expanded new plural discourses, along with the failure of Marxism to interpret the altered conjuncture. Beyond this was the explosion of collective forms of defiance that indeed could be labeled "political." The feminist movement, for example, provided a context with which both the individual and collective pursuit of subjectivity could merge as part of a newly politicized formation.[48] Once the personal and political became dialectically intertwined in this fashion, then the micro and macro spheres too could be understood as interconnected in the milieu of popular movements that sought to articulate and reshape evolving identities. From this standpoint, feminism in its different expressions was able to reappropriate definitions of gender, sexuality, and kinship—reconceptualizing the very meaning of the "private realm"—in a more critical transformative discourse. Just as shifting collective identities were integral to earlier struggles for national liberation in the third world, merging the self with the public at a time of mass mobilization, the new movements stressed empowerment through the pursuit of new meanings and identities.[49]

The historical dynamic of groups struggling for identity in and through social movements requires breaking down the division between individual and collective forms of subjectivity in much the same way that Marx believed such a dynamic would unfold in the formation of class consciousness. Everyday life, culture, and politics converge as part of a larger transformative process.[50] In the contemporary period, however, this logic is refashioned to fit the new paradigm of multiple conflicts tied to plural (and sometimes overlapping) identities—an immensely difficult problem to theorize but one that surely cannot be ignored. As Craig Calhoun writes: "The politics of identity—politics either starting from or aiming at claimed identities of their protagonists—have to be taken seriously. The struggles occasioned by identity politics need to be understood, however, not as simply between those who claim different identities but in each subject as the multiple and contending discourses of our era challenge any of our efforts to attain stable self-recognition or coherent subjectivity."[51] Viewed in this way, the formation of popular consciousness today becomes a far more intricate process than was assumed historically in either the Marxist class model or the third world national liberation model.

At this point, however, the question must be posed as to how and even whether a politics of identity gets constructed over time. Put differently, there is the critical issue of how "stable self-recognition" and "coherent subjectivity" become incorporated into an explicitly political discourse and practice. The construction of a politics of identity is in fact a matter of great complexity—far more problematic than is commonly supposed, given the diverse mediations that help shape identity in the contemporary period and the ever present influences of a depoliticized society. Moreover, in the discourse of identity there are strong pressures that can easily militate against emergence of a revitalized politics. As I have argued in earlier chapters, politics refers to an inclusive notion of citizenship, participation in a general community, the exercise of social governance, and a sense of what is distinctively public and common. In its Rousseauian vision, the very idea of politics is unthinkable without an interactive framework where modes of discourse and action can lead to a binding social contract that ensures rights, democracy, and the common good—perhaps even survival against the ominous threat of civic anarchy. In other words, a visionary, democratic politics ultimately requires forms of loyalty that transcend the dispersed, parochial identities of locale, kinship, ethnicity, and so forth; differences must either converge with or give way to the common interest. Lacking such a normative understanding of politics, the possibility of society-wide planning and legitimization processes that allow for realization of public interests and goods is ruled out, leaving private or local interests (mostly extensions of the market) to compete for hegemony. And this is precisely the dilemma encountered, in a different way, by the proliferation of dispersed identities in the new social movements, postmodernism, and multiculturalism. In the end, identity politics can have transformative implications only in a common modality of wide citizen participation and social governance.

As it turns out, the politics of identity has become a contradiction in terms, given the way it has played out during the past decade or so—identity signifying more and more an affiliation with cultural enclaves that divide and insulate while often encouraging parochial, ethnocentric, or even chauvinistic attitudes. If identity (like culture) is inevitably hard to define, its connotations nonetheless seem to have narrowed; frequently it signifies that which is natural and given rather than what is created as people struggle to establish meaning and purpose in their lives. Identity in its common usage suggests either, with the individual, some form of self-affirmation or, in a social context, one's sense of belonging to a particular racial or ethnic group. While such groups have often been the source of important resistance movements in U.S. history, today they correspond neither to unified nor organized communities nor to any particular ideological beliefs and goals. Indeed, our very understanding of identity implies a relativism that goes against broad, societal-wide belief systems that might transcend the immediacy of parochial groups. In a highly relativized world each group is inclined to seek out its own expressions of "identity," culture, and subjectivity, embracing in the process its own insular, esoteric codes, symbols, motifs, and lifestyles—a trend consonant with both postmodern theory and an academic milieu that thrives on hyperspecialization, esoteric discourses, and competitive rituals.

The deeper consequences of the identity maze, especially in its most exaggerated variants, for politics are rather far-reaching. It can readily produce a situation where, as Todd Gitlin observes, "identities harden into fortified enclaves"—a tendency comparable to the insularity of enclave ideology with its preference for local organizing (discussed in Chapter 6).[52] In both cases the public sphere is broken down into a host of rival interest groups (or "cultural" identities), each with its own unique perceptions, feelings, and discourses, and often its special claim to victim status—all constituted apart from, sometimes even *against*, the general terrain of politics. Notions of public good or the common interest may be regarded as irrelevant to the local community or even as potentially threatening to groups bent on preserving their own cultural turf. Affirmations of enclave consciousness permeate in ethnic nationalism, postmodern ("difference") feminism, gay liberation, and the "wilderness" identity of proponents of deep ecology—along with the white-male chauvinism of militias and the fierce territorial (often ethnic) loyalties of many urban gangs. This trend has been deepened (and further legitimated) by the ethos of multiculturalism that has become standard discourse not only in academic and cultural life but in corporations and government, where "diversity" is a key ingredient of public policy. The resulting fragmentation of social discourse, much of it abstracted from concrete issues and outcomes, only serves to further impede thinking about the kind of social governance needed to improve people's lives. It is social governance that, after all, functions to mediate differences and make long-range planning for societal goals possible.

This predicament is further heightened by identity concerns and by the fetishizing of subject positions, or self-determination, through symbolic discourses that are detached from political ends and means. Of course, identity has always been a vital component of social movements. In itself, however, identity does not necessarily bring people into the public sphere where they can come face to face with issues of power, material conditions, and social change; on the contrary, excessive preoccupation with identity is more likely to deflect popular attention away from such issues. The struggle for collective identity provides catharsis and perhaps some measure of *local* empowerment, but it cannot give rise to transformations in the class and power relations of society as a whole. This is not merely a case of popular groups being divided against one another instead of being united against a single power structure; rather, the issue is more specifically the way forms of resistance are rendered abstract, disconnected from real historical possibilities. Consider the fact that a number of social identities are most fully vocalized (and theorized) precisely at a time when the social foundations of such identity are drastically eroded. For example, with the globalization of markets and communications there is a resurgence of local, regional, and (in some instances) national attachments; with the homogenizing effects of commodity worship we see a return to "roots" in the form of racial, ethnic, and cultural identities; with bureaucratic rationalization we see the spread of alternative, typically antiauthoritarian, lifestyles; with the breakdown of family and neighborhood we see a reassertion of family and "local" values; with the disintegration of cities we see the carving out of gang-defined turf and community; with secularization and the decline of established religion we see the widespread search for "spiritual" and new-age values; and so on. What all these modalities share in common is a desperate quest for personhood and community in a colonizing world that denies exactly those possibilities—a search generally devoid of any effective social or political mechanism. In this milieu citizenship, to the extent it lives on, achieves meaning largely on the fringes of the public realm.

True to the contemporary ethos of antipolitics, therefore, the identity maze—referring again to its more insular expressions—amounts to something of a visceral escape from the concerns of strategy, power, and social governance. It priviledges the micro sphere of society, often behind a guise of emancipatory ideals. Genuine modes of empowerment that might contest corporate and state power are devalued at precisely the very time when strictly peripheral and symbolic elements of opposition came to be most glorified. In Gitlin's words: "Affirming the virtues of the margins, identity politics has left the centers of power intact."[53]

Viewed in this light, the preoccupation with identity and related concerns of multiculturalism, while clearly important in the formative stages of social movements, now seems to have lost its capacity for ideological expansion; goals are frequently articulated only in and through specific local constituencies, often in conflict with the interests of others (as when one community works to export its own environmental problems to another community). The complex linkages between the micro and macro, local and national, and specific identities and general societal concerns wind up obliterated, subverting the conditions of large-scale empowerment. This is why identity discourse, for the most part, has been silent about urgent social problems such as the need to rebuild the cities, the ecological crisis, technological displacement of jobs, the destructive effects of a still largely military-based economy, and the plague of civic violence and crime. As with the therapeutic model, the postmodern quest for self-affirmation is never grounded in its social and political context and thus, ironically, ends up negated by its own assumptions.

Given the vast separation between "subject positions" and dominant institutions, reducing "difference" to its more symbolic expression, local identities are readily submerged by an all-powerful global market that has much more discursive influence over people's lives.

Amid the endless play of identities, most human beings are forced into a regimen of work and consumption; they encounter daily the oppressive (and homogenizing) reality of corporate colonization. As the global culture expands with seemingly few impediments, it affirms its hegemony over those identities or subcultures that could pose a threat to the commodified world order; local attachments and loyalties are inundated by the flow of images, codes, data, and discourses to such an extent that they can exert little influence on material reality, on the world of money, jobs, goods, and technology. While a deep sense of cultural uniqueness or identity offers psychological anchorage for many, from a political standpoint such differences amount to what Russell Jacoby calls the "myth of multiculturalism."[54] In the United States, perhaps more than elsewhere, multiple cultures are reproduced in a single corporate-dominated consumer society. Identity-based groups and movements rarely uphold an ideological alternative to the way American society is organized or governed. On the contrary, postmodern themes of identity, diversity, and multiculturalism merge nicely with corporate interests in post-Fordist America, reinforcing the market emphasis on consumer lifestyles, cultivation of the self, competition, and the free flow of images. The fragments of local disgruntlement thus remain completely at home in the global market.

In modern history, identities have been forged through the constitution of social movements, labor unions, parties, states, and above all *ideologies* that articulate a connection between personal aspirations, interests, and activity in the public sphere. Organizational structures and belief systems, bound together in some way, upheld a sense of the future while imparting broader purpose to personal identities; in this fashion various allegiances (to race, ethnicity, class, locale, gender) could be incorporated into a unifying historical process, akin to Gramsci's concept of "social bloc." Liberalism, socialism, communism, anarchism, and nationalism were modern ideologies that often lent cohesive direction, however fragile at times, to dispersed oppositional movements, interests, and movements. What gave labor struggles their political explosiveness was not so much the congealing of class consciousness as such (vital as that was), but the convergence of class identities (often tied to other identities) with the universalizing power of socialist or communist ideologies. Similarly, in the United States, multiple local identities around class, ethnicity, and region were historically subsumed by the powerful convergence of liberalism and nationalism that facilitated capitalist ascendancy.

Clearly the question here is not one of identity itself but rather of how identities (or "differences") are historically formed and politically represented. The proliferation of identity discourses and groups in the United States since the 1960s has exerted a salutary influence on the culture in many ways, redefining our understanding of gender and ethnic relations, opening up new vistas and opportunities for previously marginalized sectors, and reinvigorating social movements at a time when the traditional Left seemed moribund. Multiculturalism gave rise to a heightened sense of diversity and tolerance, but, as earlier noted, a true *politics* of identity requires more: it suggests a dialectical relationship between group and public interests, between micro and macro realms, between local and societal arenas of participation. Identities that remain confined to parochial expressions of subjectivity, or that fail to transcend natural, fixed social formations (related to race, ethnicity, gender), are bound to be subordinated to hegemonic discourses; in themselves, they can never be transformative. And this is precisely the contemporary predicament of identity formations in the United States.[55] If these formations amount to a kind of cultural haven for many outside mainstream discourses, from the standpoint of oppositional politics they ultimately become an ideological trap.

There is a further dilemma that in post-Fordist society there can be no simple return to the comforts of Enlightenment rationality, nor to those universalizing ideals associated with class struggle, socialist politics, and world revolution—nor should there be. The vibrant multiplicity of discourses, identities, and movements that remains a durable feature of the postmodern epoch cannot be negated or transcended by efforts to impose grand theoretical designs. The fragments are not likely to vanish, given the immense scope and complexity of multiple and dispersed identities. Any "Leninist" or other Jacobin imposition of an overarching belief system would lead to disastrous authoritarian outcomes—in the unlikely event that it would succeed. Such a dilemma is sharpened by the depoliticizing effects of two significant factors explored in earlier chapters. First, it has become abundantly clear that identity formation must now take place in what Jonathan Friedman describes as the "single complex process of global transformations"—a process influencing development and consciousness in even the most "private" spheres (or micro spheres), in often invisible ways.[56] In one way or another, individuals must encounter powerful global forces over which they have little control, and personal reactions are predictably characterized by frustration, cynicism, and private retreat in a situation where "local" options may appear hopeless. Second, as postmodern theory correctly emphasizes, identities and allegiances increasingly take shape in and through a mass-mediated culture where images and signs work to obliterate anything resembling a unified oppositional consciousness. This combination of highly fragmented identity groups and the omnipresent force of a depoliticized society operates mightily against development of such a consciousness.

FRAGMENTS AGAINST THE WHOLE

Postmodernism and identity politics—these historically interconnected forces are rooted in the same logic of post-Fordist development that has upended long-cherished values of Enlightenment rationality that were integral to both liberal capitalism and the socialist opposition to it. The new era (in England often referred to as "new times") has disgorged a turbulent and rapidly changing civil society marked by obliteration of old social boundaries, a transformed labor force, decentered subjects, and an increasingly fragmented public life. It is the death knell of ambitious universalizing ideologies that could furnish popular consensus around emergent forms of political opposition. As Gitlin writes: "These days, it sometimes seems that the *Zeitgeist* is blowing nothing but fragments."[57] Indeed, the proliferation of fragments, or fragmented cultures, appears to capture the essence of the contemporary predicament that is often referred to as the "postmodern condition."[58]

Yet the fragments, as we have seen, capture only one side of contemporary reality; the thorny and recalcitrant dynamics of corporate colonization remain, having assumed increasingly global proportions. Contemporary society is a two-sided edifice in which a highly fluid, dispersed, and sometimes chaotic civil society coexists with a stable, rationally organized state and corporate system. Popular struggles for identity, empowerment, and broadening of the public sphere have taken off in the midst of fully institutionalized regimes of domination bent on maximizing their hegemony. Modernity has broken down old hierarchies and barriers to freedom, opening up new avenues of change while at the same time creating unprecedented concentrations of economic and political power. It has allowed for greater spheres of local autonomy while simultaneously producing tendencies toward economic globalization. Indeed, efforts to decolonize in one sense and to further colonize civil society in another have gone hand-in-hand over the past three decades. If postmodernism, new social movements, and identity politics represent in some way a challenge to modernity, then the globalizing power structure, with its reliance on bureaucracy, science, and technology, can be seen as elevating modernity to new levels. Post-Fordism paves the way toward cultural revitalization at the very moment the corporate system aggressively pursues commodification of the world. Thus, while modernity generates conditions of emancipation, it also places massive obstacles in the way of concrete *struggles* for emancipation—obstacles that, as I argue throughout this book, work ceaselessly to depoliticize the public sphere. The triumph of the systemic whole over the local fragments, if we have come to that, suggests a paralysis of transformative politics in the most dramatic sense. This paralysis should not be confused with any "end of history," however, insofar as modernity continues to be characterized by a number of explosive contradictions.

A strictly negative interpretation of post-Fordism would be highly misleading in view of widespread insurgent tendencies surfacing in the advanced industrial societies since the 1960s. For the Left, at least, a break with the past—with the different legacies' organized socialism—has been both inevitable and necessary. The era has given rise to wider and more diversified processes of social change, opening up new cultural and political terrain. As Stuart Hall writes: "This pluralization of social life expands the positionalities and identities available to ordinary people (at least in the industrialized world) in their everyday working, social, familial, and sexual lives."[59] Empowerment of minorities, women, gays, and other marginalized groups has been placed on the agenda; counterhegemonic discourses on culture, ecology, health, the body, and sexuality have entered the public realm; multiple sites of resistance and change have been legitimated; and instrumental modes of rationality tied to state and corporate domination have come under sustained critique. An entire universe of meanings has become unsettled, if not in mainstream society, then at least for growing numbers of people on the political and cultural margins. Micro and noninstitutional spheres of life such as the family have been made more open to oppositional intervention, especially in the orbit of new movements, where a renewed subversive politics has at least seemed possible.

This renaissance of civil society is augmented further by the information revolution, with its relatively open flow of knowledge and data, and global forms of mobility. As more people become alienated from increasingly remote centers of power, moreover, their capacity for networking and interaction is bolstered by the same force (global technology) that extends the regimen of domination. The resilience of civil society in the face of growing corporate colonization is a theme that shapes not only postmodern theory but also the ethos of citizen-action groups and nongovernmental organizations around the world. David Korten, who writes about the suffocating power of large corporations, can still express optimism about expanding counter forces at work in society that have "enormous capacity to rapidly network dispersed individuals and organizations that are not motivated by voluntary commitments."[60] He goes further: "Each day, more people are saying no to the forces of corporate colonialism, reclaiming their spaces, taking back responsibility for their lives, and working to create real-world alternatives to the myths and illusions of economic globalization."[61] Other writers, like Jeremy Rifkin, see oppositional potential in emergent social forces that, in Rifkin's estimation, are revitalizing civil society and inspiring new forms of "voluntary" third-sector citizen participation.

Such exuberance, while perhaps understandable for the micro level, overlooks stubborn obstacles created by vastly more powerful macro processes at work; society, though more resilient, pluralized and turbulent since the 1960s, has also been deeply depoliticized by the forces discussed in this book. Thus, the postmodern obsession with localism, fragments, and decentered subjects reveals the essence of a society caught in deep social turbulence, but simultaneously captures the logic of antipolitics. The leap from a fluid, open civil society with its multiple zones of resistance to more broad-based, organized forms of opposition that can advance a transformative agenda has scarcely been addressed by postmodern theory. How local knowledge and dispersed struggles are expected to lead to some type of transformative politics given the strong pull of fragments, powerful centrifugal forces, and the absence of universalizing ideology remains something of a mystery. There is also poor recognition of the fact that society, far from being "autonomous" or separate from macro influences, is being constantly shaped and reshaped by large-scale depoliticizing factors: corporate colonization, commodified culture, the mass media, and so forth. It is not enough to simply anticipate that struggles for the decolonization of society will have desired political outcomes. Nor can one assume that "identity" will be defined in one ideological direction rather than another.

It is tempting to conclude that all the intellectual and cultural attention paid to postmodern themes, above all in the university, amounts to just another escape from politics, affirming a shift toward the "postpolitical," where issues of state power, governance, and macro transformations are seen as archaic. There may be some truth to this. Some currents in postmodern theory, however, do strive to incorporate the emphasis on localized fragments into a larger social totality, but this is often carried forward in such an abstract discourse that the fragments are still left without vital theoretical linkages. As Kuan-Hsing Chen writes: "The irony, and perhaps the failure, of a critical postmodernism resides in its political double-bind. On the one hand, it calls for a movement toward the local, the specific, the oppressed. On the other, it continuously operates at the level of the global, the abstract, and the general. The local, the specific, and the oppressed appear to be peripheral in the postmodern spectrum."[62] Put differently, the failure of postmodernism to grasp the global system in *political* terms serves to marginalize that which is celebrated—the local and dispersed—even further.

It is possible to make sense of this predicament in yet another way: the postmodern turn takes place generally outside of, and sometimes against, the institutional–political sphere in its pursuit of new modes of social resistance and interest representation. It has had a familiar tendency to dismiss the terrain of government, parties, elections, and interest groups as hopelessly corrupt, thus in effect rejecting politics as a mechanism of change, although this stance has been moderated since the late 1970s. The great fear of centralized state power, however, was exacerbated in the wake of widespread Soviet-style communist collapse, which only further discredited the bureaucratic–centralist "command" systems of governance. The more extreme variants of "post" thinking fetishized the micro realm to such a degree that the public sphere amounted to little more than an afterthought. With renewed attention devoted to identity and fragments, references to "discourse politics," "cultural politics," and of course "identity politics" entered the lexicon, commonly superseding what had been traditionally understood as "politics," or political action. This subtle but nonetheless profound conceptual shift was accompanied by, and to some extent inspired by, a dread of instrumentalism that often led to contempt for large-scale structures of any type. Even the new populism, which was attached to the efficacy of political intervention, upheld the vision of a localized "human-scale" community. Many groups and movements adopted the view that social gains made possible through sustained public engagement at the macro level were not worth the risk of psychological or ideological corruption. Others seemed to believe that, over time, collective struggles in the micro sphere could be gradually translated into successes at the macro level—although how this process was supposed to occur usually was left unspecified. Still others expressed a quasi-anarchistic hostility toward politics *tout court* on the assumption that the widespread diffusion of antistatist activity throughout civil society would eventually give rise to a generalized system of self-management.

While the postmodern turn surely contains much that is emancipatory, there is an overriding problem. In a highly depoliticized society such as the United States, where fragments coexist with a relatively unified system of state and corporate domination linked to the war economy—that is, where pluralization extends to just one side of the equation— the fragments are much too easily neutralized, absorbed into insular and largely powerless enclaves of resistance. In such a milieu emergent forms of opposition will have great difficulty achieving political expression; if "cultural politics" empowers, it does so at best only partially. The understandable search for identity and solidarity in a world so rife with personal alienation can bring much comfort, but it inevitably produces feelings of despair and cynicism that the individual's life-world undergoes little if any change. Not surprisingly, it is this very despair and cynicism which enters into and defines so much postmodern theory. Where politics does occasionally surface, it frequently takes on the discourse of tepid, marginal interest groups—a tendency prevalent, for example, in modern U.S. environmentalism.[63] The idea of a coherent "social bloc" of oppositional forces, informed by critical ideological consensus, gains little currency where there is such a proliferation of subject positions, local agencies, and fragmented identities, each cultivating its own (blurred) domains while fiercely protecting its own sense of marginal turf.

The postmodern assault on Enlightenment values—surely a necessary corrective to blind faith in modernity—can lead to exaggerated claims that reject the very hope of social transformation carried out by means of democratic participation and social planning. Indeed, the notion of "progress" itself, whether associated with modernity or not, is often debunked in Nietzschean terms as nothing but a seductive illusion. There is an abiding fear in postmodernism of any totalizing scheme, which for intellectuals of most ideological persuasions recalls the worst authoritarian excesses of Leninist-style Jacobinism. As totality evaporates, so too, necessarily, does the commitment to teleological goals.[64] If the deep reaction against Leninism and Stalinism is understandable enough, the resulting decline of ideological universality implies a commensurate loss of faith in the human capacity to transform the world inspired by a collective action motivated by a coherent vision of the future. This deterioration of ideological vision is one of the hallmarks of contemporary antipolitics.

At a time when dispersed fragments reflecting the "postmodern condition" remain strong in American culture, the obstacles to repoliticization of the public sphere are bound to be stronger than ever. The system does not merely reproduce forms of ideological hegemony, but pulverizes discourse altogether. One result is that citizenship itself has become an increasingly devalued and problematic concept; and without the vital sense of public engagement that is basic to citizenship, the task of rebuilding society is hopeless—that is, unless we return to the simplistic orthodox Marxist notion of economic crisis as the episodic launching pad of collective subjectivity. In Philip Wexler's words: "Postmodernism is not a culture that creates a political individual characterized by critical distance, alienation, and reflexive rationality. Rather the individual subject is decentered, diffused, and fragmented."[65] Under these circumstances any all-embracing return to Enlightenment universalism, with its attachment to growth-oriented technocratic goals shared by liberalism and Marxism alike, cannot be the source of a rejuvenated politics (especially in the industrialized countries). The global ecological crisis alone makes such an option illusory. At the same time, nihilistic revolt against all dimensions of modernity will only help to deepen the culture of fragments. Wherever progressive groups and movements remain divided among rival identity enclaves fighting over their own parochial turf, power elites are free to disrupt them as the elites amass greater power and wealth, while more and more of the population sinks deeper into poverty and alienation.

A REVIVAL OF POLITICS?

I
f the nineteenth century was preeminently a time when politics was devalued or sublimated as a reaction to the Jacobin impulses of the
French Revolution, the twentieth century has witnessed just the opposite—a reassertion of politics such that state power has at times achieved
nearly Orwellian dimensions. Politics became, in its more Promethean
manifestations, an engine of the great modern revolutions: Mexican,
Russian, Chinese, Yugoslav, Algerian, Cuban, Vietnamese. It became a vehicle for what the Greeks called "architectonics," what Hobbes envisioned through his Leviathan, what Machiavelli had in mind with his epic
rendering of the "prince," and eventually what Lenin and the Bolsheviks
referred to as the vanguard party in the historic struggle to conquer state
power on behalf of transformative goals. With the success of Leninism,
politics assumed control of all aspects of life, an organizational weapon
for seizing state power, an indispensable tool of mass mobilization—the
essence of an integrative force capable (in theory) of remaking civil society in the image of an official Marxist ideology. While nineteenth-century Marxism viewed politics as more or less epiphenomenal, a reflection of underlying material forces and class structure, the irony was that
twentieth-century communist revolutions and the party-states they created wound up inverting this relationship, putting "politics in command"
of a turbulent, often recalcitrant, historical reality. Even a critical Marxist
like Gramsci could write: "One can say that man is essentially 'political'
since it is through the activity of transforming and consciously directing
other men that man realizes his 'humanity,' his 'human nature.'"[1] This
amounts to nothing less than a modern restatement of Aristotle's classical definition of *zoon politikon*, which understood politics as a kind of ethical and existential calling.

Of course, the primacy of politics was hardly confined to the Communist experience—far from it. A similar dynamic entered into the birth
of fascism, which to an extent greater even than Leninism enshrined state

power and its most authoritarian elements (hierarchy, discipline, violence, militarism) as an end itself, to be worshipped at the altar of the *volk* and the nation. Fascist regimes erected mobilization systems in Italy, Germany, Japan, Spain, Portugal, Hungary, and elsewhere in the two decades after 1920, most of which crumbled with the end of World War II. Even if reactionary authoritarianism never went so far as to overthrow the old order, politics for fascism as for communism was always a central locus of ideological legitimization, economic planning, and popular mobilization. A comparable dynamic shaped events in the third world during the postwar years, leading to traditional dictatorships and military governments in such nations as Pakistan, Chile, Indonesia, Syria, and the Philippines. Even in Western Europe and North America the idea of the Keynesian welfare state gave impetus to centralized forms of governance, including economic planning. In every region of the world "politics" was commonly understood to be the main catalyst of national independence and economic modernization, just as it had been at the time of the French Revolution.

Forces seemingly directed against this dramatic increase in the scope of politics and state power, especially in the West, began to congeal during the 1960s and had picked up momentum by the late 1970s. Where the realm of politics had been previously championed as furnishing vital space for human creativity and intervention, it was now increasingly viewed with caution, as the harbinger of abusive centralized power, bureaucracy, warfare, and even global catastrophe. Indeed, a wholesale assault on the efficacy of state governance and, to some degree, the validity of the public sphere itself was mounted first by the New Left and the counterculture and then by a variety of currents in the 1970s and 1980s: new social movements, neoliberalism, libertarianism, and postmodernism, as well as the myriad tendencies and movements explored in this volume.

The final push toward an extreme antipolitics came with the disintegration of Soviet and East European communist power that had already begun in the late 1970s with the resurgence of popular struggles to reclaim and enlarge "civil society." The various trends toward radical depoliticization seemed to crystallize in the 1990s, in the United States above all, where shrinkage of the public sphere was now being taken for granted. As David Croteau observes: "While many people abroad struggled to increase their participation in public life, to strengthen fledging democracies, and to redevelop civil society, many Americans seem to have abandoned any hope of incorporating democracy at home. The reigning political mood in America is a combination of disenchantment, cynicism, and alienation."[2]

The disintegration of political life in late-twentieth-century America poses a series of novel dilemmas and challenges that I have tried to illuminate in this volume. Many of the social phenomena explored here—metaphysics, the therapeutic culture, localism, deep ecology, urban revolt, and postmodernism, among them—intersect with and reinforce one another. While those intellectual and psychological responses to an increasingly harsh, atomized social order have deep origins in the popular movements of the 1960s and 1970s, the momentum of such responses has not noticably waned throughout the 1990s. Despite their often radically different constituencies, outlooks, and espoused goals, these modalities all share a profoundly depoliticized *modus operandi*.

As the quagmire of political decay widens, urgent social problems go unsolved. Such problems, from urban decline to technological displacement of labor to global ecological crisis, cannot be grasped, much less acted on, without looking at the national and international context of markets, finance, and communications. Yet, paradoxically, the widespread retreat from politics, so often inspired by localist impulses, comes at a time when social agendas that ignore global factors will be, more than ever, reduced to impotence. Localist withdrawal is in fact powerfully reinforced by the growing remoteness and devaluation of politics (especially state and federal politics) as increasing numbers of people turn away from difficult, frustrating public concerns toward more comfortable, manageable private ones. Of course, the private realm holds significance as a source of self-fulfillment and as a bulwark against an assortment of outside encroachments. Yet, by diminishing the life of common involvements, we negate the very idea of politics as a source of public good and social transformation.[3] In the meantime, it may not be too hyperbolic to say that the fate of the world hangs in the balance. The unyielding truth is that, even as the mood of antipolitics encapsulates more and more of American culture, it is still the vagaries of political power that will decisively shape the future of human societies.

THE TRIUMPH OF LIBERAL CAPITALISM?

The theme of a depoliticized public sphere developed in this book should not be confused with the familiar "end of ideology" or "end of history" theses that, in various incarnations, have resurfaced in the United States since Daniel Bell's seminal *The End of Ideology* nearly four decades ago. Reflecting on American political culture in the 1950s, Bell concluded that "ideology, which was the road to action, has come to a dead end."[4] For Bell and kindred observers like Seymour Martin Lipset and Edward Shils, ideology amounted to a kind of "secular religion," in that it has an all-inclusive system of beliefs, passion, and is viewed as a "lever of action" designed to change the world, to make history. Viewed thusly, ideology could be seen as a blueprint for social engineering in the manner of earlier critiques like those of Karl Popper and Hannah Arendt—a definition that focused mainly on Marxism as a uniquely totalistic and closed worldview. Advanced industrial society, according to Bell, had witnessed the exhaustion of such ideologies insofar as a "rough consensus" had emerged that the important issues were pluralism, the welfare state, and economic growth. In place of outmoded secular religions dedicated to class struggle and revolution, modern commitments revolved increasingly around issues of economic productivity and efficiency, leading to a situation in which "politics offers little excitement" or relevance; the larger, more explosive social issues had finally been settled in this view.[5] Aside from some pockets of resistance to the new consensus here and there, liberal capitalism had been triumphant.

Writing three decades later, Francis Fukuyama preferred to speak of the "end of history"—a stage where both liberal democracy and the free market constitute the "end-point of mankind's ideological evolution," where all rival ideologies (monarchism, fascism, communism, socialism, and so on) have finally been conquered or made anachronistic.[6] As a more or less intelligible evolutionary process, history has given rise to a pervasive liberal consensus regarding the main "underlying principles and institutions," that now provide the "only coherent political aspiration that spans different regions and cultures around the globe."[7] Echoing Bell, Fukuyama argues that economic modernization generates strong homogenizing pressures favoring the priorities of material abundance, technology, and consumerism, to which Fukuyama adds the obvious role of global markets and communications. Further, liberal democracy—to a far greater extent than dictatorships of either the Right or the Left—is able to solve the time-honored problem of "recognition" insofar as liberalism is the only ideology consonant with both individual freedom and popular sovereignty.[8] After the collapse of the Soviet bloc, the last barrier to worldwide liberal consensus was removed, allowing capitalist democracy to establish its hegemony as the only force possessing "universal validity."

Despite some obvious differences in nuance and context, Bell and Fukuyama make a number of interrelated assumptions that have gained wide acceptance in mainstream academic, media, and political circles. They assume that history has reached its final (political) stage and that liberal-capitalist society can satisfy the major needs and demands of the world's population, they have faith in the Enlightenment-style valuation of material growth and instrumental rationality grounded in science and technology, believe that anticapitalist ideologies seem to always give rise to extreme authoritarian methods, and, most significantly, they believe that rival systems to capitalism are obsolete if compelling issues of the day have been settled—or are at least able to be settled—in the liberal-capitalist framework. My own perspective rejects *all* of these assumptions, which are refuted daily by the immensely destructive character of capitalist growth economies, as well as the disintegration of liberal-democratic *politics,* as I have argued throughout this volume. The Bell–Fukuyama paradigm is further confounded by the appearance of oppositional ideologies (e.g., feminism, ecology, the greens, democratic socialism) that do not have the "totalitarian" or "secular religious" properties associated with orthodox and Leninist versions of Marxism. Beyond this, there is the obvious phenomenon—ignored by these writers—of deep authoritarian trends overtaking social and political life as a result of corporate colonization and bureaucratization. In paying exclusive attention to the *formal* structures and processes of liberal democracy, Bell and Fukuyama inevitably sidestep the impact of larger historical processes at work in the global political economy—an ironic shortcoming in Fukuyama given his overriding emphasis on the supposed "logic" of world history.

If we turn to Herbert Marcuse's more "critical" interpretation of the waning of oppositional politics, we find an analysis that manages to avoid the simplistic "end of ideology" and "end of history" pitfalls. Like Bell (writing earlier) and Fukuyama (later), Marcuse concludes that antisystem energies have been largely absorbed or mollified by the industrial–technological apparatus of capitalist society. Where Marcuse departs from Bell and Fukuyama, however, is in his more *dialectical* approach; in his construct, the onset of "one-dimensionality" typical of advanced capitalism blocks immediate prospects for subversive change, but it does not and cannot overcome the basic social contradictions of the system. Thus: "Contemporary society seems to be capable of containing social change— qualitative change which would establish essentially different institutions, a new direction of the productive process, new modes of human existence,"[9] but "the fact that the vast majority of the population accepts, and is made to accept, this society does not render it less irrational and less reprehensible."[10] Marcuse argues that, as industrialization advances, technology merges with commodity production to give capitalism greater "internal cohesion," enabling the system to reproduce itself more efficiently; countervailing powers (including, above all, labor) wind up so ideologically absorbed that they lose the capacity to confront "the whole" of the social order. With the spread of technological rationality the refusal to go along, to accept conformist and instrumental priorities, seems increasingly "neurotic" and "impotent."[11] Marcuse never posits an end of ideology because, from his standpoint, the system becomes even *more* ideological insofar as hegemonic beliefs (liberal capitalism, technological rationality) become firmly embedded in the very structure of production itself, tightly integrated into the daily rhythms of social life. At the same time, capitalism is subjected to explosive divisions and tensions; there can be no "end of ideology" because Marcuse, quite rightly, allows for possible future revolt—anticipated in the "great refusal" of the 1960s—as material and ideological conditions undergo far-reaching transformations. If modernity contains strong impulses toward domination and the administered society, it also contains the seeds of its own transcendence in the form of mounting social contradictions. Here Marcuse's dialectical framework permits him to avoid the naive liberal one-sidedness of Bell and Fukuyama as well as the dark pessimism of Frankfurt School theorists Adorno and Max Horkheimer, whose *Dialectic of Enlightenment*, influential though it may have been on Marcuse's thinking, seems to foreclose long-term transformative hopes.[12]

The theoretical motif of earlier chapters shares much with Marcuse—except for the obvious qualification that economic globalization adds new dimensions to the current predicament. Marcuse saw, accurately enough, that forms of ideological hegemony—however pervasive—could be fragile and shifting, allowing for the emergence of novel modes of political opposition virtually overnight. Indeed, the 1960s upheavals occurred within only a few years of the publication of *One-Dimensional Man* and strongly influenced his later work.[13] At the same time, he understood the unprecedented ideological power of both technology and commodity production in a way that foresaw the advent of corporate colonization and the impediment it would pose for social change. Here Marcuse parted company with the more optimistic rationalism of Habermas while also elaborating themes that would later be familiar in the postmodernism of Foucault, Baudrillard, and Laclau and Mouffe. Marcuse was among the first to systematically theorize the conditions of depoliticization in advanced industrial society, without at the same time yielding to the facile (and ultimately myopic) "end of ideology" thesis. Marcuse believed that, in a world shaped by instrumental rationality and consumerism, the realm of politics would become increasingly bankrupt as larger numbers of people sought out privatized modes of retreat—an outcome all the more likely as modernity destroyed larger spheres of public life, including local communities, neighborhoods, and other autonomous social spaces. The failure of modernizing alternatives such as Social Democracy and Communism to remedy the situation simply added to the mix of popular ideological defeat and withdrawal. If ideology had not yet vanished, it nonetheless lives on in its present (*system-sustaining*) form, helping to legitimate the cynical and exploitative operations of power structures; as we have seen, elite rule is more consolidated than ever, whatever the ideological rationale employed.

The recurrent belief that we have reached the "end of ideology" or "end of history" in response to increasing levels of modernization is thus quite disingenuous, since it has become clear that the only ideologies to have supposedly disappeared are *oppositional* ones. Historical conditions are presented as in fact favoring a *specific* universal ideology—liberal capitalism—that today so penetrates every area of human life that it can easily be taken for granted. The rather arbitrary theme of Bell, Fukuyama, and others—that the liberal-capitalist system has checkmated all political alternatives—ignores far too many countervailing factors to be convincing and thus lacks analytical rigor. In certain ways these ideas anticipate and inform, even if haphazardly, the postmodern obsession with the historic collapse of grand theories and metanarratives. In each case the main target of critique turns out to be Marxism, which as the main foundation of oppositional politics is regarded as completely obsolete and no longer retrievable; socialism in all its variants is pronounced as dead. But yet another factor must be taken into account, namely, that the more all-encompassing view of politics informing these theories is a profoundly *minimalist* one. Such a view coincides with the quasi-Burkean assumptions of the founders of the American Republic—a highly elitist, defensive, and restricted framework that corresponds to C. B. Macpherson's idea of a "protective democracy," a narrow pluralism with almost byzantine constitutional restraints and a limited base of suffrage that has little in common with any conception of "democracy."[14] The intention of the Founding Fathers was to temper rather than encourage or facilitate democratic participation and citizenship, much less popular movements.

THE MINIMALIST TRAP

Behind this vision there is the belief, well articulated by Michael Oakeshott, that politics cannot and should not be directed at social change. It is an outlook insisting that, whatever the particular type of ideology as such, a decidedly ambitious or transformative view of politics runs inherently counter to the natural order of things. In his seminal work, *Rationalism in Politics*, Oakeshott argued that a social engineering approach to politics was futile on its own premises. Modern totalitarian methods have such an approach, and it invariably gets carried to extremes.[15] Completely reversing the Greek notion of architectonics, Oakeshott held that it would be the worst mistake to enlist politics in the service of remaking societies by means of creative statecraft. Politics is not a realm of human fulfillment; it is the process of *adapting* new challenges to a framework of long-standing customs and traditions, much akin to the time-honored English tradition of "muddling through." The imposition of universal principles and ideals on local, immediate, changing realities not only obscures particular modes of human experience but also leads to often harsh authoritarian outcomes. Politics for Oakeshott, as for Burke, is rooted in the tangled, complex web of everyday social interaction and therefore cannot be employed for purposes of reordering society without leading to new forms of domination. Constructing tidy schemes for amorphous, recalcitrant populations is a recipe for either chaos or tyranny: ideological visions, blueprints, plans, social contracts, elaborate platforms—all are inevitably out of touch with the unpredictable rhythm and flow of people's daily lives. Thus, Oakeshott believes it is impossible to arrive at an ideal of rational politics independent of the actual *practice* of politics in a historically specific setting.

Moving from this premise, Oakeshott argues that political actors can never hope to lay out *viable* political ends or goals in advance; they can expect nothing more than a series of haphazard ad hoc maneuvers. Hence, those ideals set forth in the medium of well-articulated ideologies will in reality simply be used for cosmetic purposes by self-interested politicians as they work their way from one situation to another. Inverting Lenin's famous Jacobin formula, Oakeshott wrote that politics is essentially about *following* the mood of the times, not leading. Whatever the structure of power, ideals will inevitably be taken over by elements of corruption and opportunism and will be sidetracked by inevitable policy failures—problems that derive from the very difficulty of governance through social engineering. Anticipating later themes of postmodernism, Oakeshott deprecates the very pursuit of collective subjectivity, of political agencies that set out to transform society. The result is a devaluing of politics in the extreme. What we have in Oakeshott's work, in its most developed form, is a coherent theory of antipolitics that includes the minimalism of both conservative and liberal traditions.

But it is a very deceptive and misleading minimalism. While Oakeshott debunks political mechanisms and rational planning as either useless or dangerous, the actually existing power structure—replete with its own centralized state apparatus, institutional hierarchies, conscious designs, and, indeed, rational plans—remains fully intact, insulated from the minimalist critique. In other words, ideologies and plans are perfectly acceptable for elites who preside over established governing systems, but not for ordinary citizens or groups anxious to challenge the status quo. Such one-sided minimalism gives carte blanche to elites who naturally desire as much space to maneuver as possible. The flight from "abstract principles" rules out ethical attacks on injustices that may pervade the status quo (slavery or imperialist wars, for example) insofar as those injustices might be seen as too deeply embedded in the social and institutional matrix of the time to be the target of oppositional political action. If politics is reduced to nothing other than a process of everyday muddling-through, then people are condemned to accept the harsh realities of an exploitative and authoritarian system, with no choice but to yield to the dictates of "conventional wisdom." Systematic attempts to ameliorate oppressive conditions would, in Oakeshott's view, turn into a political nightmare. A belief that totalitarianism might result from extreme attempts to put society in order is one thing; to argue that all politicized efforts to change the world are necessarily doomed either to impotence or totalitarianism requires a completely different (and indefensible) set of premises.

Oakeshott's minimalism poses yet another, but still related, range of problems: the shrinkage of politics hardly suggests that corporate colonization, social hierarchies, or centralized state and military institutions will magically disappear from people's lives. Far from it: the public space vacated by ordinary citizens, well informed and ready to fight for their interests, simply gives elites more room to consolidate their own power and privilege. Beyond that, the fragmentation and chaos of a Hobbesian civil society, not too far removed from the excessive individualism, social Darwinism, and urban violence of the American landscape, could open the door to a modern Leviathan intent on restoring order and unity in the face of social disintegration. Viewed in this light, the contemporary drift toward antipolitics might set the stage for a reassertion of politics in more authoritarian and reactionary guise—or it could simply end up reinforcing the dominant state-corporate system. In either case, the state would probably become what Hobbes anticipated: the embodiment of those universal, collective interests that had vanished from civil society.[16] And either outcome would run counter to the facile antirationalism of Oakeshott's Burkean muddling-though theories.

In American society today elite agendas tend to be focused on the domestic and global expansion of power and markets—agendas that work precisely *against* officially espoused ideals of citizenship and civic empowerment or even the "free market." Antipolitical sentiment, whether of the sort embraced by Oakeshott, the 1960s counterculture, postmodernism, or deep ecology, only serves to reproduce and further legitimate this situation; minimalism at the level of citizen politics automatically equates with a maximalism of *elite* politics. Government itself is increasingly controlled by corporate and banking interests. Money dictates the way resources are allocated, the manner in which elections are conducted, and the outcome of legislation—not only through campaign contributions but by virtue of the influence of business interests (and business-owned media) in shaping political agendas. The obvious fact that citizens cannot match the power of multinational corporations graphically demonstrates this point. In such a milieu the "relative autonomy" of governmental structures (not to mention the vitality of civil society), appears to be diminishing day by day. As former Washington insider Richard Goodwin writes: "The grotesque amounts of money that are now pouring into the political system and the disgusting and demeaning way in which that money is spent are testimony to the mounting corruptions of politics and of government."[17] Given such growing corruption, it follows that the often heard appeals to "realism" and "pragmatism"—so typical of Oakeshott-style discourse—can only lead right back to established modes of doing business. What this suggests, for example, is that any hope of "solving" deep social problems will have to be advanced in a minimalist framework that will never go further than tepid social policies that leave business interests totally unaffected, or cosmetic reforms, or the "greening" of huge corporations that simply want to profit off environmentally-critical goods, and so forth. A much needed radical agenda geared to sustainable, egalitarian, and ecologically balanced forms of production and consumption is automatically ruled out by the minimalist scenario.

A thoroughgoing revival of politics—one that vigorously questions and seeks to go beyond the routinized liberal pragmatism favored by Oakeshott—is a precondition for transcending this historical predicament. Of course, any distinctly political imperative flies in the face of a deeply antipolitical culture where politics has such an unsavory association with money, corruption, interest peddling, scandals, PACs, bureaucracy, and largely irrelevant campaign spectacles—where indeed politics has been reduced to a farcical representation of its most enduring motifs. For most people in the United States normal politics means little more than false promises and empty discourses; it is rarely considered as a mechanism that might serve to improve people's lives. The concept of politics that informs this book, however, holds out prospects for a more empowering, participatory, transformative legacy compatible with an enlarged public sphere and the subversion of corporate hegemony. While this concept imputes an ethical and visionary dimension to politics, it also points toward the matter of *strategic* necessity in that politics constitutes the only (potential) countervailing power against corporate domination. Localized, and extrapolitical opposition can lay the groundwork for popular movements, but alone (in the absence of more generalized structural mediations) such opposition will never lead to large-scale societal change. Notwithstanding Oakeshott, therefore, an imminent retrieval of politics becomes an urgent imperative at a time when destructive global forces cannot be tamed by a pragmatic, muddling-through modus operandi.

For both instrumental and normative reasons, therefore, politics remains as central as ever to the human experience; its decay in some measure reflects the disintegration of the larger social order. From this standpoint, revitalization of the public sphere can be viewed as an end in itself, not simply because the public sphere enhances "civility" or rational public dialogue but because it enables people become "fully human," capable of making history. Such revitalization might occur by following the Greek (and Rousseauian) legacy, espoused by liberals like J. S. Mill and John Dewey who affirmed a commitment to what Macpherson calls "developmental democracy," which links expansion of democratic forms to the ideals of both human self-development and social progress. Such a concept spurns the market model of politics embraced by classical liberalism, turning instead toward a framework grounded in moral, cultural, and intellectual modes of self-directed activity that run counter to the narrow premises of "economic man." As Macpherson writes:

> Mill's model of democracy . . . has a moral vision . . . of a free and equal society not yet achieved. A democratic political system is valued as a means to that improvement—a necessary though not a sufficient means; and a democratic society is seen as both a result of that improvement and a means to further improvement [involving] an increase in the amount of personal self-development of all members of the society, or, in John Stuart Mill's phrase the "advancement of community . . . in intellect, in virtue, and in practical activity and efficiency."[18]

The vital egalitarian component of developmental politics, integral to what Robert Clarke calls "deep citizenship," conflicts with the imperatives of both market values and corporate domination, upholding instead a vision of postliberal, post-Marxist democratic politics.[19] Here the activation of the self, the growth of individual empowerment and identity, is inseparable from broader social and political goals; the enlargement of individuality and transformation of the public sphere proceed apace. Following Mill, the "citizen self" emerges as a positive value in itself. As Clarke suggests: "To act politically, to take charge of significant and meaningful aspects of one's life in the company of others and to have some share in the condition of that life, is good not merely as a means to some further end but in itself."[20] In the condition of postmodernity, moreover, this realm of citizenship is likely to be *enhanced* precisely by the growing multiplicity of positions and options for social interaction and public engagement.

The recovery of politics, therefore, demands nothing less than a revitalized citizenry prepared to occupy the public space that has either been neutralized or enveloped by corporate colonization—a prospect that goes well beyond formal liberal views of citizenship or conventional Marxist notions of class struggle. Further, extension of democratic control into every area of social life requires a subversion of normal politics, which in fact amounts to just another manifestation of antipolitics. At the same time, authentic citizenship requires the widest possible dissemination of information, skills, and attitudes essential to political efficacy. Without these, "consciousness transformation" would be all but impossible, or at least politically meaningless. Yet, the culture of antipolitics devalues precisely the democratization of such information, skills, and attitudes. Opinion makers in the United States, including academic social scientists, have for many years debunked the "excesses" of democracy and popular involvement—meaning anything beyond occasional trips to the ballot boxes—much as the authors of *The Federalist Papers* frowned on "factions" or extreme manifestations of "passion."[21]

Still, there is no way of avoiding the fact that repoliticization will have to be achieved in a context where the entire field of political activity has been fundamentally altered. A major impact of corporate colonization is what Ulrich Beck refers to as the "systematic transformation of the political"—the considerable loss of power, especially in the national state system itself, that severely reduces the capacity of political actors to plan, regulate, and intervene in social affairs, above all in the economy. As Beck observes: "The concepts, foundations, and instruments of politics (and nonpolitics) are becoming unclear, open and in need of historically new determination."[22] Where a Hobbesian-style authoritarian response to fragmentation or extreme localism cannot work owing to strong historical and cultural traditions, as is probably the case in the United States, the push toward decentralization may be increasingly likely. Many functions of government will be difficult to perform according to a model where strong leaders possess more or less unchallenged authority. Hence, a truly revitalized politics infused with strong participatory values can take advantage of post-Fordist or "postmodern" trends that conflict with the idea of a single fulcrum of politics and governance.

Multiple and potentially explosive sites of conflict typical of advanced capitalism are likely to embrace, against the pull of antipolitics, powerful elements of political rebirth: participatory democracy, a challenge to authoritarian rule, local community, linkage of the personal and the political, social forms of consumption, and so forth. Implicit in this progressive shift of focus is a rejection of instrumental (and corporate) modes of rationality that shape most institutional activity and feed into the ethos of domination.[23] A renovated politics must combine an ecological critique of rampant industrial growth, the feminist struggle for gender and social equality, community-based demands for expanded (and democratized) public services, and more severe limits on spending for the prison and military sectors. Assuming such political goals, political representation and decision making will have to break free of established institutional matrices and norms, which in turn would force a rethinking of the political enterprise. The party system, elections, interest groups, the role of money and electronic media—indeed, the structure of power itself—would have to be fully transformed.

Any future recuperation of politics will have to confront this historic shift; postmodernity, new social movements, and identity concerns cannot be dismissed as if they were an ideological illusion, as if it were possible to return to some kind of mythical homogeneous past. Moreover, efforts to "transcend" this highly fluid and dispersed historical reality by resorting to notions of imputed consciousness (what people *should* be thinking or doing) or simplistic theories of class struggle typically wind up as exercises attached to romantic images of the past. A rejuvenated public sphere will have to be built on a foundation of open, critical, engaging discourses of the *present*. The "crisis within the crisis" cannot be overcome through efforts to recapture a romanticized past, whether that past is defined by family values and free enterprise (on the right) or class struggle and unified political vanguards (on the left).

Under the transformed and highly fluid conditions of post-Fordism, therefore, repoliticization demands a rethinking of some familiar dualisms—between the social and political realms, between movements and parties, between community and governance, between the local and the global. Any effort to ignore or downplay the dispersed reality of new social movements and identity politics overlooks some unique transformative elements in the post-Fordist context and thus fails to grasp the essence of a revitalized politics for the future. Conversely, the glib celebration of "civil society" as an emancipatory realm directed against bureaucratic state power not only sidesteps the issue of corporate colonization but oversimplifies the nature of both state and civil society insofar as the boundaries that now presumably exist between the two are increasingly blurred. In the first instance we have a drift toward normal politics and statism; in the second we have an abstract antistatism that never addresses the question of how the modern state system might be transformed. Of course, it would be misleading to posit easy answers to this conundrum. At the same time, it seems safe to conclude that the seemingly infinite modes of retreat from politics I have explored in earlier chapters, and which extend across the ideological spectrum, only confound efforts to arrive at such answers. Only through general popular engagement in the public sphere, leading to democratic transformation of both civil society and the state, can we imagine the kind of political renewal needed to sustain "deep citizenship" and confront major social problems.

REVERSING THE DOWNWARD SPIRAL

What, then, about prospects for a historic retrieval of politics, for a diffusion of citizen empowerment, in the United States as we enter the twenty-first century? Despite incessant pressures toward depoliticization and the massive changes brought about by post-Fordism and economic globalization, counterpressures favoring democratization would seem to be equally powerful: demands imposed by the worsening urban crisis and environmental decay, aspirations made possible by the spread of education and literacy, greater availability of information, and the growth of divergent intellectual and cultural traditions. The tools of citizenship would appear to be more widely dispersed than at any time in history. For these and other reasons, we have witnessed (in the United States no less than in other industrialized countries), recurrent signs of political revival during the 1990s, including progressive changes in the labor movement, periodic returns to student activism, and the proliferation of third-party campaigns. Still, the narrowing of political discourse in the United States continues apace, as voter turnout statistics for the 1996 and 1998 elections seems to confirm. Urgent problems still go unnoticed or get trivialized, both among politicians and the mass media. The compelling question asked by Ronald Aronson in *After Marxism* bears repeating: "Why is it that increases in prosperity, in literacy, in societal development, even in psychological sophistication, have not led to irresistible ecological demands, calls for dismantling of nuclear weapons, and the revival of a politics of emancipation?"[24]

The sad reality is that progressive movements in the United States have been able to sustain only the most feeble ideological and organizational presence during the 1990s; surely no national coalition or party has emerged that is capable of making political inroads or framing durable visions and strategies of change. Groups and movements having an objective stake in democratization—the sine qua non of fundamental social transformation—have been in retreat and disarray on many fronts. Meanwhile, the realm of electoral and institutional politics declines even further, reinforced by the corrosive role of media and money in government. The more this logic of depoliticization takes hold, the more the very *ideals* of democratic participation, open debate, and social governance become corroded; the psychological barriers to reclaiming citizenship harden at every turn. The accompanying mood of cynicism and defeatism inevitably mirrors the workings of corporate hegemony, which functions to further pulverize and atomize an already disaffected population. Political renewal cannot take place without a vigorously democratic order in which free and equal citizens are involved in shaping their own destinies, but the structural and psychological requisites for such an order (outlined by Robert Michels nearly a century ago) seem more remote than ever.[25]

Further aggravating this situation is that, contrary to some conventional radical premises, worsening material and social conditions are now fostering a steady *downward* spiral of public life. It is easy enough to forget that civic decay most often works *against* the politicization of local struggles; the result more often is a pervasive sense of futility and despair. Deteriorating objective circumstances can be both cause and effect of a fragmented and weakened subjectivity, which naturally suggests a more complex relationship between social being (or class position) and mass ideologies than was assumed by classical Marxism. As post-Fordism comes increasingly to equate with urban decay, corporate downsizing, social cutbacks, job devaluation, and class polarization, it also gives rise to such familiar Hobbesian symptoms as civic violence, crime, family breakdown, substance abuse, environmental blight, and generalized alienation. Meanwhile, diminishing citizen politics allows elites to pursue their agenda with fewer obstacles—an agenda that includes welfare "reform" (cutbacks), deregulation of corporations, free trade, a harsher law-and-order regimen, balanced budget, and so forth. These policies have been the hallmark of contemporary neoliberal agendas favored by Democrats and Republicans alike. The outcome, as Curtis Gans argues, is an intensified "class war" from above that, in effect, serves to further pulverize civil society and intensify the social crisis.[26] An atomized and demoralized population is hardly capable of resisting corporate colonization, much less exercising even limited oversight over such areas as the workplace, technology, social investment, and public programs.

Where corporate expansion takes place with minimum controls and regulations—that is, where market priorities achieve their fullest expression—social decay and political decline may be expected to reinforce each other. If the liberal Keynesian state and its ideological equivalent (social democracy) historically upheld some notion of the public interest against the harsh vagaries of the market, then the contemporary turn toward neoliberal policies of "free market" and "free trade" inevitably destroys that long-standing but shaky equilibrium. Growing corporate power has been accompanied (and legitimated) by a return to nineteenth-century laissez-faire principles of material self-interest, extreme individualism, and social Darwinism, with the idea of developmental planning regarded as insufferably dysfunctional if not downright "socialistic." Less recognized is the fact that ideals of citizen participation, community, and civic life will surely be out of place in such a politically barren world—a world that reflects the highly splintered, competitive, and sometimes predatory nature of civil society. This last point is obviously crucial since, where local groups and movements are sharply divided against one another along enclave or identity lines the power structure will be less threatened by unified opposition. Where the great mass of people is consumed with its own parochial interests, lacking any ideology of resistance or opposition, elites are busy siphoning off more wealth and further solidifying their hold over society. In such a tribalized setting, where groups may actually *fear* the idea of merging with larger communities, interests, or social blocs, deep popular anger and resentment in the culture rarely achieve effective political articulation; indeed, they scarcely enter the public sphere in any form.

As we have seen in the case of Enzensberger's "civil wars," all the gangs, militias, mafias, cults, tribal groups, and local insurrections do not amount to a broad-based political opposition and in fact typically militate against such opposition. By approaching the public sphere as a battle zone, where disadvantaged groups typically war against one another (if only for attention), tribalization inherently fuels the mood of antipolitics. Popular mobilization under such circumstances amounts to little more than an artificial sense of collective empowerment—local, spontaneous, restricted, and ill fated.

Any future process of repoliticization will obviously have to confront and maneuver through this difficult morass. Frustrated and angry citizens are rarely able to find a political voice and in most cases simply abandon all hope; many go in the direction of insular enclaves, marginal identity groups, or privatized human-potential fads. There can be no doubt that hostility toward big business has festered for many years, fueled by events such as the junk bond and savings-and-loan scandals, but, with the growing fluidity and globalization of capital, the immense power of corporations seems to intimidate the average person. Even the largest and most economically secure unions have typically fallen into a defensive mode, desperately hoping to retain what jobs, wage structures, and benefits they have won over time. Hostility toward government can also be strong, as we have seen, but it most often instills a kind of antistatism that takes people *further away* from the public sphere; it offers no vision of democratic transformation and in fact has little to say about the macro sphere in general. Of course, in the eyes of most people government appears as a closer, more identifiable, target than even the most gargantuan corporations, which of course still claim "private" status. If such antistatism contains a definite logic, it nonetheless feeds into at least two problematic currents in the popular consciousness: it discredits the political enterprise as such, and it helps undercut the one public arena (government) that can effectively resist corporate hegemony. A resurgent "free market" ideology only deepens the paralysis of collective action while the real issue of state power—including how to reshape and democratize it—is merely pushed aside.

Despite this bleak outlook for politics, it is possible to identify certain positive developments. Although the corporate stranglehold over social and political life shows no signs of weakening, civil society in the United States does remain surprisingly fluid and resilient—witness the capacity of thousands of local organizations and movements to sustain a grassroots presence that, while now scattered and largely impotent, could provide the basis of a more unified oppositional politics. The long tradition of civic involvement in American society first chronicled by Tocqueville is still alive, even if greatly tarnished: groups dedicated to environmental, peace, women's, gay, ethnic, community, and health-care issues remain capable of organizing large constituencies that from time to time enter the public arena. Further, while macro structures seem to take on the character of impenetrable fortresses, their deep internal contradictions—above all, their authoritarianism and their inability to satisfy general human needs—render them more vulnerable than may appear on the surface. An enlightening contemporary example is the rapid disintegration of Communist regimes—once thought to be stable, monolithic "totalitarian" systems—in the U.S.S.R. and Eastern Europe in the late 1980s.

The modern retrieval of politics will have to begin with a further proliferation of social movements, the fortunes of which have dramatically ebbed and flowed over the past decades. For several reasons, grassroots movements have enjoyed greater success in the United States than in most other advanced industrial societies. As Hilary Wainwright suggests, movements in civil society constitute the single most viable alternative to both the authoritarian state and the tyrannical market; in their struggles for identity and autonomy they affirm, even if not self-consciously, a rebellion against the technocratic, paternalistic ideology of all-knowing elites across the entire institutional spectrum. As noted earlier, the New Left, the counterculture, and new social movements all shared the aim of revitalizing public space, allowing for the spread of critical discourses, local networks, cooperatives, movements, and entrepreneurial forms based in different communities. Popular struggles offer the glimpse of a renewed civil society that can stand opposed to the colonizing incursions of both state and corporations. But little of this energy has been channeled into oppositional politics at the national (or even local) level, for reasons that I have explored in this volume. In the political culture there is now a clear division between movements and parties, between social life and political activity, between the locality and the true locus of governmental power.

The crucial issue, as I see it, involves possible future entry of social movements into the political arena. Put differently, under what conditions is the politicization of these movements most likely to occur? Politicization would surely revitalize the movements themselves and the larger society while also breaking down artificial boundaries between them.[27] Everything turns on the degree to which *progressive* movement themes such as grassroots participation, social goods, and ecological sustainability can be brought into the arena of party politics and, eventually, state governance. Leaving aside right-wing authoritarian movements, social movements up to the present have followed diverging political trajectories. In the United States, elements of the civil rights, labor, antiwar, and feminist movements were absorbed by the Democratic Party, (conversely, in Europe traditional left parties [Social Democrats, Communists] built electoral strength for independent parties on the support of such constituencies). During the

1970s and 1980s new-populist coalitions were galvanized, some winning municipal power in small towns for short periods of time. Nationally, the Rainbow Coalition, established around hundreds of local chapters and tied to the presidential campaigns of Reverend Jesse Jackson in 1984 and 1988, succeeded in bringing together a unique mix of labor, community, and new-movement groups. As strictly movement-defined efforts, all of these political translations were emphatically short-lived; they either wound up absorbed into dominant party frameworks (often by design) or simply disintegrated through local inertia.

In southern Europe during the 1980s, a wave a "Eurosocialist" victories gave important new-movement constituencies what appeared to be a phase of political triumph, but the series of dramatic electoral conquests in France, Spain, Portugal, Greece, and Italy that brought socialist parties to national power very quickly soured, giving rise to neo-liberal policies in the guise of transformative ideologies.[29]

Through the 1990s the most ambitious and systematic effort to politicize new social movements and citizens' initiatives has been the European Green parties, which made their electoral breakthrough in West Germany during the early 1980s. Inspired by the German Greens' entry into the national Bundestag in 1983, kindred parties (Ecology, Radical, Green) were able to carve out a presence elsewhere in Europe, although none came close to duplicating the German successes. What made the European Greens so explosive, at least at their inception, was that, as an "antiparty party" organically tied to citizen movements but committed to electoral politics they held to ideals of internal party democracy and grassroots participation while incorporating ecological and feminist sensibilities into their programs. The Greens and allied groupings set out to build the first truly New Left *party* replete with distinctly new ways of framing ideology and organization—a radical model differing from both the Leninist (insurrectionary, Jacobin) and social democratic (reformist, bureaucratic) legacies of the traditional Left. The Greens were sometimes viewed as harbingers of a "new politics" appropriate to the post-Fordist setting, even if many activists had in mind something more akin to a single-minded environmental party. For more radical claims to gain wide currency, the Greens had to avoid disruptive internal schisms while also managing a fragile equilibrium between party politics and movement insurgencies—neither of which turned out to be possible, at least for the short run. The division between "Realo" (party-oriented) and "Fundi" (movement-oriented) Greens in Germany was soon resolved in favor of the "Realos" and their stratagem of allying with the powerful Social Democrats and working for maximum institutional leverage. In other European countries green-style parties achieved only marginal status, confined to a few local strongholds while generally lacking the original ideological vitality of the

German party. Even in Germany, however, the Greens quickly wound up thoroughly deradicalized as they drifted away from their earlier axis of support in local movements.

In the United States, where third parties have been even more unsuccessful owing to the winner-take-all system and strong two-party monopoly, greens have built some local strength in a few states (Michigan, Vermont, California) but are generally even more marginal to the political arena than their European counterparts. By 1996, when Ralph Nader ran a woeful campaign as the national Green Party's presidential candidate, their fortunes differed little from the historical failures of the Citizens Party, the Peace and Freedom Party, Libertarians, and other recent electoral alternatives. Following a decade of ideological preparation, national conferences, local meetings, grassroots organizing, and electoral work, public support for green initiatives was still extremely difficult to mobilize; all progressive third parties encounter severe limits to their electoral gains, which rarely surpass the familiar 5 percent threshold. Yet, the greens possess a special dynamism rooted in their uniquely international status—there were some 60 "ecological" parties around the world as of 1998—so they bring a more developed ideological identity and greater political acumen to the third-party project. In fact, U.S. greens eventually forged an agenda not too different from that of the larger European parties, calling for a rekindling of grassroots empowerment, the merger of social movements and electoral politics, the alliance of multiple constituencies in a broad social bloc, and an ecological model of development. Whatever their internal disagreements (and they can be explosive), greens have been united against a two-party regime they view as incapable of dealing with the ecological crisis.

The greens' deep reservoir of energy and optimism has translated into rapid membership growth in some locales throughout the 1990s. Hopes for quick electoral success were inspired by the dramatic overnight upsurge of Ross Perot, who won 18.9 percent of the presidential vote in 1992 despite having no well-entrenched party organization at his disposal. Suddenly the prospects for "third" parties competing effectively against Democrats and Republicans seemed qualitatively enhanced, far less utopian. Moreover, the very gravity of social problems seemed to work against the capacity of elites to arrive at meaningful solutions—hardly surprising in the face of the corporate hold over the political system. As independent Congressman Bernard Sanders noted in a 1997 speech, a third party is needed to do what the Republicans and Democrats are not doing: represent the needs of the working people and poor against a wealthy and powerful corporate elite who increasingly dominate our economic and political life. Although third-party overtures have been prohibitively expensive in recent U.S. history, today it is hard to imagine that a process of repoliticization could go very far without the presence of a strong third party—all the more so given the corporatist integration of the major parties.

In the 1994 national elections the Greens attracted one million total votes and won 80 municipal seats, mostly in small college towns where environmental and consumer awareness was strong. As the Greens struggle to achieve electoral breakthroughs here and there, however, they are hindered by an image that, while progressive, still conveys the interests and sensibilities of mainly young, white, affluent, countercultural sectors of the population. This liability, though not only a matter of image, is compounded by strong currents of new-age ideology that will prevent the Greens from expanding beyond their still insular environmental base. Moreover, aside from the short-lived presence of a very small "left-green" faction, the Greens have never been comfortable with an anticapitalist agenda, preferring instead to press for an ecologically balanced mode of production and consumption (referred to as "sustainable development") in the corporate framework. Yet, while they remain aligned with mostly nonurban constituencies, Greens in the United States cannot be dismissed as simply a one-track environmental party, since their agenda includes electoral reform, decentralization, consumers' rights, feminism, and sustainable economics in a broad program for social change. In California, for example, Green chapters have joined coalitions fighting NAFTA (the North American Free Trade Act) and the anti-immigration Proposition 187 and have collaborated with labor, minority, and women's organizations in a number of electoral campaigns. The Nader 1996 presidential bid, a lukewarm effort garnering less than 1 percent of the vote, did at least inject elements of anticorporate consciousness into the Greens' discourse. Despite this nuanced ideological turn, however, green politics at the end of the century still lacks a transformative edge and the capacity to carve out sizable electoral blocs.

The Greens are only one of literally dozens of third-party efforts to have entered political competition in the United States since 1980. According to Richard Winger in *Ballot Access Newsletter*, no fewer than 78 such parties ran candidates in the 1992 elections, although most were defined by single issues—the legalization of marijuana or repeal of federal income taxes, for example—and only a few were able to win even minor local offices. Parties such as the Peace and Freedom Party in California, founded in 1968 and faithful to its New Left origins well into the 1990s, have failed to break out of their tiny radical enclaves after repeated futile campaigns for high office. Their threshold is generally less than 1 percent of the turnout—far less than needed to keep supporters' hopes alive for significant representation in the political system. Few of these nongreen parties have much organic relationship to popular movements, so it would seem that their potential as agencies of repoliticization is virtually nil.

Once it became clear (by 1990) that the Rainbow Coalition had failed to achieve either independent electoral status or broadened community presence—mainly because of its strategic attachment to the Democratic Party—the progressive side of the labor movement began looking to establish a Labor Party somewhat along the lines of the British example. A group called Labor Party Advocates (LPA), headed by former Oil, Chemical, and Atomic Workers (OCAW) president Tony Mazzocchi, initiated plans in 1991 for a an independent electoral organization committed to working-class interests. Behind the slogan "the bosses have two parties. We should have at least one," LPA came into being based on the (correct) assumption that workers have never enjoyed real representation in either of the major parties and can never expect to get it so long as corporations exercise preponderant control over the electoral process. According to OCAW president Bob Wages: "It is no longer time to be timid. There is a tremendous political void in the United States. Working men and women can fill that void if we have the courage to band together." On this note the Labor Party was founded in Cleveland in June 1996 around the program "A Call to Justice," which embraced several goals: begin running candidates for office in 1998; reframe public debate around critical economic issues; and connect local organizing work with electoral campaigns. In contrast to the Greens' primary focus on *social* issues, LPA offers a contemporary social-democratic ideology revolving mainly around material issues. As it turned out, the Labor Party was founded at a time of revitalized working-class activism in the United States, reflected by leftward trends at work in the AFL-CIO leadership, democratization of the Teamsters' Union, and a new spirit of militancy in response to plant closings, wage cuts, and overall deterioration of the public sector. This was highlighted by a more critical attitude toward corporations and labor bureaucracies as well as toward the Democratic Party.

While labor obviously remains central to the emergence of any oppositional political bloc, the stubborn fact is that any party defined strictly around labor concerns will be limited in both its social composition and ideology (and therefore its electoral appeals). As of 1998 less than 15 percent of the American labor force was unionized, and this number is still on the decline; despite the recent upsurge in militancy, the level of generalized class consciousness in the United States remains extraordinarily low. More significantly, American labor still bears the cultural imprint of a Gompers-style economism along with a deep social conservatism that, in the 1980s, gave rise to the familiar "Reagan Democrats." Labor has always defended its own sectoral interests (wages, benefits, working conditions, and so on) within a well-defined capitalist social contract that, however, may be on the verge of unraveling in the face of globalizing pressures. As of the late 1990s it is far too early to judge the extent to which a strong revival of labor activism points toward fundamental long-term changes of direction for the movement. What does seem clear, however, is that labor-based parties elsewhere (including England) have lost any transformative edge they might once have possessed, resulting in part from their immersion in an outdated, increasingly narrow labor-movement ideology and culture, in part from decline of the manufacturing sector itself. Thus, while the vision set forth by LPA might appeal to progressive labor elements fed up with the procorporate policies of the Democrats, its popular base and ideology will have to be more expansive than previous "labor" electoral ventures in terms of both ideology and base of popular support.

The appearance of so many "third" parties along the political landscape, including such major efforts as that of the Libertarian Party, ironically testifies to the *closure* of American politics and the urgent need for viable mechanisms of change; the growth of alternatives (nearly all of them rather limited) is *not* evidence of political revitalization. The Libertarians, for their part, look toward a future in which the public sector as we know it today is largely dismantled and most governmental programs, regulations, and social initiatives are jettisoned. Dedicated to the classical liberal principle of unfettered pursuit of economic self-interest, they affirm the vitality of a "private" sphere with its supposed values of freedom and autonomy over the "public," which is viewed as authoritarian, wasteful, and corrupt by definition. Employing this powerfully antistatist message, Libertarians have won as much as 5 percent of the vote in a series of national and state elections. But that message is rather duplicitous. Leaving aside the impossibility of a completely unregulated and unplanned modern society, the Libertarian emphasis on the "private" hardly disguises a gigantic and expanding corporate realm that itself concentrates power and wealth in a very few hands. As with the Republican critique of "big government," there is no consistent dedication to antiauthoritarian principles, only a partial and highly selective antistatism (as I argued in Chapter 5). Further, the Libertarian idea of a diminished public sphere does not square with a revitalized citizen politics but rather suggests the triumph of Hobbesian social relations where civil society becomes more of a battle zone than ever—a return to the most extreme individualism consonant with a world of disembodied subjects where citizenship ultimately slips from view.

A more straightforward leftist foray into the jungle of third-party politics is the New Party, which since 1993 has created a presence in several states and by 1996 was able to run victorious candidates for local office, mostly in midwestern states. During the period 1996-1998 the New Party entered 225 electoral races (winning more than half of them) for representation in such bodies as school boards, city councils, zoning boards, and state legislatures. By 1998 the party was active in 15 states, with total membership of more than 12,000. The New Party modus operandi seems closest to that of the greens: establish close ties with social movements, organize at the local level, and expand gradually before pouring resources into major electoral campaigns. Like the greens, the New Party calls for an independent politics separate from the two major parties that would lay the foundations of a rejuvenated citizenship and democratize the decision-making process as part of an emergent "new public philosophy." In its literature the New Party frequently contrasts its own (progressive) mission with the agenda of the right-wing Christian Coalition, which, by means of painstaking grassroots organizing and educational activity, has broadened its influence both within and outside the Republican Party. A 1998 New Party programmatic statement lays out broad objectives, emphasizing a "party that is rooted in local communities and is unafraid to challenge the conventional wisdom of the 'market' and the media corporations and networks that parrot the pro-corporate agenda."

New Party goals are indeed ambitious: construct a "new majority" around a program of massive urban reconstruction, convert from military to social modes of consumption, create a sustainable economy, and in the process work to deepen local empowerment. To state the obvious, the struggle to attain such goals would require a fundamental remaking of American politics that, sooner or later, will run up against the immense constraints of corporate power. While the New Party agenda is more economistic and less attuned to social priorities than that of the Greens, both share the aim of a broad electoral alliance spanning a wide array of constituencies and movements. If New Party strategy is possibly more anticorporate, its model of social change is surely less visionary and more electorally focused—closer to that of the European social democracy—which leaves it vulnerable to the very flaws and limitations of the Labor Party model.

Despite minimal resources and media access, third-party initiatives have opened up public debate, inspired some novel if not particularly radical programs, and generally helped to broaden the political terrain. Their role will be crucial, indeed indispensable, to any future rejuvenation of American politics. At the same time, they face daunting structural and ideological obstacles on the road to any historic political breakthrough, since, despite the persistence of glaring social problems and the atrophy of electoral politics, major party hegemony remains unbroken. So long as Republicans and Democrats are perceived as the only "serious" options for voters, most people, however distrustful of elites, will feel they are wasting their votes by supporting minor parties. This is another reason why electoral activity by itself can never suffice: a "breakthrough" third party must be solidly grounded in a broad amalgamation of social movements—exactly what the Greens and, to a lesser extent, Labor Party Advocates and the New Party have in mind. In their 1990s incarnation, however, none of these alternatives seems capable, standing alone, of constructing the kind of social bloc needed to effectively compete with the major parties. Of all third-party campaigns, only the Greens would appear to have the kind of visionary outlook that might provide anticorporate opposition with the necessary ideological cohesion and mass appeal.

The list of failed third parties in U.S. history is a long one—Populists, Progressives, Socialists, Communists, American Independents (though they would say that they're still alive and kicking—just wait for Act 3), Citizens, Peace and Freedom, Libertarians, and the Consumer Party, to name only the most significant. Some of these parties enjoyed partial short-term successes but then either quickly disintegrated or wound up reduced to perpetual marginal status. Of course, a future third-party electoral triumph could occur virtually overnight—witness the dramatic upsurge of the British Liberals, German Greens, French Ecologists, and Canadian New Democrats, although those efforts never had to face the immense barriers posed by the American two-party stranglehold. Even in the United States, however, the rather meaningless Perot candidacy in 1992 reaped surprising electoral benefits during the course of a single, relatively brief campaign. The new historical juncture could offer space for a third-party upsurge, perhaps owing to worsening social problems, closure of the political system, and apparent readiness of large sectors of the population to vote for alternatives to the Democrats and Republicans (witness Perot's 8% showing even in 1996). One problem, however, is that the electorate has at its disposal an endless choice of minor parties, none of which can yet seriously pose a threat to the power structure. Even among the three or four most viable alternatives one finds a debilitating, often needless, fragmentation of energies and resources that in the end only subverts prospects for a unified opposition.

A deep process of repoliticization will depend on the coalescing of multiple forms of local opposition around common visions and goals, including above all the democratization of economic and political life. One such possibility could be along the lines of an independent Rainbow Party that would bring together in one organization several vital initiatives—for example, the Greens (with their radical ideology and postmaterialist social concerns), Labor (with its urban working-class agenda), and the New Party (oriented toward a new consensual social contract). Success will depend on the degree to which such a formation could win popular endorsement for a core set of beliefs, formulate a compelling notion of the general interest, and develop a *political* strategy that merges electoral campaigns and grassroots movements or insurgencies. These are lessons that, after all, the U.S. Right internalized long ago. If political renewal demands organizational wherewithal (involving some combination of movements, community groups, and parties), it surely cannot proceed far in the absence of generalized citizen empowerment. In turn, participatory culture necessitates the widest dissemination of information, skills, and attitudes vital to political efficacy, especially among groups that have been disenfranchised or marginalized. Partial development of such a culture has been the legacy of a few new-populist experiences in local communities such as Santa Cruz, California, and Burlington, Vermont, where progressive majorities were able to broaden the public sphere, opening up new arenas of citizen participation (on city councils, school boards, planning commissions) and social reform while whittling away at the influence of big business. For most of the existing depoliticized terrain, however, it is precisely the very information, skills, and attitudes vital to such a culture that are now so devalued—except of course in the elilte subculture. And corporate colonization, as we have seen, functions in myriad ways to reproduce this state of affairs daily.

THE ENLIGHTENMENT REVISITED

Because the wide diffusion of certain types of knowledge and expertise is essential to a rebirth of politics, there is the inevitable question as to whether, in a post-Fordist technological order, the global electronics revolution might facilitate such a process. In other words, will the computerized technological infrastructure help to empower ordinary people, thus functioning as a counterweight to the demobilizing ethos of antipolitics? With the democratization of knowledge and communications made possible by instant, easy, low-cost, and widely available information technology, many politicians, academics, and technical experts are convinced that social progress (including economic and political decentralization) is built into the prevailing developmental logic. Such partisans of technology believe that a huge multimedia system can link diverse regions of the world, plugging homes, workplaces schools, and communities into a gigantic network of data and images, imparting new meaning to Enlightenment ideals long held sacred, including democracy, personal autonomy, economic rationality, material prosperity, and advances in the human store of knowledge and understanding. It may be a hopeful harbinger of the future that the grandest real-world celebration of Enlightenment ideals occurs nightly in the primetime programming of America's most progressive educational television stations.

One of the more grandiose if not unabashedly utopian scenarios inspired by the high-tech revolution is that championed by Alvin and Heidi Toffler, who view the informational order as a powerful and irrepressible force behind worldwide democratization. (This theme has been picked up and enlarged upon by such disparate partisans as Newt Gingrich and President Clinton.) For the Tofflers, the new technology represents a "quantum leap forward" that will force a complete jettisoning of old structures and values that are "no longer fitted to the needs to a rapidly changed world." As we move headlong into the "third wave" of development, the age-old ideals of direct citizen participation and local decision making can no longer be deferred or repressed. Thus: "Using today's far more advanced computers, satellites, telephones, cable, polling techniques, and other tools, not to mention the Internet and other communications networks, an educated citizenry can for the first time in history begin making many of its own political decisions." This means "we can no longer solve our problems with the ideologies, the models, or the leftover structures of the second-wave past [industrial society]."[30] In the Tofflers' view, this epochal transformation is more or less inevitable, reflecting "a gigantic shift of information flows in society. We are . . . undergoing a fundamental demassification of communication as the power of central networks wanes. We are seeing a stunning proliferation of cable, cassette, computer, and private electronics mail systems, all pushing in the same decentralist direction." They conclude: "So long as the decision load of the social systems expands, therefore, democracy becomes not a matter of choice, but of evolutionary necessity; the system cannot run without it."[31]

Although the Tofflers never clearly specify the presumed relationship between information technology and democratization, it would be absurd to deny the importance of this new wave—especially for greater dissemination of information and data around the world and for the rapidity of communications and decision making. Corporations can use the new technology to gain competitive advantage in markets and enhance their profits; financial institutions can use it to speed up global transactions; governments can use it to improve decision-making adaptability; and of course individuals (at least those most fully wired into the system) can use it for a variety of personal and work functions. Many technophiles also believe that social movements and community groups can lay hold of computer networks to facilitate their goals, including efforts to challenge the status quo. One longtime activist deeply involved in alternative media argues that the World Wide Web "is where the political future of this country is going to be formed." He envisions radical possibilities through electronic newspapers and magazines transmitted on the Internet, a kind of computerized "free press" helping to connect people and serving as a clearinghouse of information vital to citizens engaged in social change. He foresees a technologically driven "new era of activism" with its "new sense of values" corresponding to the imminent revival of social movements and politics. As the Web democratizes the flow of information, more people are now in a position to voice their opinions, criticize the power structure, even aspire to "publish" their views in the unfolding electronic neighborhood.[32]

Yet, as we acquire the unprecedented ability to move data, ideas, and symbols around the globe, it is much too easy in the flush of technological anticipation to sidestep some critical questions, such as, Who will ultimately own and control this far-flung medium, and for what purposes? What social forces and interests are in the best position to shape informational technology? Given the depoliticized character of American society, can greater access to information by itself contribute to citizen empowerment and help break down the social division of labor? Does the increasing *centrality* of computers to the functioning of modern society reinforce long-standing trends toward instrumental rationality? Indeed, does the new technology—like all previous historical forms of technology—contain inherent epistemological and political biases that might short-circuit its emancipatory potential?

There can be no doubt that technology, far from being a simple neutral instrument, is *always* shaped by wider social forces and processes, is *always* an artifact of its particular historical times. More than that, technology generally takes on the character of those social structures in which it is embedded; it is an integral part of elaborate networks of institutions, norms, and processes that help shape and regulate most of what takes place in society.[33] This generalization seems all the more compelling in an era when computer technology seems to command a quasi-religious reverence. To answer such questions we need to first confront a basic reality: that ownership and control of what will be the most lucrative enterprise of the twenty-first century (projected in 1998 to generate revenues of more than $4 trillion annually by the year 2000) is falling more and more into the hands of global communications megacorporations. This vast new structure of corporate domination extends the global reach of such media giants as the TV networks, Disney/ABC, Microsoft, IBM, Apple, Time Warner, Bell Atlantic, and AT&T. Often forgotten is the fact that the take-off in computer technology, including the much celebrated information superhighway, occurred at a time when the global corporate order had already been well established. The bulk of modern-day technology is controlled by perhaps no more than 100 of the largest multinational companies and banks, representing unparalleled economic power and wealth. By the late-1990s these entities, operating in an increasingly fluid investment and trade environment, were able to control more than $5 trillion in assets. As theoretically "private" institutions, the multinationals have been burdened with little accountability, globally or domestically, meaning that there is no corporate democracy or citizenship in any meaningful sense. Moreover, these megafirms have accumulated sufficient economic and political power to severely reduce the influence national governments can have on their functioning. As Herbert Schiller writes: "The important duties of government have been appropriated, silently for the most part, by these giant private economic aggregates [that are] the leading force in promoting deregulation and privatization of industry, in all countries notably but not exclusively in the telecommunications sector."[34]

The multinationals are competing fiercely across the planet to control people's access to information and with it their perception of reality. Such corporate aspiration toward greater economic and ideological domination, facilitated at every turn by the new technology, contradicts the Tofflers' simplistic faith in democratization growing out of the informational regimen. In the present circumstances we are more likely to witness an increasing *closure* of cyberspace, with its narrowing consequences for public discourse and political activity. Here Schiller refers to an "electronically organized total environment" that has the potential to "colonize virtually every realm of social space."[35] Clearly, what the Tofflers and other technological partisans overlook is the way in which huge centers of economic power can so decisively shape new developmental agendas.

The entire media and communications infrastructure has actually been globally centralized, and to a lesser extent commodified, for many years. Whether in the form of TV, cable, or computers, the privileged interests have been able to set the electronics agenda, while the vast majority of people—even in the most highly industrialized countries—enter the system mainly as passive agents or consumers, "choosing" and "interacting" in only the most limited ways. The system now in place is, of course, a marvelously efficient instrument for gathering data and sending messages. But it is another matter for ordinary people, especially in marginalized sectors of the economy, to be able to register genuine choices, feelings, and critical opinions—the very basis of a democratic public sphere—through an electronic world that does so little to encourage inputs that can have political meaning.[36] Among its many functions, computer technology plays a key role in centralizing and rationalizing the power of corporations, banks, governments, and military structures around the world; it reinforces the process of globalization at the very same moment it enhances information flows—again, quite at odds with the Tofflers' optimistic, decentralizing scenario. Elite policies that contribute to worsening poverty, wars, social dislocation, and ecological crisis now depend on technology not only for efficiency but for purposes of enhanced control and legitimation. Computers have come to represent a vital component of intellectual (and cultural) capital: by expanding the store of knowledge, transmitting messages, and processing data with great rapidity, computers help break down global boundaries and thus smooth the flow of technical and material resources both within and between countries. Informational capitalism is therefore infinitely more fluid and mobile, which naturally corresponds to the imperatives of the global market. Knowledge and data become vital ingredients of an emergent techno-capitalism that, on the whole, reproduces the social division of labor in even more authoritarian guise—a reality easily concealed by the appearance of open access made possible by the perpetual flow of data and images in cyberspace.

The vision of a more open and democratic public sphere enlivened by computer technology, by increasing popular access to communications networks such as the Internet, fails to take into account deep cultural and psychological obstacles embodied in the whole paradigm of technological discourse. There is no way of avoiding the question of precisely what kind of citizen-empowerment messages get transmitted in cyberspace. We know that global informational technology is already thoroughly permeated with such capitalist values as: a tough, aggressive individualism, an intensely competitive ethos, commodified images, and an instrumental rationality. Leaving aside naive assumptions regarding technological "neutrality," any cyberspace-oriented struggles for citizen empowerment would have to move through this fully established public sphere. It is worth noting here that when individuals participate in this technology they most frequently do so in the context of the insular, privatized realm of home or office; rarely do they enter into the life of ongoing community-based groups and movements, which of course depend on sustained human interaction. Thus "citizenship" that takes shape in cyberspace, no matter how open and popularly accessible the medium, will probably lack the *social* concreteness and immediacy long understood as a precondition for democratic involvement and decision making. The world of the Internet, which has revolutionized the flow of information and images, nonetheless favors somewhat anonymous and detached modes of communication—highly appealing to those with the time and resources (a tiny minority of the global population) but hardly a step in the direction of a repoliticized public sphere.

As modern technology expands and becomes more integral to daily life, the seductions of a more or less detached form of cyber discourse are all the greater, thus in effect *reducing* popular impulses toward sustained (and demanding) forms of social interaction and community involvement. Much like TV, the computer is a manifestly privatizing medium, except of course that the computer allows for endless journeys into "virtual reality." No doubt much of what gets transmitted is intrinsically valuable and helps reduce the burden of work and of an assortment of business transactions.

But the *public* dimension of the new technology needs to be assessed quite differently. In his seminal work *The Cult of Information,* Theodore Roszak writes that one of the great seductions of computers is that "you can create your own universe, and you can do whatever you want with that. You don't have to deal with people."[37] Or at least one does not have to deal with people in the direct personal sense, much less in the context of ongoing collective action; indeed, the very format militates against such engagement. What this means is that so much human choice and decision making can be detached from the actuality of existing institutional arrangements. While the information superhighway furnishes creative (and profitable) outlets for people in the professional and educated strata, its more general impact is predictably quite different: a strengthening and relegitimation of elite power. In Roszak's words: "The bureaucratic managers, the corporate elites, the military and surveillance agencies are all able to make good use of computerized data to obfuscate, mystify, intimidate, and control. Because they overwhelmingly own the sources and machinery of data, the cult of information lends a mystique to their dominance."[38]

This last point requires further elaboration, since it runs counter to one of the great myths of American pragmatism and capitalist modernity—that technology (buttressed by a steady flow of information) can be a tool, perhaps even a panacea, for solving major social problems ranging from pollution to crime to sickness to world hunger. As Neil Postman writes: "In specialized contexts, the value of calculation, speed, and voluminous information may go uncontested. But the 'message' of computer technology is comprehensive and domineering. The computer argues, to put it baldly, that the most serious problems confronting us at both personal and public levels require technological solutions through fast access to information otherwise unavailable."[39] Pushed to its extreme (as with the Tofflers) the argument for technocratic intervention as a full-scale solution to age-old dilemmas winds up sidestepping the always thorny realm of conflicting social interests, power relations, and of course *politics*. Technology is viewed as following its own essentially benevolent course, producing roughly determined outcomes (with some timely nudges here and there)—democratization, improved health care and housing, reversal of the ecological crisis, and so forth.

The technocratic belief that computers can, and probably will, serve as an emancipating instrument runs deep in American culture. Yet, this ideology obscures the fact that we have more sophisticated machines today than ever before—and a much greater abundance of information regarding every topic imaginable—yet many urgent problems (health, crime, substance abuse, urban decay, the environmental crisis) continue to fester and worsen with each passing day, and indeed are often *exacerbated* by too much reliance on technology. As an example of the latter, Jeremy Rifkin concludes in *The End of Work* that technological displacement of jobs could reach catastrophic levels by the year 2010, resulting in unemployment (and semiemployment) rates far higher than today.[40] To the degree that such conditions did not appear simply because of deficiencies in technology or information, it is highly unlikely they will be *solved* by recourse to precisely that same technology and information. As I have argued, the politics of citizen empowerment demands considerably more than that, including structural mechanisms that allow for open and critical discourse, social firmaments of community and collective involvement, a struggle for new (democratized) forms of social governance—none of which technology alone can provide.

One key question posed by the ascendancy (and grandiose claims) of modern technocratic culture is: what can democratic values ultimately mean in a setting where public intervention faces so many structural and ideological barriers, where the public sphere is so devalued, where great social challenges are so ignored or trivialized, where indeed the whole technological agenda has become so commodified? If existing patterns continue, the informational utopia of cyberspace will turn out to be just another interactive but depoliticized arena where choice and debate go little further than everyday consumer decisions, than the on-line search for a variety of personal, work-related, and simply random electronic connections. Any distinctly public endeavor beyond this is likely to take on more of an artificial character—virtual, detached, fleeting—than real. In the words of Chris Carlesson: "Perhaps the loss of public space has driven the dreamers into cyberspace, with the only thriving 'public communities' found on the Internet bulletin boards."[41]

TRANSCENDING THE "MORBID SYMPTOMS"

Writing from the terrifying depths of Italian fascism in the 1930s, Antonio Gramsci observed in his *Prison Notebooks* how the "crisis of authority" in Europe gave rise to a wholly transformed political milieu in which the old ideologies had lost their relevance and the search for new ones, especially among the popular strata, had led to a host of bizarre and irrational responses. He wrote about the loss of ruling-class consensus where "the great masses have become detached from their traditional ideologies and no longer believed what they used to believe," part of a crisis that "consists precisely in the fact the old is dying and the new cannot be born"—the reflection of an interim period in which "a great variety of morbid symptoms appears." Gramsci added: "The death of the old ideologies takes the form of skepticism with regard to all theories and general formulae; of application to the pure economic fact, and to a form of politics which is not simply realistic in fact."[42] Although Gramsci's historical setting was a far remove from turn-of-the-millennium United States, the validity of his insights—which seemingly anticipated the "postmodern condition"—appears to be universal in his perception that the crisis of authority (or hegemony) is typically accompanied by the spread of a multitude of anti-political ideas and movements.

Interpreting the depoliticization of American society in this conceptual framework, one could say that an immense power structure has extended its institutional and economic hold over large domestic and global populations, but its *ideological* domination has in many ways become more fragile as the many examples of popular antipolitical, and often antistatist, sentiments would seem to attest. The myriad expressions of political retreat analyzed in this volume do not exhaust the wide range of responses to the "crisis of authority," but they are arguably *definitive* of the current situation. These expressions share a common understanding that politics today is hopelessly remote, instrumentalized, and without ethical parameters, that it cannot serve as a viable agency of collective action. What runs through the various discourses of antipolitics is a struggle for identity and purpose largely *outside* the public sphere; human choices regarding values or ethics are forced into the local, micro, privatized realms of existence, in effect acknowledging precisely what is absent from the discourse of normal politics. The "morbid symptoms" that Gramsci believed would accompany the breakdown of hegemony are thus entirely understandable and even predictable, sometimes even salutary. An emotionally driven hostility toward the state, a rejection of "strategic thinking," a depleted sense of political efficacy defined by widespread passivity, cynicism, and fatalism—all these phenomena make sense as part of the context of this depoliticized quest for purpose. A politics disconnected from public values and ethics, that has no relationship to any future plan or vision, amounts to an enterprise that most will regard as bankrupt. The historic erosion of long-established ideologies is both the cause and effect of this tendency.

The complex social conditions underlying this shift in political culture are of course very real; as we have seen, depoliticization is more than a matter of individual or small group psychology, more than a function of irrationalism, civil privatism, or millenarian escapades. Our analysis hinges on the unprecedented corporate penetration of civil society and, by logical extension, the deep impact of economic globalization on political life around the world. Other factors enter into the picture: media culture, consumerism, bureaucracy, technological rationality, post-Fordist social fragmentation. Given such multiple and overlapping factors at work, the tide of antipolitics might seem to be insurmountable, irreversible. The general mood is such that we should not be terribly surprised to find a profound diminution of those public values associated with citizenship, democratic participation, and the common good—a total absence of the traditional Greek ideal of *zoon politikon* that leaves us powerless at a time of pressing challenges. As Benjamin Barber writes: "We are left stranded by this melancholy history in an era where civil society is in eclipse and where citizens have neither home for their civic institutions nor voice with which to speak even within nation-states normally committed to democracy."[43]

There can be little doubt, then, that future struggles to reclaim politics for (and by) an empowered citizenry will face a Sisyphean battle, especially since the most troublesome obstacles remain firmly in place. And traditional ideological legacies—nationalism, liberalism, socialism, communism—can no longer offer adequate progressive guideposts for emergent centers of resistance and opposition. The truth may be that such ideologies have in themselves contributed enormously to the decline of political interest, passion, and commitment since the 1970s, at least in the industrialized countries. We know that popular disaffection from the old ideologies has played a catalytic role in the contemporary rise of antipolitics. In one nation after another claims surrounding these ideologies (to ensure freedom and democracy, guarantee national self-determination, end poverty, facilitate social equality, and so on) have been soundly discredited, as shown not only in the fall of Communism but in the failure of liberal capitalism (or social democracy) to insert itself effectively into the ideological void.

Probably no ideology has contributed more to the present impasse than liberal capitalism, the developmental logic and ethical presuppositions of which stand in conflict with the imperatives of an open, participatory, dynamic public sphere. Ostensibly "democratic," contemporary liberal capitalism corrodes the very fiber of political life. The remarkable material success of the U.S. economic model has occluded this reality, often concealing the deep ethical and political vacuum created by Enlightenment rationality and laissez-faire market principles; tarnished as these might be, they still serve to legitimate global capitalism. While corporate priorities and consumer values are on the rise around the world, only in the United States are liberal-capitalist ideas worshiped by elites and opinion makers as a virtual civic religion in which social progress becomes equated with endless material growth, individual self-interest, the triumph of the marketplace, and the celebration of science and technology. Sadly, however, these very principles scarcely conceal a global economic machine veering out of control that levels everything in its path, leaving behind a socially dislocated and atomized mass public bereft of political moorings.

Despite its undeniable contributions to the historic struggles for individual freedom, human rights, and consensual governance, modern liberalism still adheres to a free-market ethos and possessive individualism that conflicts with such distinctly public ideals as the common interest, civic participation, social ethics, economic planning and regulation, and "sustainable development." Given such an enfeebled public dimension, and owing to the deep impact of corporate colonization, politics winds up reduced to little more than a series of power machinations in which rival dominant groups compete for institutional and material advantage, all legitimated by the charade of electoral campaigns. The idea that politics might serve as a vehicle for generalized citizen involvement or movements for social change is nullified in the name of competing plural "interests." Whatever the original intentions of classical liberals who fought an ongoing battle against feudal privilege and monarchical absolutism, modern liberal thinking is far too organically connected to both corporate domination and governmental power, to the realities of social hierarchy, to have much in the way of a democratizing thrust. As William Ophuls observes: "The liberal paradigm of politics is moribund. Liberal politics has become an increasingly naked struggle for power played out in a media arena before an electronic mob."[44] Modern liberalism is perfectly compatible with a truncated, elitist version of political life in which the majority of people are effectively disenfranchised, reduced to manipulable objects even as they enjoy formal legal and political rights, even as traditional democratic ideals are paid official lip service. The ideology, with all of its emphasis on laws, procedures, and rituals, ultimately turns against its own premises. In Michael Sandel's words: "The procedural republic cannot secure the liberty it promises, because it cannot sustain the kind of political community and civic engagement that liberty requires."[45]

In many ways the ethos of modern liberalism actually feeds into the return to a quasi-Hobbesian state of nature where atomized individuals and group interests compete apart from an ethical system; turbulence in civil society, however, may be perfectly compatible with the consolidation of *hegemonic* interests—assuming that such turbulence does not get out of control. The decay of civic life has for some time gone hand in hand with vigorous reassertion of market or corporate principles, which might seem to lead to greater social and personal autonomy but in fact generates exactly the opposite, namely, enhanced authoritarian control over civil society along with a growing, media-abetted social conformism.

From this standpoint it seems abundantly clear that recent efforts by politicians and social scientists to resuscitate the theme of civil society as a bastion of emancipatory forces and impulses is completely misplaced. The idea that some unmediated notion of civil society—all spheres of human activity not subsumed by "the state"—corresponds to inherently democratic values and practices is scarcely borne out by contemporary developments; indeed the very emergence of a depoliticized society indicates an altogether different course. The reality is that civil society, with the end of the cold war, has come to embrace a turn toward privatization, toward a neoliberal emphasis on market capitalism that is fully compatible with the growth of corporate colonization and economic globalization. The dense network of local and voluntary organizations (including the familiar NGOs) trumpeted by many as a major step toward democratization turns out to be not only antistatist but antipolitical in the deepest meaning of the term. Hence, the widespread view that rejuvenation of civil society will offer a viable alternative to the presumably malignant nation-state is nothing but a myth.[46]

It would be foolhardy to think that repoliticization of American society can advance in the repressive ethos of liberal capitalism; indeed the theory and practice of antipolitics shapes the very core of modern liberalism. To be sure, the system reproduces itself through social and political beliefs tied to myths of the free market and individualism, and to the seductions of consumerism, which may be said to constitute a political ideology. Such an ideology, however, narrows and devalues politics as an essential form of human activity. Still, however irrelevant these myths might be to an understanding of social reality, their legitimating function points to a crucial imperative—namely, that political opposition too requires a coherent ideology, one that goes beyond instrumental rationality and economic self-interest, one that embodies a transformative vision. At the same time, the search for alternatives gives rise to its own conundrum in that the most powerful twentieth-century ideologies have now exhausted their potential. Social democratic reformism, for example, has turned into an even more bureaucratized and statist model of capitalism—slightly more attuned to social and welfare priorities but without even the pretense of an alternative to liberal-capitalist class and power structures. The Soviet model, firmly embedded in the tradition of Leninist centralism, could once have laid claim to historical "success" defined in terms of winning and holding state power but now stands fully discredited after its collapse (a victim of the internal contradictions of bureaucratic centralism). Similarly, an insurrectionary strategy (Leninist or otherwise) seems doomed to failure in post-Fordist society where conditions permitting a vanguard's seizure of power simply do not exist. At the other end of the spectrum, localist alternatives tied to anarchism, council communism, and radical strains of the new social movements appear confined to the margins, lacking viable social agencies or institutional levers of change. Often motivated by spontaneous impulses, localism generally remains trapped, powerless to articulate a public language or develop into a sustained political force. The localist predicament is aggravated, moreover, by the increasingly *global* character of issues, problems, and conditions that movements and parties must ultimately confront today. As the old ideological discourses lose their intellectual and psychological capacity to generate oppositional politics, the irresistible popular drift toward *anti*politics—including those "morbid symptoms" described by Gramsci—becomes all the more understandable.

The difficult struggle for organizational and ideological alternatives relevant to the post-Fordist historical context—that is, for a revitalized language and vision of politics, for a reinvention of politics—is thus indispensable to hopes for repoliticization. Such a task poses dauntless challenges, for it will have to overcome a political culture steeped in cynicism, withdrawal, and passivity; it will have to reverse the powerful trend toward antipolitics. Political renewal depends on recovery of precisely those concerns that a depoliticized society so thoroughly devalues, namely, collective consumption, social planning, citizen involvement, and the imposition of public controls over capital. The kind of "deep citizenship"needed to reverse depoliticization will have to be inclusive, generalized, public, attuned to demands for social equity—and sensitive to multiple definitions of the common good. Implicit here is a constantly broadening public sphere in which rules of the game become unsettled, where the institutional fabric is no longer approached as fixed, natural, and static—where, in other words, the whole terrain of politics can be redefined and reshaped to incorporate expanded citizenship. An enlarged public sphere implies transcendence of the dichotomy civil society versus state, local versus national, community versus political, indeed national versus global—in a way that allows for a thoroughgoing discourse of democratization at all levels, in all spheres. Viewed from this angle, the point is not to embrace some fetishized notion of civil society *against* the state, for example, but rather to anticipate a lengthy process of social transformation inclusive of both. It should hardly need repeating that the *existing* federal government in the United States—corrupt, repressive, undemocratic, and replete with the security state, the military–industrial complex, and a bloated prison system—is not the one that must be protected and extended. The real choice for the twenty-first century will not be statism versus antistatism, but rather which model of governance makes sense.[47] Surely without *some* powerful (yet democratized) governing bodies, no amalgam of social forces or popular movements can hope to confront the awesome presence of multinational corporations.

Repoliticization can never take place unless change-oriented groups and movements begin to unify their social, largely prepolitical, struggles around distinctly common, public aims such as social equality, democratization of civic life, full employment, universal health care, and sustainable forms of development. It also demands a thoroughgoing merger of ethics and politics. The ethics in question are derived from neither the exchange values of the market nor the instrumentalism of Enlightenment rationality but rather from a variety of universal discourses—civic democracy, com-

munity, ecology, feminism, and so forth. At the same time, political renewal would owe little to the Jacobin tradition, embracing instead populist, radical-democratic ideals that counter the repressive thrust of
corporate colonization and the downward spiral toward what Ophuls calls
a "combination of ecological collapse and inner decay."[48] In this pan-
orama one can say that politics is upheld as a source of self-*actualization,*
as the Greeks insisted, rather than the self-abnegation and loss of autonomy usually associated with authoritarian rule; development of self and
society are thus no longer opposed but are integrally connected. As
Gramsci observed, "critical understanding of self takes place... through a
struggle of political 'hegemonies' and opposing directions, first in the ethical field and then in that of politics proper, in order to arrive at the working out at a higher level of one's own conception of reality." From this
standpoint, "progressive self-consciousness" is grounded in the unfolding
of historical processes where human beings arrive at a "single and coherent conception of the world" grounded in ethics and politics and "a conception of reality that has gone beyond common sense" and has finally become a "critical conception."[49]

This Gramscian view of politics—or, more specifically, of political revitalization grounded in the simultaneous transformation of self and society—is a distant remove from the present unfortunate state of affairs
where historical conditions reinforce the culture of anti-politics at every
turn. In the United States, at least, the multiple expressions of a depoliticized culture that I have explored in these pages are neither rigidly fixed
nor immune to explosive social contradictions that permeate any highly
stratified, geopolitically overextended order. As the system begets further
crisis and polarization, its vulnerability to breakdown and extreme conflict
increases; what remains to be known is precisely the content and *direction*
of change. Despite a lengthy period of conservative hegemony, many progressive movements and organizations have survived into the late 1990s,
even if most of them wound up marginalized or assimilated into the orbit
of institutionalized normal politics. Whether such movements and organizations can be repoliticized and the "morbid symptoms" of antipolitics
given new ideological direction—and whether those popular forces can enter into, and help democratically transform, the public sphere—will be the
most urgent issue facing the United States and the world in the early
twenty-first century.

POSTSCRIPT:
THE YEAR 2000

As this book goes to press, the U.S. presidential campaign for the year 2000—trumpeted by some as possibly an epochal moment in American political history—is already in full swing, with several hopefuls in the two major parties (along with several independents) tenaciously vying for crucial resources and jockeying for position as the race begins to take shape. If the campaign is to be appreciated as a political event rather than a media or cultural spectacle, the indicators are rather dismal: Virtually every major trend identified in the preceding pages (the narrowing of political debate, closure of the public sphere, the power of corporate colonization, erosion of citizen interest in politics) seems more visible than ever. Although opinion leaders continue to champion the virtues of democratic participation and civic culture, the process of depoliticization, at both elite and popular levels of belief and activity, follows its relentless logic. The main presidential contenders, Republican George W. Bush and Democrat Al Gore, seem bent on staging an electoral campaign notable for little more than the candidates' obsession with fundraising, with outdistancing each other in the money stakes. Already this pallid contest is being labeled the "money primary" or the "wealth campaign," reflecting the candidates' desperate search for high impact in the most advanced media culture the world has ever known. (At this writing Bush alone has built a war chest of over $60 million, the money coming from an array of wealthy folks; legal, medical, and financial special interest groups; and corporate lobbies fully a year before the actual election.) Meanwhile, worsening social problems—the fate of the environment, crises in work and education, the decline of urban life, the need for universal medical care, the debilitating war on drugs, foreign relations with Russia and China—have more or less vanished from the public agenda.

They have been obscured by platitudinous blatherings about "growth" in the U.S. economy, Bush's alleged cocaine habit of 30 years ago, and Gore's supposedly bland personality. As the race for funds and trivial gossip substitute for open, honest, genuine debate, the political system heads further toward immobility, indeed absurdity, while corporate elites go about their business with a minimum of intervention or disruption from the much despised "political" realm.

Under present conditions, it will make no difference to the American people which of these money-hungry candidates eventually ends up in the White House: Corporations will continue to be free to exploit the labor force mercilessly while downsizing whenever it fits their interests, the earth will still be plundered, the U.S. military will continue to bomb small, defenseless countries, the prison–industrial complex will absorb more funds (and inmates), and the cancer rate will be just as astronomically high. The much ballyhooed ideal of citizenship—the presumed lifeline of modern democracy—will be further devalued. Two outside presidential contenders with initially little hope of success, John McCain and Bill Bradley, have made known their disgust with the whole process. McCain denounced the system as "an elaborate influence-peddling scheme in which both parties conspire to stay in office by selling the country to the highest bidder," and Bradley complained that "democracy shouldn't be a commodity that is bought and sold," but in the face of corporate riches flooding into electoral politics of late neither McCain nor Bradley would be able to win their primaries or the election without financial support that would compromise their credibility on this point. Nor would the quirky antipolitics candidacy of Hollywood celebrity Warren Beatty matter very much aside from its comedic impact. Beatty's potential candidacy presumably has something to do with his movie *Bullworth*, a film about a U.S. senator who suffers a breakdown and decides to finally tell the truth (through the medium of rap music) about the corrupting influence of big money in American politics. Of course a Beatty campaign would add to the mockery and absurdity of the political arena—a move that might be especially appropriate for the year 2000. In a postmodern media culture Beatty's independent "candidacy" would easily overshadow whatever real issues might get posed.

In this historical context there should be little wonder that just 15 percent of Americans polled by the Pew Research Center in July 1999 said they were paying very close attention to the ostensibly critical 2000 presidential campaign—a figure that is even lower for those under age 30. The phenomenon explored in this book of declining public interest in and trust of government and politics reflects a mass disaffection considerably deeper than resentment over scandals, corruption, lying, and so forth. It has little to do with the actual character of governmental institutions and practices, although such factors do contribute. Many observers have blamed the growing antipolitical milieu on residual effects of the 1960s counterculture or the ideological impact of technology, but such explanations (while plausible in some ways) remain too simplistic. The answer must be found elsewhere: in the massive concentration of economic and political power exacerbated by the global spread of multinational capitalist corporations. Today the power of centralized elites has become more formidable, and more difficult to challenge from below, than at any time in history.

The theme of corporate colonization was dramatized in a Bill Moyers PBS special entitled "Free Speech for Sale," which aired in June 1999. The conclusion reached in this generally mainstream program could not have been more stark, nor more frightening: "The corporations no longer participate in the public debate; they simply buy it." Moyers carefully documented how the public realm has been transformed into a commodified electronic square, how independent electoral challenges are so easily neutralized by the influence of big money, how the average person is systematically and deliberately kept in the dark about such crucial issues as the role of tobacco interests, the war on drugs, the economic impact of "free" trade, what corporations are doing to the environment, and the dangers of nuclear power. He showed how, in keeping with the terms of the 1996 Telecommunications Act, the federal government has given away billions of dollars' worth of priviledges to huge media giants like AT&T and Bell Atlantic without even the semblance of a discussion of such give-aways in the mainstream media or among political leaders. A FAIR (Fairness and Accuracy in Reporting) study in August 1999 revealed what by now should hardly be startling: that mainstream TV news programming devotes just 2 percent of its total air time to the concerns of working people, such as jobs, wages, plant closings, social cutbacks, health and safety issues, child care, and so forth. As FAIR put it, the major networks saw fit to devote only 13 minutes over a full year to job safety and health issues while, during that same period, 16 workers on average died *daily* at the workplace with more than 650,000 suffering from back injuries and repetitive-motion injuries. How can citizenship be meaningful in a public sphere so thoroughly emptied and depoliticized, where issues of work, health, and survival have become so invisible, where all we seem to know about presidential candidates is what goes on in their *private* lives?

The sad truth is that even ostensibly "radical" alternatives to the regime of corporate colonization seem to have been assimilated into the matrix of political business-as-usual. Take the 1998 triumph of Jerry Brown in his candidacy for mayor of Oakland, California. For many years Brown has championed one or another version of new-age, green, and radical politics, insisting (most recently in his "We the People" organization and his Pacifica radio program) that the deadly influence of money in American politics should be fully eliminated in the interest of a revitalized citizenry. Brown's year-long tenure in office has served to reduce his liberatory visions to empty rhetoric: His overriding agenda at Oakland City Hall has been to help create an environment friendly to big business, high tech, the military, and law enforcement—the very interests he may want to cultivate if he is "going mainstream," as he seems to be trying to do. This assimilation of radical agendas, familiar to students of European political history, turns out to be doubly tragic insofar as a major "oppositional" politician like Jerry Brown has not only succumbed to the logic of corporate colonization but has further devalued the grassroots efforts made on behalf of his rejuvenated governmental mission. Betrayals of this sort will only reinforce what has become the hallmark of a depoliticized society: retreat from the public sphere, hatred of "big government" and its politicians (however radical), a turn toward civil privatism, incapacity to pursue struggles for social change and the public good. In a crisis-ridden world where so much depends on the power of government and the public sector to counter the global reach of corporate behemoths, such debilitating antipolitical trends can only have a catastrophic outcome.

NOTES

Notes to INTRODUCTION

1. Robert Kaplan, "Was Democracy Just a Moment?" *Atlantic Monthly* (December 1997), 71.
2. *Los Angeles Times* (January 4, 1998).
3. *Los Angeles Times* (December 27, 1998).
4. In a letter to the *Los Angeles Times* (November 26, 1998), actor Woody Harrelson writes: "Does anyone else think it peculiar that we live in a society where our government does not stop companies from dumping toxic sludge into our rivers and oceans, encourages the spraying of six trillion tons of pesticides per year into our farmland, uses our tax dollars to subsidize cutting down ancient trees, has a history of subsidizing the growing of tobacco products that kill people every day and at the same time will put you in jail for using a plant [marijuana] that has been proved to help people who are in pain? . . . This government has no problem controlling the governed. The question is: Who will control the government?"
5. Bill Clinton will most likely go down in history as the "balanced-budget president," although while in office he also helped to legitimate a renewed assault on the welfare state (sometimes referred to as "big government") while simultaneously implementing the antilabor free trade agreement, NAFTA, and a draconian crime bill—all issues in the conventional Republican agenda. Indeed, Clinton will probably be remembered as more of a "Republican" president than George Bush, from whom Clinton inherited commitments to tax reductions, lessened social investment, free trade, law and order, and upholding the "new world order." If Clinton's deft ability to steal the thunder of American conservatives helps to explain the right-wing vendetta against him, it also goes a long way toward explaining the paradox of the president's overwhelming popularity amid what is presumably one of the most severe crises in White House history; apparently, most people attach little or no significance to all the ranting and raving that takes place inside the Washington Beltway or on the airwaves. This is yet another sign of waning popular interest in the public sphere, where even the previously tepid debates between conservatives and liberals, Republicans and Democrats, have largely vanished from sight.

6. On the corporate hijacking of environmental agendas, see Timothy W. Luke, *Ecocritique* (Minneapolis: University of Minnesota Press, 1998), ch. 3; Brian Tokar, *Earth for Sale* (Boston: South End, 1997), chs. 1–3; and Joshua Karliner, *The Corporate Planet* (San Francisco: Sierra Club Books, 1997).

7. Robert Reich, *Locked in the Cabinet* (New York: Vintage, 1997), 101.

8. Ibid., 137–138; italics in original.

9. Aristotle, "The Politics," in Michael Curtis, ed., *The Great Political Theories* Vol. 1 (New York: Avon, 1981), 64.

10. Ibid., 65.

11. Ibid., 66.

12. Ibid.

13. Antonio Gramsci, "State and Civil Society," in Quintin Hoare and Geoffrey Nowell Smith, eds., *Selections from the Prison Notebooks* (New York: International Publishers, 1971), 249.

14. Antonio Gramsci, "The Modern Prince," in Hoare and Smith, eds., *Selections*, 130.

15. Antonio Gramsci, "The Study of Philosophy," in Hoare and Smith, eds., *Selections*, 333.

16. Hannah Arendt, *On Revolution* (New York: Viking, 1965), 215.

17. See John Schwarzmantel, *The Age of Ideology* (New York: New York University Press, 1998), 159.

18. Jamin Raskin, "Dollar Democracy," *The Nation* (May 5, 1997).

19. C. Wright Mills, *The Power Elite* (New York: Oxford University Press, 1956).

20. See Herbert I. Schiller, *Information Inequality* (New York: Routledge, 1996).

21. David McChesney, in *Extra!* (November 12, 1997).

22. By 1997 there were roughly 9 million Americans living in gated communities of one kind or another; see Edward J. Blakely and Mary Gail Snyder, *Fortress America* (Washington, DC: Cato Institute, 1997).

23. Mike Davis, *Ecology of Fear* (New York: Henry Holt, 1998), 363–364.

24. On the general deterioration of the public sphere, see Zillah Eisenstein, *Global Obscenities* (New York: New York University Press, 1998), 21–30; Michael Sandel, *Democracy's Discontent* (Cambridge, MA: Harvard University Press, 1996), chs. 1, 9; William Greider, *Who Will Tell the People?* (New York: Simon and Schuster, 1992); and Nina Eliasoph, *Avoiding Politics* (New York: Cambridge University Press, 1998).

25. David Croteau, *Politics and the Class Divide* (Philadelphia: Temple University Press, 1995), 4.

26. *Los Angeles Times* (January 12, 1998).

27. Michael Parenti, *Land of Idols* (New York: St. Martin's, 1994), viii.

28. James C. Scott, *Domination and the Arts of Resistance* (New Haven: Yale University Press, 1990), ch. 7.

29. On the depoliticizing effects of modern technology, see Herbert Marcuse, *One-Dimensional Man* (Boston: Beacon, 1964); Langdon Winner, *Autonomous Technology* (Boston: MIT Press, 1982); Theodore Roszak, *Cult of Information* (New York: Pantheon, 1986); Neil Postman, *Technopoly* (New York: Vintage, 1993); and David Noble, *The Religion of Technology* (New York: Penguin, 1998).

30. Hilary Wainwright, *Arguments for a New Left* (Cambridge, MA: Blackwell, 1994), 262.

31. *Los Angeles Times* (December 28, 1998).

32. See Paul Kennedy, *The Rise and Fall of the Great Powers* (New York: Random House, 1987).

33. James Petras and Morris Morley, *Empire or Republic?* (New York: Routledge, 1995), 104.

34. William Ophuls, *Requiem for Modern Politics* (Boulder, CO: Westview, 1997).

35. Ibid., 5.

36. On the historic conflict between capitalism and democracy, see Samuel Bowles and Herbert Gintis, *Democracy and Capitalism* (New York: Basic Books, 1987), chs. 1–3; Robert N. Bellah, Richard Madsen, William M. Sullivan, Ann Swidler, and Steven M. Tipton, *The Good Society* (New York: Vintage, 1992); and Ellen Meiksins Wood, *Capitalism versus Democracy* (London: Verso, 1998).

37. Ronald Inglehart, *Modernization and Postmodernization* (Princeton, NJ: Princeton University Press, 1997), 20–27.

38. Ulrich Beck, *The Reinvention of Politics* (Cambridge, MA: Polity, 1997), 136.

39. On this point, see Scott, *Domination and the Arts of Resistance*, chs. 6, 7, and E. J. Hobsbawm, *Primitive Rebels* (New York: Norton, 1959).

40. On the theme of a revitalized, expanded public sphere, see Nancy Fraser, "Rethinking the Public Sphere," in Henry Giroux and Peter McLaren, eds., *Between Borders* (New York: Routledge, 1994), 74–98.

Notes to CHAPTER 1

1. On Fukuyama's ideas, see Francis Fukuyama, *The End of History and the Last Man* (New York: Free Press, 1992).

2. On the eclipse of modern ideologies, see Schwartzmantel, *The Age of Ideology*, chs. 7, 8.

3. See Christopher Lasch, *The Revolt of the Elites* (New York: Norton, 1995), ch. 2.

4. Robert Borosage in *The Nation* (December 11, 1995).

5. Martin P. Wattenberg, *The Decline of American Political Parties* (Cambridge, MA: Harvard University Press, 1994).

6. *Los Angeles Times* (October 21, 1996).

7. Wattenberg, *The Decline of American Political Parties*, ix.

8. C. B. Macpherson, *The Life and Times of Liberal Democracy* (New York: Oxford University Press, 1979), ch. 4.

9. E. J. Dionne, Jr., *Why Americans Hate Politics* (New York: Simon and Schuster, 1993), 23.

10. Robert K. Landers, "Why America Doesn't Vote," *Editorial Research Reports* (1988), 84–86.

11. Daniel Hellinger and Dennis Judd, *The Democratic Facade* (Pacific Grove, CA: Brooks/Cole, 1992).

12. Michael Y. Delli Carpini and Scott Keeter, "Stability and Change in the U.S. Public's Knowledge of Politics," *Public Opinion Quarterly* (Spring–Winter 1991), 607.

13. *Los Angeles Times* (March 4, 1996).

14. Robert Putnam, *Making Democracy Work* (Princeton, NJ: Princeton University Press, 1993), ch. 6.

15. See Zillah Eisenstein, *Global Obscenities*, 21–23.

16. David Croteau, *Politics and the Class Divide*, 13.

17. On the feminist redefinition of public space, see Chantal Mouffe, "Feminism, Citizenship, and Radical Democratic Politics," in Judith Butler and Joan W. Scott, eds., *Feminists Theorize the Political* (New York: Routledge, 1992), 369–384.

18. Susan Tolchin, *The Angry American* (Boulder, CO: Westview, 1996).

19. See James A. Morone, *The Democratic Wish* (New York: Basic Books, 1990), 329.

20. Marcuse, *One-Dimensional Man*.

Notes to CHAPTER TWO

1. Macpherson, *The Life and Times of Liberal Democracy*, 43.

2. Ibid., 79.

3. Bellah et al., *The Good Society*, ch. 4.

4. See Bowles and Gintis, *Democracy and Capitalism*, ch. 1.

5. See R. Jeffrey Lustig, *Corporate Liberalism* (Berkeley: University of California Press, 1982), ch. 9.

6. On the development of the New Left ideology, see Wini Breines, *The Great Refusal* (South Hadley, MA: Praeger, 1982), and George Katsiaficas, *The Imagination of the New Left* (Boston: South End, 1987).

7. See Walter Truett Anderson, ed., *Rethinking Liberalism* (New York: Avon, 1983).

8. Greider, *Who Will Tell the People?*, 11; on this point see also Hellinger and Judd, *The Democratic Facade*.

9. Greider, *Who Will Tell the People?*, 44.

10. See Putnam, *Making Democracy Work*, 178–183.

11. It is not only leftists who detect a profoundly elitist, antidemocratic tendency at work in American politics. For a mainstream example, see Michael Lind, "To Have and Have Not," *Harper's* (June 1995).

12. Dionne, *Why Americans Hate Politics*, 332.

13. Eliasoph, *Avoiding Politics*, 250.

14. Sheldon Wolin, "What Is Revolutionary Theory Today," in Chantal Mouffe, ed., *Radical Democracy* (London: Verso, 1991), 241.

15. H. Mark Roelofs, *The Poverty of American Politics* (Philadelphia: Temple University Press, 1992), 209.

16. *Newsweek* (February 26, 1996).

17. Jeremy Rifkin, *The End of Work* (New York: Tarcher, 1995).

18. Quoted in *Newsweek* (February 26, 1996).

19. See Andrew Hacker, *Two Nations* (New York: Ballantine, 1992).

20. Elliott Currie, *Reckoning: Drugs, the Cities, and the American Future* (New York: Hill and Wang, 1993), 3. For a more recent critique of this problem, see Dan Baum, *Smoke and Mirrors* (Boston: Little, Brown, 1996).

21. Diana Gordon, *The Return of the Dangerous Classes* (New York: Norton, 1994).

22. Robert C. Aldridge, *First Strike!* (Boston: South End, 1983).

23. See Douglas Kellner, *The Persian Gulf TV War* (Boulder, CO: Westview, 1992).

24. Joshua Karliner, *The Corporate Planet*, ch. 2.

25. Albert Gore, *Earth in the Balance* (Boston: Houghton Mifflin, 1992).

26. Mark Dowie, "American Environmentalism: A Movement Courting Irrelevance, *World Policy Journal* (Winter 1991–1992), 83–94.

27. Tom Schachtman, *The Inarticulate Society* (New York: Free Press, 1995), ch. 7.

Notes to CHAPTER 3

1. Stanley A. Deetz, *Corporate Colonization* (Albany, NY: SUNY Press, 1992).

2. See Bowles and Gintis, *Capitalism and Democracy*, ch. 2, on this historic conflict between two competing forces.

3. Patricia Aufderheide, *Communications Policy and the Public Interest* (New York: Guilford Press, 1999), 22–23.

4. Ibid., 62.

5. Robert W. McChesney, *Corporate Media and the Threat to Democracy* (New York: Seven Stories Press, 1997), 34.

6. Greider, *Who Will Tell the People?* 336.

7. See Robert Reich, *The Work of Nations* (New York: Vintage, 1992), chs. 10, 11.

8. Ibid., 112.

9. Ibid., 124.

10. Jean-Marie Guehenno, *End of the Nation-State* (Minneapolis: University of Minnesota Press, 1995), 20.

11. William Greider, *One World, Ready or Not* (New York: Simon and Schuster, 1997), 18.

12. Hans Magnus Enzensberger, *Civil Wars: From L.A. to Bosnia* (New York: New Press, 1993), 14.

13. Ibid., 17, 18.

14. Murray Bookchin, *From Urbanization to Cities* (London: Cassell, 1992), 22.

15. Ibid., 22.

16. Lauren Langman, "Neon Cages: Shopping for Subjectivity," in Rob Shields, ed., *Lifestyles of Consumption* (London: Sage, 1992), 67.

17. Herbert I. Schiller, *Culture, Inc.* (New York: Oxford University Press, 1991), 89.

18. Todd Gitlin, "Television's Anti-Politics," *Dissent* (Winter 1996), 78.

19. Kellner, *Persian Gulf TV War.*

20. On the ways in which the mass media induce widespread passivity, see Edward S. Herman and Noam Chomsky, *The Manufacturing of Consent: The Political Economy of the Mass Media* (New York: Pantheon, 1988), and Michael Parenti, *Inventing Reality* (New York: St Martin's, 1993).

21. The convergence of media spectacle and the search for personal and group identity is theorized in the work of Guy Debord, *The Society of the Spectacle* (New York: Zone Books, 1995), and Jean Baudrillard, *Simulations* (New York: Semiotexte, 1983).

22. For a trenchant analysis of corporate colonization in the global context, see Eisenstein, *Global Obscenities*, and Greider, *One World*, part 1.

23. As Ophuls, *Requiem for Modern Politics*, shows, the profound mass alienation from politics has its origins in the whole Enlightenment project. See especially pages 266–278. 24. On the growing concentration of global capital, see Greider, *One World*, part 3, and Karliner, *The Corporate Planet*, ch. 1.

25. For an extended discussion of the requirements for a participatory citizenship, see Paul Barry Clarke, *Deep Citizenship* (London: Pluto, 1996), chs. 4, 7.

Notes to CHAPTER 4

1. Enzensberger, *Civil Wars*.

2. See Tom Athanasiou, *Divided Planet: The Ecology of Rich and Poor* (Boston: Little, Brown, 1996), ch. 1.

3. William Greider, "Global Warning," *The Nation* (January 13, 1997).

4. Athanasiou, *Divided Planet*, 58.

5. Greider, "Global Warning."

6. Alvin and Heidi Toffler, *Creating a New Civilization* (Atlanta: Turner Publications, 1994).

7. Aristotle, "The Politics," 64–101.

8. Ibid., 64.

9. Ibid., 65.

10. *The Republic of Plato*, translated by F. M. Cornford (New York: Oxford University Press, 1963), 55.

11. Ibid., 177.

12. Sheldon Wolin, *Politics and Vision* (Boston: Little, Brown, 1960), ch. 1.

13. Jean-Jacques Rousseau, *The Social Contract* (New York, 1967), 22.

14. Ibid., 70.

15. See T. H. Marshall, *Class, Citizenship, and Social Development* (New York: Anchor, 1965).

16. Hannah Arendt, *The Human Condition* (New York: University of Chicago Press, 1958).

17. John Shotter, "Psychology and Citizenship: Identity and Belonging," in Bryan S. Turner, ed., *Citizenship and Social Theory* (London: Sage, 1993), 121–131.

18. On the concept of "totalitarian democracy," see J. L. Talmon, *The Rise of Totalitarian Democracy* (Boston: Praeger, 1952).

19. Gramsci, "The Study of Philosophy," 326.

20. Ibid., 360.

21. Gramsci, "State and Civil Society," 248–249.

22. Frances Fox Piven and Richard Cloward, *Poor People's Movements* (New York: Vintage, 1979), introduction.

23. Herbert Marcuse, *Counterrevolution and Revolt* (Boston: Beacon, 1971), xii.

24. Ibid., xiii.

25. On the role of 1960s popular movements in broadening the public sphere, see Sara Evans, *Personal Politics* (New York: Vintage, 1979); Breines, *The Great Refusal*; Katsiaficas, *The Imagination of the New Left*; and James Miller, *Democracy Is in the Streets* (New York: Simon and Schuster, 1987).

26. See Miller, *Democracy Is in the Streets*, introduction.

27. Ibid., 333.

28. Piven and Cloward, *Poor People's Movements*, ch. 4.

29. Erich Fromm, *Escape from Freedom* (New York: Avon, 1969).

30. Jürgen Habermas, "The Public Sphere: An Encyclopedia Article," in Stephen Eric Bronner and Douglas Kellner, eds., *Critical Theory and Society* (New York: Routledge, 1989), 137.

31. Ibid., 136.

32. See Janet Biehl, *Rethinking Ecofeminist Politics* (Boston: South End, 1991), 140.

33. On the expansion of civic affairs in the United States during the nineteenth century, see Alexis de Tocqueville, *Democracy in America*, translated by George Lawrence (New York: Harper and Row, 1969), 189–261.

34. See Dionne, *Why Americans Hate Politics*. See also Robert Putnam's well-known essay "Bowling Alone: America's Declining Social Capital," *Journal of Democracy* (January 1995).

35. Fraser, "Rethinking the Public Sphere," 90.

36. See the discussion of "protective democracy" in Macpherson, *The Life and Times of Liberal Democracy* (New York, 1977), ch. 2.

37. See Wolin, *Politics and Vision*, ch. 2.

38. Ibid., 417.

39. Robert Michels, *Political Parties* (New York: Collier, 1962).

40. Max Weber, "Politics as a Vocation," in *From Max Weber*, translated and edited by H. H. Gerth and C. Wright Mills (New York: Oxford University Press, 1946), 77–128.

41. V. I. Lenin, "What Is to Be Done?" in Robert C. Tucker, ed., *The Lenin Anthology* (New York: Norton, 1975), 12–114.

42. A. J. Polan, *Lenin and the End of Politics* (Berkeley: University of California Press, 1984), 130.

43. Herbert Marcuse, *One-Dimensional Man*.

44. Max Horkheimer and Theodor W. Adorno, *Dialectic of Enlightenment* (New York: Continuum, 1972).

45. Theodor Adorno, "The Culture Industry Reconsidered," in Bronner and Kellner, *Critical Theory and Society*, 135.

Notes to CHAPTER 5

1. Benjamin Barber, *Jihad versus McWorld* (New York: Ballantine, 1995), 295.

2. Dionne, *Why Americans Hate Politics*, ch. 1.

3. Marcuse, *One-Dimensional Man*.

4. Breines, *The Great Refusal*.

5. Theodore Roszak, *The Making of a Counterculture* (Berkeley: University of California Press, 1968), xxvi.

6. Carl Boggs, "Rethinking the Sixties Legacy: From New Left to New Social Movements," in Sanford M. Lyman, ed., *Social Movements: Critiques, Concepts, Case-Studies* (New York: New York University Press, 1995).

7. See Roszak, *The Making of a Counterculture*, and Charles Reich, *The Greening of America* (New York: Bantam, 1970) on the role that personal and cultural transformation played in the New Left and the counterculture.

8. Reich, *The Greening of America*, 389–390.

9. Fritjof Capra, *The Turning Point* (New York: Simon and Schuster, 1982).

10. Christopher Lasch, *The Culture of Narcissism* (New York: Warner Books, 1979), 43.

11. On the evolution of the Proposition 13 movement in California, see Clarence Y. H. Lo, *Small Property versus Big Government: Social Origins of the Property Tax Revolt* (Berkeley: University of California Press, 1990), and David O. Sears, *Tax Revolt* (Cambridge, MA: Harvard University Press, 1985).

12. Howard Jarvis, *I'm Mad as Hell* (New York: Bantam, 1979), 6.

13. For Rothbard's classic libertarian statement, see "Confessions of a Right-Wing Liberal," *Ramparts* (June 1968). See also various contributions to the journal *Libertarian Review*. For a general elaboration of libertarian views, see William S. Maddox and Stuart A. Lilie, *Beyond Liberal and Conservative* (Washington, DC: Cato Institute, 1984).

14. For a summation of Libertarian Party electoral efforts, see J. M. Hazlett, *The Libertarian Party and Other Minor Parties in the United States* (Jefferson, NC, 1992).

15. Seymour Melman, *The Demilitarized Society* (Montreal: Black Rose, 1989).

16. Theodore Roszak, "America after Affluence: An Era of Limits and Values," in Anderson, *Rethinking Liberalism*, 29.

17. See, for example, Samuel P. Huntington, *American Politics: The Promise of Disharmony* (Cambridge, MA: Harvard University Press, 1981).

18. Roger Griffin, *The Nature of Fascism* (New York: Routledge, 1993), ch. 3.

19. See David H. Bennett, *The Party of Fear* (Chapel Hill: University of North Carolina Press, 1995).

20. On the Koresh phenomenon in the Branch Davidians, see Marc Breault and Martin King, *Inside the Cult* (New York: Clarendon, 1993).

21. Hobsbawm, *Primitive Rebels*, chs. 4–6.

22. Ibid., 68–70.

23. William W. Zellner, *Countercultures* (New York: St. Martin's, 1995), ch. 1.

24. Ibid., 4, 5.

25. Ibid., 49.

26. Ibid., 52.

27. Ibid., 65.

28. See Chip Berlet and Matthew N. Lyons, "Militia Nation," *The Progressive* (June 1995).

29. James William Gibson, *Warrior Dreams* (New York: Hill and Wang, 1994).

30. Ibid., introduction.

31. Ibid., 11.

32. *Los Angeles Times* (January 4, 1997).

33. See *The Unabomber Manifesto: Industrial Society and Its Future* (Berkeley, CA: Jolly Roger Press, 1995), 4.

34. Zellner, *Countercultures*, ch. 5.

35. See Joe Conason, Alfred Ross, and Lee Colkorinos, "The Promise Keepers Are Coming," *The Nation* (October 7, 1996).

36. Hobsbawm, *Primitive Rebels*, 104–105.

37. See Zeev Sternhell, *The Birth of Fascist Ideology* (Princeton, NJ: Princeton University Press, 1994), 18.

38. Griffin, *The Nature of Fascism*, 26, 35.

39. On this point, see Fromm, *Escape from Freedom*.

40. On Mussolini's views and the development of Italian fascism, see Griffin, *The Nature of Fascism*, ch. 3.

41. John H. Kautsky, *Political Change in Underdeveloped Countries* (New York: Wiley, 1962), 101, 103.

42. Griffin, *The Nature of Fascism*, 112.

43. See Enzensberger, *Civil Wars*, 9–71.

44. Barber, *Jihad versus McWorld*, introduction.

45. On the political impact of globalization, see Greider, *One World, Ready or Not*, part 1.

46. Barber, *Jihad versus McWorld*, 7.

47. Ophuls, *Requiem for Modern Politics*, 226.

48. On the incipient totalitarian features present in rationalized state capitalism, or "techno-capitalism," see Lauren Langman, "From Total Administration to the Surveillance State" (unpublished manuscript).

Notes to CHAPTER 6

1. See Fukuyama, *The End of History*.

2. Hobsbawm, *Primitive Rebels*, chs. 4–6.

3. Gramsci, "State and Civil Society," 238–243.

4. For Reich's views on the emergence of reactionary populism in Europe, see *The Mass Psychology of Fascism* (New York: Farrar, Straus, Giroux, 1970). Fromm's ideas are set forth in *Escape from Freedom*.

5. See Louise Hay, *You Can Heal Your Life* (New York: Bantam, 1979).

6. Marilyn Ferguson, *The Acquarian Conspiracy* (Los Angeles: Tarcher, 1980), and Marianne Williamson, *A Return to Love* (Los Angeles: Tarcher, 1981).

7. Mark Satin, *New Age Politics* (New York: Dell, 1978).

8. Parenti, *Land of Idols*, 17.

9. James Redfield, *The Celestine Prophecy* (New York: Warner Books, 1993).

10. Ibid., 106, 223.

11. Ibid., 239.

12. Corinne McLaughlin and Gordon Davidson, *Spiritual Politics* (New York, 1994), 4.

13. Ibid., 14.

14. Ibid., 20.

15. Ibid., 26–28.

16. Ibid., 237, 238.

17. Ibid., 421.

18. Theodore Adorno, *The Stars Down to Earth* (Heidelberg: Carl Winter, 1957).

19. Ibid., 27.

20. Ibid., 40.

21. Ibid., 66.

22. Fromm, *Escape from Freedom,* ch. 2.

23. Ibid., 133.

24. Janet Biehl, *Rethinking Ecofeminist Politics*, 6. For a more positive view, see Irene Diamond and Gloria Orenstein, *Reweaving the World: The Emergence of Ecofeminism* (San Francisco: Sierra Club Books, 1990).

25. Biehl, *Rethinking Ecofeminist Politics*, 134–135.

26. Jürgen Habermas, *Legitimation Crisis* (Boston: Beacon, 1973).

27. Parenti, *Land of Idols*, 21.

28. Dana L. Cloud, " 'Socialism of the Mind': The New Age of Post-Marxism," in Herbert W. Simons and Michael Billig, eds., *After Postmodernism* (London: Sage, 1994), 222–251.

29. See Harold Bloom, *The American Religion: The Emergence of the Post-Christian Nation* (New York: Simon and Schuster, 1992).

30. See, for example, Cloud, "Socialism of the Mind," and Parenti, *Land of Idols.*

31. Paul Wachtel, *The Poverty of Affluence* (Philadelphia: New Society Publishers, 1989).

32. See Richard Hofstadter, *Anti-Intellectualism in American Life* (New York: Vintage, 1966).

33. Russell Jacoby, *Social Amnesia* (Boston: Beacon, 1975), 51.

34. Ibid., 64.

35. Guy Debord, *Comments on the Society of the Spectacle* (London: Verso, 1988), 29, 87.

36. See Robert Hughes, *The Culture of Complaint* (New York: Warner Books, 1994) and Charles L. Sykes, *A Nation of Victims* (New York: St. Martin's, 1992).

37. See Steven Best and Douglas Kellner, *The Postmodern Turn* (New York: Guilford Press, 1997), on the linkage between identity formations, politics, and the mass media.

38. On this point, see Cloud, "Socialism of the Mind."

39. Sykes, *A Nation of Victims*, ch. 4.

40. See, for example, Sara Evans, *Personal Politics.*

41. Sykes, *A Nation of Victims*, 146.

42. This denigration of the public realm is visible in the work of John Bradshaw and M. Scott Peck, among others. See John Bradshaw, *Bradshaw On: The Family* (Deerfield Beach, FL: Health Communications, 1988), and M. Scott Peck, *The Road Less Traveled* (New York: Simon and Schuster, 1988).

43. Stanton Peele, *Diseasing of America* (Lexington, MA: Lexington Books, 1985).

44. Ibid., 28.

45. Ibid., 255.

46. Wendy Kaminer, *I'm Dysfunctional, You're Dysfunctional* (New York: Vintage, 1993), conclusion.

47. See Peele, *Diseasing of America*, ch. 9 and Kaminer, *I'm Dysfunctional, You're Dysfunctional*, 158.

48. Kaminer, *I'm Dysfunctional, You're Dysfunctional*, conclusion.

49. Wachtel, *The Poverty of Affluence*, 219

50. On classical populism in the United States, see Lawrence Goodwyn, *The Populist Moment* (New York: Oxford University Press, 1978).

51. Saul Alinsky, *Reveille for Radicals* (Chicago: Universeity of Chicago Press, 1946).

52. For a sampling of works on new populism, see Harry Boyte, *The Backyard Revolution* (Philadelphia, 1980); Martin Carnoy and Derek Shearer, *Economic Democracy* (White Plains, NY: M. E. Sharpe, 1980); and Mark Kann, *Middle-Class Radicalism in Santa Monica* (Philadelphia: Temple University Press, 1986).

53. See Kann, *Middle-Class Radicalism*, for a critical account of the new-populist experience in Santa Monica, California, during the 1980s.

54. Karen Paget, "Citizen Organizing: Many Movements, No Majority," *The American Prospect* (Summer 1990).

55. Boyte, *The Backyard Revolution*, 7.

56. Carl Boggs, *Social Movements and Political Power* (Philadelphia: Temple University Press, 1986), ch. 4.

57. Allan Heskin, *Tenants and the American Dream* (New York: Praeger, 1983), ch. 1.

58. Joseph M. Kling and Prudence S. Posner, "Class and Community in an Era of Urban Transformation," in Kling and Posner, eds., *Dilemmas of Activism* (Philadelphia: Temple University Press, 1990), 14.

59. Sidney Plotkin, "Community and Alienation: Enclave Consciousness and Urban Movements," in Michael Peter Smith, ed., *Breaking Chains* (New Brunswick, NJ: Transaction Publishers, 1991), 14–15.

60. Ibid., 15.

61. Ibid., 17–18.

62. Allan Heskin, *The Struggle for Community* (Boulder, CO: Westview, 1991).

63. Ibid., ch. 3.

64. See Sidney Plotkin and William E. Scheuerman, "Two Roads Left: Strategies of Resistance to Plant Closings in the Monongahela Valley," in Kling and Posner, *Dilemmas of Action*, 193–217.

65. Ibid., 211.

66. Kann, *Middle-Class Radicalism*, 261.

67. Robert Fischer, *Let the People Decide* (New York: Macmillan, 1994).

68. John Stuart Mill, *On Liberty* (New York: Meridian, 1962), 129–130.

69. Fischer, *Let the People Decide*, 230.

70. On the linkage between globalization of the capitalist economy and urban decay, see Petras and Morley, *Empire or Republic?* ch. 3.

71. Hobsbawm, *Primitive Rebels*, ch. 7.

72. Tony Martin, "From Slavery to Rodney King: Continuity and Change," in Haki R. Madhubuti, *Why L.A. Happened* (Chicago: Third World Press, 1993), 35.

73. Mike Davis, *L.A. Was Just the Beginning* (Westfield, NJ: Open Media, 1992), 4.

74. Madhubuti, *Why L.A. Happened*, xiv.

75. On the alienation of participants in the uprising, see Anna Devere Smith, *Twilight: Los Angeles 1992* (New York: Doubleday, 1994).

76. bell hooks, "Let Freedom Ring," in Madhubuti, *Why L.A. Happened*, 242–243.

77. Mike Davis, "In L.A., Burning All Illusions," *The Nation* (June 1, 1992), 744.

78. *Los Angeles Times* (December 18, 1996).

79. Dwight Conquergood, "For the Nation! How Street Gangs Problematize Patriotism," in Simons and Billig, *After Postmodernism*, 204, 212.

80. "Bloods/Crips Proposal," in Madhubuti, *Why L.A. Happened*, 274–282.

81. George Sessions, ed., *Deep Ecology for the Twenty-First Century* (Boston: Shambhala, 1995), introduction, xxi.

82. Stephan Bodian, "An Interview with Arne Naess," in Sessions, *Deep Ecology*, 28.

83. Ibid., 30, 32.

84. Fritjof Capra, "Deep Ecology: A New Paradigm," in Sessions, *Deep Ecology*, 20.

85. Ibid., 21. For a further refinement of these views, see Capra's *The Turning Point*. The film *Mindwalk*, directed by Berndt Capra, is based on this book.

86. Jack Turner, "Gary Snyder and the Practice of the Wild," in Sessions, *Deep Ecology*, 45.

87. Sessions, "Deep Ecology and the New Age Movement," in Sessions, *Deep Ecology*, 290.

88. Murray Bookchin, *The Philosophy of Social Ecology* (Montreal: Black Rose, 1990), 41–42. See also Bookchin's "Social Ecology versus Deep Ecology," in *Socialist Review* (July–September 1988).

89. Reich, *The Greening of America*.

90. Peter Dickens, *Society and Nature* (Philadelphia: Temple University Press, 1992), 192.

91. Cecile Jackson, "Myths of Ecofeminism," *New Left Review* (March–April 1995), 129.

92. Ibid., 129.

93. Bookchin, "Social Ecology versus Deep Ecology," 22.

94. Timothy W. Luke, *Ecocritique*, 22, 25.

95. Rudolf Bahro, *From Red to Green* (London: Verso, 1984), 212. Bahro says, "I believe that human evolution began to go wrong with the English industrial revolution."

Notes to CHAPTER 7

1. Inglehart, *Modernization and Postmodernization*, ch. 10.

2. See, for example, Steven Best and Douglas Kellner, *Postmodern Theory: Critical Interrogations* (New York: Guilford Press, 1991), which remains one of the most comprehensive attempts to forge a synthesis bringing together currents of Marxism, postmodernism, and Critical Theory; see especially pages 256–304.

3. Ronald Aronson, *After Marxism* (New York: Guilford Press, 1995), 171.

4. On the postmodern break with the past, see Barry Smart, *Modern Conditions, Postmodern Controversies* (New York: Routledge, 1992), especially chs. 2, 6. For a more critical assessment of this "break," see Terry Eagleton, *Illusions of Postmodernism* (London: Verso, 1996).

5. Best and Kellner, *Postmodern Theory*, 283.

6. Alex Callinicos, *Against Postmodernism* (New York: St. Martin's, 1989).

7. Ibid., 164.

8. On the depoliticization of theoretical work in the academic Left, see Russell Jacoby, *Dogmatic Wisdom* (New York: Doubleday, 1994); Lawrence C. Soley, *Leasing the Ivory Tower* (Boston: South End, 1995); and Carl Boggs, *Intellectuals and the Crisis of Modernity* (Albany, NY: SUNY Press, 1993).

9. Barbara Epstein, "Why Poststructuralism Is a Dead End for Progressive Thought," *Socialist Review* (vol. 25, no. 2, 1995), 96–97.

10. A good deal of postmodern theory, especially Jean Baudrillard's contribution in the area of media simulations (entitled *Simulations*), owes a profound debt to Guy Debord's *The Society of the Spectacle*.

11. Jean Baudrillard, *In the Shadow of Silent Majorities* (New York: Semiotexte, 1983), 25–26. This essay originally appeared in 1978.

12. See Richard Rorty, *Contingency, Irony, and Solildarity* (Cambridge, UK: Cambridge University Press, 1989), and Carol Gilligan, *In a Different Voice* (Cambridge, MA: Harvard University Press, 1982); see also Nancy Fraser, *Unruly Practices* (Minneapolis, 1989).

13. Fredric Jameson, *The Political Unconscious* (New York: Cornell University Press, 1981); Ernesto Laclau and Chantal Mouffe, *Hegemony and Socialist Strategy* (London: Verso, 1985); and Alain Touraine, *The Voice and the Eye* (Cambridge, UK: Cambridge University Press, 1981).

14. Laclau and Mouffe, *Hegemony and Socialist Strategy*.

15. For a thorough discussion of discourse theory from a Marxist standpoint, see Norman Geras, "Post Marxism?" *New Left Review* (May–June 1987), 40–82; see also Best and Kellner, *Postmodern Theory*, 192–204.

16. Laclau and Mouffe, *Hegemony and Socialist Strategy*, ch. 4.

17. Ibid., 111.

18. Epstein, "Why Poststructuralism," 85.

19. Jacoby, *Dogmatic Wisdom*, 182.

20. See Donna Haraway, *Simians, Cyborgs, and Women* (New York: Routledge, 1991); Judith Butler, *Bodies That Matter* (New York: Routledge, 1993); and Drucilla Cornell, *The Philosophy of the Limit* (New York: Routledge, 1992).

21. Teresa L. Ebert, *Ludic Feminism* (Ann Arbor: University of Michigan Press, 1996).

22. Ibid., 184.

23. Leslie Gotfrit, "Women Dancing Back," in Henry A. Giroux, ed., *Postmodernism, Feminism, and Cultural Politics* (Albany, NY: SUNY Press, 1991).

24. Ibid., 181.

25. Ibid., 183.

26. Ibid., 183–184.

27. Ibid., 188.

28. Philip Wexler, "Citizenship in the Semiotic Society," in Bryan S. Turner,

ed., *Theories of Modernity and Postmodernity* (Newbury Park, CA: Sage, 1990), 164–169.

29. Ibid., 174.

30. Norman Denzin, The Cinematic Society (Newbury Park: Sage, CA., 1995).

31. Zygmunt Bauman, *Intimations of Postmodernity* (New York: Routledge, 1992), 200–201.

32. Murray Bookchin, *Re-Enchanting Humanity* (New York: Cassell, 1995), 175.

33. Marcuse, *One-Dimensional Man*; see also Terry Eagleton, *Illusions of Post-modernism*, 22, 64.

34. Bauman, *Intimations of Postmodernity*, 200.

35. Ibid.

36. Boggs, *Social Movements and Political Power*, ch. 5.

37. John Stockwell, *The Praetorian Guard* (Boston: South End, 1991), 13.

38. For an excellent discussion of the popular support that was mobilized behind the Persian Gulf war in 1991, see Kellner, *The Persian Gulf TV War*.

39. Seymour Melman, "Military State Capitalism," *The Nation* (May 20, 1991).

40. On the relationship between a militarized economy and the declining social infrastructure, see Melman, *The Demilitarized Society*, and Petras and Morley, *Empire or Republic?*, ch. 2.

41. See Carl Boggs, "Social Movements, the War Economy, and the Dilemmas of Political Strategy," *New Political Science* (Winter 1993), 3–16.

42. Barbara Epstein, in her *Political Protest and Cultural Revolution* (Berkeley: University of California Press, 1991), shows both the positive and negative sides of efforts by the peace movement and other activist groups to go beyond the realm of normal politics.

43. On this point, see Melman, *The Demilitarized Society*,, ch. 5.

44. Claus Offe, "Reflections on the Institutional Self-Transformation of Movement Politics: A Tentative Stage Model," in Russell J. Dalton and Manfred Kuechler, eds., *Challenging the Political Order: New Social and Political Movements in Western Democracies* (New York: Oxford University Press, 1990), 238.

45. See Piven and Cloward, *Poor People's Movements*, ch. 4.

46. See especially Jacques Derrida, *Margins of Philosophy* (Chicago, 1981).

47. On the decentering of political agency, see Alberto Melucci, *Nomads of the Present* (London, 1989).

48. See Sheila Rowbotham et al., *Beyond the Fragments* (Boston: Alyson Press, 1979), on the role of identity concerns in shaping the feminist movement.

49. On the centrality of identity politics in the forging of third-world liberation movements, see Frantz Fanon, *The Wretched of the Earth* (New York: Grove, 1963); Paulo Freire, *Pedagogy of the Oppressed* (New York: Continuum, 1972), and Eric Wolf, *Peasant Wars in the Twentieth Century* (New York: Harper and Row, 1969).

50. Regarding the significance of culture in the making of working-class consciousness, see E. P. Thompson's classic *The Making of the English Working Class* (New York: Vintage, 1963).

51. Craig Calhoun, ed., *Social Theory and the Politics of Identity* (Cambridge, MA: Blackwell, 1994), 19–20.

52. Todd Gitlin, *The Twilight of Common Dreams* (New York: Holt, 1995), 145.

53. Ibid., 236

54. See Russell Jacoby, "The Myth of Multiculturalism," *New Left Review* (November–December 1994).

55. Lauren Langman, "The End of Political Man (and Woman), in Alberto Gasparini, ed., *Nation, Ethnicity, Minority, and Border* (Gorizia, Italy: ISIG, 1998), 15–36.

56. Jonathan Friedman, *Cultural Identity and Global Process* (Newbury Park, CA: Sage, 1994), 190.

57. Gitlin, *The Twilight of Common Dreams*, 168.

58. David Harvey, *The Condition of Postmodernity* (Oxford, UK: Oxford University Press, 1989).

59. Stuart Hall, "The Meaning of New Times," in David Morley and Kuan-Hsing Chen, eds., *Stuart Hall: Critical Dialogues in Cultural Studies* (London: Routledge, 1996), 234.

60. David Korten, *When Corporations Rule the World* (West Hartford, CT: Kumarian Press, 1995), 297.

61. Ibid., 294.

62. Kuan-Hsing Chen, "Post-Marxism: Between/Beyond Critical Postmodernism and Cultural Studies," in Morley and Chen, *Stuart Hall*, 321.

63. On the depoliticization of the American environmental movement, see Mark Dowie, "American Environmentalism."

64. Dick Hebdige, "Postmodernism and the 'Other Side,' " in Morley and Chen, *Stuart Hall*, 174–200; see also Eagleton, *Illusions of Postmodernism*.

65. Philip Wexler, "Citizenship," 169.

Notes to CONCLUSION

1. Gramsci, "The Study of Philosophy," 360.

2. Croteau, *Politics and the Class Divide*, 4.

3. Wolin, in Mouffe, *Radical Democracy*.

4. Daniel Bell, *The End of Ideology* (New York: Free Press, 1960), 393.

5. Ibid., 403–405.

6. Fukuyama, *The End of History*, xiii.

7. Ibid.

8. Ibid., 42.

9. Marcuse, *One-Dimensional Man*, xii.

10. Ibid., xiii.

11. Ibid., 9.

12. Horkheimer and Adorno, *Dialectic of Enlightenment*.

13. See, for example, Marcuse's *An Essay on Liberation* (Boston: Beacon, 1969), and *Counterrevolution and Revolt*.

14. See Macpherson, *The Life and Times of Liberal Democracy*, ch. 4.

15. Michael Oakeshott, *Rationalism in Politics* (London: Allen and Unwin, 1962).

16. As John Keane observes, the dialectic between civil society and the state has broken down in modern society—surely one crucial element in the larger pro-

cess of depoliticization analyzed in this volume. See Keane, *Democracy and Civil Society* (London: Verso, 1988), 61.

17. *Los Angeles Times* (January 30, 1997).

18. Macpherson, *Life and Times*, 47.

19. Paul Barry Clarke, *Deep Citizenship*.

20. Ibid., 110.

21. For an example of this scholarship, see Huntington, *American Politics*.

22. Ulrich Beck, *Risk Society* (London: Sage, 1992), 191.

23. Wainwright, *Arguments for a New Left*, 191.

24. Aronson, *After Marxism*, 176.

25. Robert Michels, *Political Parties*, ch. 1.

26. Herbert J. Gans, *The War against the Poor* (New York: Basic Books, 1995).

27. See my discussion of social movements and the state in *Social Movements and Political Power*, ch. 6.

28. See Piven and Cloward, *Poor People's Movements,* chs. 3 and 4.

29. Boggs, *Social Movements and Political Power*, ch. 4.

30. Toffler and Toffler, *Creating a New Civilization*, 98–99.

31. Ibid., 101, 103.

32. *Los Angeles Times* (March 14, 1996).

33. See, for example, Langdon Winner's argument in *Autonomous Technology*.

34. Schiller, *Information Inequality*, 94.

35. Schiller, *Culture Inc.*, chs. 5–7.

36. On the profoundly antidemocratic character of most modern technology, see Winner, *Autonomous Technology*; Postman, *Technopoly*; and Roszak, *The Cult of Information*.

37. Roszak, *The Cult of Information*, 68.

38. Ibid., 208.

39. Ibid., 119.

40. Rifkin, *The End of Work*.

41. Chris Carlsson, "The Shape of Truth to Come: New Media and Knowledge," in James Brook and Iain A. Boal, *Resisting the Virtual Life* (San Francisco: City Lights, 1995), 242.

42. Gramsci, "State and Civil Society," 275–276.

43. Barber, *Jihad versus McWorld*, 284.

44. Ophuls, *Requiem for Modern Politics,* 29.

45. Sandel, *Democracy's Discontent*, 24.

46. See David Rieff's contribution to "Civil Society and the Future of the Nation-State," *The Nation* (February 22, 1999).

47. Sandel, *Democracy's Discontent*, 269.

48. See Michael Clough's contribution to "Civil Society . . . ," *The Nation* (February 22, 1999).

49. Gramsci, "The Study of Philosophy," 333–334.

INDEX

Public sphere; *see also* Social crisis; Social
  response
anarchism, 99, 117–118
antipolitics
  global ecology and, 91–95
  modernity and, 111–112
commodification of, 78–85
  economic restructuring, 78–79
  media and, 82–85
  personal consumption, 80–82
  post-Fordism, 78–79, 80, 85
  television and, 82–85
  urban decline, 79–80
decline of, 117–122
global ecology, 89–95
  antipolitics and, 91–95
  corporate cover-up, 90–91
  corporate elitism and, 90–91
  crisis of, 89–90
  social movements, 92–94
Leninism, 99–100, 120–121
liberalism, 99, 114–116
Marxism, 99–101, 116–117
modernity, 108–114
  antipolitics, 111–112
  kinship demise, 109
  necessary changes, 113–114
  political centrality, 108–110
  political culture, 110–111
  public opinion, 108
social crisis and, 45–47
  democracy, 46
  depoliticization, 45–47
  elitism, 46
  Reagan election, 45
social movements
  civil rights, 104–105
  feminism, 105–106
  global ecology and, 92–94
  New Left, 103–104, 106, 107
  traditional political discourse, 102–108
traditional political discourse, 95–108
  anarchism, 99
  Antonio Gramsci, 100–102
  Aristotle, 95, 96
  citizenship, 97–98
  civic consciousness, 95–97
  civil rights movement, 104–105
  feminist movement, 105–106
  Greek culture, 95–97
  Jacobinism, 99, 100–101, 107

Leninism, 99–100
liberalism, 99
Marxism, 99–101
New Left movement, 103–104, 106,
  107
Plato, 95, 96, 99
Rousseau, 95, 96–97, 99
social movements, 102–108
statecraft, 98–102, 103, 106–108

Race relations, 53–54, 55–56
  civil rights movement, 104–105
  drug policy and, 55–56
  incarceration rates, 53, 55
  poverty, 53
Rainbow Coalition, 27, 263
Rationalism in Politics (Oakeshott), 249–
  251
Reagan, Ronald, 45
Reckoning (Currie), 55
Redfield, James, 172
Republic, The (Plato), 96
Republican Party; *see* Political party sys-
  tem
Right-wing antipolitics, 135, 136–137
  cults, 138–146, 153–156
  Aryan Nations, 149
  Davidians, 138, 139–140
  Dobson organization, 153–154
  government legitimacy and, 138
  Heaven's Gate, 139, 141
  militias, 144–147, 149–150
  Montana Freemen, 138, 145–146
  Moonies, 154
  Oklahoma City bombing, 138, 144,
    149
  Posse Comitatus, 143
  Promise Keepers, 154–155
  Ruby Ridge, 138, 149
  skinheads, 141–142
  survivalists, 142–144
  Viper Militia, 146
  terrorism, 150–153
Roszak, Theodore, 272
Rousseau, 8, 95, 96–97, 99
Route 2 Project (Los Angeles), 190–191
Ruby Ridge, 138, 149

Satin, Mark, 170–171
Saxon, Kurt, 143, 144
Scott Paper, 52

ABOUT THE AUTHOR

CARL BOGGS has written two books on Antonio Gramsci, an Italian Marxist of the early twentieth century and one of the seminal thinkers of the modern period, and he has written extensively on contemporary social and political theory, social movements, political sociology, and European politics. He is the author of *The Impasse of European Communism* (Westview, 1982), *The Two Revolutions: Antonio Gramsci and the Dilemmas of Western Marxism* (Boston: South End Press, 1984), *Social Movements and Political Power* (Temple University Press, 1986), *Intellectuals and the Crisis of Modernity* (State University of New York Press, 1993), and *The Socialist Tradition* (Routledge, 1996). He has been a columnist at the *L.A. Village View* and hosted radio programs at KPFK in Los Angeles. He taught for six years in the sociology department at UCLA, most recently from 1993 to 1996. For the past 12 years he has been a professor of social sciences at National University in Los Angeles.